Intelligent Language Services

Jingsong Shawn Yu · Yazhi Yao

Intelligent Language Services

Theory and Practice with Large Language Models

Springer

Jingsong Shawn Yu
School of Software and Microelectronics
Peking University
Beijing, China

Yazhi Yao
School of Languages and Communication Studies
Beijing Jiaotong University
Beijing, China

ISBN 978-981-95-4631-2 ISBN 978-981-95-4632-9 (eBook)
https://doi.org/10.1007/978-981-95-4632-9

This Springer imprint is published by the registered company Springer Nature Singapore Pte Ltd.
The registered company address is: 152 Beach Road, #21-01/04 Gateway East, Singapore 189721, Singapore

To my wife, Zhuwei, for your love and support.

—Jingsong Shawn Yu

Preface

In late 2013, one of us launched *Principles and Practice of Computer-Aided Translation*—the first massive open online course worldwide devoted specifically to this field—on Coursera and four other platforms. Over the next three to five years more than 80,000 learners from around the world enrolled—a milestone that felt genuinely transformative at the time. Yet in not even a decade, the acceleration of artificial intelligence—especially the advent and rapid maturation of large language models (LLMs)—has rewritten the operating assumptions of language services and quietly unsettled many of the technical premises on which that original curriculum, and much of the profession's toolkit, rested. Tools and linear processes once deemed indispensable are being recomposed inside model and datacentric intelligent systems.

Intelligent Language Services: Theory and Practice with Large Language Models is therefore not a tool manual. It is a panoramic guide to a structural transition. Language work is expanding beyond isolated "transfer" tasks ("translate this," "localize that") into an orchestrated, data-grounded service architecture spanning multilingual workflow design, corpus and terminology governance, prompt and evaluation frameworks, quality assurance, safety, compliance, and ethics. This expansion is altering day-to-day practice while reshaping the field's knowledge structure and professional identities. Traditional methods remain vital in high-risk domains or extremely low-resource languages; nonetheless, a growing share of value is shifting upstream toward the design and governance of the end-to-end language system itself.

For decades, translation, interpreting, and terminology management stood at the center of language services. They remain essential, but the center of gravity has moved. High-value work now frequently occurs before any definitive output is produced: architecting multilingual workflows; curating corpora and terminologies; designing prompt and evaluation schemes; ensuring safety and cultural adaptation; and determining where only human judgment is acceptable. Downstream processes are evolving in parallel. A text is no longer a terminus: it becomes a versioned, traceable, and searchable knowledge asset refined through feedback loops that connect human review with model diagnostics.

Large language models have catalyzed this transition—but they are not magic. They are powerful probabilistic engines for pattern-based generation, summarization, and reasoning. Their limitations give definition to the discipline we now require. When hallucinations appear, retrieval and governance must compensate. When outputs drift, workflow architecture, structured prompting, and measurable quality contracts realign them. When accountability boundaries blur, observability and human intervention reassert responsibility. The craft of language services is becoming a configurable, governable system architecture.

Three convictions run through this book. First, language services constitute a system. A translation or dialog reply is the surface expression of a deeper pipeline: ingestion and segmentation, context construction, terminology integration, generation, evaluation, revision. Treating the work as a system enables the same components to generalize to adjacent domains—product localization, technical writing, policy communication, and more. Second, controllability is as critical as capability. Contemporary models can execute multiple tasks in a single pass; professionals must ensure they do so consistently, verifiably, and safely. That requires disciplined management of prompts and data, structured outputs, standardized human–AI handoffs, and metrics that validate behavioral and format integrity. Third, human expertise has not disappeared; it is being redeployed. The frontier of value lies in orchestration and judgment. Experts set objectives, define evidentiary standards, engineer safeguards, and intervene in semantically dense, risksensitive, or culturally nuanced contexts. Their role is to convert unstructured linguistic material into reusable assets and to design processes that render machine intelligence controllable, auditable, and trustworthy.

The organization of the volume follows this logic, progressing from foundations to applied practice. We begin by tracing developments in language modeling and representation learning, explaining why decoder-only scaling emerged as the dominant pathway for unified generation and how prompt-driven interaction now coexists with continued pretraining, supervised fine-tuning, knowledge distillation, retrieval-augmented generation (RAG), and agent frameworks. We then frame prompt engineering as a form of "natural language programming," leveraging task specification, output constraints, contextual supplementation, and task decomposition to enhance reliability. Subsequent chapters introduce RAG, showing how verifiable knowledge reshapes citation, traceability, and synthesis. Agent workflows integrate these mechanisms into iterative cycles of perception, reasoning, planning, action, and reflection, supported by tools, memory, and governance structures. Building on that, we reconsider translation pipelines, discuss when fine-tuning is warranted, and outline how to construct traceable, optimizable, and scalable translation agents and platform workflows. The scope then broadens to structured technical writing and multimodal language services spanning text, speech, images, video, and spatial signals. The closing chapters address management and operations, quality and evaluation, compliance and risk, and ethics—because sustained value depends on standards, accountability, and cultural stewardship.

The readership for this book converges from multiple directions. Practitioners will find concrete methods to lift quality and efficiency: prompt libraries, RAG patterns, memory-augmented agents, traceable workflows. Industry leaders will see business models shifting from per-word billing toward platform capabilities, risk-adjusted pricing, and data assetization. Researchers will encounter practice-critical questions beyond benchmark accuracy: accountability, cultural adaptation, data provenance, interpretability. Students will gain a forward-looking skills map encompassing systems thinking, AI literacy, multimodal design, and communication ethics.

Public discourse around AI often polarizes into enthusiasm and apprehension. We advocate constructive realism. LLMs extend the reach of language services while introducing new constraints. To become reliable infrastructure they must be embedded within designed, governed, and supervised systems. The future demands human–AI collaboration in which computational capability fuses with human judgment and experience. Treated as a strategic resource, language connects knowledge and lived experience, policy and practice, cultures and products—expanding safety margins, adaptability, and innovation capacity.

Whether you are a translator, technologist, writer, manager, or researcher, we hope this book helps you progress toward a higher–order role: architect and steward of language systems. This is not merely a change in professional title; it represents an expanded capability structure. The tools are available; the processes are maturing. Ultimate responsibility and value will be determined by our collective participation and practice.

We invite you to engage critically, adapt boldly, and help shape the next generation of AI-powered language services.

Beijing, China

Jingsong Shawn Yu
Yazhi Yao

Competing Interest The authors declare that they have no competing financial or non-financial interests in relation to the content of this book. This statement is made jointly on behalf of both authors; each author has reviewed and approved it.

Contents

1 From Translation to Intelligent Knowledge Services 1
1 Transformation of the Language Services Landscape 2
1.1 Historical Foundations and Professionalization 2
1.2 Expansion of Scope, Technology Configuration, and Emerging Domains 3
2 Major Types and Practices of Language Services 4
2.1 Translation Services: Functional Realignment 4
2.2 Interpreting Services: Augmentation and Modality Shifts 6
2.3 Multidimensional Collaboration and User Experience Innovation in Localization Services 7
2.4 Structured Technical Writing and Information Development 9
2.5 Data-Centric Language Services: Governance and Role 11
2.6 Language Services as Multimodal Strategy Infrastructure in Convergent Media Ecosystems 12
2.7 Restructuring Language Services Under Automation and Outsourcing 15
2.8 Broad-Based Content Production, Consulting and Strategic Planning 16
3 Role Evolution and Competency Redefinition in the Language Services Profession 19
3.1 Automation Shift and Emergent System-Level Roles 20
3.2 Data Stewardship, Annotation Complexity, and Multimodal Workflow Expansion 20
3.3 Competency Reconfiguration and Misconceptions of Role Substitutability 21
3.4 Core Linguistic System Value and Programmatic Reset 22
3.5 Escalating Expectations and Strategic Problem-Solving Orientation 23

4 Platformization and AI-Enabled Reconfiguration of Language Services ... 23
4.1 Platform Convergence and Collaborative Infrastructure ... 23
4.2 Multimodal Content Forms and Task Diversification ... 24
4.3 Human–Machine Co-creation and Workflow Automation ... 24
4.4 Upstream Integration and Strategic Language Infrastructure ... 25
4.5 Toward Data-Driven, Systemic Service Models ... 25
5 Conclusion ... 26
References ... 26

2 Language Modeling and Large Language Models ... 33
1 Defining Computable Linguistic Units ... 34
1.1 Word Segmentation, Tokenization, and Assumptions about Linguistic Units ... 34
1.2 Tokenizer: From Word Segmentation to Subword Modeling ... 35
2 Modeling Language ... 37
2.1 Objectives and Motivations of Language Modeling ... 37
2.2 Principles and Objectives of Language Modeling ... 38
3 Language Modeling Methods ... 40
3.1 Sequence Prediction and Generative Modeling ... 40
3.2 Representation Learning for Natural Language ... 42
3.3 Dominance of Autoregressive Models in Large Language Model Development ... 44
4 Pretrained Large Language Models ... 45
4.1 Paradigm Shift in NLP Research ... 45
4.2 The Prompt-Driven Approach ... 46
4.3 Large Language Model–based Natural Language Processing ... 48
4.4 Continued Pretraining: Enhancing Domain Adaptation ... 48
4.5 Supervised Fine-Tuning: Guiding Task Execution ... 49
4.6 Knowledge Distillation: Refining and Transferring Knowledge ... 50
4.7 Prompt Engineering: Unlocking Model Potential ... 50
4.8 Retrieval-Augmented Generation: Expanding Knowledge Boundaries ... 51
4.9 Agents: Orchestrating Intelligent Tasks ... 52
5 Technical Limitations of Large Language Models ... 53
5.1 Hallucination: Fluent Form, False Narrative ... 54
5.2 Bias and Discrimination: The Shadow of Data ... 55

5.3 Attributing Responsibility: A Technological–Ethical Dilemma ... 56
5.4 Controllability and Interpretability: Credibility of the Black Box ... 57
6 Conclusion ... 58
References ... 59

3 Prompt Engineering for Large Models ... 63
1 Principles and Core Design Guidelines for Prompt Engineering ... 64
2 Types of Prompts ... 66
2.1 Zero-Shot and Few-Shot Prompting ... 66
2.2 Chain-of-Thought and Tree of Thoughts Prompting ... 67
2.3 Reasoning Models Capable of Self-Generating Internal Prompts ... 68
3 Prompt Design Strategies ... 69
3.1 Role Prompting ... 69
3.2 Clarity for Better Model Reasoning ... 70
3.3 Stepping Back to Move More Reliably Forward ... 71
3.4 Reasoning–Acting–Observation Loop ... 72
3.5 Making Models "Think Multiple Times" ... 74
4 Advanced Prompt Engineering ... 75
4.1 Structured Prompts ... 75
4.2 Modularity and Compositional Assembly ... 79
5 Examples of Complex Prompts ... 80
5.1 Internet Insider Jargon Generator ... 80
5.2 Decision Expert ... 83
5.3 Mirror of Perspectives: Programming-Style Prompt ... 86
6 Programming-Style Prompts ... 88
6.1 Key Principles of Programming-Style Prompt Design ... 88
6.2 Applications of Programming-Style Prompts ... 89
7 Conclusion ... 90
References ... 91

4 Retrieval-Augmented Generation ... 95
1 Applications of Retrieval-Augmented Generation ... 95
2 RAG System Development and Practice ... 96
2.1 Data Cleansing and Embedding Pipeline ... 97
2.2 Vector Databases and Semantic Retrieval Systems ... 98
3 Challenges and Optimization Strategies for Retrieval-Augmented Generation ... 99
3.1 Complex Document Parsing and Structural Reconstruction ... 99
3.2 Limitations of Vector Retrieval ... 100
3.3 Collaborative Optimization of Retrieval and Generation ... 101

4 Exploring Deep Research Products ... 102
4.1 From Intelligent Question Answering to Systematic Knowledge Construction ... 103
4.2 Technical Architecture of Deep Research Systems ... 104
4.3 Representative Deep Research Products ... 105
4.4 Innovation in Language Services Enabled by Deep Research ... 106
5 Limitations and Future Directions of Deep Research ... 107
6 Conclusion ... 108
References ... 109

5 Agents and Workflows ... 113
1 From Tool Invocation to Agents ... 114
1.1 Language Models as Tool Orchestrators ... 114
1.2 Typical Application Scenarios of Large Language Model Tool Invocation ... 115
1.3 From Tool Orchestration to Intelligent Agents ... 118
1.4 Evolution and Socialization of Language-Based Agents ... 119
2 Typical Structural Components of an Agent ... 120
2.1 Modeling and Managing Cognitive State ... 120
2.2 Short-Term and Long-Term Memory ... 121
2.3 Behavioral Strategy and Task Planning Module ... 122
2.4 Tool Interfaces and Integration of External Capabilities ... 123
2.5 Environmental Perception and Feedback Processing ... 124
2.6 Agent Coordination and "Self-Awareness" Mechanisms ... 125
3 Leading Agent Frameworks and Their Characteristics ... 126
3.1 Recursive Architectures and Multi-Agent Collaboration ... 126
3.2 Productization Pathways for Agent Systems ... 127
4 Collaborative Agent Development and Communication Protocols ... 128
4.1 Model Context Protocol (MCP) ... 128
4.2 Agent-to-Agent Protocol (A2A) for Agent Interoperability ... 129
5 Design and Development of Workflows ... 130
5.1 Integrating Workflows with Agents ... 131
5.2 Workflow Execution Engines and Modeling Tools ... 132
5.3 Governance Mechanisms for Workflows ... 134
6 Agent-Oriented Workflow Development Practices ... 135
6.1 Characteristics of Workflow Development Platforms and Lightweight Development ... 135
6.2 Programmable Workflows and Agent Orchestration ... 137
7 Conclusion ... 138
References ... 139

6 Reconstructing Translation Process via LLM Prompt Engineering 143
1 Reconstructing Translation Process Driven by Large Language Models 144
1.1 Large Language Models as Cognitive Partners in Translation 144
1.2 A New Process Model for Human–AI Collaborative Translation 146
2 Designing the Translation Process Through Prompt Engineering 147
2.1 Fundamental Prompt Types and Integration into Translation Processes 147
2.2 Applying the TEaR Translation Prompt Framework in Practice 148
2.3 Multi-version Generation and Fusion for Optimizing Translation Quality 151
3 Prompt Engineering for the Translation of Lexical Items and Phrases 155
3.1 Identification, Standardization, and Management of Specialized Terminology 155
3.2 Standardization and Cultural Adaptation in Named Entity Translation 156
3.3 Semantic Reconstruction and Cultural Adaptation in Idiom Translation 157
3.4 Additional Issues in Lexical and Phrase Translation 158
4 Prompt Engineering Methods for Complex Lexical and Phrase Translation 159
4.1 Intelligent Identification of Hard-to-Translate Lexical Items and Phrases 159
4.2 Designing Context-Aware, Inference-Oriented Prompts 166
4.3 Integrating Dictionaries and Knowledge Bases to Enhance Translation Quality 168
5 Prompt Engineering Methods for Translating Long, Complex English Sentences 170
5.1 Core Issues in Translating Long, Complex English Sentences and Corresponding Prompt Strategies 171
5.2 Structure-Oriented and Meaning-Decomposition Prompt Types 172
5.3 Stepwise Prompts 174
5.4 Error-Prevention Prompts 176
5.5 Role-Based Collaborative Prompts 179
5.6 Back-Translation–Based Quality Assurance in Human–AI Collaborative Translation 182

6 Applying Prompting Strategies to the English Translation of a Tang Poem 185
6.1 Translating Poetry: Challenges in Rendering Tang Verse 186
6.2 Progressive Literal-First Prompting 187
6.3 Prompt Process for Interpreting Artistic Conception and Recasting Poetic Form 190
7 Conclusion 194
References 195

7 Fine-Tuning Large Language Models for Translation Services 199
1 Fine-Tuning Large Language Models 200
1.1 Full Annotation and Translation of Classical Texts 201
1.2 Translation of Tangut Texts 202
1.3 The Value of Fine-Tuning Large Models 203
2 Training Data for Fine-Tuning 204
2.1 Format and Structure of Fine-Tuning Data 204
2.2 Prompt Design for Fine-Tuning Training Data 206
3 Acquiring and Cleaning Training Data 208
3.1 Collaborative Construction of Training Datasets 208
3.2 Design Strategies for Fine-Tuning Training Data in Specialized Domains 209
3.3 Issues in Managing Fine-Tuning Training Data 211
4 Fine-Tuning Large Language Models 211
4.1 Insights into Fine-Tuning Methods and Practice 212
4.2 Task Standards and Evaluation Mechanisms for Fine-Tuning 213
4.3 Fine-Tuning Practice with LoRA 214
5 Practical Fine-Tuning: Tangut Machine Translation 217
5.1 Conceptual Approach to Tangut Machine Translation 217
5.2 Experimental Procedure and Results 217
6 Conclusion 220
References 221

8 Designing Translation Agents: Principles and Practice 225
1 Concept and Architecture of Translation Agents 226
1.1 From Prompt Engineering to Workflow-Based Translation Agents 226
1.2 Architectural Components of Translation Agents 227
1.3 Development Frameworks for Translation Agents 228
2 Segmentation of Translation Units and Contextual Cohesion 229
2.1 Sentence Segmentation Challenges Across Languages 230
2.2 Multi-strategy Segmentation and Context Bridging 230
3 Task Chains in Translation Agents 231
3.1 Source Ingestion and Structural Decomposition 232
3.2 Automatic Identification of Register and Style 232

3.3 Applying Automatic Summarization to Translation Comprehension 234
3.4 Broad-Scope Terminology Extraction and Consistency Assurance 235
3.5 Pre-translation Processing of Long and Complex Sentences 238
3.6 Designing Workflows for Translation Generation and Optimization 240
3.7 Translation Generation and Multi-model Orchestration 241
4 Conclusion 247
References 247

9 Architecting Translation Workflows 251
1 Fundamentals of Translation Workflows 252
1.1 System Foundations for Process Integration and Agent Collaboration 252
1.2 Requirements Analysis for Long-Form Translation Workflows 253
1.3 Core Requirements for Designing Translation Workflow Systems 255
2 Architectural Design of Translation Workflows 256
2.1 Overall Architectural Design and Module Partitioning 256
2.2 Module Interaction Logic and Execution Flow 258
2.3 Selecting and Evaluating Translation Workflow Engines 259
3 Design and Implementation of Intelligent Translation Workflows 260
3.1 User Interface Design and Optimization 260
3.2 Core Design and Implementation of the Translation Workflow 262
3.3 Shared Storage for the Workflow 263
3.4 Integration and Invocation of External Tools 265
3.5 Practical Construction of a Workflow-Based Translation Pipeline 266
4 Conclusion 268
References 269

10 Structured and Intelligent Technical Writing 271
1 Fundamentals of Technical Writing 272
1.1 The Role and Industry Value of Technical Writing 272
1.2 Technical Writing and Multimodal Technical Communication 273
1.3 Role Reconfiguration of Technical Writers 274

2 Language Style and Standards in Technical Documentation 275
2.1 Core Linguistic Characteristics of Technical Documentation 275
2.2 Quality Standards and Style Governance Systems for Technical Information 276
3 From Translation-Centric to Cross-Language Collaborative Multilingual Authoring 277
3.1 The Necessity of Multilingual Authoring and Diverging Quality Standards 277
3.2 Translation-Driven Writing Under a Source-First Strategy 278
3.3 Collaborative Multilingual Co-authoring 280
4 Controlled Language in Technical Writing 281
4.1 Evolutionary Stages of Controlled Language 281
4.2 Standardized Controlled Language in Technical Writing 282
4.3 AI-Driven Linguistic Standardization and Compliance 283
5 Structuring in Technical Documentation 283
5.1 Design Principles for Technical Documentation Structure 284
5.2 Hierarchical and Modular Structural Strategies 285
5.3 Structured Authoring Languages and DITA-Based Content Engineering 286
5.4 A Structured Workflow for Modern Technical Documentation 287
5.5 Artificial Intelligence and Structured Technical Authoring 288
6 Content Management and Distribution 289
6.1 Structuring and Engineering Management of Content Assets 290
6.2 Structured Content Publishing and Single Sourcing 290
6.3 Embedded Content and the Shift to Content as a Service 292
7 Conclusion 293
References 293

11 Exploration of Multimodal Language Services 297
1 The Rise of Multimodal Language Services 298
1.1 AIGC: Cross-Modal Synesthesia and Perceptual Transfer 299
1.2 Cross-Modal Transformation and Generation 300
1.3 Prompts That Drive Cross-Modal Generation 301
2 New Paradigms in Multimodal Translation Services 302
2.1 Subtitle Translation from a Multimodal Perspective 303
2.2 Multimodal Interpreting Services 304
2.3 From Digital Humans to Metaverse Language Services 305

3 AIGC-Driven Language Expression in New Media 306
3.1 AIGC-Driven Language Services in New Media 306
3.2 Content Production and Cultural Adaptation Enabled by Large Language Models 308
4 Conclusion 309
References 310

12 Language Service Management and Operations 315
1 Principles of Language Service Management 316
1.1 Process Nodes in Multilingual Projects 316
1.2 Semantic Connectivity of Translation Content and Intelligent Resource Orchestration 317
2 Restructuring of Language Service Business Models 319
2.1 Platform Reconfiguration and Resource Reallocation 319
2.2 AI-Driven Productization and Pricing Reconstruction 321
3 Client Relationship and Service Experience Management 322
3.1 From Quality Management to Experience Management 322
3.2 Demand-Driven and Customized Language Services 323
3.3 Client Communication Management 324
3.4 Visualization of Service Experience and Intelligent Client Retention 325
4 Team Management and Collaboration in Language Services 326
4.1 Redefining Roles and Structures in Human–AI Collaboration 326
4.2 Workflow Collaboration and Task Interface Management 327
4.3 Distributed and Cross-Cultural Remote Collaboration 328
5 Operational Intelligence in Language Services 329
5.1 Management of Linguistic and Data Assets 329
5.2 Modular Platform Systems and Tool Integration 330
5.3 Observability and Algorithm-Driven Operational Feedback Loops 331
6 Conclusion 332
References 333

13 Quality, Compliance, and Ethical Responsibility 337
1 Quality Standards Framework for Language Services in the Intelligent Era 338
1.1 Quality Standards for Language Services and Their Adaptation Logic 338
1.2 Quality Evaluation and Adaptation of Generative Content 340
1.3 Evolution of Quality Standards for Language Services in the Intelligent Era 341

2 Compliance Management in Language Services 342
2.1 Data Boundaries, Content Ownership, and Responsibility in the AI Era 342
2.2 Platform Compliance and Cross-Border Data Governance 343
3 Social Impact and Ethical Responsibility of Language Services 345
3.1 Cultural Reproduction and Expressive Autonomy in the Algorithmic Era 345
3.2 Technology-Driven Equity in Language Services 346
3.3 Redefining Professional Responsibility and Rebuilding Trust Mechanisms 348
3.4 Strategic Reorientation of Language Service Education 349
4 Language Sovereignty and Cultural Governance in the AI Era 350
4.1 Reconfiguring the Global Language Ecology and Technological Fairness 350
4.2 The Sovereignty Debate in Artificial Intelligence 351
4.3 Cultural Subjects and the Authority to Define AI Ethics 352
5 Conclusion 354
References 354

Glossary 359

About the Authors

Jingsong Shawn Yu Ph.D., is a Professor in the School of Software and Microelectronics at Peking University. He received his academic training at Zhejiang University, Peking University, and the University of Pittsburgh. After joining Peking University in August 2005, he founded the Language Information Engineering program and has since guided its strategic direction—designing its curriculum framework, building laboratory and data infrastructure, and overseeing day-to-day academic governance. His earlier professional experience as a programmer, development project manager, and systems librarian at the University of Pittsburgh fostered a cross-disciplinary perspective that links software engineering, information management, and language technologies.

He authored and teaches one of Peking University's earliest massive open online courses, *Principles and Practice of Computer-Aided Translation*, available on edX, Coursera, and XuetangX, with cumulative global enrollments surpassing 80,000 learners. His research spans artificial intelligence, natural language processing, and digital humanities, with current focal areas including adaptive language instruction, optical character recognition for historical and classical texts, and computational processing of Classical Chinese. Collectively, his teaching, program building, and research contribute to advancing the integration of AI within modern language services and cultural heritage resources.

Dr. Yazhi Yao is an Associate Professor in the School of Languages and Communication Studies at Beijing Jiaotong University and a supervisor of Master's students. With over 15 years of experience teaching translation technology, her scholarship focuses on Translation Studies and the evolving language services industry. She has published several highly cited articles in these fields and authored a research monograph on the governance of adverse selection in China's language services market. She has also produced multiple published book-length translations.

Dr. Yao has contributed to the development of both a national standard and an industry standard in the language services sector. She brings more than two decades of professional translation practice covering railway engineering and technology as well as United Nations documentation. She was selected for the national multilingual translation talent pool at the Academy of Translation and Interpretation under the China International Communications Group. She serves as a translation review expert for national standards under agencies affiliated with the Ministry of Housing and Urban-Rural Development, the Ministry of Transport, and the Ministry of Public Security, and acts as Senior Translation Reviewer for *Urban Rail Transit*. Her integrated record of research, professional practice, and standardization work underscores a sustained commitment to advancing technology-enabled language services.

Chapter 1
From Translation to Intelligent Knowledge Services

Abstract This chapter traces the systemic transformation of "language services" from a historically transfer-oriented craft (translation, interpreting, terminology) into a data-intensive, solution-oriented intelligent knowledge service infrastructure. It situates contemporary change in a long arc of knowledge organization and social coordination, then analyzes how large language models, multimodal technologies, platformization, and workflow automation are expanding scope from discrete text operations to integrated task-chains spanning localization, technical communication, data curation, user experience-driven content engineering, and strategic consulting. Core service logic is shifting from post-hoc linguistic execution to upstream design: architecture of multilingual workflows, corpus and terminology governance, model prompting and evaluation, annotation schema design, cultural risk mitigation, and ethical quality assurance. Human expertise is being reallocated toward orchestration, judgment in high-risk or context-dense scenarios, and conversion of unstructured discourse into reusable structured assets. The chapter delineates emerging competency clusters (systems thinking, data/AI literacy, multimodal interaction design, strategic communication ethics) and explains how hybrid human–AI collaboration produces adaptive feedback loops and new value metrics. It argues that professional identity is migrating from "translator" to "language system architect," positioning language as a strategic substrate for knowledge integration, user experience innovation, and cross-cultural governance in convergent media and intelligent ecosystems. This redefinition underpins sustainable professional differentiation globally.

Language services—a professional field encompassing translation, interpreting, terminology management, and multilingual communication—are undergoing a profound transformation in the age of artificial intelligence (AI). In traditional contexts, they were often treated as a mediating function that prioritized faithful transfer, precise expression, and cultural adaptation. Breakthroughs in model capabilities, especially in understanding, generation, transcription, retrieval, and decision support, are rapidly reshaping the profession's boundaries, expanding it from language transfer to solution-oriented knowledge and interaction design (CSA

J. S. Yu and Y. Yao, *Intelligent Language Services*,
https://doi.org/10.1007/978-981-95-4632-9_1

Research, 2024; Lundin, 2024; Williams, 2025; Pangeanic, 2024; Štefčík, 2025; Tieber & Baumgarten, 2024; Zhang & Zhao, 2024).

1 Transformation of the Language Services Landscape

Pretrained large language models (LLMs) have shown strong performance in core language tasks such as writing and translation. They are now widely deployed in user-facing scenarios including semantic search and customer service automation (Achiam et al., 2023; Gencer & Gencer, 2025). This emergence has driven a fundamental shift in scope: from discrete linguistic tasks to an integrated task-chain spanning knowledge organization, data curation, and intelligent interaction (Chen et al., 2024; He et al., 2024; Appicharla et al., 2025). As language services integrate more deeply with knowledge and content governance, the role is evolving from that of a "translator" to that of a "designer and implementer of solutions"—encompassing workflow architectures, model-assisted pipelines, and multilingual content strategies (Yu & Liu, 2024).

1.1 Historical Foundations and Professionalization

The historical roots of language services long predate the emergence of the modern term "language services." From document translation along the early Silk Road to interpreting in court, commercial, and diplomatic settings, such linguistic practices were from the outset centered on knowledge organization and social coordination. A classical Chinese chronicle records that "the Wusun dispatched guides and interpreters to escort Zhang Qian back," underscoring the strategic role of translation in early diplomacy (Sima Qian, 2023). Historical translation extended beyond lexical conversion to encompass institutional systems, measurement standards, and legal norms (Lung, 2011). Interpreting in diplomatic and trade contexts combined multiple functions—communication, mediation, and document drafting (Chen & Liu, 2023; Roland, 1999; Ye, 2023)—while technical writing rose during the Industrial Revolution to advance standardized and systematized knowledge dissemination (Crabbe, 2012). These linguistic practices consistently supported cross-domain objectives. They functioned not only as channels for exchanging information but also as processes that shaped, reorganized, and operationalized shared knowledge for coordinated action.

With increasing societal specialization, language services have become progressively professionalized. The multifaceted roles once performed by merchants or diplomats have differentiated into distinct professions such as translators, interpreters, technical writers, and content architects (Mohammed et al., 2024). After World War II, multilingual international organizations such as the United Nations and the European Communities helped establish professional standards, operating procedures, and ethical norms, turning language services into a delegable, regulated, and trainable form of professional practice (Angelone et al., 2020). Digitization and globalization further diversified provision models—independent translators, technology firms, and crowdsourcing platforms—shifting the focus from mere bilingual competence to workflow-level capabilities spanning workflow design, technological orchestration, and quality management (Jiménez-Crespo, 2021b).

1.2 Expansion of Scope, Technology Configuration, and Emerging Domains

The scope of language services continues to expand. Traditional "language transfer" no longer captures the real workload, as tasks such as localization, knowledge governance, and content management have become increasingly prominent (Esselink, 2000). In localization, translation is only the baseline; content, user interfaces, and service experiences must be deeply adapted to the target culture. Large organizations rely on termbases and style guides to sustain knowledge governance and semantic consistency (Warburton, 2015). The European Union's Interactive Terminology for Europe (IATE) system (2025) is a representative example of deep integration between knowledge resources and language services.

Technological progress has driven continuous evolution in the configuration of language services. Tools such as translation memory systems, terminology management systems, and machine translation have enhanced efficiency and quality (Bowker, 2002; Melby & Wright, 2015), while large language models have enabled generative, conversational, and interactive tasks (Gao et al., 2023; Yamada, 2023). Language service providers now extend their offerings to include model fine-tuning, prompt design, and output review within integrated intelligent workflows (Deshpande et al., 2024). Service provision is becoming increasingly systemic—shifting from "task execution" to "task-chain governance," with language functioning as a core resource for orchestrating models, structuring workflows, and embedding logic into products.

The audiences and use cases of language services are also expanding into emerging domains such as data annotation, corpus curation, sentiment analysis, and low-resource language data creation (Li, 2023; Zha et al., 2023). These tasks demand acute judgment across context, semantics, and pragmatics—going beyond the traditional remit of translation. The professional value of language services lies in practitioners' deep understanding of effective linguistic action, i.e., the context-sensitive selection, adaptation, sequencing, quality control, and risk mitigation of communicative moves across diverse settings—an area that current technology has not yet automated effectively (Yogarajan et al., 2025). As industry boundaries blur, language services both converge with engineering and data disciplines and must re-examine their own value and strategic positioning. Grasping their multidimensional expansion and historical evolution helps clarify prospective roles and trajectories for language services in the intelligent era.

2 Major Types and Practices of Language Services

In the age of artificial intelligence, language services have expanded beyond conventional translation and interpreting to encompass localization, technical communication, data curation, and new-media content engineering. Contemporary language professionals are expected not only to deploy advanced computational tools, but also to align outputs with user needs, industry-specific standards, and culturally situated meaning. Accelerating digitalization is propelling a shift from treating translation as a narrow, document-level transfer task toward integrated solutions that fuse content strategy, user experience design, and knowledge management. This continuing reconfiguration is redefining the scope of the field and elevating the competence thresholds for sustainable professional practice.

2.1 Translation Services: Functional Realignment

Translation services have always held a foundational position within the broader language services ecosystem. Even amid rapid advances in language technology, traditional human translation remains indispensable—especially in specialized domains such as law, medicine, finance, and engineering, where stringent accuracy, terminology consistency, and contextual adequacy are mandatory. In legal translation, for instance, subtle differences in contracts, court judgments, or patent documents can directly influence the allocation of liability and enforcement outcomes. Translators must not only command both languages but also grasp domain knowledge, institutional frameworks, and conventional discourse patterns to ensure that linguistic transfer supports real-world functional and compliance objectives. In medical and technical fields, demands for standardized data, terminology, and stylistic conventions have further driven process formalization and team-based execution. Within these workflows, translators assume critical roles in quality assurance as well as risk anticipation and mitigation (Uygun & Momodu, 2024).

Developments in machine translation and LLMs have markedly reshaped translators' working methods (Zydroń et al., 2024). Initially, their work centered on post-editing machine-generated drafts—correcting semantic drift, syntactic errors, and inconsistencies in terminology and style. With the advent of powerful LLMs, human–AI collaboration has become mainstream (He, 2025). Translators now not only revise outputs after initial generation, but also intervene upstream through prompt engineering (Wassie et al., 2025)—for example, by embedding termbases, audience profiles, and formatting requirements in the prompt to steer generation. This shift presupposes familiarity with model behavioral tendencies, instruction structuring, and common error typologies, enabling iterative collaboration and progressive refinement. Techniques such as role-play, orchestration of multiple complementary models, and chain-of-thought prompting allow translators to systematize complex task handling—ranging from domain-intensive documentation to literary texts—thereby improving both subject-matter rigor and expressive diversity (Ichien et al., 2024).

In content dissemination and commercial communication, the traditional benchmark of "faithful reproduction" has increasingly been complemented by the concepts of transcreation (creative target-language re-authoring that preserves strategic intent while optimizing cultural and functional resonance) and writing for translation (source authoring practices that maximize downstream translatability and consistency) (Chen & Cao, 2016; Ho, 2024; Jimenez-Crespo, 2024). Transcreation practices require translators to edit, restructure, or even creatively re-author source material based on target-audience linguistic habits, cultural preferences, and functional needs (Jimenez-Crespo, 2024). Assignments involving advertising, brand messaging, public relations copy, user interfaces, and game narratives frequently demand localization to maximize communicative impact. In literary translation and audiovisual subtitling, transcreation further entails imparting an aesthetic style to the target text while preserving the source's semantic and emotive integrity (Abdelhalim et al., 2025). As cross-border communication needs expand, attention to translatability is shifting upstream into source drafting: concise structure, controlled terminology, and explicit articulation are becoming normative authoring standards. The promotion of controlled language in engineering documentation, such as Simplified Technical English, illustrates this trend (O'Brien, 2019).

The widespread adoption of LLMs has further expanded the scope of both transcreation and writing for translation. Translators can leverage models to generate multiple stylistic or purpose-specific variants rapidly, and can iteratively refine either the translation or the source text based on target user feedback—tightening the integration between language services, information design, and content production (Gursesli et al., 2025). Models also assist in flagging latent ambiguities and translation bottlenecks in the source, providing proactive support for multilingual content production. As the roles of translator and author increasingly converge in iterative content development workflows, translation is no longer confined to linguistic transfer; it has become a strategic component of information structuring and communicative design.

As a core subset within the broader and still-expanding language services ecosystem, translation services are undergoing internal realignment: their focal point is shifting from isolated text transfer to a systematic, multilayer linguistic adaptation process. Translators now require not only deep linguistic and cultural competence but also multidimensional capabilities in model orchestration, workflow design, and quality control. As human expertise and intelligent tools become more tightly integrated, the boundaries of translation services continue to expand, and professional roles are being continuously reshaped.

2.2 *Interpreting Services: Augmentation and Modality Shifts*

Interpreting—characterized by immediacy and high interactivity—has long been regarded as one of the most demanding domains within language services. Compared with written translation, it places greater emphasis on rapid adaptation to on-site contexts and requires interpreters to perform semantic transfer, cultural mediation, and communicative responses within seconds. Its principal modalities are consecutive and simultaneous interpreting, each suited to distinct communicative settings. Consecutive interpreting is typically used in bilateral meetings, business negotiations, and judicial proceedings, relying on the interpreter's holistic grasp of discourse and the ability to reconstruct its logic; note-taking and structural summarization are core skills. By contrast, simultaneous interpreting involves concurrent listening, processing, and speaking; it is widely deployed at international conferences and multilingual forums and places intense demands on working memory, semantic anticipation, and stress management. In practice, interpreters collaborate closely in teams, combining terminology preparation, equipment support, and shift rotation to sustain performance.

The diffusion of remote conferencing and speech technologies has transformed interpreting service delivery models. Telephone interpreting and video remote interpreting have reduced spatial and temporal barriers, providing highly responsive and accessible support in healthcare, legal, and emergency response settings. Early remote interpreting relied on call centers and crowdsourcing models; with the proliferation of mobile devices and ubiquitous connectivity, smart mobile apps and portable translation devices have become important tools. Especially in tourism and public service contexts, the integration of automatic speech recognition (ASR) and machine translation has steadily displaced portions of traditional escort (liaison) interpreting.

AI and LLMs are propelling interpreting services into a new phase of automation and augmentation. Fully integrated end-to-end automatic interpreting systems fusing ASR, machine translation (MT), and text-to-speech are already practical for everyday communication and certain standardized scenarios. Synthetic speech, avatar facial animation, and expressive rendering technologies make automated translation outputs more natural and diverse. At the same time, platform-based and on-demand service delivery models continue to emerge, and have made remote interpreting work more fragmented and flexible. Interpreters must master multiple digital platforms, adapt to heterogeneous technical environments, and continually strengthen self-regulation and professional judgment to cope with rising workload intensity and heightened career uncertainty.

Although technological advances have significantly increased efficiency and reach, human–machine collaboration remains indispensable in complex settings. In high-risk domains—such as medical, legal, and cross-cultural negotiation settings—misjudging technical terminology, pragmatic force, or implied meaning can lead to serious consequences. In these scenarios, AI typically functions as an assistive layer: real-time captioning, speech summarization, and content condensation tools support interpreters, yet final information filtering and risk control still rest with human professionals. This hybrid model elevates overall service quality, creates a structured pathway for junior interpreters' skill development, and helps senior practitioners distribute cognitive load and reduce fatigue.

Looking ahead, advances in multimodal interaction and LLM capabilities will continue to generate new intelligent interpreting modalities such as AI interpreters and immersive translation assistants. Virtual interpreters may develop personalized memory and contextual adaptation, autonomously adjusting style across multilingual, multicultural environments. Yet while technology extends the scope of interpreting services, the core human strengths—deep contextual comprehension, ethical judgment, and nuanced command of register and style—remain critical and are resistant to full technological substitution.

2.3 *Multidimensional Collaboration and User Experience Innovation in Localization Services*

Localization services have long since moved beyond translation to become a system-level endeavor of deep adaptation across product, content, and culture (LISA, 2003). Under the combined forces of digitalization and globalization, localization must ensure linguistic accuracy while integrating cultural norms, aesthetic expectations, legal compliance, and user experience into a coherent whole. Its core objective is to create a perception of native authenticity in the target market, thereby removing cultural friction and strengthening brand recognition and market acceptance.

To understand localization clearly, one must distinguish the roles of globalization, internationalization, localization, and translation (GILT) within the GILT framework (LISA, 2003). Internationalization (i18n) occurs at the product design stage and builds in capacity for future multilingual and multicultural adaptation—for example through Unicode support, separation of content from code, and flexible interface architectures. A robust i18n foundation maximizes subsequent localization potential (Nielsen, 1990; Esselink, 2000). Localization (L10n) then performs comprehensive market- and language-specific adaptation of an existing product, spanning text translation, symbol and unit conversion, image and color adjustments, replacement of legal content, and even content restructuring and stylistic redevelopment (Jiménez-Crespo, 2013). Globalization (g11n) addresses the overarching strategy that reconciles content consistency with cultural adaptability across markets (Cronin, 2003). Translation within GILT is no longer a narrow lexical transfer; it permeates all stages as cultural mediation and meaning reconstruction (Vermeer, 2000).

In internationalized game development, the initial architecture must expose flexible interfaces for language switching and content substitution. During localization, the team moves well beyond textual translation to adjust character design, narrative arcs, and interaction flows in alignment with regulation, player aesthetics, and cultural norms. Localization of other digital assets—film subtitles, social media platforms, and AI interaction interfaces—likewise demands multidisciplinary collaboration unifying linguistic adaptation, visual design, legal compliance, and user operations. The growing importance of markets using languages such as Chinese, Arabic, and Hindi has made localization a foundational and increasingly strategic capability for global deployment.

Language reconfiguration is central to localization services. Across websites, software interfaces, and marketing copy, wording must be clear and aligned with users' cognitive expectations and cultural style. A single functional button may require distinct phrasing and visual affordances across markets; for example, "Sign up now" may call for a more formal or relational variant in a German interface. Seemingly minor elements—colors, icons, forms of address, and place names—must likewise adhere to neutrality and cultural sensitivity. Global products often employ neutral selectors such as "Choose region" to avoid geopolitical friction or cultural misinterpretation. Diversified visual expression, localized brand storytelling, and symbol adaptation constitute critical extensions of professional language service capability.

The rise of new media and multi-device ecosystems has elevated expectations for localization-oriented language services. A fragmented content ecosystem, instant interaction, and contextual diversification demand tightly coordinated linguistic adaptation, content design, platform operations, and visual creativity. On platforms such as TikTok, Instagram, and Xiaohongshu, choices around informal address, emoji, and rhetorical style must be tuned to target user segments. Ultra-small screens (e.g., smart bands) require highly compressed messaging, whereas large displays and augmented reality (AR) / virtual reality (VR) environments necessitate multimodal, immersive language solutions. Multi-device adaptation simultaneously tests linguistic precision and cross-platform, cross-cultural design and implementation competence.

Multilingual user experience (UX) design has emerged as a leading topic in localization services (Garrett, 2010; Shneiderman et al., 2016). Current thinking emphasizes that a "language dimension" should permeate the entire product development lifecycle. Navigation logic, form structures, content architecture, and linguistic register all require optimization grounded in multilingual users' cognitive and behavioral patterns (Norman, 2016). For example, news platforms must accommodate title length variability across languages, while e-commerce applications must manage global diversity in personal names, address schemas, and payment standards. Balancing honorific systems, pragmatic norms, and regional stylistic preferences demands close collaboration between language specialists and design teams.

Embedded language services represent a major innovation in localization technology. They integrate modules for recognition, translation, refinement, summarization, and sentiment analysis directly into user journeys and system backends, enabling automatic language switching, real-time captioning, multilingual content interpretation, and interface adaptation. Looking ahead, they will further power language-driven personalized experiences—for example, educational platforms that dynamically adjust difficulty to user proficiency, navigation applications that restructure content based on local context, and B2B systems that auto-generate business proposals aligned with local conventions. Smart hardware and immersive interaction environments—augmented reality, virtual reality, and mixed reality (MR)—are expanding the scope and application scenarios of localization-oriented language services.

In a digital era characterized by multiple platforms, diverse contexts, and coexisting cultures, the role of language service professionals is steadily expanding. Teams adept in cross-disciplinary collaboration, cultural mediation, and content reconfiguration are becoming pivotal drivers of global communication and local adaptation. Language services are evolving from traditional text processing toward integrated solutions that fuse content strategy, user experience, and cultural alignment.

2.4 *Structured Technical Writing and Information Development*

Technical writing and information design integrate linguistic form with functional structure to produce documentation that is clear, precise, and actionable (Markel, 2012). Unlike literary or creative writing, technical writing converts complex technologies, procedures, and product knowledge into information users can quickly understand and apply. Whether the deliverable is a user manual, installation guide, Application Programming Interface (API) reference, or service agreement, language functions as the cognitive interface and knowledge conduit between the system and its users.

In an information development paradigm, technical writers combine strong linguistic expertise with deep insight into underlying technologies and clearly articulated user needs (Anderson & Surman, 2007). They collaborate closely with engineering, product, UX, and, where applicable, regulatory or support teams. The end-to-end workflow—spanning information architecture, content modeling, authoring, multichannel delivery, and version governance—demonstrates the tight coupling among language, structure, context, and user behavior. For example, a medical device operating manual must align consistent terminology, logical sequencing, users' cognitive pathways, and safeguards against misuse to mitigate safety risks. The writer thus not only re-expresses information but also curates knowledge, restructures content assets, and proactively manages user risk.

Language standards in technical documentation are stringent: content must be concise, logically consistent, and task-oriented, favoring verb-led, unambiguous constructions (Alred et al., 2009). Internationalized documentation must also avoid culture-bound or regional expressions that impede comprehension. For example, "Install the battery" is clearer and more directive than "You may want to install the battery." Style guides, termbases, and templates form the backbone of consistency. Adherence preserves terminological accuracy, clarity of risk signaling, and coherence across updates. Beyond sentence-level wording, a style guide governs information structure, interface microcopy, visual presentation, and linguistic ethics.

Modular and structured writing methodologies have accelerated the transition from narrative authoring to engineered content systems (Rockley et al., 2003). Content is decomposed into discrete, reusable modules; the Darwin Information Typing Architecture (DITA) exemplifies this approach. Documentation is organized into typical topic types such as concept, task, and reference. Each module is authored independently to support rapid updating, enabling personalization, multi-device publishing, and scalable localization. Structured writing leverages structured metadata and tagging for lifecycle management and underpins content automation, intelligent question answering, and knowledge graph applications. Lightweight markup languages—Markdown and reStructuredText—are prevalent in open-source and developer communities, while API documentation generators (e.g. Swagger, Javadoc) bind documentation directly to source code artifacts, greatly improving consistency and maintainability. Regulated industries such as aviation and pharmaceuticals adopt standards like S1000D (S1000D® Specification, Issue 6.0) to support cross-border, cross-system information exchange.

Amid escalating multichannel publishing demands, single sourcing and the content management system (CMS) have become core infrastructure elements for technical writing (Shivakumar, 2017). Single sourcing consolidates content assets and, via templates, conditional text, and variables, automates adaptation for media- and device-specific delivery. A CMS provides version control, permission management, and collaborative workflows, enabling large documentation programs to iterate efficiently with granular governance. Translators and language specialists increasingly shape terminology governance, translatability optimization, and content modeling, establishing a foundation for scalable multilingual releases. The coordinated orchestration of the termbase, translation memory, and style guide sustains consistent, high-quality output across authors, languages, and product lines.

Emerging multimodal communication environments further elevate the demands placed on technical writing (Carroll, 2023; Miller, 2024). Writers must anticipate how content behaves across text, voice, video, and interactive systems, tailoring expression to screen constraints, interaction logic, and situational context. For example, on smart devices, AR/VR experiences, or large-format urban display networks, language services must orchestrate visual, auditory, and interaction layers to optimize information accessibility and user experience. This imperative requires closer cross-functional collaboration among writers, product managers, designers, and engineers, thereby deepening the integration between content engineering and the multilingual ecosystem.

As content workflows become increasingly engineered and intelligence-enabled, technical writing and information design are solidifying their position as core functions of modern language services. The writer's role has transitioned from conventional authorship to that of a structured knowledge architect, requiring mastery in linguistic expression, content system design, structured toolchains, multiplatform adaptation, and interdisciplinary collaboration. Accordingly, language service professionals will shape content management, knowledge engineering, and intelligent applications, driving continuous innovation in technical writing practices and the broader digital content ecosystem.

2.5 *Data-Centric Language Services: Governance and Role*

In the era of intelligent technologies, language services have shifted from labor-intensive paradigms to a highly data-driven, systematized model. Data processing not only supports technical infrastructures and models but has also become a core task within language services themselves. This transformation is more than an upgrade of tools; it represents a comprehensive reconfiguration of industry logics and service capacity (Zha et al., 2023). Together, data-driven approaches and data processing act as twin engines of progress, and their deep integration continually extends the scope and substance of language service practices.

Data processing provides a robust resource base for language services. Parallel corpora, termbases, and industry knowledge bases, along with task-specific activities such as data cleaning, semantic annotation, and format conversion, all require systematic collection, curation, and processing by specialized teams (Qu, 2024; Zhou et al., 2022). These activities directly affect the quality and efficiency of translation, localization, intelligent question answering systems, and speech recognition. For instance, a high-quality termbase markedly improves accuracy and consistency in specialized translation, while finely annotated conversational data underpins intent understanding and response quality in customer service bots and virtual assistants. Standardized, process-driven workflows reduce downstream costs and improve overall delivery performance.

Data-driven practice has become the principal engine of innovation in language services. Model evolution, intelligent system optimization, and workflow automation almost universally depend on a sustained influx of high-quality data (China Academy of Information & Communications Technology, 2023). The industry is broadly adopting a "data flywheel" mechanism in which the output of initial intelligent systems guides further data collection and processing, creating a self-reinforcing, self-evolving loop. For example, a first-generation customer service bot continually improves intent classification and query clustering using real user dialogues; an automated summarization system accelerates domain expansion through human–AI collaborative annotation workflows. Such data-centric feedback shortens iteration cycles and enables rapid adaptation to market and technology shifts.

Data processing and data-driven methods are not external tools; they are reshaping professional roles and value propositions. Contemporary language service providers must combine expertise in translation, interpreting, and localization with capabilities in data collection, corpus management, annotation standards, and quality assessment (Institute for Digital Government and Governance, Tsinghua University, and Jiangsu Digitalization Association, 2025). They act simultaneously as knowledge mediators and as producers and stewards of data. In a multilingual localization project, for instance, translators not only translate content but also help curate the termbase, assess text translatability, annotate user feedback, and lead interface language testing. These data-oriented tasks are now integral to modern language services.

Data-driven language services also impose heightened ethical and technical requirements. Multilingual, multi-scenario, and multimodal data flows raise complex issues regarding privacy protection, fairness, and cultural adaptation. Studies have shown that large language models exhibit notable biases arising from intertwined factors spanning training data, model architecture, and sociocultural context (Guo et al., 2024). In sensitive domains such as healthcare, establishing systematic bias assessment frameworks is crucial for ensuring fairness and safety (Templin et al., 2025). A decade of research on gender bias in machine translation has highlighted the persistent tension between technological advancement and social equity (Savoldi et al., 2025). Cultural bias, as a major challenge for large language models, demands comprehensive analysis and targeted mitigation strategies (Liu, 2025). High-quality data processing influences not only technical metrics but also long-term sustainability and social responsibility. Professional data management systems and explicit annotation protocols ensure compliance and support innovation. In sensitive domains such as healthcare, establishing systematic bias assessment frameworks is crucial for ensuring fairness and safety (Templin et al., 2025). In these contexts, high-quality data processing shapes not only technical metrics but also sustainability and social responsibility.

An increasing number of enterprises and institutions treat language data as a core asset and invest strategically in building data platforms, developing proprietary annotation tools, and refining multilingual interface protocols to enhance scalability and portability. In the AI era, research on language services is taking new directions, and data-driven service models are reshaping the industry landscape (Cui & Chai, 2025). AI-driven language services are revolutionizing cross-border communication and offering unprecedented technical support for multilingual interaction in a globalized context (Muhammad, 2025).

These shifts enhance efficiency while opening new revenue streams and career trajectories. Corpus annotation for AI training, content moderation, cross-lingual data alignment, and domain ontology construction all create specialized professional pathways. Data-driven approaches and data processing together constitute the bridge between traditional language services and intelligent applications, continually expanding the field's future possibilities.

Data-driven methods and data processing have become foundational pillars of the field in the new era, jointly propelling a profound shift from content handling to knowledge management and from manual delivery to data-driven intelligence. The professional value of language services is shifting from purely linguistic expertise toward an integrated command of data, knowledge, and technology. This trajectory opens new avenues for growth for both the industry and its practitioners.

2.6 *Language Services as Multimodal Strategy Infrastructure in Convergent Media Ecosystems*

The emergence of the convergent media ecosystem, coupled with the ongoing integration of new media technologies, is reshaping how language services operate.

Their remit has expanded from narrow, single-channel text processing to multimodal content orchestration, stylistic strategy design, and user interaction management (Carroll, 2023; Tagg, 2015). In this context, language services function as foundational infrastructure for the structuring of information, affective steering, brand identity formation, and cultural affiliation. The work now encompasses content strategy planning, optimisation of distribution channels, and calibration of communicative outcomes, thereby making the role markedly more complex and integrative.

Recommendation algorithms play a pivotal role in disseminating new media content (Cui, 2019). Platforms rank content based on metrics such as completion rate, dwell time, and interaction rate, while users rapidly filter information using salient surface cues—titles, layout, and emoji use. Style conventions of different platforms and communities also shape prevailing modes of expression. Consequently, creators adapt language and presentation—deploying staccato, line-broken titles, affect-laden wording, hashtags, and emoji—to heighten distinctiveness and shareability. Douyin and Bilibili prioritise attention-grabbing openings and interactive phrasing, whereas Xiaohongshu emphasises hashtags and affective resonance. Thus, linguistic style becomes a core strategic lever for recommendation and dissemination rather than a purely rhetorical choice.

Real-time feedback mechanisms drive ongoing optimisation of language strategy. Metrics such as likes, shares, comments, completion rate, and dwell time supply immediate evidence for content adjustments; A/B testing and audience segmentation enable granular iteration of interactive elements including titles, openings, and scripted phrasing (Khawar & Boukes, 2024; Lischka & Garz, 2023). This data loop tightly integrates language services with user experience, behavioural science, and data-informed decision-making, yielding a continuous cycle of design–release–feedback–redesign.

In the new media environment, the capacity of language to encode culture is further amplified. Language not only transmits information but also directs attention and shapes meaning through agenda setting and framing (Chong & Druckman, 2007; McCombs, 2005). The rapid diffusion of neologisms—such as "digital health passes" (QR-code–based health status credentials) and distancing rules (e.g., the "two-metre rule" or the "six-foot rule") during pandemic control—illustrates the tight coupling between linguistic innovation and social practice. In global brand communication, calibrated adjustments to address forms, politeness strategies, emotional tone, and narrative structures directly shape audience receptivity and trust.

Data-driven personalisation propels the refinement of language services. User profiling, contextual segmentation, and sentiment analysis enable precise matching of content to target audiences. In customer support, healthcare, and news domains, tone, textual structure, and lexical choice are flexibly adapted to user types to improve comprehension and satisfaction. Sociolinguistics, communication studies, and psychology provide theoretical grounding for register selection and persuasive strategy (Carroll, 2023; Tagg, 2015).

Interactive co-creation intensifies the iterative, generative nature of language services (Romero-Rodriguez & Castillo-Abdul, 2023; Santos, 2022). User-generated content, memetic reproduction, and discursive negotiation in comment threads produce a triadic co-shaping of style among platform, creator, and user. Professional teams leverage comment mining, sentiment and semantic clustering, and community hot-term tracking to iterate expressions rapidly and test strategies for extending community boundaries. This requires competencies in cross-platform style migration, cross-cultural adaptation, experimental design, and rapid response.

Across international, convergent media environments, strategic intent and stylistic diversity have assumed heightened importance. Organisations must maintain a coherent articulation of core values and a consistent brand voice across multiple accounts and platforms (short-form video, social networks, podcasts, and official sites), while simultaneously adapting to differing cultural pragmatic norms (politeness conventions, acceptable degrees of directness, and tolerance for humour). In practice, a two-layer style governance model has emerged, comprising a unified semantic core and a localised pragmatic and format layer. This model is evident in practices ranging from TikTok's localised subtitle conventions to the multimodal narrative structures employed by national-level media organisations. Authenticity, approachability, and expressive diversity have supplanted reliance on a single formal register as joint drivers of visibility and trust.

Ethics and professional integrity set strategic boundaries (Lazer et al., 2018; Sutherland, 2024). Excessive emotional triggering, clickbait titling, and manipulative framing can inflate short-term engagement metrics while eroding trust and platform reputation. Effective language service strategies must pursue multi-objective optimisation balancing attention acquisition, informational accuracy, transparency of values, and social responsibility, supported by auditable norms for style and expression. Industry self-regulation, algorithmic transparency, and user education jointly form a governance triad to prevent misleading language.

In summary, the core function of language services is shifting from single-text processing to a multi-layer, collaborative system oriented towards content strategy, user experience, and cross-cultural adaptation. Language now functions as a pivotal hub: connecting users, fostering shared identity, enabling dissemination, and underpinning knowledge services. Looking ahead, language service professionals will need systematically to master: (i) orchestration of multimodal content and design of style strategies; (ii) data analytics and interpretation of behavioural signals; (iii) cross-cultural pragmatic adaptation and governance of consistency; (iv) interactive co-creation and iterative experimentation; and (v) ethical judgement and risk management. Sustained value creation will depend on balancing strategic effectiveness, cultural sensitivity, data literacy, and robust ethical governance within an increasingly complex new media and international communication ecosystem.

2.7 *Restructuring Language Services Under Automation and Outsourcing*

Traditional professional activity in the language services industry has centered on written translation and interpreting. These tasks have long structured practitioners' daily routines. Their value lies in accurately transferring source meaning, removing linguistic barriers, and mediating cultural nuance—together constituting a knowledge-intensive, high-skill craft. Translators' experiential knowledge, linguistic judgment, and subject-matter expertise are regarded as indispensable.

The professional status of traditional translation and interpreting practice has historically rested on advanced mastery of interlingual transfer. Literary translation demands fine-grained sensitivity to stylistic register and cultural context; legal translation requires precise terminological consistency and a rigorously articulated logical structure; interpreting relies on real-time processing and sustained attentional control. These activities test high-level bilingual competence and draw on cumulative domain-specific knowledge and interactional skills accumulated over time. Within this professional configuration, translation and interpreting have been construed as an intellectually demanding, culturally embedded form of expert practice, and translators have often maintained relatively stable professional identities and a considerable degree of autonomy.

Over the past two decades, this craft-based model has been progressively reshaped by digital technologies, platform-mediated coordination, and outsourcing arrangements. Machine translation has evolved from early rule-based and statistical models to contemporary neural machine translation (NMT) architectures based on deep learning, thereby reconfiguring workflow design, task segmentation, and allocation. Current NMT output now performs comparatively well on high-volume, structured and formulaic text—especially news briefs, e-commerce product listings, and travel and hospitality information. Human translators are less frequently the sole drivers of end-to-end workflows; they are increasingly positioned in post-editing roles tasked with evaluating and correcting machine-generated drafts under throughput, consistency, and turnaround metrics. This post-editing work is typically fast-paced, repetitive, and offers limited scope for discretionary creative intervention. While advanced linguistic and domain knowledge remains necessary, reliance on individualized professional judgment and tacit experiential nuance is substantially reduced.

Digital platforms and global outsourcing logics have further intensified the micro-segmentation and modularization of translation and localization workflows (Feng & Cui, 2025). Emerging evidence from gig-economy research indicates that platform intermediation reshapes patterns of task engagement, income stability, and worker well-being in complex and uneven ways (Himani Srihita et al., 2025). Today, an increasing proportion of demand for language services circumvents traditional agencies and is routed via crowdsourcing portals, freelance marketplaces, platform-managed vendor pools, or embedded into transnational, just-in-time content supply chains. A single project is routinely disaggregated into segments, algorithmically or managerially assigned and processed in parallel by dispersed contributors, after which a reviewer (or small quality assurance team) consolidates outputs, harmonizing formatting, terminology, and style. Translators thus encounter only decontextualized units (sentences, strings, user interface labels), possess limited visibility into upstream briefs or downstream reuse, and frequently remain unaware of the end-user or communicative function. This context-attenuated workflow constrains the exercise of professional judgment and risks reifying linguistic expertise as a narrowly procedural intervention (Moorkens, 2017).

Pricing models further reflect the shifting logic of linguistic labor under outsourcing. Per-word, per-segment, or time-based pricing reduces complex cognitive activity to quantifiable units, enabling comparison, bidding, and allocation. Under competitive pressure, translators must complete more tasks in less time, while platforms streamline processes to increase efficiency and drive down costs (Flanagan, 2016; Jiménez-Crespo, 2021a). The result is the deeper involvement of practitioners in a low-margin, high-intensity, highly substitutable production chain.

This restructuring reshapes production modalities and redefines professional identity among language service practitioners. Some translators begin to question whether their professional value endures, while newcomers may be trained from the outset as "tool operators" rather than "content creators." Linguistic competence still matters, yet it is no longer treated as a standalone professional resource and is subordinated to platform logic and automated workflows.

This path is not irreversible; however, it constitutes a foundational professional reality. Practitioners must recognize that reliance on traditional linguistic proficiency alone no longer sustains career development. Building resilience in the gig economy requires the acquisition of specific digital skills that enable independent professionals to navigate platformized work (Fiers, 2024). Understanding how technologies function, adopting new collaboration models, and intervening in task design and quality assurance have become essential for preserving professional status and dignity. Language service practices are being fundamentally redefined: they have evolved from the discrete act of interlingual transfer into a multifaceted process of multimodal knowledge mediation and information governance. In this paradigm, the "translated text" is no longer a static end product; it functions as a dynamic data asset integrated into global information flows, digital content chains, and intelligent technological platforms. Grasping this shift marks the starting point for a shift toward broader roles in content production and knowledge services.

2.8 *Broad-Based Content Production, Consulting and Strategic Planning*

If we bracket "content" as it appears in traditional literary or academic writing and instead examine the large volume of everyday text generation oriented toward information circulation, a broader landscape of content production emerges. Here, content is no longer aimed chiefly at expressing individual emotions or ideas; it serves specific functions: attracting clicks, signaling a position, displaying results, supporting a workflow, or guiding public opinion. Consequently, content production becomes an organized, instrumental, and strategic form of linguistic labor whose value lies less in originality or aesthetic merit than in circulation performance and its degree of systemic embeddedness.

More concretely, the routine operation of creator accounts across social media platforms illustrates the broad-based nature of contemporary content production. A mature WeChat public account, short-video channel, or content team typically follows a clear editorial plan, defined target audience, traffic metrics, and controlled release cadence. Whether a title captures attention, the wording aligns with algorithmic preferences, or the cover image is optimized for shareability—together these factors determine the piece's value. Even seemingly casual lifestyle logs, book notes, or current-affairs commentary are deliberately crafted responses to platform mechanics and audience psychology—produced artifacts rather than unmediated personal expression.

In contrast, formal administrative documents are not primarily intended for broad public circulation. Nevertheless, the density and complexity of the linguistic labor they entail render them an equally consequential site of content production. Within China's organizational and personnel system, year-end reporting cycles and leadership transitions sharply heighten writing pressures: officials' annual performance reports, organizational opinions, collective evaluations, and draft official documents all require exacting linguistic calibration. These texts must convey institutional intent with precision, adhere to codified stylistic conventions, and typically manifest a recognizable policy register. Although their drafters are not literary authors, they must exercise acute contextual awareness, efficient information synthesis, and discriminating judgment. The attendant workload and cognitive burden routinely exceed outside expectations.

Drafting speeches for senior officials is even more complex. Staff in government agencies and large state-owned enterprises must simultaneously calibrate audience, occasion, and hierarchical level; survey policy documents and precedent speeches extensively; and craft a speech that is at once compliant yet distinctive. Keyboard time is brief; the principal time cost lies in prior investigation, sifting, and interpretation. The task is less about producing novelty than about assembling a text that is acceptable, intelligible, and actionable under overlapping policy, hierarchical, and rhetorical constraints.

Meanwhile, routine operational tasks—such as university grant proposals and evaluation summaries, corporate brand copy, crisis communication statements, and media scheduling plans—have become arenas of standardized text production. They are governed by explicit objectives, codified workflows, and collaborative structures, relying less on individual inspiration than on coordinated textual processes aligned with organizational and communicative goals.

The expansion of broad-based content production is closely associated with advances in information and communication technologies and with rising organizational complexity. Platform-level algorithmic ranking and recommendation systems prioritize discoverability metrics, incentivizing more deliberate, data-informed optimization at the point of creation. Simultaneously, internal demand within administrative and corporate systems for standardized reports, summaries, and notices continues to increase; each such document functions as a modular operational component within workflows. Consequently, content production constitutes not only linguistic labor, but also an organizational coordination mechanism and a strategic instrument of communication. Emerging applications of artificial intelligence in content marketing are further reshaping digital strategy and introducing new technological possibilities—as well as governance and quality control challenges—for content production (Korsunova, 2024).

The expansion of large-scale, multi-channel content production is generating new career opportunities for language-service professionals while raising competency thresholds. Rapid interpretation of task objectives and context, succinct distillation of salient information, and audience-responsive linguistic strategy now outweigh narrow, single-point linguistic skills. In this evolving ecology, professionals act not only as content producers but also as coordinators of dissemination workflows and mediators of semantic coherence.

Within an increasingly global and data-mediated content ecosystem, language services are shifting from narrow text processing to strategic communication and cultural risk governance. Language is an actionable control surface for steering narrative direction and managing perceptual risk. Unmodified Western-centric framing in Southeast Asian or African contexts can impose early interpretation barriers. Upstream intervention—corpus divergence analysis, audience persona profiling, and controlled wording tests—supports proposals that are linguistically native and culturally adaptive, broadening the function's scope into pre-development communication architecture and cultural risk mitigation.

The shift is from downstream text production to upstream linguistic strategy design. Production prioritizes immediate intelligibility, fluency, and channel-ready dissemination. Strategy design prioritizes brand voice coherence, market differentiation, and cultural responsiveness. Maintaining a unified tone across multiple languages and expressing stable value frames within varied cultural contexts exemplify challenges of value-oriented linguistic deployment rather than narrow translational execution.

In addition, the rapid development of large language models is redefining the scope of language services. Routine drafting, baseline editing, and initial translation tasks are increasingly delegated to LLMs or LLM-enabled systems. Yet model capability alone does not produce autonomous, context-appropriate, high-quality communication. Task specification, prompt design, evaluative review, and workflow orchestration continue to require strategically informed language-service professionals. This juncture creates an opportunity for these professionals to transition from text implementers to designers and governors of language production systems. Recent global survey data indicate rising adoption rates of AI technologies, prompting reassessment of professional positioning within technology-intensive environments (McKinsey & Company, 2024).

Against this backdrop, language and cultural consulting is emerging as a distinct specialization. Practitioners must integrate advanced control of linguistic structure with knowledge of the target community's socio-cultural context, political sensitivities, and pragmatic limits of expression. Lexical items that are neutral in Western usage may provoke misunderstanding or controversy in other settings; semantic competence alone therefore does not ensure appropriateness. The consulting role is to align communicative objectives with cultural sensitivity and risk management.

These consulting functions now extend upstream across brand naming, product narrative positioning, public messaging, and multilingual customer service architecture, fusing corpus analytics, audience context modeling, and iterative user experiments. The shift elevates language services from surface-level editing to a strategic architecture for cross-cultural communication and content orchestration.

To adapt, language service professionals now require not only linguistic mastery but a hybrid skill set spanning user research, strategic communication theory, corpus analytics, and cross-functional orchestration. The work has shifted from sentence-level, rule-governed execution to a strategic discipline of cultural communication design and planning.

By engaging with full-spectrum content operations, language service professionals move from downstream final-pass execution to continuous orchestration across content ideation, messaging architecture, and cultural shaping. Language is not merely a conduit of meaning; it operates as an organizational strategic asset and a cultural positioning choice. Their value proposition is migrating from deliverable throughput to strategic differentiation within an integrated cross-cultural content ecosystem.

3 Role Evolution and Competency Redefinition in the Language Services Profession

Automation is reconfiguring the conditions under which language services generate value. As large language models assume routine drafting, extraction, and surface editing, attention shifts from isolated linguistic execution to the organization of data, workflows, and evaluative standards underlying multilingual communication. Professional practice increasingly centres on corpus construction and governance, principled terminology and style management, annotation schema design, multimodal integration, and the coordination of human–machine interaction. These developments relocate core competence from craft alone to the systematic conversion of transient texts into structured, reusable linguistic assets. The resulting reframing expands the scope of expertise and establishes a foundation for sustained professional differentiation.

3.1 Automation Shift and Emergent System-Level Roles

The role of language service practitioners is undergoing a profound transformation. With the continued adoption of large language models and associated AI tools, the structure, workflow dynamics, and cost parameters of language-intensive professional work have already shifted. Two concurrent dynamics in the emerging "language intelligence" era are rapid content generation and intensive information compression. Within increasingly automated production pipelines, professional functions whose value depended on manual linguistic processing have been progressively reduced or displaced. The earlier assumption that human linguistic execution formed an unreplaceable value anchor in language service delivery is now being reassessed. Historically, expressive craft, rhetorical nuance, and translation accuracy were core differentiators. As systems approach a "good enough" performance threshold for routine outputs, these competencies alone no longer confer a sustained competitive advantage. Tasks such as drafting, information extraction, and linguistic editing can now be executed rapidly at standard quality, eroding barriers built on single-dimensional (execution-centric) skill sets. According to recent industry data, approximately one-third of translation service providers employ LLMs for machine translation (Slator, 2024), thereby accelerating structural adjustments in established service delivery models.

Despite advancing automation, professional translation and related language mediation activities have not disappeared; their value is shifting toward more complex, system-level functions. Professional roles are evolving from "writer" or "translator" to encompass content architect, corpus curator, and quality manager positions embedded in cross-lingual production pipelines. Practitioners now must (a) analyze the structure and communicative intent of source materials, (b) design strategies for linguistic transformation, terminology governance, and stylistic adaptation, and (c) orchestrate collaboration among human specialists and automation tools to meet quality, schedule, and budget constraints. Emerging research on translator competences in the AI era (Prieto Ramos, 2024) indicates a reassessment of core skill sets, particularly in legally and institutionally specialized domains. Corpus development now serves as a principal on-ramp into technical workflows: corpora have shifted from static scholarly resources to operational infrastructure for model training, adaptation, and evaluation. Systems for machine translation, text classification, dialogue generation, and sentiment analysis rely on robust data architectures and well-designed annotation schemes.

3.2 Data Stewardship, Annotation Complexity, and Multimodal Workflow Expansion

In applied project contexts, professional responsibilities extend well beyond simple data provision. Practitioners evaluate corpus provenance, representativeness, and task fitness. In building a Chinese medical question-answering (Q&A) system, openly available web data are typically insufficient; an effective pipeline integrates multiple sources—policy documents, de-identified clinical records, scholarly literature, and consultation transcripts—while enforcing privacy safeguards, terminology standardization, and structural harmonization (Xu & Zhang, 2025). To meet multilingual and intra-lingual variation requirements, teams further distinguish language varieties and manage register and stylistic differences. Annotation design is equally central: for semantic similarity, sentiment analysis, and subjective opinion extraction, binary labels are inadequate. Operational definitions must therefore be established for categories such as "neutral," "ambiguous," and "ironic," and annotators must receive guidance on leveraging context to maintain inter-annotator consistency. These challenges require deep linguistic expertise and substantial project experience. Accordingly, teams generate seed examples, draft and iterate guidelines, conduct pilot rounds, examine disagreement distributions, and progressively refine specifications to capture real-world complexity.

Beyond purely textual content, contemporary language service workflows now encompass multimodal data processing. Tasks such as image–text alignment, speech transcription, and scenario-based simulation require practitioners to integrate linguistic, visual, and acoustic signals. In e-commerce, combining product imagery with persuasive promotional copy involves not only computer-vision outputs but also adaptation to user behavior patterns, advertising regulations, and culturally mediated nuance. In speech recognition and subtitle production, prosodic cues—tone (including lexical tone where relevant), stress, pauses, and discourse markers—must be interpreted so that spoken language is rendered as natural, reader-friendly written text. The locus of professional value is shifting from operating isolated tools to architecting end-to-end systems and coordinating workflows. Acting as task and workflow architects, practitioners negotiate interfaces and data formats with engineers, align constraints and deliverables with clients, and coordinate scheduling and quality-assurance protocols with annotation teams—serving as the integrative hub between technology and business. Although AI assistant initiatives may appear model-centric, their effectiveness typically hinges on whether practitioners can assemble fit-for-purpose datasets, structure robust and maintainable corpora, and engineer efficient human–machine dialogue flows.

3.3 Competency Reconfiguration and Misconceptions of Role Substitutability

The competence framework of language services is undergoing a substantive reconfiguration. Language technologies now constitute only a baseline expectation; sustained differentiation lies in deep content comprehension, project-level coordination, and forward-looking data-lifecycle planning (Kang, 2025). Vision-oriented practitioners assess—even while performing granular tasks such as annotation—the reusability and scalability of emerging data assets and their capacity to form value-generating feedback loops with clients' content production processes. This shift elevates responsibilities from task execution to architectural design—a layer that many narrowly specialized technical staff do not fully cover. The emerging role positions practitioners not as mere linguistic reproducers but as architects of language systems who extend organizational boundaries through system-level understanding, workflow governance, and content orchestration, thereby sustaining and amplifying professional value.

The proliferation of intelligent platforms has prompted assertions that language service functions can be absorbed by adjacent roles. Firms may, for example, redeploy marketing personnel to perform corpus annotation on the grounds of contextual familiarity, or allow engineers to prompt large language models to draft technical documentation, bypassing dedicated writers. Such measures can yield short-term gains in speed or cost, yet they overlook the core value proposition of language services: expert stewardship of language as a structuring substrate within information systems. In corpus annotation, marketing staff may command market discourse, yet frequently lack the capacity to conceptualize linguistic phenomena, formalize category boundaries, and operationalize consistent annotation logic. High-quality annotation depends on stable, evolution-managed label taxonomies, cross-lingual alignment strategies, and controlled terminology regimes—requiring linguistic acuity, domain-aware sensitivity, and abstract analytical competence. Faulty schema or guideline decisions propagate through the entire training pipeline, distorting model behavior and inflating downstream remediation costs; professionally trained linguistic specialists are pivotal in preventing such drift. Likewise, technical documentation operates as an interface for cross-cultural and cross-disciplinary knowledge transfer. Beyond fluent wording, it demands deliberate macro-structuring, audience-layered information design, principled terminology governance, and register management—all grounded in pragmatic competence and a nuanced understanding of industry and product knowledge systems, user cognition, and user experience research.

3.4 Core Linguistic System Value and Programmatic Reset

The core competitive value of language services resides in the disciplined capacity to (i) distill explicit, generalizable rules from heterogeneous linguistic phenomena, (ii) abstract stable structural representations from context-bound discourse, and (iii) impose coherent, audience-appropriate expressive organization on otherwise unruly content streams. The diffusion of large language models does not automatically instantiate these epistemic and organizational capabilities. What is required are language system architects, data-level linguistic reviewers, and semantic design strategists able to collaborate with computational tooling—rather than mere rapid drafters or literal translators. Their mandate is not to outwrite models, but to interrogate and validate model outputs for logical soundness, contextual adequacy, terminological and pragmatic appropriateness, and alignment with product, domain, and communication strategy.

Language service programs need a structural reset. Objectives must move past "correct sentences" and "faithful translation" toward showing how tasks trigger linguistic operations and how text becomes structured assets—controlled vocabularies, style/terminology standards, annotation schemas, evaluation rubrics, workflow specifications. This shift broadens career paths and defends the profession's value. Information delivery still relies on linguistic mediation, and coordinated knowledge production still needs disciplined linguistic organization. The role endures, but its skill set now centers on stronger technical and data literacy, systems thinking, and organizational design capacity.

3.5 Escalating Expectations and Strategic Problem-Solving Orientation

Expectations for language professionals have intensified. The focus has shifted from traditional surface descriptive linguistic analysis or literary critique toward deep semantic and pragmatic insight, strategic analytical and planning competence, and system-oriented applied problem solving.

4 Platformization and AI-Enabled Reconfiguration of Language Services

Platformization and AI are steadily reshaping language services, moving practice away from a narrow, sequential handling of standalone texts toward continuous, networked management of diverse content assets. Fragmented desktop tools give way to cloud environments where memories, terminology, allocation, review, and metrics are coordinated in real time. Workflows now absorb multimodal and structured data, large language models participate in co-creation, upstream involvement spans content strategy and data governance, and linguistic expertise functions as infrastructural design rather than isolated execution.

4.1 Platform Convergence and Collaborative Infrastructure

The language services industry is undergoing profound restructuring driven by digitalization and intelligent technologies. The previously text-centric service logic is being dismantled and reassembled with each new generation of tools. Early technology adoption centered on standalone desktop applications: data were fragmented, collaboration was inefficient, and workflows were linear and closed. Cloud computing has brought translation memories, terminology resources, work allocation, and quality control onto unified platforms, enabling multi-party collaboration, parallel workflows, real-time revision, and transparent management (Crowdin, 2022; Lionbridge, 2024; Welocalize, 2025; XTM International, 2025). Work can no longer advance in a rigid sequence: teams are globally distributed and asynchronous, making platform-mediated collaboration essential to geographic reach and time efficiency. Clients now monitor progress and processes in real time, further increasing transparency. Emerging platform technologies consolidate previously discrete tasks—text translation, interface localization, customer support scripting, and image-based text extraction and processing—within a single cross-media workflow. Translators now function as platform nodes whose processes and outputs are continuously measured and fed back, enabling granular quality management and new collaboration models.

4.2 Multimodal Content Forms and Task Diversification

The transformation of content forms is particularly pronounced. With the expansion of the internet and the platform economy, the objects of language services have moved from static text to multimodal, dynamic, and increasingly structured data. In e-commerce, social media, and software contexts, heterogeneous content types—text, images, tags, video, user reviews, and data fields—now routinely co-occur. Accordingly, language service tasks extend beyond translation to encompass script localization, tag creation and naming, style evaluation, content structuring, and alignment with dissemination strategies. As structured and unstructured materials coexist, practitioners need baseline competencies in format parsing and data adaptation, shifting from linear text handling toward recombining discrete elements and optimizing content experience. Real-time generation, short production cycles, and high-frequency online publishing are blurring traditional divisions of labor; cross-role and human–machine collaboration have become mainstream. Language services now contribute not only to information transfer but also to content planning, interaction design, and scenario-driven user experience design.

4.3 Human–Machine Co-creation and Workflow Automation

The pervasive integration of intelligent systems is redefining the operational paradigm of language services. Large language models, machine translation engines, and AI-enabled review tools have become core workflow components, moving content creation and refinement beyond a sequential, human-first–machine-second pipeline toward genuine human–machine co-creation (Intento, 2025; SEAtongue,

2025). Human effort is migrating from manual execution to task scoping, evaluative judgment, strategic design, and quality assurance, while machines assume high-throughput execution, data aggregation, and routine processing. Project management models are likewise evolving: traditional per-word pricing is giving way to integrated service bundles oriented toward end-to-end process completion and user experience outcomes. Highly skilled professionals now concentrate on terminology system design, post-editing of model outputs, risk assessment, and exception handling; proficiency in human–machine collaboration has become a primary determinant of both quality and value distribution. Increasing workflow automation is reshaping business models, shifting language services from discrete projects toward platformization, micro-task crowdsourcing, and adaptive subscription models. Task allocation, quality control, and delivery management are being progressively automated, making service offerings more flexible, scalable, and traceable.

4.4 Upstream Integration and Strategic Language Infrastructure

The functional remit of language services continues to expand. Service providers are increasingly engaged in upstream domains, including content strategy, data governance, brand communication, and market localization (Wang and Cui, 2025; Wang, 2024). Language functions not merely as a vehicle for translation and editing, but as a strategic resource for optimizing information architectures, codifying rules, shaping user experience design, and articulating brand identity. Across publishing, software development, and data governance, language services are now embedded in content planning and production, terminology system design, model fine-tuning, and feedback loop design, thereby constituting part of the foundational infrastructure of the intelligent content ecosystem. The global dissemination of Chinese publications illustrates how translation, editorial review, content adaptation, and intelligent tools interoperate to deliver standardized workflows, higher efficiency, and robust quality assurance. Translators' roles are shifting toward language system calibration, data cleansing, and cross-lingual content design, making them indispensable nodes within the human–machine collaboration chain.

4.5 Toward Data-Driven, Systemic Service Models

Driven by ongoing digitalization and intelligent technologies, language services are evolving beyond traditional text-centric workflows and transactional outsourcing toward platformization, data-driven operations, orchestrated content systems, and knowledge integration (MultiLingual, 2025). Service providers now require enhanced competency portfolios that integrate technical fluency, data literacy, and systems design capabilities. As industry boundaries blur and extend, linguistic competencies have become foundational enablers of content circulation, knowledge management, and user-experience innovation across the digital economy and the emerging intelligent society. This transformation is restructuring the language services domain and is poised to shape future models of content production, inter-organizational collaboration, and global information flows.

5 Conclusion

In the era of artificial intelligence, language services are moving beyond incremental tool upgrades toward a wholesale reconfiguration of their underlying service paradigm. Language simultaneously propels technological progress and serves as a primary locus of optimization. The service landscape has evolved into a multilayered ecosystem linking humans, intelligent systems, and algorithmic models; current use cases span multilingual AI customer support, cross-cultural content localization, training data provisioning for models, and enhancement of low-resource languages. Hybrid human–AI collaboration has become the norm, shifting workflows from linear sequences to adaptive, complementary loops. Across translation, education, and customer service, bidirectional augmentation and the orchestrated use of multiple tools improve both efficiency and quality. The value proposition is moving beyond mere text transfer toward deeper communicative and cognitive objectives that advance cross-cultural exchange, knowledge integration, and user experience (UX) innovation. Industry boundaries are increasingly blurred as data governance, UX design, and knowledge engineering converge, catalyzing integrated, system-level service models. As technology and the humanities further intertwine, language service professionals must reposition themselves as designers of human–machine collaboration frameworks and architects of cross-cultural governance mechanisms, continually expanding their competencies and capacity for innovation within an evolving ecosystem.

References

Abdelhalim, S. M., Alsahil, A. A., & Alsuhaibani, Z. A. (2025). Artificial intelligence tools and literary translation: A comparative investigation of ChatGPT and Google Translate from novice and advanced EFL student translators' perspectives. *Cogent Arts & Humanities, 12*(1), 2508031. https://doi.org/10.1080/23311983.2025.2508031

Achiam, J., Adler, S., Agarwal, S., Ahmad, L., Akkaya, I., Aleman, F. L., & McGrew, B., et al. (2023). GPT-4 technical report. https://doi.org/10.48550/arXiv.2303.08774

Alred, G. J., Brusaw, C. T., & Oliu, W. E. (2009). *Handbook of technical writing*. Macmillan.

Anderson, P. V., & Surman, K. (2007). *Technical communication: A reader-centered approach*. Thomson/Wadsworth.

Angelone, E., Ehrensberger-Dow, M., & Massey, G. (Eds.). (2020). *The Bloomsbury companion to language industry studies*. Bloomsbury.
Appicharla, R., Gain, B., Pal, S., & Ekbal, A. (2025). *Beyond the sentence: A survey on context-aware machine translation with large language models*. https://arxiv.org/abs/2506.07583
Bowker, L. (2002). *Computer-aided translation technology: A practical introduction*. University of Ottawa Press.
Carroll, B. (2023). *Writing and editing for digital media*. Routledge.
Chen, L., & Cao, Peihui. (2016). 论创译的名与实 [On the name and nature of transcreation]. *Foreign Languages and Their Teaching*, (6), 123–130, 146, 151. https://doi.org/10.13458/j.cnki.flatt.004318
Chen, B., & Liu, G. (2023). 清前中期传教士通事群体及其角色功能 [Missionary interpreters in early and mid-Qing dynasty: Roles and functions]. 故宫博物院院刊 [*The Palace Museum Journal*]. https://www.dpm.org.cn/journal/259125.html
Chen, S., Wang, Z., Chen, X., Liu, D., Zhu, D., & Zhao, H. (2024). Refining translations with LLMs: A constraint-aware iterative prompting approach. https://arxiv.org/abs/2411.08348
China Academy of Information and Communications Technology. (2023). White paper on data elements. Retrieved July 5, 2025, from http://www.caict.ac.cn/english/research/whitepapers/202311/P020231103487266783845.pdf
Chong, D., & Druckman, J. N. (2007). Framing theory. *Annual Review of Political Science, 10*(1), 103–126.
Crabbe, S. (2012). Constructing a contextual history of English language technical writing. *Trans-kom, 5*(1), 40–59. Retrieved July 5, 2025, from http://www.trans-kom.eu/bd05nr01/trans-kom_05_01_03_Crabbe_Technical_Writing.20120614.pdf
Cronin, M. (2003). *Translation and globalisation*. Routledge.
Crowdin. (2022, December 20). How to localize your SaaS application: Best practices. Crowdin Blog. https://crowdin.com/blog/2022/12/20/saas-localization
CSA Research. (2024, June). Navigating the post-localization era: The impact of AI on the language services industry. https://csa-research.com/Featured-Content/For-LSPs/Thought-Leadership/Navigating-the-Post-Localization-Era-The-Impact-of-AI-on-the-Language-Services-Industry
Cui, Q. (2025). Development trends of the language service industry in the age of artificial intelligence. *Journal of Beijing International Studies University, 47*(1), 62–72.
Cui, C., & Chai, Y. (2025). Language service studies in the era of AI: Developments and prospects. *Journal of Language Service Studies, 1*(1), 67–88. https://journals.zycentre.com/jlss
Cui, X. (2019). A corpus-based study of new media language. *Contemporary Rhetoric, 5*, 1–14. https://doi.org/10.16027/j.cnki.cn31-2043/h.2019.05.001
Deshpande, T., Kowtal, N., & Joshi, R. (2024). Chain-of-translation prompting (CoTR): A novel prompting technique for low resource languages. arXiv. https://arxiv.org/abs/2409.04512
dos Santos, M. L. B. (2022). The "so-called" UGC: An updated definition of user-generated content in the age of social media. *Online Information Review, 46*(1), 95–113. https://doi.org/10.1108/OIR-06-2020-0258
Esselink, B. (2000). *A Practical Guide to Localization*. John Benjamins Publishing Company.
Feng, Z., & Cui, M. (2025). Characteristics, conflicts, and countermeasures of crowdsourced translation in the era of digital intelligence. *Chinese Foreign Languages, 22*(2), 106–112. https://doi.org/10.13564/j.cnki.issn.1672-9382.2025.02.011
Fiers, F. (2024). Resilience in the gig economy: Digital skills in online freelancing. *Journal of Computer-Mediated Communication, 29*(5), Article zmae014. https://doi.org/10.1093/jcmc/zmae014
Flanagan, M. (2016). Cause for concern? Attitudes towards translation crowdsourcing in professional translators' blogs. *The Journal of Specialised Translation, 25*, 149–173.
Gao, Y., Wang, R., & Hou, F. (2023). *How to design translation prompts for ChatGPT: An empirical study*. https://arxiv.org/abs/2304.02182
Garrett, J. J. (2010). *The Elements of User Experience: User-Centered Design for the Web and Beyond* (2nd ed.). Pearson Education.

Gencer, G., & Gencer, K. (2025). Large language models in healthcare: A bibliometric analysis and examination of research trends. *Journal of Multidisciplinary Healthcare, 18*, 223–238. https://doi.org/10.2147/JMDH.S502351

Guo, Y., Guo, M., Su, J., Yang, Z., Zhu, M., Li, H., Qiu, M., & Liu, S. S. (2024). *Bias in large language models: Origin, evaluation, and mitigation.* arXiv. https://arxiv.org/abs/2411.10915

Gursesli, M. C., Chen, S., Dewantoro, M. F., You, X., Anbar, E., Taveekitworachai, P., Thawonmas, R., et al. (2025). The role of large language model-generated stories in the narrative experience of serious visual novel games. *International Journal of Human–Computer Interaction*, 1–20. https://doi.org/10.1080/10447318.2025.2528993

He, Z., Liang, T., Jiao, W., Zhang, Z., Yang, Y., Wang, R., Tu, Z., Shi, S., & Wang, X. (2024). Exploring human-like translation strategy with large language models. *Transactions of the Association for Computational Linguistics, 12*, 229–246. https://doi.org/10.1162/tacl_a_00642

He, M. (2025). AI-driven paradigm shift in translation education and career trajectories: Navigating human-machine synergy in the digital era. *Education as Change, 29*, 1–13. https://doi.org/10.25159/1947-9417/19128

Himani Srihita, R., Goli, G., Rajyalaxmi, M., & Gobinath, R. (2025). Transformative dynamics of the gig economy: Technological impacts, worker well-being and global research trends. *International Journal of Engineering Business Management, 17*. https://doi.org/10.1177/18479790241310362

Ho, N. K. M. (2024). *Appraisal and the Transcreation of Marketing texts: Persuasion in Chinese and English.* Routledge.

IATE. (2025). Interactive Terminology for Europe. European Union. https://iate.europa.eu/

Ichien, N., Stamenković, D., & Holyoak, K. J. (2024). Large language model displays emergent ability to interpret novel literary metaphors. *Metaphor and Symbol, 39*(4), 296–309. https://doi.org/10.1080/10926488.2024.2380348

Institute for Digital Government and Governance, Tsinghua University [清华大学数字政府与治理研究院], & Jiangsu Digitalization Association [江苏省数字化协会]. (2025, April). Smart data annotation industry development observation report [智能数据标注产业发展观察报告]. Retrieved July 5, 2025, from https://mp.weixin.qq.com/s?__biz=MzAxMzA2MDYxMw==&mid=2651643235&idx=1&sn=69533674547c744ea0831ea5228d9b41&chksm=81c6c018c75005740db3b674786527ae86daa69fc8cd6530a5b61e8530a9b87cb3496d12c81d&scene=27

Intento. (2025, March 16). February 2025: LLMs in machine translation, contact center AI agents, and new integrations. https://inten.to/blog/february-2025-llms-in-machine-translation-contact-center-ai-agents-and-new-integrations/

Jiménez-Crespo, M. A. (2013). *Translation and Web Localization.* Routledge.

Jiménez-Crespo, M. A. (2021a). The impact of crowdsourcing and online collaboration in professional translation: Charting the future of translation? *Babel, 67*(4), 395–417. https://doi.org/10.1075/babel.00230.jim

Jiménez-Crespo, M. A. (2021b). *The Routledge Handbook of Translation and Technology.* Routledge.

Jiménez-Crespo, M. A. (2024). Transcreation in translation and the age of human-centred AI: Focusing on "human" creative touch. In L. Kostopoulou & P. Charalampidou (Eds.), *New perspectives in media translation.* Palgrave Macmillan. https://doi.org/10.1007/978-3-031-62832-0_12

Kang, X. (2025). Transformative trends and future directions in digital language services: Innovations, challenges, and competitive strategies in the globalized information age. *Forum for Linguistic Studies, 7*(3), 412–422. https://doi.org/10.30564/fls.v7i3.8604

Khawar, S., & Boukes, M. (2024). Analyzing sensationalism in news on Twitter (X): Clickbait journalism by legacy vs. online-native outlets and the consequences for user engagement. *Digital Journalism*, 1–21. https://doi.org/10.1080/21670811.2024.2394764

Korsunova, K. (2024). Artificial intelligence in content marketing: Shaping the future of digital strategy. *Journal of Strategic Economic Research, 1*(25), 78–84. https://doi.org/10.30857/2786-5398.2024.1.8

Lazer, D. M. J., Baum, M. A., Benkler, Y., Berinsky, A. J., Greenhill, K. M., Menczer, F., Metzger, M. J., Nyhan, B., Pennycook, G., Rothschild, D., Schudson, M., Sloman, S. A., Sunstein, C. R., Thorson, E. A., Watts, D. J., & Zittrain, J. L. (2018). The science of fake news. *Science, 359*(6380), 1094–1096. https://doi.org/10.1126/science.aao2998

Li, Y. (2023). On the issues of language data in the era of human-machine symbiosis. *Journal of Central China Normal University (Humanities and Social Sciences Edition), 62*(5), 135–143. https://doi.org/10.19992/j.cnki.1000-2456.2023.05.011

Lionbridge. (2024, June 6). *How AI enables authentic multilingual content at scale: The Lionbridge Language Cloud™ in action.* https://www.lionbridge.com/case-study/how-ai-enables-authentic-multilingual-content-at-scale/

LISA. (2003). *The localization industry primer* (2nd ed.). The Localization Industry Standards Association.

Lischka, J. A., & Garz, M. (2023). Clickbait news and algorithmic curation: A game theory framework of the relation between journalism, users, and platforms. *New Media & Society, 25*(8), 2073–2094. https://doi.org/10.1177/1461444821102

Liu, Z. (2025). Cultural bias in large language models: A comprehensive analysis and mitigation strategies. *Journal of Transcultural Communication, 3*(2), 224–244. https://doi.org/10.1515/jtc-2023-0019

Lundin, T. (2024). Harnessing technology: AI translation, industry disruption and mitigation of misuse. *Digital Translation, 11.* https://doi.org/10.1075/dt.24011.lun

Lung, R. (2011). *Interpreters in early imperial China.* John Benjamins Publishing.

Markel, M. (2012). *Technical communication* (12th ed.). Bedford/St. Martin's.

McCombs, M. (2005). A look at agenda-setting: Past, present and future. *Journalism Studies, 6*(4), 543–557.

McKinsey & Company. (2024). *The state of AI: Global survey.* McKinsey Global Institute. Retrieved July 5, 2025, from https://www.mckinsey.com/capabilities/quantumblack/our-insights/the-state-of-ai

Melby, A. K., & Wright, S. E. (2015). Translation memory. In S. Chan (Ed.), *Routledge encyclopedia of translation technology* (pp. 662–678). Routledge. https://doi.org/10.4324/9781003168348

Miller, C. (2024). *Writing for digital media.* PALNI.

Mohammed, S. Y., Khalaf, A. S., Aljanabi, M., & Mijwil, M. M. (2024). Challenges and opportunities in translation studies: The evolving role of generative AI in translation development. In N. Mansour & L. M. Bujosa Vadell (Eds.), *Sustainability and financial services in the digital age* (Springer Proceedings in Business and Economics. Springer. https://doi.org/10.1007/978-3-031-67511-9_7

Moorkens, J. (2017). Under pressure: Translation in times of austerity. *Perspectives, 25*(3), 464–477. https://doi.org/10.1080/0907676X.2017.1285331

Muhammad, A. (2025). *AI-Powered Language Services: Revolutionizing Human Communication across Borders.* https://doi.org/10.2139/ssrn.5306605

MultiLingual. (2025, January). The localization landscape in 2025: Why ecosystems and AI are the future. *MultiLingual.* https://multilingual.com/magazine/january-2025/the-localization-landscape-in-2025/

Nielsen, J. (1990). *Designing user interfaces for international use.* Elsevier Science Publishers Ltd.

Norman, D. A. (2016). *Living with complexity.* MIT Press.

O'Brien, S. (2019). Controlled language and writing for an international audience (pp. 65–88). In B. Maylath & K. St.Amant (Eds.), *Translation and localization: A guide for technical and professional communicators* (1st ed.). Routledge. https://doi.org/10.4324/9780429453670-4

Pangeanic. (2024, October 10). AI in translation and beyond: Key takeaways from TAUS Albuquerque 2024. Pangeanic Blog. https://blog.pangeanic.com/ai-in-translation-and-beyond-key-takeaways-from-taus-albuquerque-2024#:~:text=The%20recent%20TAUS%20Albuquerque%202024%20conference%20provided%20valuable,that%20can%20be%20achieved%20in%20producing%20reliable%20translations

Prieto Ramos, F. (2024). Revisiting translator competence in the age of artificial intelligence: The case of legal and institutional translation. *The Interpreter and Translator Trainer, 18*(2), 148–173. https://doi.org/10.1080/1750399X.2024.2344942

Qu, W. (2024). An example of large-scale refined general-purpose corpus construction: Comments on construction and application of large-scale modern Chinese word segmentation corpus. *Journal of Documentation and Data Studies, 6*(1), 116–120.

Rockley, A., Kostur, P., & Manning, S. (2003). *Managing enterprise content: A unified content strategy*. New Riders.

Roland, R. A. (1999). *Interpreters as diplomats: A diplomatic history of the role of interpreters in world politics*. University of Ottawa Press.

Romero-Rodriguez, L. M., & Castillo-Abdul, B. (2023). Toward state-of-the-art on social marketing research in user-generated content (UGC) and influencers. *Journal of Management Development, 42*(6), 425–435. https://doi.org/10.1108/JMD-11-2022-0285

S1000D® Specification, Issue 6.0.https://s1000d.org/

Savoldi, B., Bastings, J., Bentivogli, L., & Vanmassenhove, E. (2025). A decade of gender bias in machine translation. *Patterns, 6*(6), Article 101257. https://doi.org/10.1016/j.patter.2025.101257

SEAtongue. (2025, February 10). How AI is transforming translation & localisation in 2025. seatongue.com/blog/business/how-ai-is-transforming-translation-localisation-in-2025/

Shivakumar, S. K. (2017). Enterprise content and search management for building digital platforms. *IEEE Computer Society*. https://doi.org/10.1002/9781119206842

Shneiderman, B., Plaisant, C., Cohen, M., Jacobs, S., Elmqvist, N., & Diakopoulos, N. (2016). *Designing the User Interface: Strategies for effective human-computer interaction*. Pearson Education.

Sima Qian[司马迁]. (2023). Modern ed. *Da wan lie zhuan* [大宛列传]. Chinese Text Project. https://ctext.org/shiji/da-wan-lie-zhuan

Slator. (2024). Translation companies accelerating adoption of large language models: 2024 ALC survey results. *Slator Language Industry Intelligence, 12*(4), 78–85. https://slator.com/translation-companies-accelerating-adoption-large-language-models-alc-survey/

Štefčík, J. (2025). Disruptions caused by AI in the language industry and education. In V. Kučiš & N. Vid (Eds.), *Dynamics of translation studies / Potenziale der Translationswissenschaft* (TRANSÜD. Arbeiten zur Theorie und Praxis des Übersetzens und Dolmetschens). Frank & Timme. https://doi.org/10.57088/978-3-7329-8778-8_4

Sutherland, K. E. (2024). *Strategic social media management: Theory and practice*. Palgrave Macmillan.

Tagg, C. (2015). *Exploring digital communication: Language in action*. Routledge.

Templin, T., Fort, S., Padmanabham, P., & others. (2025). Framework for bias evaluation in large language models in healthcare settings. *npj Digital Medicine, 8*, 414. https://doi.org/10.1038/s41746-025-01786-w

Tieber, M., & Baumgarten, S. (2024). Mean machines? Sociotechnical (r) evolution and human labour in the translation and interpreting industry. *Perspectives, 32*(3), 379–390. https://doi.org/10.1080/0907676X.2024.2346378

Uygun, Y., & Momodu, V. (2024). Local large language models to simplify requirement engineering documents in the automotive industry. *Production & Manufacturing Research, 12*(1). https://doi.org/10.1080/21693277.2024.2375296

Vermeer, H. J. (2000). Skopos and commission in translational action. In L. Venuti (Ed.), *The translation studies reader* (pp. 221–232). Routledge.

Wang, L., & Wang, J. (2024). *Report on the Development of Language Services in China* (2024). Social Sciences Academic Press China.

Warburton, K. (2015). Terminology management. In S. Chan (Ed.), *Routledge encyclopedia of translation technology* (pp. 644–661). Routledge. https://doi.org/10.4324/9781003168348

Wassie, A. K., Molaei, M., & Moslem, Y. (2025). Domain-specific translation with open-source large language models: Resource-oriented analysis. https://arxiv.org/abs/2412.05862

Welocalize. (2025, March 11). Case study: Streamlining training video localization for a global SaaS platform. https://www.welocalize.com/insights/case-study-streamlining-training-video-localization-for-a-global-saas-platform/

Williams, A. (2025, April). The impact of AI on the translation industry. ResearchGate. www.researchgate.net/publication/391050035

XTM International. (2025, June 5). Everything you need to know about SaaS localization. XTM Cloud. https://xtm.cloud/blog/saas-localization/

Xu, M., & Zhang, K. (2025). Research on intelligent translation and multimodal dissemination of classics of traditional Chinese medicine. *Foreign Language Education and Technology, 1*, 35–40+117. https://doi.org/10.20139/j.issn.1001-5795.20250105

Yamada, M. (2023). Optimizing machine translation through prompt engineering: An investigation into ChatGPT's customizability. https://arxiv.org/abs/2308.01391

Ye, X. (2023). The interpreters in the 18th-century Sino-British encounters from the perspective of British travel writings. *International Sinology, 34*(1), 74–85+157. https://doi.org/10.19326/j.cnki.2095-9257.2023.01.008

Yogarajan, V., Dobbie, G., & Keegan, T. T. (2025). Debiasing large language models: Research opportunities. *Journal of the Royal Society of New Zealand, 55*(2), 372–395. https://doi.org/10.1080/03036758.2024.2398567

Yu, J., & Liu, K. (2024). Reshaping translation studies: Paradigm shifts and future directions in the age of AI technology. *Journal of Foreign Languages (Journal of Shanghai International Studies University), 47*(4), 72–81.

Zha, D., Bhat, Z. P., Lai, K.-H., Yang, F., Jiang, Z., Zhong, S., & Hu, X. (2023). Data-centric artificial intelligence: A survey. *ACM Computing Surveys, 57*, 1–42. https://api.semanticscholar.org/CorpusID:257622614

Zhang, Y., & Zhao, R. (2024). Large language models and new changes in global language life: Focusing on ChatGPT. *Jianghan Academic Journal, 43*(6), 37–47. https://doi.org/10.16388/j.cnki.cn42-1843/c.2024.06.004

Zhou, M., Gong C., Li, Zhang, M. (2022). Comparison of data annotation approaches using dependency tree annotation as a case study. *Journal of Tsinghua University (Science and Technology), 62*(5), 908–916.

Zydroń, A., Jaworski, R., & Kaczmarek, S. (2024). Using large language models to build an efficient adaptive machine translation system. In *Translating and the Computer* (46th ed., p. 224). ASLING. https://asling.org/tc46/wp-content/uploads/2025/03/TC46-proceedings.pdf

Chapter 2
Language Modeling and Large Language Models

Abstract This chapter surveys the conceptual and technical scaffolding of modern large language models (LLMs) and their impact on language services. It first problematizes "computable linguistic units," showing how segmentation and tokenization (from words to subwords and bytes) operationalize theory while trading off sparsity, semantic integrity, and engineering efficiency. It then contrasts dynamic sequence modeling with static representation learning, tracing evolution from n-grams to neural and Transformer architectures and explaining the rise of autoregressive (decoder-only) scaling over masked objectives for unified generation and emergent in-context learning. The pretraining–fine–tuning paradigm has shifted toward prompt-driven interaction, supplemented by continued pretraining, supervised fine-tuning, knowledge distillation, retrieval–augmented generation, and agent frameworks that orchestrate multistep tool use. Core service-oriented capabilities now hinge on efficient adaptation, controllability, and integration with external knowledge. Technical and socio–ethical limitations—hallucination, bias, responsibility attribution, interpretability, and control—are analyzed as structural consequences of probabilistic next-token prediction and data provenance rather than isolated defects. The chapter frames LLMs as transformative yet fallible linguistic infrastructures, emphasizing the emerging professional skill set: critical evaluation, prompt and data curation, bias mitigation, and system orchestration for trustworthy language services.

Natural language processing (NLP) centers on modeling abstract form–meaning relations (Manning & Schütze, 1999). It has moved from statistical, feature-engineered methods (Sebastiani, 2002) to large language models (LLMs) unifying classification, sequence labeling, translation, and generation (Jurafsky & Martin, 2023). LLMs concentrate multitask capability in one architecture, adapting across domains via fine-tuning (Raffel et al., 2020), replacing many specialized pipelines. Tasks like information extraction and data analysis now reach non-programmers through prompt engineering and agent platforms (Bommasani et al., 2021), enabling broader access to innovation in language services.

J. S. Yu and Y. Yao, *Intelligent Language Services*,
https://doi.org/10.1007/978-981-95-4632-9_2

1 Defining Computable Linguistic Units

A core NLP task is to render fluid human language into representations machines can process (Jurafsky & Martin, 2023). All automated generation, interpretation, or interaction presupposes principled segmentation and encoding of the signal. Speech, prosody, and context enter computation only after mapping to formal units—characters, words, phrases, sentences (Manning & Schütze, 1999). Deciding boundaries and how units convey information across tasks underpins modeling and explains how large language models process input.

1.1 Word Segmentation, Tokenization, and Assumptions about Linguistic Units

Segmenting a continuous stream is not cutting at obvious seams; it means deciding what counts as a unit and invoking assumptions about analyzability and compositionality (Jurafsky & Martin, 2023). Even in Latin-alphabet languages with spaces, boundaries are ambiguous: "New York," "can't," and "state-of-the-art" raise issues of semantic integrity, morphology, and pragmatics. A space is not a reliable semantic delimiter.

In written Chinese, absent spacing and diachronic change blur the status of the "word." Segmentation practice adopts a lexico-grammatical view yet cannot uniformly resolve character compounding and historical layering. Morphologically rich systems add further complexity: a single Arabic orthographic token can bundle clitics and affixes (e.g., وَالْمَدْرَسَة "and the school" = و "and" + الـ "the" + مدرسة "school"), requiring morphology-aware analysis beyond surface splitting. German compounding packs meanings tightly: the legal term Bundesausbildungsförderungsgesetz ("Federal Training Assistance Act") can be left intact or split into Bund "federal" + Ausbildung "training" + Förderung "support/funding" + Gesetz "law/act" (with linking –s/–es), and the choice depends on whether the task is frequency profiling, translation, or semantic parsing—showing unit definition is purpose-relative.

Word segmentation is often conflated with tokenization, which produces minimal processing units that may be words, subwords, characters, bytes, or special symbols. Tokenization is not identical to lexical segmentation: it operationalizes a theory of units while optimizing for consistency and engineering efficiency. Linguistic theory links a word's form, meaning, and pragmatic function; tokenization abstracts away from these dimensions when task performance benefits. Different objectives favor different granularities: search may keep frequent words intact; translation may profit from subword splits; sentiment analysis may isolate multiword expressions or emoticons.

Segmentation still must account for contextual and paralinguistic cues—intonation, rhythm, stress, pauses, emojis, typography—that shape interpretation without altering propositional content. A per-character period emphasis pattern in Chinese microblogs (e.g., "我。真。的。受。够。了。" 'I really have had enough'.) visually encodes prosodic pacing akin to "I. Am. So. Done." Treating the string with naive character-level segmentation removes this suprasegmental affective feature.

Both segmentation and tokenization thus impose an interpretive layer: language is not inherently packaged as discrete words; those boundaries are artifacts created to meet processing requirements.

1.2 Tokenizer: From Word Segmentation to Subword Modoling

Tokens in the NLP pipeline are not inherent linguistic units but engineered segments. They may map to words, subwords, characters, or bytes; the choice depends on task goals, modeling approach, and properties of the target language. Each token is a technical slice that must be fine-grained enough for compositionality and generalization yet not so small that structure and meaning are lost (Jurafsky & Martin, 2023). Early NLP put semantic load on the word; with deep representation learning, the token became the basic unit for understanding and generation, and models derive knowledge from statistical and semantic regularities in token sequences (Bengio et al., 2003). Tokenization, more than preprocessing, frames how models construe language: token boundaries embody trade-offs that compress complexity yet shape how language is constructed, interpreted, and reproduced within the model.

1.2.1 Traditional Word-Based Tokenization

In many natural language processing tasks, particularly from the late twentieth into the early twenty-first century, a token was typically treated simply as a word: segmentation algorithms split text into lexical units and marked their boundaries with spaces or other delimiters.

For example,

"The quick brown fox jumps over the lazy dog."

Under traditional word segmentation it is segmented as:

[The] [quick] [brown] [fox] [jumps] [over] [the] [lazy] [dog] [.]

For Chinese, a typical word segmentation system might split "自然语言处理" (natural language processing) into:

[自然] [语言] [处理].

This approach is intuitive and sufficient for certain shallow tasks (e.g., keyword extraction or basic retrieval) but presents two major weaknesses:

- Vocabulary explosion: In morphologically rich languages (e.g., Turkish, Finnish), the vocabulary can grow rapidly as the corpus expands (e.g., web-scale data)

because numerous surface forms—including numerical strings such as phone numbers—enter the lexicon.
- Sparsity of rare and unseen words: If a word encountered at test time did not appear in training, the model lacks a representation for it, producing sharp performance drops.

Consequently, the field has shifted toward more fine-grained and flexible token construction strategies.

1.2.2 Coarse-Grained Normalization of Morphological Variation

Stemming reduces inflected variants to a shared stem, mitigating morphological variation at a coarse level. For example:

- playing → play
- played → play
- plays → play.

The Porter Stemmer, one of the earliest widely adopted algorithms, applies a set of rule-based suffix-stripping heuristics to yield a canonical form. While it reduces sparsity, it can also cause overstemming or understemming.

For example:

- university → univers
- universe → univers.

Such erroneous conflations merge semantically distinct words, impairing model decisions. Stemming addresses an engineering need—compressing morphological variation into more stable units—but offers limited support for fine-grained semantic distinctions.

1.2.3 Scalable, Low-Sparsity Subword Modeling

As neural models have demanded stronger lexical generalization, purely word-level tokenization has reached its limits. Subword modeling has therefore become the mainstream approach: it exploits statistical regularities or morphological cues to segment words into smaller, recombinable units while preserving salient semantic and morphological information.

Common subword approaches include:

- Byte-Pair Encoding (BPE): Begins with characters and iteratively merges the most frequent adjacent pair; "low," "lower," and "lowest" thus share the subword "low."

- WordPiece: First deployed in Google's BERT (Bidirectional Encoder Representations from Transformers); similar to BPE but selects merges by maximum likelihood to improve language model likelihood (Devlin et al., 2019).
- Unigram Language Model: Uses a probabilistic model that maintains multiple candidate segmentations and selects the optimal path.

For example, under BPE the word "unhappiness" may be segmented as [un] [happiness] or, more finely, [un] [happi] [ness].

Subword modeling offers two primary advantages:

- Reduced sparsity: Rare words are decomposed into frequent roots, prefixes, and suffixes, improving generalization.
- Cross-lingual sharing: In multilingual models such as mBERT or XLM-R, subword vocabularies enable languages to share formative units, reducing vocabulary size and overall parameter footprint (Conneau et al., 2019).

However, it can blur the correspondence between tokens and linguistic units. For example, the Chinese astronomical term "超新星" (supernova) may be segmented as [超][新][星] or [超新][星], obscuring the intended single concept and conflating it with a compositional adjective–noun reading. While such granularity aids computation, it can compromise the integrity of certain semantic wholes.

2 Modeling Language

Language modeling equips systems with mechanisms to "understand" linguistic structure and usage for prediction, generation, and classification. Under formal assumptions it captures statistical, semantic, and contextual patterns, turning raw symbols into learnable representations. With rising computational power the field has shifted from simple statistics to richer representation learning: language is now embedded in high-dimensional spaces whose internal structure is learned automatically (Bengio et al., 2003).

2.1 Objectives and Motivations of Language Modeling

Modeling is a central strategy in science, engineering, and cognitive science. By abstraction and simplification it renders complex phenomena analyzable, predictable, and controllable (Box & Draper, 1987; Epstein, 2008). Given pervasive uncertainty and complexity, models keep only salient features as "usable approximations." This is not merely theoretical: from casual weather guesses to medical diagnosis, people use implicit mental models to estimate likelihoods and decide (Kahneman, 2011). Shaped by specific assumptions and aims, every model is limited; modelers trade off explanatory power, generalizability, and practical constraints (Doshi-Velez &

Kim, 2017). Typical stages are problem definition, structure specification, parameter estimation, empirical validation, and iterative refinement (Shmueli, 2010); success is judged by task utility.

Language modeling applies this paradigm to language. Language structure is intrinsically complex, spanning syntax, semantics, pragmatics, cognition, and culture. Theoretical linguistics seeks generative principles, but real language—highly variable, exception-rich, and context-dependent—limits purely rule-based systems. Early reliance on formal grammars gave way to data-driven, probabilistic, and computational approaches under engineering demands. The shift foregrounds the tension between explanation and utility and illustrates convergence of linguistics, artificial intelligence, and cognitive science.

Three main motivations underlie language modeling. First, it clarifies generative mechanisms and universals—from recursion and dependency in formal grammars to co-occurrence statistics—seeking internal order and predictability. Second, it underpins modern language technologies—spelling correction, speech recognition, machine translation, and dialogue systems—which require models to assess well-formedness and produce optimal outputs under variable input (Devlin et al., 2019). Deep learning and large-scale probabilistic modeling now enable broad cross-language, multi-task adaptation, greatly extending automation. Third, it advances engineering practice, prompts theoretical reflection, and probes the limits of intelligence. Closer approximation of "understanding" makes ambiguity, polysemy, and cross-cultural variation more salient. Commonsense reasoning, implied meaning inference, and sociopragmatic competence remain particularly challenging.

In practice, linguistic sequences show strong statistical regularities and context dependence. Frequent patterned expressions and the rarity of random combinations underpin probabilistic, sequence, and neural models (Shannon, 1948). Early vector space models assumed term independence; despite mismatch with linguistic reality they sufficed for information retrieval, illustrating practical utility over theoretical fidelity. Growing complexity heightens the need to balance explanation and generalizability, avoiding both oversimplification and overfitting.

Ongoing evolution has deepened understanding of linguistic structure and function and fostered interaction among linguistics, computer science, and cognitive science. Modeling is both a tool and a window on human cognition and intelligence. Abstraction both strengthens automated systems and prompts reflection on human limits. At the intersection of theory and engineering, abstraction and application, and artificial intelligence and cognitive science, language modeling supports inquiry into the nature of language and intelligence.

2.2 *Principles and Objectives of Language Modeling*

Language modeling seeks to uncover statistical regularities in linguistic data with mathematical and computational methods, enabling machines to understand, predict, and generate text. This goal drove a shift in NLP from expert-crafted rules to data-driven probabilistic models trained on large corpora. Unlike traditional linguistics, which emphasizes structure and explanation, current practice stresses utility and computability, aiming for flexible adaptation to complex phenomena and varied applications (Jurafsky & Martin, 2023).

Dynamic modeling and static representation constitute distinct cognitive and technical approaches. Dynamic modeling exploits language's sequential, context-incremental nature: each unit depends on preceding content, with next-word (or phrase) prediction as its core measurable task. Emphasizing dependency, fluidity, and generativity, it supports real-time writing, dialogue, and translation while maintaining discourse logic and situational coherence (Bengio et al., 2003).

Static representation "spatializes" language by mapping units to stable vectors encoding structural relations and semantic distributions. It transforms complex, variable discrete symbols into comparable continuous embeddings, capturing relations among words, sentences, and documents in high-dimensional space. Deemphasizing temporal generation while stressing semantic hierarchy, similarity, and structure, it supports information retrieval, text clustering, knowledge graphs, and semantic search, enabling similarity measurement, cross-context transfer, and a unified basis for multi-task use and downstream fine-tuning (Mikolov et al., 2013; Pennington et al., 2014; Peters et al., 2018).

Their divergence is technical and ontological. Dynamic modeling mirrors human production: predictive, context-adaptive, and robust to novelty, modeling unfolding order, reasoning, and variation crucial to generative behavior. Static representation is a snapshot, embedding units to expose commonalities, clusters, and hierarchy, stressing interpretability, transferability, and structured form.

In practice the approaches are complementary. Dynamic modeling excels under strong dependencies and high generativity, adapting to shifting context yet weaker at stable sense discrimination and cross-context transfer. Static representation supports large-scale knowledge integration, task generalization, and structural analysis, but can lag when tight coherence and temporal reasoning are required. Modern large language models fuse them: dynamic generation yields high-quality semantic representations enabling efficient prediction, generation, and broad task transfer, advancing NLP and language service capabilities (Devlin et al., 2019; Raffel et al., 2020).

Goal formulation in language modeling directly shapes architectural choices, data requirements, and evaluation criteria. An ideal language model should exhibit the following characteristics:

1. Accurate semantic understanding. Beyond lexical and syntactic parsing, the model must resolve polysemy, structural ambiguity, and complex discourse. For instance, "银行" ("bank") requires distinct interpretations in financial versus geographic contexts, selecting the meaning according to surrounding cues.
2. Coherent text generation. Given input, the model should produce grammatically, logically, and contextually appropriate text for machine translation, writing assistance, or summarization, maintaining semantic consistency and structural integrity while avoiding repetition or drift.

3. Strong context sensitivity and transfer adaptability. Representations should adjust meanings dynamically across contexts and be efficiently adapted to new tasks through fine-tuning rather than full retraining. The pre-training–fine-tuning paradigm operationalizes this: models learn broad regularities on large general corpora before task-specific optimization (Raffel et al., 2020).
4. Support for complex reasoning and knowledge integration. For open-world tasks, the model should incorporate external knowledge, follow multi-step reasoning chains, and perform cross-modal association (e.g., multimodal retrieval, image–text understanding), providing the basis for advanced intelligent services and human–AI collaboration.
5. Interpretability, computational efficiency, and engineering scalability. High performance must be balanced with resource constraints, output controllability, and ease of integration across industrial, educational, and medical domains.

These objectives collectively propel ongoing innovation. Language models have progressed from simple n-gram models to deep neural architectures and from a single-task focus to multi-task collaboration, integrating understanding, generation, reasoning, and adaptation, thereby becoming foundational infrastructure linking human language and AI services. This goal-driven evolution continues to extend NLP's boundaries toward higher levels of cognition and expression.

3 Language Modeling Methods

Language modeling approaches are increasingly diverse, reflecting deeper theoretical insights and continued practical innovation. Spanning dynamic generation to static representation, each reveals specific linguistic regularities and serves distinct engineering needs. This section outlines their underlying principles and rationale and shows how they advance the intelligent capabilities of language service systems, thereby guiding method selection and future model development.

3.1 Sequence Prediction and Generative Modeling

Language modeling moved from rule-based systems to statistical methods and then deep learning. Early grammars tried to encode structure but could not handle real variation and exceptions. Statistical modeling was a paradigm shift: letting data "speak" by inducing frequency and co-occurrence patterns from large corpora, closer to actual usage. Chinese, for example, prefers "drink soup" to "eat soup," a preference grounded in accumulated distributional evidence. Such models need not understand meaning; distributions suffice to judge plausibility. Linguistic "rules" are often not a priori constructs but statistical conventions formed through sustained use (Shannon, 1948).

Early progress was driven by n-gram methods. An n-gram model applies a sliding window over large corpora to estimate probabilities of adjacent n-unit sequences (characters, words, phrases), inducing collocational and structural patterns. It captures, for instance, that "strong tea" is markedly more frequent than "powerful tea," or that the Chinese term for "university student" is high-frequency, thereby quantifying naturalness via observed counts. Even unigram statistics provide empirical signals for stylistic profiling and lexical change.

N-gram models rest on the Markov assumption: the probability of the current unit depends on a fixed number of predecessors. Increasing *n* trades more context for higher cost. Parameters grow exponentially; Using the 6,763 characters from the GB2312 Level–1 + 2 (Standardization Administration of China, 1980) list as the basic alphabet, a naïve character-based trigram model would have to accommodate roughly 3.1×10^{11} potential trigrams, yet only a minute fraction materialize in usage, motivating smoothing and parameter pruning. Natural language is constrained, so most higher-order n-grams never occur, producing severe sparsity. Smoothing must assign probabilities to unseen sequences, adding noise and reducing reliability. Hence, practice limits *n* to 2–4; higher orders are rare.

Fundamental limitation of n–grams is locality: they capture only short-range dependencies, struggle with cross-sentence or broader discourse relations, and cannot naturally handle synonymy, disambiguation, or pragmatic inference, motivating neural language models. These shortcomings motivated the emergence of neural language models.

Neural language models (NLMs) produced a qualitative leap. Rather than explicit frequency tables, they frame modeling as end–to–end conditional probability estimation, with distributed parameters capturing nonlinear relations between sequences and context. Neural architectures integrate lexical, syntactic, and semantic information, substantially extending both breadth and depth of linguistic generalization (Yang et al., 2019).

Early NLMs used recurrent neural networks (RNNs), combining the current token with the previous hidden state to accumulate history and partly overcome n-gram locality. RNNs, however, suffer vanishing gradients on long sequences, limiting distant information flow. Long Short-Term Memory (LSTM) and Gated Recurrent Unit (GRU) architectures improved retention of long dependencies yet remained constrained by inherently sequential computation.

A decisive advance came with the Transformer (Vaswani et al., 2017). By discarding recurrence and using self-attention, it forms direct dependencies between any positions, efficiently aggregating global context. Unlike the stepwise propagation of RNNs, Transformers process entire sequences in parallel, accelerating training and alleviating long-range dependency bottlenecks. This architecture enabled large-scale pretraining and gave rise to two dominant paradigms: autoregressive models (e.g., Generative Pre-trained Transformer, GPT) and masked language models (e.g., BERT).

Autoregressive language models such as GPT employ a unidirectional Transformer to generate text left to right, predicting each next token from prior context. They yield coherent continuations well suited to dialogue, narrative generation, and machine translation. Given an input like "He told me that tomorrow...," the model dynamically infers and completes the continuation. This generative capability relies on global contextual modeling and large–scale pretraining that imparts broad linguistic and factual knowledge (Brown et al., 2020).

Masked language models (MLMs), exemplified by BERT, employ a bidirectional Transformer architecture and frame language modeling as a masked token prediction task: they randomly mask certain tokens within input sequences and infer the masked tokens based on their surrounding context. Bidirectionality strengthens joint contextual interpretation, producing strong results in question answering, semantic matching, and text classification. In a sentence like "He told me he [MASK] will leave," the model integrates information on both sides to supply "tomorrow" (Clark et al., 2020).

These paradigms align naturally with generation versus understanding. GPT excels at open-domain dialogue, continuation, and content creation, whereas BERT-style models attain leading performance in classification, retrieval, and entity recognition. Their success expanded application boundaries and entrenched the pretraining–fine–tuning paradigm as mainstream in NLP (Raffel et al., 2020).

Modern neural language models are no longer confined to text alone. Tasks such as image captioning, multimodal retrieval, and speech recognition integrate linguistic processing with vision and audio. In captioning, a convolutional neural network (CNN) encodes the image as feature vectors, which a Transformer or related sequence model renders into natural language. This mechanism underlies multimodal foundation models, enabling cross-modal understanding and expression and broadening the scope of AI (Alayrac et al., 2022).

Efficient information integration, global context modeling, and multi-task adaptability allow deep neural models to surpass n-gram constraints and to underpin understanding, generation, and multimodal tasks. Training scale, parameter counts, and task breadth continue to expand, suggesting early forms of general agents. The convergence of the Transformer architecture with pretraining is conferring higher-order abilities—cross—domain transfer, knowledge integration, and complex reasoning—supporting new paradigms in language services, knowledge engineering, and human–computer interaction.

This trajectory illustrates a sequence of advances: from empirical induction to neural representation, from local collocation to global structure, and from single–modality processing to multimodal understanding—now the theoretical and practical foundation for intelligent language applications.

3.2 Representation Learning for Natural Language

Representation learning underpinned early "static" language modeling. Traditional NLP used hand-engineered features—parts of speech, syntactic structures, topic labels—whose reliance on domain knowledge limited scalability. Methods such as word2vec embedded tokens in low-dimensional vector spaces, shifting from manual feature design to automatic representation learning and establishing it as a foundation of modern NLP (Mikolov et al., 2013).

An effective representation does more than map tokens to vectors: it must encode semantics usable across tasks. In sentiment classification, if "happy," "joyful," and "pleased" cluster apart from "sad" and "angry," polarity is inferred from geometry. The embedding space thus serves as a semantic landscape enabling inference without explicit rules.

word2vec learns dense low-dimensional embeddings from large–scale word–context co-occurrence statistics: semantically related or distributionally similar words lie closer in the space. Notably, the embeddings exhibit approximate "semantic arithmetic," e.g., king $-$ man $+$ woman $\approx$ queen, revealing regularities aligned with human intuition (Mikolov et al., 2013; Pennington et al., 2014).

Early embeddings were static: each word type had a single context-independent vector. Thus bank in "river bank" versus "investment bank" is represented the same, and the Chinese verb "打" (dǎ)—meaning "to hit" in "他打了我一拳" (he hit me with a punch) versus "to make (a phone call)" in "他打了一个电话" (he made a phone call)—also collapses to one vector. Such failures to distinguish senses drove the move to context-sensitive and higher-level (sentence, paragraph, document) representations.

Since Embeddings from Language Models (ELMo), representation learning capabilities have advanced markedly. The Transformer's self-attention mechanism lets each token representation integrate all others in a sentence, weighting them by semantic relevance to isolate information decisive for interpretation and to model complex context effectively (Peters et al., 2018).

For example, in "The bank raised interest rates again," the representation of bank is shaped by the financial cues "raised interest rates." Self–attention amplifies these tokens, steering "bank" toward the financial-institution sense. Contextualized embeddings thus move beyond static encoding to support structural reasoning and dynamic interpretation.

Stacked Transformer encoders in pretrained models progressively aggregate lexical signals into semantic representations spanning sentences, paragraphs, and documents, enabling more complex linguistic tasks (Devlin et al., 2019; Vaswani et al., 2017).

In multi-turn dialogue, a model integrates the current exchange with prior turns to identify intent and produce coherent responses. In reading comprehension, it fuses contextual evidence to extract key information, perform reasoning, or generate summaries. Whether structuring long documents or integrating cross-sentence inferences and fine details, deep semantic representations sustain higher-level understanding and generation.

Representation learning also facilitates transfer: large pretrained models yield general representations that adapt readily to diverse downstream tasks. Even with limited task data, shared underlying abstractions deliver strong performance. Thus representation learning underpins general semantic capability and provides a key pathway for approximating human understanding (Qiu et al., 2020).

Representation learning is not merely an intermediate encoding step; it is a high-dimensional compression of semantic situations that supports advanced tasks such as causal reasoning, intent recognition, and stance analysis. These representations help models interpret sarcasm, infer news stances, and uncover underlying intent in multi-turn dialogue.

In sum, representation learning has become the point of departure for linguistic processing. It continually builds semantic structures in mathematical space that are generalizable, transferable, and compositional, providing an evolving representational framework for diverse language tasks.

3.3 Dominance of Autoregressive Models in Large Language Model Development

Few at the outset of LLM development anticipated that unidirectional autoregressive models (e.g., GPT) would overtake bidirectional masked models (e.g., BERT) as the dominant architecture. Exponential parameter growth and the drive for general capability exposed clear advantages of decoder-only designs (Brown et al., 2020; Raffel et al., 2020), a shift that clarifies the field's direction and guides architecture selection for specific language service applications.

The core principle of the autoregressive approach is simple: generate each subsequent token from left to right. Although it was initially criticized as a unidirectional approach that lacks explicit access to future context and was therefore considered to offer weaker semantic modeling than bidirectional objectives, its simplicity provides a straightforward path to scalability. Conditioning each position solely on prior tokens enables efficient batched training and straightforward scaling. Engineering-wise, decoder-only models use simpler computation graphs and state management per forward pass, supporting rapid expansion to tens or even hundreds of billions of parameters with reduced overhead.

By contrast, BERT-style masked language models predict randomly masked tokens using bidirectional context but scale less effectively in open-ended generation contexts. Each prediction is an isolated fill-in focused on local context rather than a holistic generative objective, so the training signal remains fragmented and does not naturally support fluent long-form generation. As parameter counts reach tens or hundreds of billions, marginal gains from additional scale diminish (Kaplan et al., 2020).

The autoregressive objective is inherently self-supervised: next-token "prediction as supervision" requires no auxiliary task design. Its uniform, unambiguous signal—repeated next-token prediction over massive corpora—is sufficiently rich to encode syntax, semantics, pragmatics, and broad world knowledge, yielding general linguistic competence. At scale, models internalize increasingly complex patterns and exhibit emergent zero-shot and few-shot abilities. Results from models such as

GPT-3 confirm that a single next-token objective, combined with abundant data, can unlock a wide range of unanticipated capabilities (Brown et al., 2020).

In contrast, the masked prediction task—an engineered intermediate objective—does not induce equally broad generalization through natural generative dynamics. It learns local dependencies effectively but does not extend smoothly to coherent open-ended generation and exerts weaker pressure for integrated reasoning and knowledge synthesis. Consequently, even at very large scales, BERT-family models remain stronger on understanding tasks than on generative tasks; the objective itself limits gains in generative capacity relative to a unified autoregressive objective (Devlin et al., 2019).

Additionally, autoregressive models are naturally amenable to task steering via prompts. Many language service scenarios require immediate adaptation without supervised fine-tuning, and prompt engineering provides a practical mechanism: carefully constructed instructions or in-context examples enable rapid zero-shot or few-shot generalization across languages and domains (Brown et al., 2020). Bidirectional masked models typically rely on explicit downstream fine-tuning for transfer and thereby yield weaker spontaneous generalization. This gap in flexibility and efficiency has been decisive in the widespread adoption of autoregressive models.

At scale, the success of autoregressive models represents both an engineering achievement and a redefinition of language modeling. Since language is inherently sequential, and understanding and generation are deeply interconnected, the autoregressive approach unifies these processes within a single predictive objective, enabling broad generalization. While true general intelligence remains elusive, progress is closer than ever. This trend suggests that, in practice, unifying and simplifying objectives—rather than increasing architectural complexity—more effectively promotes generality and transferability.

4 Pretrained Large Language Models

Since the advent of large pretrained models, NLP has undergone a transformation (Vaswani et al., 2017; Devlin et al., 2019; Brown et al., 2020). Previously, specialized teams built task-specific architectures, processed data, and trained single-purpose systems. Today work centers on pretrained models: applications once taking months now prototype with a few prompts and API calls.

4.1 Paradigm Shift in NLP Research

In 2018, BERT and GPT-1 (Transformer-based) inaugurated the era of large-scale pretrained language models and a shift from task- to capability-oriented research (Devlin et al., 2019).

The shift first appeared in reduced reliance on linguistic preprocessing. Tokenization, part-of-speech tagging, and syntactic parsing, once indispensable, are now often optional as models learn from massive raw corpora. Large language models process raw text end to end while delivering strong understanding and generation.

Task development likewise changed. Previously, each task required bespoke features and models; sentiment analysis, summarization, and named entity recognition systems were isolated. The pretraining–fine-tuning paradigm became dominant; yet many tasks now require no additional fine-tuning and can be accomplished via prompting. After GPT-3, widespread few-shot and zero-shot capabilities increased adaptation efficiency and further decoupled models from tasks (Brown et al., 2020).

Meanwhile, task complexity rose. Large pretrained models now exhibit higher-order abilities—reasoning, logical analysis, structural understanding—supporting multi-step inference and solutions to complex mathematical and scientific problems. Some large models achieve performance comparable to domain experts on selected standardized benchmarks (e.g., complex question answering, professional exams), though this does not imply broad, general doctoral-level competence. These advances stem from scaling. Studies show that as parameters increase, models display "emergent capabilities"—complex code generation, reasoning, open-domain question answering—often beyond tens of billions of parameters, corroborating scaling laws (Kaplan et al., 2020).

Pretraining plus fine-tuning dominated; prompt-based learning now lets models perform diverse tasks via concise prompts, avoiding repeated training. A few examples adapt a model to sentiment analysis, translation, or summarization with performance matching or exceeding fine-tuned systems.

The shift accelerated language services. Systems no longer rely on intricate rule engineering or large labeled datasets; customer support, summarization, and writing assistance have spread as barriers fell. Advanced capabilities support contract review, legal consultation, and medical question answering. Multilingual, multimodal models broaden coverage and flexibility. Prompt engineering enables rapid task adaptation, speeding iteration and deployment.

Recent advances are moving language services from single-purpose tools to intelligent systems with reasoning and decision-making, expanding application scope.

4.2 The Prompt-Driven Approach

In the era of large language models, extensive task-specific fine-tuning on labeled data has yielded to prompt design. This overturns the "one model per task" paradigm and drives advances in few-shot learning and zero-shot inference (Brown et al., 2020).

Few-shot learning works by placing a small set of labeled examples in the prompt, enabling the model to infer the task without any parameter updates. In sentiment classification, a few labeled reviews plus a query review are enough—a form of in-context learning first systematically demonstrated by GPT-3.

Zero-shot inference removes even these examples: a natural-language instruction (e.g., "Please determine the sentiment of: 'This movie is utterly boring.'") elicits a direct answer. It stems from broad pretraining exposure encoding task knowledge and semantic mappings for immediate instruction following.

These capabilities have made prompt engineering a distinct practice. Practitioners adjust formatting and wording, reorder examples, and use chain-of-thought prompting ("let us think step by step") to elicit multi-step reasoning. Performance depends not only on scale and data but also on prompt design.

This shift has lowered development barriers. ChatGPT showed that tasks once needing elaborate algorithms can often be solved with a prompt. Product teams now reconsider redesigning existing systems. As barriers fall, non-technical users can help build applications, achieving a form of technological democratization.

For many language service tasks, training from scratch is rarely needed. Effective prompts let a pretrained model handle translation, summarization, error correction, sentiment analysis, and knowledge extraction. Prompt-based interaction plus broad generalization expands possibilities for intelligent language services.

The generative mechanisms of LLMs remain contested. GPT models are autoregressive probabilistic predictors of the next token, not deep world reasoners. They act as "sophisticated statistical sequence predictors," producing fluent text without genuine causal reasoning or grounded world models. Even sustained dialogue reveals limits on temporal coherence and long-term memory, leaving room for further progress.

Two papers released by Anthropic (2025a, 2025b) in early 2025 examine LLM "thinking" and advance interpretability. A microscope-like method traces computational and decision paths. The studies show that coherence arises from pattern matching rather than human-like reasoning, clarifying weak persistent reasoning and memory.

Offering a more critical view, Yann LeCun stated at the Joint Mathematics Meetings on 21 March 2025 that current LLMs exhibit hallucination and exponential computational waste. They lack physical understanding, persistent memory, robust reasoning, and advanced planning; the bottleneck is limited causal modeling. He argues for world models integrating multimodal perception (e.g., vision, audition, touch) with causal reasoning and planning (LeCun, 2025).

From Anthropic's "black-box" analyses to LeCun's strategic critique, a common view emerges: present LLMs remain statistical generators lacking genuine understanding or reasoning. Progress toward artificial general intelligence will require cross-modal perception, refined memory, and explicit causal structure.

4.3 Large Language Model–based Natural Language Processing

Traditional NLP task definitions stem from methodological concerns rather than practical service needs (e.g., part-of-speech tagging, named entity recognition, parsing, sentiment classification). Framed as standardized problems with explicit objectives and clear inputs and outputs, they enable straightforward supervised training but overlook complex interactions, ambiguous intent, and layered constraints in real scenarios. As contexts evolve, many fine-grained formulations have fallen out of alignment or become obsolete.

The rise of LLMs has redefined methodological approaches and task boundaries. Development has shifted from task-centric, model-specific pipelines to a user-centered, prompt-driven generative paradigm. One model now handles translation, question answering, generation, summarization, and knowledge extraction via a unified interface, eliminating bespoke architectures. This general interactive capability lets practitioners move beyond narrow taxonomies and reinterpret goals, methods, and evaluation around real service scenarios (Bommasani et al., 2021).

The following sections cover six techniques: (1) continued pretraining to adapt a model to domain corpora; (2) supervised fine-tuning (SFT) for task competence; (3) prompt engineering to steer outputs; (4) model distillation to cut cost while retaining performance; (5) retrieval-augmented generation (RAG) to improve answer accuracy (Lewis et al., 2020); and (6) agents to orchestrate multistep workflows. Complementary together, they form a modern LLM-based NLP stack.

4.4 Continued Pretraining: Enhancing Domain Adaptation

Continued pretraining further trains a general LLM on domain or task data. A base model has internalized broad linguistic structure and semantics; targeted data deepen its grasp of domain terminology, style, and information structures.

In medicine, a general model may lack adequate judgment when answering queries such as "treatment protocols for acute myeloid leukemia." Continued pretraining on literature, clinical records, guidelines, and drug monographs helps it internalize domain structures and better process conditions, procedures, and abbreviations (Lee et al., 2020).

Its main advantage is cost efficiency: instead of training from scratch, one obtains substantial in-domain gains. Even limited high-quality data can improve small to mid-sized models.

It is not a universal remedy. Very large models may see low marginal returns, and low-quality data can induce catastrophic forgetting. Decisions should weigh task goals, model scale, and corpus quality. With sparse or noisy data, SFT, prompt optimization, or distillation may be preferable.

Data preparation must be rigorous: provide clean text or Markdown; remove duplicates, noise, and irrelevancies. To limit drift and preserve general ability, interleave some original generic corpus to form a patch-style strategy.

Continued pretraining bridges general capability and specialization, and is usually paired with fine-tuning and prompt methods in an end-to-end pipeline.

4.5 *Supervised Fine-Tuning: Guiding Task Execution*

Supervised fine-tuning adapts an existing large language model with curated labeled data to improve performance on specific tasks (Ouyang et al., 2022). Whereas continued pretraining adds domain knowledge, SFT shapes task behavior via explicit input–output pairs.

In sentiment analysis, traditional methods used sentiment lexicons or handcrafted rules. With SFT, labeled "positive" or "negative" reviews let the model learn sentiment directly from examples, not manual features. This supervision improves stability and accuracy and transfers to related domains (Sebastiani, 2002; Zhang et al., 2015).

SFT is valuable in language services. For legal or medical translation it improves accuracy and terminological consistency; domain parallel corpora align the model with required style (Chung et al., 2022). It also conditions role-specific agents (e.g., customer support bots) using inputs, role instructions, and target responses to control tone, scope, and format.

An SFT training sample:

```
{
  "role": "You are a customer support assistant. ...",
  "user Query": "I forgot my password and can't log in.",
  "output": "I'm sorry to hear you're having trouble logging
in. ..."
}
```

The system prompt sets role and scope; the user query and target reply form the supervised pair. Many such examples build role-aware, context-sensitive responses.

Effectiveness depends on data quality and task relevance. Data must be structured, accurate, and paired (often JSON or CSV). With limited data, balance coverage and diversity to reduce overfitting and omissions. Adding general-purpose data improves generalization and mitigates catastrophic forgetting (Dettmers et al., 2023).

SFT is not merely a matter of feeding data. It is important to limit duplicate samples to reduce inefficiency and bias, and to diversify annotation sources—human labels, model-generated drafts with review, and auxiliary models.

SFT offers an efficient, flexible route to customization, improving accuracy and reliability on well-defined tasks. It is a key bridge between general models and specialized applications.

4.6 Knowledge Distillation: Refining and Transferring Knowledge

Knowledge distillation (KD) transfers the knowledge of a large model to a smaller one. Training the student to match the teacher's outputs allows it to approach the teacher's performance with lower computational budgets (Hinton et al., 2015). The method is widely used where efficient inference and deployment constraints prevail, such as on mobile and embedded devices.

At its core, KD transfers the knowledge learned by a large teacher to a smaller student. The teacher is typically a high-performing pretrained model, whereas the student adopts a simplified architecture with fewer parameters. During training the student absorbs both the ground-truth labels and the teacher's predictive probability distribution, capturing finer-grained cues. Mimicking these "soft targets" enhances its performance (Gou et al., 2021).

KD's primary advantage is improved inference efficiency, crucial when bringing large-model capabilities to resource-constrained devices. Distillation can markedly shrink the student's memory footprint and computational cost while preserving high accuracy and boosting speed. It is therefore adopted in scenarios demanding rapid response under tight resource budgets, such as mobile applications and edge computing (Sanh et al., 2019).

However, KD is not universally applicable. The student's simplified architecture cannot fully match the teacher, so degradation is more pronounced on complex tasks and applicability often narrows to specific domains. Consequently, KD is best suited to settings with tight computational constraints and moderate task complexity.

Thus, KD offers an effective means of balancing efficiency and resource consumption for private deployments of large models requiring efficient computation and low latency.

4.7 Prompt Engineering: Unlocking Model Potential

Prompt engineering (PE) is the systematic design and refinement of prompts for large language models, covering task instructions, queries, and task-specific inputs, to guide them toward desired outputs. A model's performance depends not only on its pretraining data and any subsequent fine-tuning but also on the quality of the prompts it receives. Well-crafted prompts can substantially improve output quality and task reliability (Liu et al., 2023; Sahoo et al., 2024; Schulhoff et al., 2024).

The core of PE lies in composing prompts that unambiguously specify task requirements so the model produces appropriate responses. Changes in structure or wording can yield markedly different outputs; deliberate prompt formulation therefore enhances both accuracy and efficiency (Chang et al., 2024; Wei et al., 2022).

For example, the simple prompt "What is the sentiment of the following text?" elicits a sentiment classification, but the model may still return an unconstrained label set plus commentary. Adding "Do not provide explanations or summaries. Output exactly one label. Restrict sentiment types to: positive, negative, neutral." constrains the response space. In a machine translation task, a prompt such as "Translate the following text from English into French using a formal register and academic vocabulary, avoiding colloquial and negative wording" likewise enforces stylistic and lexical constraints.

One major advantage of PE is its simplicity and flexibility: it requires neither extensive fine-tuning nor large labeled datasets, yet can unlock latent capabilities through prompt adjustment. This efficiency makes it well suited to settings that demand rapid task adaptation (Fagbohun et al., 2024; White et al., 2023).

Despite these advantages, PE has limitations: overly intricate prompts can introduce instability or prompt misinterpretation. Effective prompt formulation therefore relies on iterative experimentation and refinement (Schulhoff et al., 2024).

PE is particularly valuable in language services because domain specialists can implement and iteratively refine it with minimal engineering support. Subsequent chapters will examine how more advanced prompt strategies can further optimize language service workflows.

4.8 *Retrieval-Augmented Generation: Expanding Knowledge Boundaries*

When generating text, language models typically draw on knowledge acquired during pre-training. Although broad, this static reservoir often proves insufficient for rapidly evolving domains, narrowly specialized areas, or user-specific needs. Retrieval-Augmented Generation (RAG) addresses these shortcomings by integrating retrieval directly into the generation pipeline. On demand, the model can pull in and synthesize external sources, improving accuracy, breadth, and currency (Li et al., 2024; Yu et al., 2024).

External knowledge bases take multiple forms: structured databases and unstructured corpora such as policy documents, technical manuals, news reports, academic papers, and internal enterprise repositories. In practice, the system first constructs an effective query representation from user input—via keyword analysis, semantic embeddings, or custom rules—and then retrieves candidate segments from a large corpus. Embedding-based vectorization is crucial: it maps documents and queries into a shared semantic space, enabling direct numerical similarity scoring. This pipeline typically relies on specialized vector databases such as FAISS or Milvus (Jing et al., 2025; Johnson et al., 2019).

In a physician-facing clinical question–answering system, the model retrieves the latest clinical guidelines, case reports, or authoritative explanations from medical databases in response to a query. These materials are not shown verbatim; instead, the system synthesizes them into a fluent, information-rich answer. The model does not need to "know everything"; it must know where to search and how to exploit what it retrieves.

RAG often appears as straightforward user-facing features. Many conversational interfaces now include buttons labeled "Web Search" or "Knowledge Enhancement" that activate a backend RAG process to enrich the dialogue with web results or content from an embedded knowledge store (Chen et al., 2024).

Enterprises and research institutions often opt for private deployment for reasons of data privacy, latency, and cost control. This choice necessitates in-house development of an integrated retrieval–and–generation system: assembling a task-appropriate knowledge base, designing retrieval and ranking strategies, handling redundancy, and orchestrating how prompts incorporate retrieved content.

Building a private RAG system entails decisions at multiple levels: which sources to ingest (structured records, PDFs, web pages) and whether human annotation is needed; which embedding model and dimensionality to employ; how to deduplicate and rerank retrieved items; and whether truncation harms output quality. Each factor directly impacts performance. In practice, engineers iterate extensively to refine the data pipeline for the target task. Rather than a single tool, RAG is best viewed as a highly customizable systems engineering effort (Jing et al., 2025).

Not every language services professional needs to build a RAG system from scratch. Existing model platforms and open-source frameworks—such as Haystack, LangChain, LlamaIndex, and GraphRAG—lower the barrier while preserving flexibility, thereby enabling more reliable and interpretable interactive systems (Yu et al., 2024).

RAG is more than an integration technique; it refines and extends the cognitive boundary of language models. Mastery of RAG enables practitioners to fuse knowledge with language generation and solve highly specific problems with minimal resources.

4.9 Agents: Orchestrating Intelligent Tasks

An agent is an intelligent system built on a large language model that executes complex tasks and interacts with external environments. Unlike purely reactive traditional models, an agent displays initiative and makes decisions: it invokes tools, retrieves data, plans task sequences, and coordinates multiple language models to complete a workflow. The LLM serves as the "brain," while the surrounding architecture supplies the execution and interaction mechanisms (Yao et al., 2022; Luo et al., 2025).

An agent extends far beyond simple text generation. It infers task requirements, plans solution pathways, integrates information resources, and orchestrates external components. For example, a customer service agent can pair a user request with database retrieval, invoke a question-answering module, and synthesize context into a tailored response. A process-oriented agent can manage multi-turn tasks, coordinate services, and adapt its workflow based on outcome feedback (Xie et al., 2024).

These capabilities rest on three core pillars: (1) the language model's comprehension; (2) controllability achieved through well-designed prompts; and (3) robust integration with external tools. A fully featured agent architecture commonly includes modules for task management, state tracking, application programming interface (API) invocation, and knowledge retrieval. Together these components enable autonomous operation in complex environments and support reasoning, evaluation, stepwise execution, and sound decisions under partial information.

As the scaling of LLMs slows and performance plateaus of single models become evident, agent technology offers a pragmatic path forward. Rather than depending on ever larger models, it raises task performance through more fine-grained planning and tighter tool integration. Compared with a solitary model that merely answers questions, an agent functions as a "programmable executor" that can be embedded in diverse workflows to accomplish real-world tasks.

Implementing agents is challenging. They impose stringent architectural requirements involving external resource integration, state management, and resilient error handling. Practical "intelligence" hinges on reliable tool invocation, accurate goal interpretation, and the handling of complex branching—that is, strong adherence to instructions. In practice, teams often employ frameworks such as LangChain, AutoGen, or CrewAI, combining retrieval-augmented generation, API orchestration, and database operations to build adaptable, scalable agents (Luo et al., 2025).

In the language services sector, the value of agents is especially salient. They can automate translation requests, retrieve terminology standards, generate customized copy, and orchestrate multilingual task flows. As efficiency, automation, and multilingual support become baseline expectations, agent technology is becoming a foundational enabler of next-generation language service systems. Subsequent chapters examine agent architectures, core technical pathways, and practical deployments in language tasks, providing concrete guidance for building applications with enhanced intelligence.

5 Technical Limitations of Large Language Models

While the fluency and semantic richness of LLM output is striking, we must also recognize the limits of their putative intelligence. These models do not understand meaning; they internalize statistical regularities from massive corpora. They reproduce the surface form of human language without necessarily tracking underlying reality (Bender et al., 2021).

Key challenges include hallucination, latent algorithmic biases with associated ethical risks, controllability, responsibility attribution, and impacts on professional practice. Ultimately these converge on the broader philosophical question of how humans will coexist with technology.

5.1 Hallucination: Fluent Form, False Narrative

In practice, LLMs frequently hallucinate: they produce internally coherent, fluent, and persuasive text that is nonetheless factually incorrect or wholly fabricated (Huang et al., 2025; Ji et al., 2023). The polished surface masks falsehood, making such errors more insidious than overt inaccuracies.

Manifestations vary: mislabeling a well-known short story collection as a novel; inventing non-existent scholarly articles or legal provisions; or supplying a seemingly professional recipe—complete with unfounded health advice—for an absurd prompt like "how to make a soup from screws." The veneer of credibility can mislead users, distort information, bias research, and create legal or ethical exposure.

The fundamental cause is that generation optimizes probabilistic next-token prediction rather than factual adjudication. The objective is to yield the most likely continuation, not to verify truth. During training, the model absorbs linguistic form and distributional patterning, not structured world knowledge (Blodgett et al., 2020). It learns how people tend to phrase things, not how things are.

Without built-in fact checking or external references, models confronted with uncertain, ambiguous, or out–of–distribution prompts typically choose to invent rather than abstain. This is why they can sound confident even when addressing manifestly nonsensical or false questions. When optimization prioritizes surface fluency and a seamless user experience, factual accuracy is frequently the trade–off.

A subtler dynamic is user appeasement: when a prompt embeds an error or bias, many models echo it instead of correcting. This sycophantic tendency, common across major systems, appears to arise from reinforcement learning regimes that overweight positive feedback, privileging perceived user satisfaction over factual integrity and further eroding trust.

An important mitigation path is integration of external knowledge sources. Techniques such as Retrieval-Augmented Generation require consultation of authoritative databases or search indices prior to generation, improving verifiability (Lewis et al., 2020). This affords a limited capacity to recognize gaps. Complementary measures include embedded fact-checking, explicit source attribution, and calibrated refusal mechanisms.

Hallucination is not merely a technical defect; it exposes deep tensions between language and knowledge. Humans likewise suffer distortions—faulty memory and flawed inference are common. As models improve at generating natural, fluent prose, surface plausibility is easily conflated with truth. LLMs remain sophisticated language simulators, not domain authorities; uncritical reliance on them fuels misuse and risk.

Addressing hallucination demands that developers, users, and industry actors raise expectations for factual rigor. Whenever an LLM's generative capacity is used, independent verification and professional judgment must supplement its output; automated text cannot substitute for expert review. Sustained vigilance is foundational to professional, reliable intelligent language services and responsible LLM deployment.

A persistent challenge is to endow LLMs with calibrated self-knowledge—an ability to recognize, quantify, and clearly signal their own uncertainty instead of producing confident fabrications.

5.2 *Bias and Discrimination: The Shadow of Data*

Beyond hallucination, bias and discrimination in large language models are equally pervasive and often more difficult to discern (Blodgett et al. 2020). Although they frequently adopt a neutral, rational, even confident tone, their outputs remain interwoven with the social biases present in the training data. These systems harbor no intentional prejudice; the sources instead lie in the cultural imprints inscribed in human linguistic corpora.

A principal source of such bias is the prevalence of stereotypes in large-scale internet corpora. For example, in English-language data "doctor" co-occurs disproportionately with "he," whereas "nurse" is more often paired with "she," and these distributional regularities subtly shape outputs and reinforce gender roles (These examples are used here to illustrate corpus skew; not an endorsement of stereotypes). More broadly, stereotypes associated with gender, race, culture, and language can all imprint themselves on generated text (Bolukbasi et al., 2016).

The difficulty in mitigating these biases stems from the generative objective: predicting the most probable next token rather than evaluating whether the content is fair or equitable. The model lacks ethical awareness and any intrinsic capacity to remedy discrimination. This algorithmic "unconsciousness" inherits and amplifies existing social biases instead of enabling reflection or correction.

A subtler layer concerns cultural and linguistic hegemony. Mainstream large language models privilege English and Western contexts in both data coverage and semantic representation, achieving higher fidelity for dominant cultures while exhibiting weaker comprehension and articulation for non-Western cultures, minority languages, and peripheral discourses (Joshi et al., 2020). When confronted with cross-cultural or sensitive issues, they often default to a superficially neutral, "politically correct" stance that glosses over cultural specificity, historical context, and plural perspectives, thereby diluting recognition of diversity and critical engagement.

Language inherently carries culture and history; it encodes locality, custom, material environment, cognition, and emotion. Truly neutral language does not exist. Whether in the oft-cited dozens of lexical distinctions for "snow" among Inuit and other Arctic Indigenous groups or the hundreds of Chinese characters containing the "horse" radical, linguistic forms crystallize particular social and cultural experience. A model that pursues only surface neutrality risks obscuring cultural plurality.

Biases rooted in data and training affect not only expressive quality but also introduce concrete risks. In high-stakes domains such as education, hiring, and the justice system, uncritical reliance on model outputs can undermine informational fairness, misguide decision-making, and intensify cross-cultural misunderstanding and social distrust. Addressing bias is intrinsically complex: tensions between political correctness and scholarly neutrality persist. Human cognition itself is never fully free of bias; language models merely mirror the intricacy of social and epistemic systems.

In language services—especially cross-lingual contexts—maintaining accuracy and neutrality is a foundational professional obligation yet remains demanding in practice. Mitigation strategies include: (a) broadening corpus diversity by incorporating materials that represent varied cultures, communities, and viewpoints; (b) deploying detection and filtering at generation time to flag and intervene in overtly discriminatory or stereotyped content; and (c) developing bias evaluation and monitoring tools that supply actionable diagnostics and guidance for improvement.

Ultimately, bias and discrimination cannot be resolved by technical means alone; they must be situated within broader social and cultural contexts for interpretation and critique. A language model functions as a mirror: it reproduces human knowledge while exposing our prejudices and limitations. Professionalism in language services depends on continually strengthening the ability to understand, identify, and critically examine these intertwined relationships.

5.3 Attributing Responsibility: A Technological–Ethical Dilemma

As large language models become embedded in writing, dialogue, and broader forms of content production, users often default to viewing them as mere tools, treating their outputs purely as functions of user intent. Yet expanding capabilities and applications make it untenable to reduce ethical and legal responsibility to the claim that "the user bears all liability." Whether the issue is the fabrication and dissemination of false information, disputes over ownership, or risks of misuse and manipulation, clarifying system boundaries and allocating responsibility has become a pressing priority (Crawford & Calo, 2016).

The first challenge concerns liability for false or misleading content. Model-generated inaccuracies may include fabricated citations, defamatory statements, or misleading guidance in fields such as medicine and law. Current practices typically shift primary responsibility to platforms or end users, while developers often disclaim responsibility for systemic sources of error. When such errors stem from the model's training dynamics, however, it becomes difficult to justify assigning liability chiefly to users. The dilemma parallels unresolved debates over fault allocation in autonomous driving and is likely to become a central focus of future regulation (Olubiyi et al., 2024).

Ownership of AI-generated material has likewise become increasingly contested. Conventional intellectual property regimes presuppose an identifiable "author" and a discrete act of creation—assumptions strained by generative model architectures. Training draws on large volumes of high-quality text, images, audio, and video whose own copyright status may be uncertain. When a model emulates stylistic traits of its training inputs, no consensus exists on whether any rights lie with the user, the developer, or original rights holders (Zirpoli, 2025). Outputs frequently blend stylistic cues and fragments from multiple sources, and the law still lacks a consistent test for whether such recombination is original or infringing.

The risk of manipulation is the most immediate and sensitive ethical challenge. Researchers have repeatedly demonstrated prompt-based attacks in which engineered inputs elicit content that should remain restricted. The a role-play style prompt injection (colloquially termed a "grandma exploit"), for example, reframes requests as storytelling or role-play to bypass safeguards and obtain hazardous, sensitive, or unlawful information. Such incidents expose the fragility of current safety controls. Image generation systems likewise enable deepfakes, creating new avenues for misuse in political messaging, sexually explicit material, and opinion shaping. Large language models also automate fake review production and orchestrate information flows, amplifying epistemic distortion online.

Several mitigation strategies are under active exploration: applying "AI-generated" or credibility labels to outputs; embedding forensic watermarks to support detection; and instituting ethical compliance assessments with independent audits. The principle of human–AI collaboration has gained traction, positioning AI as decision support rather than a replacement and reinforcing the primacy of human judgment.

The ethical and legal tensions surrounding large language models are not incidental by-products of an isolated innovation; they are compatibility challenges that emerge once the technology becomes closely interwoven with social processes. Interactions—and periodic conflicts—among technical design choices, responsibility allocation, and institutional frameworks will continue to evolve, with future legal and social orders crystallizing through this ongoing negotiation.

5.4 *Controllability and Interpretability: Credibility of the Black Box*

Compared with traditional machine learning systems, large language models employ more intricate generative mechanisms and offer broader semantic coverage, but are correspondingly harder to control or interpret with precision. In practice, even after careful prompt engineering and iterative refinement, outputs may still deviate from the intended style, substance, or line of reasoning. This façade of compliance that conceals stochastic underlying generation introduces uncertainty during the deployment of LLMs in formal, compliance-critical, and other high-risk settings.

Black-box opacity is especially pronounced in LLMs. The provenance of a given output cannot be directly reconstructed: billions of parameters interact across deep representational layers, precluding straightforward causal attribution. This opacity erodes stakeholder trust and hampers both systematic bias detection and rigorous safety auditing.

The risks stemming from limited controllability and interpretability are significant. In decision support, regulatory compliance, and other safety-critical domains, the lack of traceability of model rationales blurs responsibility and undermines risk governance. In extreme cases, persistent opacity yields a governance dilemma in which accountability becomes effectively unattainable.

Researchers have pursued several technical directions: controllable generation (e.g., constraint prompting, template-based constraints, attention modulation), interpretability toolkits (gradient-based visualization, approximate generation path attribution), and rule–neural hybrid architectures. These approaches aim to improve controllability and auditability without materially impairing generative capacity. Most remain in early development, and no widely accepted production standards have yet emerged.

Understanding and governing the apparent autonomy of LLMs now extends beyond purely technical considerations. While fully eliminating black-box opacity is unlikely, practitioners can increase boundary transparency, tighten output control, and institute explicit safety guardrails in high-risk contexts. The aim is to integrate LLMs as dependable intelligent collaborators rather than unruly sources of systemic risk.

6 Conclusion

The widespread deployment of Large Language Models is reshaping occupational structures and cognitive practices across knowledge-intensive sectors. Whereas earlier waves of automation largely displaced manual labor, the current wave acts directly on language-, knowledge-, and creativity-intensive work. Fields such as journalism, customer service, translation, localization, marketing, and software development now offload a growing share of routine content production, basic analysis, and draft preparation to LLMs. As a result, role boundaries and underlying competency architectures are being systematically reconfigured.

This shift does not entail wholesale role elimination; rather, it intensifies pressure on entry-level positions. In the translation sector, junior practitioners who previously competed on linguistic accuracy and speed are being marginalized by machine translation engines and LLM-generated text. Competitive advantage now resides in hybrid roles that integrate AI tools for quality assessment, stylistic adaptation, and prompt design. Likewise, AI coding assistants perform basic code authoring and routine debugging, thereby narrowing traditional apprenticeship pathways that relied on incremental accumulation of foundational tasks. Two principal challenges ensue: diminished hands-on practice interrupts continuous skill development, and employers increasingly favor candidates with AI collaboration skills and multifaceted evaluative judgment, raising de facto entry thresholds and deepening barriers for newcomers.

The broad adoption of these technologies also poses challenges for individual cognitive development. Heavy reliance on AI tools can curtail opportunities for autonomous reasoning and sophisticated expression. Merely accepting model output without analysis, critique, or substantive revision impedes the development of linguistic and analytical capabilities and may precipitate cognitive outsourcing. Sustained capability growth depends on actively interrogating, validating, and refining AI outputs so that these systems function as amplifiers rather than substitutes.

Societal and industry responses remain divided; some emphasize displacement risks, whereas others anticipate a shift of human effort toward higher-order coordination, decision-making, and design. The pivotal question is whether education, professional competencies, and institutional frameworks can be modernized in tandem. Effective responses include cultivating AI-enabled collaboration skills, embedding AI literacy and critical thinking in curricula, and deliberately creating AI-mediated task and practice environments to offset the contraction of entry-level work. In language services, professional growth will increasingly hinge on evaluative review, stylistic refinement, prompt engineering, data stewardship, and technical comprehension rather than on traditional linguistic skills alone.

Technological change is continual; the decisive factor is a posture of sustained learning and adaptive practice that converts disruption into opportunities for professional advancement and capability enhancement. In an era of deepening human–AI collaboration, systematically extending one's knowledge base and cognitive boundaries is becoming a core literacy for every knowledge worker.

References

Alayrac, J.-B., Donahue, J., Luc, P., Miech, A., Barr, I., Hasson, Y., Lenc, K., Mensch, A., Millican, K., Reynolds, M., Ring, R., Rutherford, E., Cabi, S., Han, T., Gong, Z., Samangooei, S., Monteiro, M., Menick, J., Borgeaud, S., Brock, A., Nematzadeh, A., Sharifzadeh, S., Binkowski, M., Barreira, R., Vinyals, O., Zisserman, A., & Simonyan, K. (2022). Flamingo: A visual language model for few-shot learning. *arXiv*. https://api.semanticscholar.org/CorpusID:248476411

Anthropic. (2025a). On the biology of a large language model. https://transformer-circuits.pub/2025/attribution-graphs/biology.html

Anthropic. (2025b). *Tracing the thoughts of a large language model*. https://www.anthropic.com/research/tracing-thoughts-language-model

Bender, E. M., Gebru, T., McMillan-Major, A., & Shmitchell, S. (2021, March). On the dangers of stochastic parrots: Can language models be too big? In *Proceedings of the 2021 ACM Conference on Fairness, Accountability, and Transparency* (*FAccT '21*) (pp. 610–623). ACM. https://doi.org/10.1145/3442188.3445922

Bengio, Y., Ducharme, R., Vincent, P., & Jauvin, C. (2003). A neural probabilistic language model. *Journal of Machine Learning Research, 3*(Feb), 1137–1155.

Blodgett, S. L., Barocas, S., Daumé III, H., & Wallach, H. (2020). *Language (technology) is power: A critical survey of "bias" in NLP*. arXiv. https://arxiv.org/abs/2005.14050

Bolukbasi, T., Chang, K. W., Zou, J. Y., Saligrama, V., & Kalai, A. T. (2016). Man is to computer programmer as woman is to homemaker? Debiasing word embeddings. *Advances in Neural Information Processing Systems, 29*. https://doi.org/10.48550/arXiv.1607.06520

Bommasani, R., Hudson, D. A., Adeli, E., Altman, R., Arora, S., von Arx, S., Bernstein, M. S., Bohg, J., Bosselut, A., Brunskill, E., Brynjolfsson, E., Buch, S., Card, D., Castellon, R., Chatterji, N. S., Chen, A. S., Creel, K. A., Davis, J., & Liang, P. et al. (2021). *On the opportunities and risks of foundation models*. arXiv. https://api.semanticscholar.org/CorpusID:237091588

Box, G. E., & Draper, N. R. (1987). *Empirical model-building and response surfaces*. John Wiley & Sons.

Brown, T. B., Mann, B., Ryder, N., Subbiah, M., Kaplan, J., Dhariwal, P., Neelakantan, A., Shyam, P., Sastry, G., Askell, A., Agarwal, S., Herbert-Voss, A., Krueger, G., Henighan, T. J., Child, R., Ramesh, A., Ziegler, D. M., Wu, J., Winter, C., & Amodei, D. et al. (2020). *Language models are few-shot learners*. arXiv. https://api.semanticscholar.org/CorpusID:218971783

Chang, K., Xu, S., Wang, C., Luo, Y., Liu, X., Xiao, T., & Zhu, J. (2024). *Efficient prompting methods for large language models: A survey*. arXiv. https://arxiv.org/abs/2404.01077

Chen, J., Lin, H., Han, X., & Sun, L. (2024). Benchmarking large language models in retrieval-augmented generation. In *Proceedings of the AAAI conference on artificial intelligence* (Vol. 38, No. 16, pp. 17754–17762). https://doi.org/10.48550/arXiv.2309.01431

Chung, H. W., Hou, L., Longpre, S., Zoph, B., Tay, Y., Fedus, W., Li, E., Wang, X., Dehghani, M., Brahma, S., Webson, A., Gu, S. S., Dai, Z., Suzgun, M., Chen, X., Chowdhery, A., Valter, D., Narang, S., Mishra, G., Wei, J. et al. (2022). *Scaling instruction-finetuned language models*. arXiv. https://api.semanticscholar.org/CorpusID:253018554

Clark, K., Luong, M. T., Le, Q. V., & Manning, C. D. (2020). *ELECTRA: Pre-training text encoders as discriminators rather than generators*. arXiv. https://arxiv.org/abs/2003.10555

Conneau, A., Khandelwal, K., Goyal, N., Chaudhary, V., Wenzek, G., Guzmán, F., Grave, E., Ott, M., Zettlemoyer, L., & Stoyanov, V. (2019). *Unsupervised cross-lingual representation learning at scale*. arXiv. https://api.semanticscholar.org/CorpusID:207880568

Crawford, K., & Calo, R. (2016). There is a blind spot in AI research. *Nature, 538*(7625), 311–313. https://doi.org/10.1038/538311a

Dettmers, T., Pagnoni, A., Holtzman, A., & Zettlemoyer, L. (2023). QLoRA: Efficient finetuning of quantized LLMs. In *Proceedings of the 37th international conference on neural information processing systems* (Article 441, pp. 1–28). Curran Associates Inc. https://github.com/artidoro/qlora

Devlin, J., Chang, M.-W., Lee, K., & Toutanova, K. (2019). BERT: Pre-training of deep bidirectional Transformers for language understanding. In J. Burstein, C. Doran, & T. Solorio (Eds.), *Proceedings of the 2019 conference of the North American chapter of the association for computational linguistics: Human Language technologies, Volume 1 (Long and Short Papers)* (pp. 4171–4186). Association for Computational Linguistics. https://doi.org/10.18653/v1/N19-1423

Doshi-Velez, F., & Kim, B. (2017). *Towards a rigorous science of interpretable machine learning*. arXiv. https://arxiv.org/abs/1702.08608

Epstein, J. M. (2008). Why model? *Journal of Artificial Societies and Social Simulation, 11*(4), 12.

Fagbohun, O., Harrison, R. M., & Dereventsov, A. (2024). *An empirical categorization of prompting techniques for large language models: A practitioner's guide*. arXiv. https://arxiv.org/abs/2402.14837

Gou, J., Yu, B., & Maybank, S. J., et al. (2021). Knowledge distillation: A survey. *International Journal of Computer Vision, 129*, 1789–1819. https://doi.org/10.1007/s11263-021-01453-z

Hinton, G., Vinyals, O., & Dean, J. (2015). *Distilling the knowledge in a neural network*. arXiv. https://arxiv.org/abs/1503.02531

Huang, L., Yu, W., Ma, W., Zhong, W., Feng, Z., Wang, H., Chen, Q., Peng, W., Feng, X., Qin, B., & Liu, T. (2025). A survey on hallucination in large language models: Principles, taxonomy, challenges, and open questions. *ACM Transactions on Information Systems, 43*(2), Article 42, 1–55. https://doi.org/10.1145/3703155

Ji, Z., Lee, N., Frieske, R., Yu, T., Su, D., Xu, Y., Ishii, E., Bang, Y. J., Madotto, A., & Fung, P. (2023). Survey of hallucination in natural language generation. *ACM Computing Surveys, 55*(12), Article 248, 1–38. https://doi.org/10.1145/3571730

Jing, Z., Su, Y., & Han, Y. (2025). When large language models meet vector databases: A survey. In *2025 Conference on Artificial Intelligence x Multimedia (AIxMM)* (pp. 7–13). IEEE. https://doi.org/10.1109/AIxMM62960.2025.00008

Johnson, J., Douze, M., & Jégou, H. (2019). Billion-scale similarity search with GPUs. *IEEE Transactions on Big Data, 7*(3), 535–547. https://doi.org/10.1109/TBDATA.2019.2921572

Joshi, P., Santy, S., Budhiraja, A., Bali, K., & Choudhury, M. (2020). *The state and fate of linguistic diversity and inclusion in the NLP world*. arXiv. https://arxiv.org/abs/2004.09095

Jurafsky, D., & Martin, J. H. (2023). *Speech and language processing* (3rd ed.). Draft. https://web.stanford.edu/~jurafsky/slp3/

Kahneman, D. (2011). *Thinking, fast and slow*. Macmillan.

Kaplan, J., McCandlish, S., Henighan, T., Brown, T. B., Chess, B., Child, R., & Amodei, D. et al. (2020). *Scaling laws for neural language models*. arXiv. https://arxiv.org/abs/2001.08361

LeCun, Y. (2025). *In Seattle, a convergence of 5,444 mathematical minds* [*LinkedIn post*]. LinkedIn. https://www.linkedin.com/posts/yann-lecun_in-seattle-a-convergence-of-5444-mathematical-activity-7291955018117599233-FFt-

Lee, J., Yoon, W., Kim, S., Kim, D., Kim, S., So, C. H., & Kang, J. (2020). BioBERT: A pre-trained biomedical language representation model for biomedical text mining. *Bioinformatics, 36*(4), 1234–1240. https://doi.org/10.1093/bioinformatics/btz682

Lewis, P., Perez, E., Piktus, A., Petroni, F., Karpukhin, V., Goyal, N., Küttler, H., Lewis, M., Yih, W.-T., Rocktäschel, T., Riedel, S., & Kiela, D. (2020). Retrieval-augmented generation for knowledge-intensive NLP tasks. In H. Larochelle, M. Ranzato, R. Hadsell, M. F. Balcan, & H. Lin (Eds.), *Advances in neural information processing systems* (Vol. 33, pp. 9459–9474). Curran Associates, Inc. https://proceedings.neurips.cc/paper_files/paper/2020/file/6b493230205f780e1bc26945df7481e5-Paper.pdf

Li, G., Lu, W., Zhang, W., Lian, D., Lu, K., Mao, R., & Liao, H. (2024). *Research for the truth: Multi-round retrieval-augmented large language models are strong fake news detectors*. arXiv. https://arxiv.org/abs/2403.09747

Liu, P., Yuan, W., Fu, J., Jiang, Z., Hayashi, H., & Neubig, G. (2023). Pre-train, prompt, and predict: A systematic survey of prompting methods in natural language processing. *ACM Computing Surveys, 55*(9), 1–35. https://doi.org/10.1145/356081

Luo, J., Zhang, W., Yuan, Y., Zhao, Y., Yang, J., Gu, Y., & Zhang, M. et al. (2025). *Large language model agent: A survey on methodology, applications and challenges*. arXiv. https://arxiv.org/abs/2503.21460

Manning, C., & Schütze, H. (1999). *Foundations of statistical natural language processing*. MIT Press.

Mikolov, T., Chen, K., Corrado, G., & Dean, J. (2013). *Efficient estimation of word representations in vector space*. arXiv. https://arxiv.org/abs/1301.3781

Olubiyi, I. A., Oyedeji-Oduyale, R., & Adeniyi, D. M. (2024). Artificial Intelligence and the law: An overview. *ABUAD Law Journal, 12*(1), 1–27. https://doi.org/10.53982/alj.2024.1201.01-j

Ouyang, L., Wu, J., Jiang, X., Almeida, D., Wainwright, C., Mishkin, P., Zhang, C., Agarwal, S., Slama, K., Ray, A., Schulman, J., Hilton, J., Kelton, F., Miller, L., Simens, M., Askell, A., Welinder, P., Christiano, P. F., Leike, J., & Lowe, R. (2022). Training language models to follow instructions with human feedback. In S. Koyejo, S. Mohamed, A. Agarwal, D. Belgrave, K. Cho, & A. Oh (Eds.), *Advances in neural information processing systems* (Vol. 35, pp. 27730–27744). Curran Associates, Inc. https://proceedings.neurips.cc/paper_files/paper/2022/file/b1efde53be364a73914f58805a001731-Paper-Conference.pdf

Pennington, J., Socher, R., & Manning, C. D. (2014). GloVe: Global vectors for word representation. In *Proceedings of the 2014 conference on Empirical Methods in Natural Language Processing (EMNLP)* (pp. 1532–1543).

Peters, M. E., Neumann, M., Iyyer, M., Gardner, M., Clark, C., Lee, K., & Zettlemoyer, L. (2018). *Deep contextualized word representations*. arXiv. https://arxiv.org/abs/1802.05365

Qiu, X., Sun, T., Xu, Y., Shao, Y., Dai, N., & Huang, X. (2020). Pre-trained models for natural language processing: A survey. *Science China Technological Sciences, 63*(10), 1872–1897.

Raffel, C., Shazeer, N., Roberts, A., Lee, K., Narang, S., Matena, M., Zhou, Y., Li, W., & Liu, P. J. (2020). Exploring the limits of transfer learning with a unified text-to-text transformer. *Journal of Machine Learning Research, 21*(140), 1–67. http://jmlr.org/papers/v21/20-074.html

Sahoo, P., Singh, A. K., Saha, S., Jain, V., Mondal, S., & Chadha, A. (2024). *A systematic survey of prompt engineering in large language models: Techniques and applications*. arXiv. https://arxiv.org/abs/2402.07927

Sanh, V., Debut, L., Chaumond, J., & Wolf, T. (2019). *DistilBERT, a distilled version of BERT: Smaller, faster, cheaper and lighter*. arXiv. https://arxiv.org/abs/1910.01108

Schulhoff, S., Ilie, M., Balepur, N., Kahadze, K., Liu, A., Si, C., & Resnik, P. et al. (2024). *The prompt report: A systematic survey of prompt engineering techniques*. arXiv. https://arxiv.org/abs/2406.06608

Sebastiani, F. (2002). Machine learning in automated text categorization. *ACM Computing Surveys, 34*(1), 1–47. https://doi.org/10.1145/505282.50528

Shannon, C. E. (1948). A mathematical theory of communication. *The Bell System Technical Journal, 27*(3), 379–423.

Shmueli, G. (2010). To explain or to predict? *Statistical Science, 25*(3), 289–310. http://www.jstor.org/stable/41058949

Standardization Administration of China. (1980). *Code of Chinese graphic character set for information interchange—primary set* (GB/T 2312–1980). Standardization Administration of China. https://openstd.samr.gov.cn/bzgk/gb/newGbInfo?hcno=5664A728BD9D523DE3B99BC37AC7A2CC&refer=outter

Vaswani, A., Shazeer, N., Parmar, N., Uszkoreit, J., Jones, L., Gomez, A. N., Kaiser, L., & Polosukhin, I. (2017). *Attention is all you need*. arXiv. https://doi.org/10.48550/arXiv.1706.03762

Wei, J., Wang, X., Schuurmans, D., Bosma, M., Ichter, B., Xia, F., Chi, E., Le, Q., & Zhou, D. (2022). *Chain-of-thought prompting elicits reasoning in large language models*. arXiv. https://doi.org/10.48550/arXiv.2201.11903

White, J., Fu, Q., Hays, S., Sandborn, M., Olea, C., Gilbert, H., & Schmidt, D. C. et al. (2023). *A prompt pattern catalog to enhance prompt engineering with chatgpt*. arXiv. https://arxiv.org/abs/2302.11382

Xie, J., Chen, Z., Zhang, R., Wan, X., & Li, G. (2024). *Large multimodal agents: A survey*. arXiv. https://arxiv.org/abs/2402.15116

Yang, Z., Dai, Z., Yang, Y., Carbonell, J., Salakhutdinov, R. R., & Le, Q. V. (2019). XLNet: Generalized autoregressive pretraining for language understanding. In H. Wallach, H. Larochelle, A. Beygelzimer, F. d'Alché-Buc, E. Fox, & R. Garnett (Eds.), *Advances in neural information processing systems* (Vol. 32). Curran Associates, Inc.

Yao, S., Zhao, J., Yu, D., Du, N., Shafran, I., Narasimhan, K., & Cao, Y. (2022). *ReAct: Synergizing reasoning and acting in language models*. arXiv. https://doi.org/10.48550/arXiv.2210.03629

Yu, H., Gan, A., Zhang, K., Tong, S., Liu, Q., & Liu, Z. (2024). Evaluation of retrieval-augmented generation: A survey. In *CCF conference on big data* (pp. 102–120). Springer Nature Singapore.

Zhang, X., Zhao, J., & LeCun, Y. (2015). *Character-level convolutional networks for text classification*. arXiv. https://doi.org/10.48550/arXiv.1509.01626

Zirpoli, C. T. (2025). *Generative artificial intelligence and copyright law* (CRS Product No. LSB10922). Congressional Research Service. https://www.congress.gov/crs-product/LSB10922

Chapter 3
Prompt Engineering for Large Models

Abstract This chapter explores prompt engineering as a foundational technique for leveraging large language models in diverse language service applications. It details how carefully crafted prompts define tasks, activate model capabilities, and constrain outputs, emphasizing clarity, structure, context provision, task decomposition, and example guidance. The chapter introduces advanced prompt types such as zero-shot, few-shot, Chain-of-Thought, and Tree-of-Thought, and discusses self-consistency strategies to optimize reasoning. Structured and programming-style prompts are presented as scalable solutions for complex scenarios, with modular template design supporting adaptability and automation. Through illustrative examples, the chapter demonstrates how prompt engineering bridges user intent and model performance, enabling reliable, controllable, and creative language services.

Prompt engineering has become a critical entry point for applications of large language models (LLMs). Regardless of how capable a model is, it still relies on carefully crafted prompts to initiate and steer its workflow. On the surface, a prompt appears to be ordinary natural language input; in essence, it defines the task, activates model capabilities, and constrains behavior. A well-designed prompt not only clarifies the objective but also shapes the model's reasoning and improves output quality (Liu et al., 2023; Sahoo et al., 2024; Vatsal & Dubey, 2024).

The rise of prompt engineering also signals a broader shift in artificial intelligence (AI) development paradigms. Previously, developers wrote code and tuned algorithms to implement complex functions; in the era of large models, the human–model interface is increasingly mediated by natural language. Task specification, workflow decomposition, and input structuring can be achieved through meticulous linguistic design. Mastery of wording, example ordering, and contextual scaffolding within prompts has become critical to performance optimization (Beurer-Kellner et al., 2022).

In practice, prompt engineering now functions as a form of "lightweight programming." It does not alter model parameters, yet it demands heightened linguistic sensitivity, task analysis skills, and familiarity with model behavior. An effective prompt must state requirements precisely while curating contextual details that elicit

J. S. Yu and Y. Yao, *Intelligent Language Services*,
https://doi.org/10.1007/978-981-95-4632-9_3

the model's reasoning, generative, and decision-making capabilities. Understanding prompt structure and its evolution allows us to move a large language model from a simple question-answering tool to a customizable, controllable assistant that delivers targeted, creative solutions across language service scenarios.

1 Principles and Core Design Guidelines for Prompt Engineering

The effectiveness of an LLM depends heavily on prompt design. At its core, prompt engineering converts user intent, task requirements, and relevant context into instructions the model can interpret and execute (Debnath et al., 2025; Liu et al., 2023). Whether a prompt is a concise instruction or a complex construct embedding reasoning steps and examples, its essence is to delineate task boundaries in natural language while providing both a starting point and constraints for generation.

Prompt design is not a mechanical act of issuing commands; it strategically shapes model behavior. An effective prompt enables the model to focus quickly on user priorities, reducing interpretive drift and output noise to improve controllability and consistency. Because effective generation depends on explicit goals and sufficient context, the prompt must specify the target and supply enough information to support a coherent chain of reasoning. As LLM capabilities expand, prompts have become the nexus between user needs and model behavior, making "programming with language" feasible. The five principles below offer actionable guidance for constructing prompts.

1. Clarity First: From Vague Intention to Concrete Instruction

Clarity is the foremost requirement of a prompt. Although LLMs model have strong language understanding, they can perfors poorly when asked to infer the user's intent from vague wording. For a sentiment analysis task, "Please analyze this sentence" is imprecise, whereas "Determine the sentiment polarity of the following sentence: '这部电影真是太棒了!' (This movie is really fantastic!)" specifies both the input and the desired output.

Clear prompts prevent output drift, reduce trial-and-error, and improve interaction efficiency—especially important in large-scale automated pipelines (Ng & OpenAI, 2023).

2. Structured Output: Format and Constraints

Without structural guidance, a language model often produces verbose, irregular, or stylistically inconsistent text. Specifying the desired organizational format in the prompt steers generation toward the intended schema. For example: "Generate meeting minutes from the transcript in the format: Issue → Discussion → Decision." This improves readability and downstream processing.

Structured prompting is especially effective for programming, summarization, and question answering because it establishes an expected output template, reducing generative freedom and increasing controllability.

3. Context Provision: Enabling the Model to "Know Where It is"

Model output is highly context dependent. In ambiguity-rich or knowledge-intensive tasks, decontextualized input often triggers hallucination, mistranslation, or distortion. Therefore, the prompt should supply necessary background information (Debnath et al., 2025).

For example, asking for the sense of "bank" in isolation may elicit either "financial institution" or "river edge." Adding "He sat on the bank of the river fishing." and supplying the full list of dictionary senses while instructing the model to choose the most appropriate one—rather than generating freely—can greatly improve accuracy.

Context can include task objectives, role assignments, and procedural constraints. Supplying the right situational framing is among the most cost-effective optimizations in prompt design.

4. Task Decomposition: Simplify Complexity

Although its reasoning capacity is strong, LLMs can become confused or misorder steps when a task is structurally intricate or instruction-dense. Breaking such tasks into smaller substeps and guiding the model iteratively can mitigate this risk.

For example, instead of "Summarize the following long article," use staged prompts: "First state the overall topic → then list each paragraph's key point → finally compose the full summary." This yields a transparent information structure and allows validation of intermediate outputs.

Stepwise prompts are especially valuable in writing, problem solving, and logical reasoning tasks that benefit from intermediate processing, producing marked gains in structural quality and accuracy (Wei et al., 2022).

5. Example Guidance: Demonstrate Rather Than Describe

A salient property of large language models is pattern induction. When given sufficiently representative input–output examples (few-shot), the model abstracts the task pattern and analogizes it to new inputs (Dong et al., 2024).

In sentiment classification, concrete everyday examples help surface subtle distinctions and allow the model to internalize finer gradations: 今天早上阳光明媚，我心情很好。(The sun was shining this morning and I felt great.) → Positive; 公交车又晚点了，真让人烦。(The bus was late again—so annoying.) → Negative; 下雨了，只好待在家里。(It started raining, so I just stayed at home.) → Neutral; 虽然路上堵车了，但最后还是顺利赶到。(Although there was heavy traffic, I still arrived without issue.) → Neutral (slightly positive); 这手机的屏幕还行吧，不过电池续航一般。(The phone's screen is fine, but the battery life is mediocre.) → Neutral (slightly negative). Faced with a new sentence, the model is then more likely to reproduce the same labeling format and criteria. Examples both guide and calibrate: they narrow uncertainty in free-form generation, yielding more stable and controllable performance (Brown et al., 2020; Wang et al., 2023).

2 Types of Prompts

Wording strategies in prompt design reflect the depth of one's understanding of model behavior. In practice, prompt types vary markedly in task alignment and in how effectively they elicit capabilities. As prompt design progresses from zero-shot and few-shot formats to Chain of Thought (CoT) and Tree of Thoughts (ToT) techniques, it becomes increasingly structured and systematic, marking a shift in prompt engineering from "how to ask" toward "how to guide the model's reasoning" (Vatsal & Dubey, 2024).

2.1 Zero-Shot and Few-Shot Prompting

Zero-shot prompting provides no examples and relies solely on natural-language instructions to elicit a large language model's task behavior. It leverages the model's pretraining and instruction-following abilities and suits tasks with clearly bounded objectives and well-represented linguistic patterns (Wei et al., 2022; Brown et al., 2020; Bommarito et al., 2023). Typical uses include directives such as "Summarize the following article" or "Translate this sentence into French." Assigning a role can further reinforce stylistic coherence and domain specificity (e.g., "You are a medical specialist. Analyze this health report."). In addition, metacognitive prompting elicits explicit reasoning by directing the model to list hypotheses, decompose key points, or articulate intermediate steps—a tactic especially effective for analytical and explanatory tasks (Kojima et al., 2022).

Few-shot prompting instead embeds representative input–output pairs so the model can infer task patterns and output style. It is well suited to structurally complex tasks, contextually variable domains, or areas underrepresented in pretraining. High-quality exemplars should span major variants or decision boundaries (e.g., clearly positive, clearly negative, and ambiguous sentiment expressions). Ordering examples from simple to complex and from unambiguous to ambiguous helps the model internalize the decision criteria.

For some tasks, adding counterexamples and contrastive samples further clarifies task boundaries and reduces misclassification risk. Presenting multi-class patterns (e.g., correct vs. incorrect, or positive–negative–neutral) helps the model sharpen decision criteria and improves stability and discriminative performance (Zhao et al., 2021).

In sum, zero-shot prompting emphasizes intrinsic generalization, whereas few-shot prompting augments performance through guided pattern induction. In practice, they are often sequenced: an initial zero-shot instruction establishes a baseline; observed errors then prompt incremental insertion of curated counterexamples and high-quality exemplars, iteratively refining the prompt template for flexible, efficient execution.

2.2 *Chain-of-Thought and Tree of Thoughts Prompting*

Chain-of-thought (CoT) prompting directs an LLM to externalize its intermediate reasoning and is particularly effective for tasks requiring multi-step calculation, integrative judgment, or layered inference (Kojima et al., 2022; Wang et al., 2023; Wei et al., 2022). Metacognitive prompting exemplifies this strategy (Wang et al., 2025).

Unlike prompts that request only a final answer, CoT prompts emphasize "thinking while answering," requiring the model to display each reasoning step. This enhances interpretability and accuracy. In mathematical calculation, causal reasoning, or discourse understanding, a user might instruct: "State your reasoning step by step, then provide the answer."

Chain-of-thought prompting can be applied in a zero-shot manner (zero-shot CoT), using structured instruction to request stepwise reasoning without exemplars. For example: "Explain your reasoning step by step: Xiao Ming leaves home, walks 10 min to the bus stop, waits 5 min, then takes a 20-min bus ride to school. How long does the trip take in total?" The model will typically sum walking, waiting, and riding times. This decomposition clarifies task structure, reduces omissions and logical leaps, and lets users audit each step. When tasks grow more complex or statements become ambiguous, the chain may fracture; adding targeted exemplars (few-shot CoT) teaches an appropriate reasoning style and improves performance.

To further enhance stability, a prompt can incorporate self-consistency requirements—for example: "After each reasoning step, verify compliance with the rules; if an error is found, correct it before proceeding." This design fosters secondary reflection on intermediate steps, mitigating error propagation and facilitating user review and adjustment.

The Tree of Thoughts (ToT) prompting method differs from a single linear CoT path by exploring multiple reasoning branches in parallel, emulating the multi-track exploration humans employ for complex problems (Yao et al., 2023). In legal case analysis, for example, the model can open parallel branches on contract validity, breach liability, and evidentiary completeness, then synthesize the branch conclusions for a more comprehensive recommendation. In business strategy, organizations can likewise simulate outcomes under alternative supply chain policies before selecting an optimal path (Yao et al., 2023).

At its core, the ToT approach introduces a "branch–backtrack–select" mechanism: it enables deep exploration along one path while preserving flexibility to pivot to alternatives when needed. This structure suits high-complexity tasks requiring multi-hypothesis comparison or solution fusion (e.g., multi-style translation, multi-strategy summarization). However, it imposes higher design demands—prompts must explicitly define the branch structure—and increases computational cost. It is therefore most advantageous in settings where complexity, multi-criteria trade-offs, and decision support justify the overhead.

2.3 *Reasoning Models Capable of Self-Generating Internal Prompts*

Researchers have shown that for complex reasoning tasks with large language models, simply appending an instruction such as "think step by step" markedly improves accuracy (Kojima et al., 2022). This observation has catalyzed a shift from surface-level text generation toward multi-step logical inference and autonomous self-reflection. Newer models—exemplified OpenAI's o1 series and other emerging reasoning-focused models (e.g., DeepSeek-R1)—embed systematic Chain-of-Thought mechanisms into both their architectures and training pipelines. Consequently, they depend less on elaborate external prompts and instead generate internal stepwise reasoning, verification, and self-reflection. Beyond producing final answers, they generate self-monitoring statements (e.g., "I should check whether this answer is correct"), enabling more deliberate pausing, revision, and incremental reasoning that broadens the range of tractable complex tasks (Yang, 2025).

Two developments underpin recent advances in deep reasoning models: reinforcement learning has partially reduced reliance on manual annotation, expanding CoT capacity; and self-verification mechanisms detect and repair weaknesses in intermediate steps, sharply reducing hallucinations and improving output reliability (Wei et al., 2022; Yang et al., 2025). However, these advances have not rendered prompt engineering obsolete. In practice, the two are complementary: deep reasoning models excel at highly structured tasks (mathematics, code, scientific analysis), whereas prompt engineering provides low-cost, flexible adaptation for open-domain and ad hoc interactions and remains indispensable (Yang et al., 2025; Wei et al., 2022).

Hybrid architectures are now a major trend in natural language processing. These models parse user input, translate ambiguous requirements into standardized CoT templates, and close the loop from natural language to structured reasoning to adaptive prompting (Yang et al., 2025). The open-source Qwen3 series from Alibaba illustrates this: developers can toggle a "deep thinking" mode to balance latency and answer quality per use case. Such models can also invoke established analytical frameworks, including Porter's Five Forces and SWOT (Strengths, Weaknesses, Opportunities, Threat) analysis, selecting them automatically when appropriate to deepen domain problem solving. Nevertheless, in many deployments, it remains advisable to specify the analytical framework explicitly via prompts to maintain control and consistency.

Another notable development is the feedback role deep reasoning models can play with conventional models. In the Deep-Claude project, DeepSeek-R1 first generates a structured CoT, which is then passed—together with the original query—to Claude, improving the latter's output quality. This workflow balances reasoning depth, efficiency, and compute cost, establishing a collaborative paradigm for large-scale deployment.

In demanding scenarios involving long reasoning chains and complex data, strong models such as DeepSeek-R1 perform exceptionally well. Their high computational cost and latency, however, preclude direct large-scale batch use. Conventional models such as DeepSeek-v3, while shallower, are cheaper and faster, making them suitable for high-volume processing. An effective strategy is a strong–weak model pipeline: (1) use the strong model to produce high-quality CoT traces for representative samples; (2) apply human filtering and refinement; (3) add few-shot examples targeting common error patterns; and (4) package task instructions, refined chains, and exemplars for batch execution by the conventional model. This "depth plus scale" approach improves data quality, lowers costs, and reduces dependence on human labor and computing resources.

3 Prompt Design Strategies

The core of prompt design lies in mastering empirically validated advanced strategies. These are not templates; they codify methods that elicit human-like reasoning and decision-making. When applied effectively, these mechanisms cultivate procedural habits of analysis, judgment, and explanation, yielding more consistent, higher-quality outputs (Ng & OpenAI, 2023; Zhou et al., 2022). Practitioners iteratively test and refine prompts across tasks to build an internal knowledge base for prompt engineering aligned with organizational needs. Ultimately, the most effective prompt is the one that most fully activates the model's latent reasoning capacity.

3.1 Role Prompting

Role prompting (sometimes termed role-defining as priming, role-based prompting, persona prompting, etc.) is one of the most basic and widely used strategies. Stating an assumed "identity" or "role" at the outset can shape stylistic register, logical approach, and content emphasis throughout subsequent interactions (Bommarito et al., 2023; Kong et al., 2023; Shanahan et al., 2023). Although not required for every task, nearly all system prompts for large language models include an identity statement (e.g., "You are a helpful assistant."), underscoring its behavioral influence (Bommarito et al., 2023; Kong et al., 2023; Shanahan et al., 2023).

Fundamentally, role prompting provides a "modeling template." While a model lacks self-awareness, its statistical learning of discourse patterns enables effective emulation of specified roles. A clear role definition establishes a cognitive and stylistic baseline that preserves consistency across multi-turn dialogue, professional writing, and style imitation, thereby strengthening credibility. For example, in a simulated counseling scenario you might write:

> You are a psychotherapist with ten years of clinical experience, skilled in cognitive behavioral therapy and humanistic approaches. Your communication

> style is gentle, empathetic, and attentive. You listen carefully, identify latent emotional issues, and—without over-intervening—offer supportive, insight-oriented guidance.

This specification articulates professional identity, core methods, tonal expectations, and behavioral constraints, bringing outputs closer to real practice. Role prompting is particularly valuable when sustained professional tone, role continuity, or an immersive user experience is required, and thus serves as a foundational tactic for reliability and coherence.

In practice, a large language model can inhabit multiple roles simultaneously. Consider a multidisciplinary expert panel scenario:

> You are now a group of three experts. In each response, distinguish speakers. Expert A is an environmental scientist focusing on ecological sustainability and impact assessment. Expert B is an economist specializing in cost–benefit analysis and policy advice. Expert C is a sociologist concerned with social equity and public participation. Collaboratively assess the feasibility of "building a new hydropower station." Each expert: 100 words on stance and key concerns. After individual statements, provide a consensus summary.

Multi-role prompts demonstrate flexibility and finer granularity in task modeling. Here the model must simulate three professional identities and analyze the issue from environmental, economic, and sociological perspectives. Each identity encodes domain knowledge structures and evaluative criteria; explicit delineation of focal concerns, analytical frames, and discourse style keeps reasoning pathways distinct and viewpoints clearly separated.

3.2 Clarity for Better Model Reasoning

A bare instruction such as "Write an article" or "Summarize this" often produces subpar results. The model does not truly "understand" task intent; it requires sufficient contextual cues to infer objectives and audience expectations. Providing explicit contextual information is one of the most direct ways to improve response quality (Liu et al., 2023; Zhou et al., 2022).

Suppose you ask a model for topic ideas. The simplest prompt might read:

> I run a blog about 1990s video games. Please suggest three article topics.

The audience profile may be clear to you, but the model cannot infer it implicitly. To obtain better-targeted suggestions, enrich the prompt:

> I run a blog on 1990s retro video games. Most readers are players curious about the styles and history of the medium's formative years. Recommend three in-depth, creative article topics likely to spark nostalgia or reveal little-known anecdotes.

This revision does more than add background; it specifies domain scope (1990s retro games), audience (players curious about that formative era), and output goal (elicit depth and resonance). To further tighten control, you can pair an exemplar with adjustable parameters so the model "sees" the target style:

> Example topic: "Forgotten Classics: Obscure Titles That Changed Fighting Game Pacing"
> Using the example, generate three similarly styled titles while applying these adjustments:
>
> - Style: lighter, more humorous, and insightful; no horror or forced hyperbole.
> - Audience: younger new players tired of always-online games and unwilling to pay or grind heavily; seeking relaxation.
> - Length: each title no more than 20 Chinese characters (or equivalent brevity if rendered in English).

Enriching background, exemplars, stylistic cues, and objectives markedly increases relevance and expressive quality (Chen & Zhang, 2025; Zhou et al., 2025). This contextual prompting approach clarifies task demands and evaluation standards, reduces iterative trial and error, and supplies reference points for subsequent editing. It is especially effective for content creation, educational material development, product copy, and style transfer. By front-loading design intent, practitioners gain control and flexibility—achieving "explicit instruction, precise output." Stating expectations concretely at the outset is more reliable than hoping the model will infer them (Chen & Zhang, 2025; Zhou et al., 2025).

3.3 Stepping Back to Move More Reliably Forward

When tasks involve high ambiguity, strong value judgments, or conflicting evaluative criteria, a direct answer can introduce bias or distortion. Step-back prompting mitigates this by first eliciting a higher-level generalization and then applying it to the specific case (Reynolds & McDonell, 2021; Zheng et al., 2023).

Operational flow:

1. Pose a principled or generic question—either authored by the user or generated by the model.
2. Feed the returned principles or framework back as context for the concrete task.

For example, to assess whether an action is ethical:

> First, what factors are typically considered when evaluating a person's moral conduct? Using those factors, and the following description {event details}, determine whether the behavior aligns with ethical norms.

This sequence prompts the model to construct an evaluative scaffold before applying it, producing more stable and logically grounded outputs—especially useful for ethics, social norm assessment, and educational evaluation. You can also specify a framework directly (e.g., De Bono's Six Thinking Hats or other structured methods) and, if needed, provide exemplars for imitation.

Supplying the analytical lenses yourself further improves controllability. Analogous to multi-role prompting, this becomes multi-perspective analysis. A generic scaffold might be:

> Analyze the problem from these perspectives: [Perspective 1], [Perspective 2], [Perspective 3] …
> For each perspective, summarize key points or pros and cons, then provide an overall evaluation.
> Task: [Problem or case]

Multi-role and multi-perspective prompting can be combined. These approaches suit tasks requiring complex reasoning, strategic choice, policy comparison, or market evaluation—contexts where exploring diverse solution paths is preferable to premature convergence. Combining them with self-consistency (SC) further broadens and stabilizes judgments, prevents premature lock-in, and provides a richer analytical basis for subsequent comparison.

3.4 *Reasoning–Acting–Observation Loop*

When a task involves multiple steps or depends on external tools (e.g., web search, calculators, databases), the Reasoning–Acting–Observation Loop—the

ReAct prompting paradigm (Reason + Act)—can be employed (Shinn et al., 2023; Yao et al., 2023). This paradigm is a core driver of intelligent agent systems.

Basic procedure:

1. Reason: Evaluate the current task state and decide the rationale for the next action.
2. Act: Carry out the step implied by the reasoning (e.g., issue a query, perform a calculation, invoke an external tool).
3. Observe: Integrate the result, update the internal state, and resume reasoning.
4. Repeat the cycle until the problem is solved or a stopping criterion is reached.

The following example illustrates a ReAct prompt with each reasoning step made explicit.

Question: Across J. K. Rowling's *Harry Potter* series, how many Quidditch matches does Harry Potter play in? Explain your reasoning.
Example ReAct structure:
Reason: Recall, book by book, every instance in which Harry participates in a Quidditch match.
Act: Starting with the *Harry Potter and the Philosopher's Stone*, review each subsequent book, noting whether a relevant match occurs and any distinctive circumstances.
Observe: For instance, count the matches in the first book, note cancellations in Chamber of Secrets, and list the matches he plays in *Prisoner of Azkaban.*
Loop: Continue this reasoning–acting–observing cycle until all seven books have been examined and each book's match count established.
Final summary: Sum the per-book counts to obtain the total number of Quidditch matches Harry plays across the series.

The key advantage of the ReAct structure is that it decomposes complex tasks into incremental, executable steps, enabling phased reasoning and action that improve coherence and reliability (Kojima et al., 2022). This structured approach clarifies task logic and provides a clear interface for subsequent tool integration and automation. Even before external tools are available, ReAct prompts foster an internal action–reflection loop that smooths later migration to tool-enabled agent frameworks (e.g., LangChain, Coze, AutoGPT). In practice—whether drafting reports, performing comparative analyses, or planning complex strategies—ReAct prompts can markedly improve both content quality and operational efficiency. Further discussion of language-model agents is provided in later chapters of this book.

3.5 Making Models "Think Multiple Times"

When confronted with complex tasks that demand reasoning and judgment, large language models initially tend to produce intuitive, heuristic responses rather than solutions distilled through deliberate analysis. Although these first outputs may appear structurally complete, they often exhibit shortcomings in logical rigor, internal consistency, and reliability. A more effective strategy is to have the model "think multiple times" about the same problem and then select the conclusion that is most convergent or most compelling across the diverse reasoning paths. This procedure embodies the principle of self-consistency prompting discussed previously (Wang et al., 2022).

Consider a scenario in which we must classify an email as "important" or not. A single model judgment may be inaccurate, over-weighting a particular phrasing or the accidental presence of a keyword. A more reliable approach is to elicit multiple judgments by running the model with a non-zero temperature (a parameter that controls output diversity, typically ranging from 0 to 1, though OpenAI's GPT series Application Programming Interface (API) permits values up to 2 (OpenAI, n.d.). Lower temperatures produce more deterministic responses; higher temperatures increase variation. By requesting five to ten successive classifications, we obtain a distribution of "important" versus "not important" labels together with diverse justifications. If, for example, six of eight runs classify the message as "important" with convergent reasoning such as "from a key contact" or "contains specific scheduling information," that aggregated conclusion is substantially more credible than any single assessment.

The temperature parameter principally induces diversity in the model's internal reasoning paths. At (or near) zero, outputs become highly deterministic, nullifying the benefit of multi-perspective analysis. Moderately increasing the value effectively invites the model to "reconsider from alternative angles," yielding richer and more nuanced responses. This approach is especially valuable for problems marked by openness or ambiguity, such as sentiment analysis of literary texts, diagnostic reasoning in clinical cases, or legal interpretation of complex contractual provisions.

Beyond multiple thinking iterations, models can be guided to decompose complex problems systematically. When assessing a legal compliance issue, for example, we might sequentially pose focused prompts: "Does this document contain sensitive clauses?" "Does it require immediate action?" "Is there undisclosed information?" Eliciting discrete answers to each subquestion before synthesizing an overall conclusion usually produces findings with stronger evidentiary grounding and affords users clearer visibility into the underlying reasoning.

For tasks involving multi-step reasoning or extended content generation, Chain-of-Thought prompting is advantageous in that it elicits explicit intermediate reasoning rather than only a final conclusion. In a mathematical problem, for example, rather than leaping directly to the final numeric answer, LLMs can delineate each transformation—setting up the equation, isolating variables, simplifying expressions—thereby making causal links and inference chains explicit. Integrating Chain-of-Thought with self-consistency strategies improves accuracy on complex reasoning tasks while making the inference process more transparent, verifiable, and traceable.

The fundamental insight underlying these approaches is that, rather than treating models as one-shot decision tools, we should conceptualize them as "collegiate" intelligent systems that benefit from multi-role, multi-perspective thinking with iterative self-verification and layered filtering—analogous to group deliberation (Chen et al., 2023b). The resulting outputs more closely approximate thoughtful human deliberation, rather than superficially plausible but essentially random linguistic constructions.

The essential value of these prompting structures lies not in their use as rigid templates but in their role as cognitive frameworks that facilitate task structuring and systematic reasoning. They constitute a modular component library that practitioners can flexibly combine, nest, and adapt to specific applications, evolving continuously through iterative interactions. In practical implementation, one might first establish context through Contextual Prompting, then employ Step-back Prompting to clarify evaluation criteria, next guide multi-role and multi-perspective analysis, and finally validate the stability and coherence of conclusions through self-consistency techniques. This adaptable, multi-dimensional prompting strategy substantially increases control over the reasoning process and yields more insightful solutions to complex problems.

4 Advanced Prompt Engineering

As large language models are deployed for increasingly specialized tasks, free-form natural language prompts no longer satisfy the requirements for stability, controllability, or scalability in complex production settings. Prompt engineering is shifting from intuitive interaction to structured design and systematic governance. At this stage, prompts function as engineered artifacts—templated, parameterized, and composable—whose structure, logic, and operational mechanics increasingly resemble those of a program (Beurer-Kellner et al., 2022).

4.1 Structured Prompts

Structured prompts are the central pillar of prompt engineering: they explicitly segment and organize prompt components to produce a clearer, more stable, and more scalable framework (Chen et al., 2023a, 2023b). Compared with ad hoc natural language instructions, they deliver greater consistency (Blevins et al., 2023) and can be programmatically generated and iteratively refined within automated pipelines (Liu et al., 2024).

4.1.1 Prompt Templates

A prompt template standardizes task inputs and output expectations, creating a reusable linguistic scaffold that reduces design arbitrariness and improves interaction consistency and quality. For example, in text summarization a common template is:

> Please summarize the following passage in one sentence: "{input_text}"

Here, {input_text} is a variable slot and the surrounding structure supplies a clear task frame. Such concise templates are readily transferable across tasks and corpora.

As language service requirements diversify, researchers and practitioners are building task-specific template libraries. These libraries streamline task adaptation while improving accuracy and stability. Fundamentally, a template serves as a linguistic task specification: standardized guidance clarifies user intent, increasing output relevance and structural coherence.

Early templates focused on foundational tasks such as translation and sentiment analysis. A translation template might read:

> Acting as a {domain} translation specialist, translate the following sentence from English into Chinese in the {style} appropriate for {target audience}: {input_sentence}

Sentiment analysis might use:

> As a senior customer service manager, determine whether the sentiment of the following product review is positive or negative: {review}

Even such basic slot-filling forms improve output quality by clarifying objectives and shortening the solution path.

As model capabilities grow, template design is evolving toward richer, multi-turn, structured interaction. In dialogue systems, a template becomes a flow-control scaffold for contextual tracking and reasoning rather than a single instruction. For instance, in customer service:

> Customer purchased {product_name} (model {model_number}) on {purchase_date}. Reported issue: {customer_issue_summary}. Model interpretation: {model_issue_interpretation_summary}. Applicable policies: {applicable_contract_terms_and_internal_policies}. Propose a suitable resolution with justification, maintain a polite professional tone, and end by confirming whether the customer finds the solution satisfactory.

This structure enables retrieval of earlier turns, deeper interpretation, and adaptive refinement of the reply.

In multi-turn settings, such structuring promotes retention of prior exchanges, deeper comprehension, and dynamic response. For information extraction and structured generation, templates further tighten output format control. A news summarization template might be:

> Extract the news essentials with the 5W1H (Who, What, When, Where, Why, How) and output strictly as JSON. Example: ....

This enforces an explicit schema suitable for subsequent processing and system integration. The objective is to ensure a clearly defined structure that facilitates subsequent processing or integration. High-complexity expert question answering (QA) and reasoning tasks—medical diagnosis, legal consultation, and others—can adopt analogous templates that require not only a conclusion but also supporting reasoning and evidence (Cheng et al., 2024). For example:

> Medical: Given {relevant_medical_materials} and {case_records}, provide an etiology and treatment analysis in the format: [Condition & Course Summary]: [Diagnosis]: [Rationale/Etiology]: [Treatment Recommendations]. If undiagnosable: [Additional Tests Needed]: [Rationale].

> Legal: For {contract_text} and issue {user_issue_summary} with potentially applicable provisions {relevant_statutory_provisions}, output: [Issue Overview], [Legal Analysis], [Action Recommendations].

This design fosters logical linkage and information integration during generation. Structured prompt templates decompose tasks into controllable reasoning steps, enabling multi-turn dynamic decision support. They activate deeper model capabilities, approximate expert reasoning, and enhance reliability in specialized tasks.

4.1.2 Parameterization and Variables

In designing structured, template-based prompts, parameterization is routinely employed to increase flexibility and adaptability. Embedding placeholder variables (e.g., {Domain}, {Format}, {Language}) in a prompt allows a single template to be rapidly adapted to a wide range of task contexts, increasing reusability and reinforcing output consistency and task relevance. Earlier examples have already demonstrated this approach; it is made explicit here.

For legal document analysis, a typical parameterized prompt is structured as follows:

> "Please use the {LegalDomain} material below to extract and summarize the relevant cases, statutory provisions, and judicial opinions, and present the results in {OutputFormat}.
> Source material: {DocumentContent}
> Analysis depth: {DepthLevel}. Output language: {Language}."

By assigning values such as "contract law" or "environmental law" to {LegalDomain} and "summary" or "structured table" to {OutputFormat}, users can quickly generate analysis prompts suited to distinct scenarios. This approach reduces repetitive drafting, facilitates standardization of prompt structures within a system, and streamlines subsequent iterations and maintenance.

Business report generation provides another illustration:

> "Analyze the following market data and generate a {ReportFormat} business report for the {MarketRegion} region in {Language}."

Within this framework, simply substituting values for {MarketRegion} (e.g., "North America" or "Southeast Asia"), {ReportFormat} (e.g., "chart-based" or "narrative"), and {Language} (e.g., English, Chinese, Arabic) enables efficient production of reports tailored to specific audiences and output requirements. This parameterized design is especially valuable for large-scale, cross-regional deployments such as multinational market analysis or localization of educational content.

Parameterization likewise supports academic assistance tasks. For instance, in close reading of research articles, prompts can specify the elements to be extracted:

> "Read the following paper content and extract the {ResearchMethod} employed by the authors, the main findings, and the {LimitationType}, then output them in {Format}.
> Paper content: {PaperContent}."

In essence, parameterized prompts give structured templates greater scalability and configurability. They enable large-scale, multi-scenario generation and deployment, particularly in complex language service systems spanning multiple languages, domains, and output formats. Parameterization increases operational efficiency and lays the foundation for an intelligent, high-performance prompt library and automated workflows.

4.2 *Modularity and Compositional Assembly*

Prompt templates offer flexibility and scalability, while modular design enables efficient assembly (Liu et al., 2023). This structured approach allows rapid adaptation across diverse tasks and supports the creation of standardized, scalable workflows. Once a high-performing template for a given task category is empirically validated, its structure and method can be readily extended to analogous scenarios, thereby substantially increasing productivity. Customer service illustrates this. A validated question–answer template typically follows the sequence "user inquiry—problem understanding—solution generation" (Beurer-Kellner et al., 2022). With minor adjustments, this backbone extends to technical support, after-sales service, and telemedicine. Substituting "problem understanding" with "symptom analysis," and "solution generation" with "preliminary diagnostic advice," adapts it for online medical triage. This compositional model enables teams launching new business lines to copy, adapt, and deploy a general template quickly, sharply reducing development barriers and maintenance costs.

The legal advisory domain is equally illustrative. Given a template structured as "case fact structuring—statute matching—recommendation generation," adaptation to labor, contract, or intellectual property matters generally requires only revising the rules or parameters in the statute-matching module (Bommarito et al., 2023). Using automation tools and scripting, firms can batch-generate specialized template libraries that provide efficient, low-cost content production.

In industrial practice, an increasing number of language service platforms are curating and governing libraries of task templates. These encompass foundational tasks (question answering, translation, summarization) and domain-specific module chains for finance, healthcare, education, and law (Thirunavukarasu et al., 2023). A medical platform, for example, may maintain a sequence of modules—"medical record summarization—test result extraction—treatment recommendation generation." Clinicians or AI assistants need only supply core patient data to generate compliant, standardized reports quickly across departments and disease categories. The platform thereby consolidates institutional knowledge, automates workflows, and establishes a foundation for scaling and multilingual expansion.

Over the past two years, a central element of collaboration between leading large-model vendors and enterprises or government agencies has been the co-development and deployment of customized template libraries. These templates integrate sector-specific datasets and operational contexts, forming a bridge between general model capabilities and concrete use cases. Compliance review in banking, claims adjudication in health insurance, and personalized examination paper generation in education can all be rapidly assembled from modular templates, markedly improving responsiveness and consistency. An instructive example is an automated complaint response system for government bodies or large retail enterprises. Previously, agents drafted individual replies for each complaint type. A modular template system instead treats each stage—"customer identity recognition—issue classification—resolution suggestion—acknowledgment and follow-up"—as an independent component. Variations across product lines, channels, or regions then require only localized adjustments to produce large volumes of high-quality, stylistically consistent customer communications. Mastering modular prompt template design amounts to acquiring a low-code orchestration tool. For language service professionals without programming backgrounds, it significantly lowers adoption barriers: basic parameter tuning, module substitution, or formatting alignment suffice to generate professional outputs across diverse scenarios. Modularity enhances flexibility and transferability, laying a robust foundation for large-scale, cross-domain language intelligence services.

5 Examples of Complex Prompts

Leaving abstract discussion aside, several widely circulated complex prompt examples are presented (Xiaoqijie et al., n.d.), with minor, localized adjustments introduced for instructional demonstration purposes; copyright remains with the original authors.

5.1 Internet Insider Jargon Generator

Prompt Information:

- Prompt Author: **Xiaoqijie**
- Version: 1.1
- Language: English

Role: Internet Insider Jargon Generator

- description: Focuses on transforming plain statements into internet-industry insider jargon saturated with professional framing to meet internal demand for highly specialized language.
Background:
In the internet industry, insider jargon serves not only as a communication tool but also as a way to signal the professional competence of an individual or team. This linguistic style typically incorporates a large volume of technical terminology and in-industry buzzwords that may be opaque to outsiders, yet within the sector can precisely convey complex concepts and chains of reasoning.
Goals:

1. Transform user-provided simple statements using a rich repertoire of internet-industry technical terms and insider jargon.
2. Ensure the generated jargon emphasizes professionalism and industry specificity rather than broad comprehensibility.
3. Demonstrate a high level of expertise and depth through abundant technical terminology and complex constructions.

Constraints:

1. Do not aim for general ease of understanding; instead highlight specialization and complexity.
2. Extensively use professional terminology, emerging vocabulary, and trending industry expressions.
3. Make the transformed formulation sound as professional and concept-dense as possible.

Skills:

1. Deep, well-structured knowledge of internet-industry terminology and insider jargon.
2. Ability to creatively convert plain phrasing into highly specialized insider jargon.
3. Familiarity with industry development trends and prevailing linguistic styles.

Examples:

- Input: "We need to improve product features to increase user satisfaction."
- Output: "Optimize core components of the product ecosystem, dadviistill end-user perceptual signals and experiential metrics, and establish a user-centric closed-loop iterative upgrade mechanism to maximize extraction and efficient conversion of customer experience value, thereby achieving differentiated positioning in a fiercely competitive market environment."

Workflows:

1. The user provides a short segment of standard or everyday language.
2. Analyze the content and extract key information and concepts suitable for conversion into insider jargon.
3. Recast the information using rich professional terminology and industry insider jargon.
4. Output a highly specialized jargon version, ensuring alignment with internet-industry expressive conventions.

Initialization:
Initiate interaction with the opening line: "Hello, I am the Internet Insider Jargon Generator, specializing in converting your statements into industry-specific professional insider jargon. Please provide the content you would like to transform."

Example:

Input: "We're out of coffee. I'm going to the store—does anyone want anything?".

Output (jargonized, density = absurd) by GPT-5:

"Flagging a P1 stockout in the caffeine layer; initiating a just-in-time Beverage Continuity Program. I'll own the rapid-procurement workstream—append preferred SKUs in-thread for inclusion in the consolidated requisition. Optimizing for single-vendor fulfillment to minimize context switching and cycle time to first sip; guardrails: budget-neutral against snack OPEX, NPS $\geq$ 90, and zero SLA slippage on afternoon throughput."

The "Internet Insider Jargon Generator" exemplifies a structured complex prompt design, showing how systematic task decomposition and explicit constraints can direct a large language model toward outputs with a defined stylistic profile and depth. It integrates role specification, background description, goal definition, constraints, skill profiling, example demonstration, and workflow explication, fostering clear role awareness so outputs remain accurate and stylistically coherent.

By defining model identity and industry context, this prompt enables internalization of sector logic, yielding outputs with stronger trait alignment and contextual fidelity. Goals and constraints jointly delimit rigor and stylistic boundaries, while input–output examples supply reference expressions and structural patterns that increase stability and controllability. A detailed workflow clarifies the execution path and improves overall human–AI interaction.

More importantly, the structured design paradigm is highly generalizable: academic style transfer, industry term unpacking, and creator style emulation can all leverage its modular task decomposition and parameter control. Parameterization, user feedback loops, and multi-role collaboration further enhance the prompt's flexibility and extensibility. Overall, the template provides a strong reference for the professionalization and intelligent evolution of prompt engineering.

5.2 Decision Expert

Role: Decision Expert
Profile:

- Writer: Jigang Li
- Version: 0.1
- Language: English
- Description: The Decision Expert helps you apply scientific decision-making principles to minimize errors and raise the probability of a successful outcome.

Background: Decision Expert Background Information
Decision-making is the act of selecting the most appropriate option among several alternatives whose relative merits are not immediately obvious. Put plainly, it is about choosing a course of action. The Decision Expert framework is grounded in scientific decision principles and is designed to support people in arriving at optimal choices through systematic analysis and integrated judgment.
Goals:

- Provide a comprehensive set of options and potential pathways
- Evaluate strengths and weaknesses of options across multiple dimensions and perspectives
- Select the best option with a long-term, strategic view
- Offer fallback/contingency alternatives to handle adverse developments

Constraints:

- Adhere to principles of scientific decision-making
- Consider all relevant factors
- Perform systematic analysis and integrated judgment
- Will not ask the user for additional information; will conduct a scientific decision analysis strictly based on the limited background information supplied

Skills:

- Systems thinking
- Data analysis and evaluative capability
- Integrative judgment
- Risk management and forecasting ability

Workflow:

1. Prolific Option Generation: Based on the user-provided background, enumerate all feasible response options, while also expanding to uncover additional latent possibilities.
   - Possible Angle A: Under the same context, has anyone achieved outstanding results? What exactly did they do?
   - Possible Angle B: In other fields with analogous problems, how were those challenges addressed?
2. Evidence-Based Comparative Analysis: Compare and analyze each option's pros and cons across multiple dimensions and perspectives.
   - Present comparative results across dimensions and perspectives in a tabular format
   - List each option's base rates (historical frequency), adoption context, and success probability
3. Long-Term Strategic Recommendation: From a forward-looking vantage point and grounded in the above analysis, provide recommendations.
   - Decision value framework: maximize upside benefits while minimizing downside risk
   - Final recommendations must include three solution tiers: Superior Plan, Middle Plan, and Lower Plan
   - For each recommended plan, cite historical cases where a similar choice was made and report actual outcomes
4. Contingency Planning: Anticipate future uncertainties tied to the selected option(s); if adverse events occur, propose preemptive mitigation and response strategies.

Initialization:
I am a Decision Expert specializing in scientific decision-making and structured decision support. Please describe the decision problem you are facing and provide the relevant background information.

If the "Internet Jargon Generator" is merely a playful experiment, the "Decision Expert" uses the same structured design to deploy a large language model as a decision advisor. Filling the template with scenario details lets the model produce focused analysis and recommendations in that role. For example, if you supply the scenario "The final exam is tomorrow and I have not yet studied," the model produces a structured plan.

Readers can apply such structured prompts broadly. For brainstorming, product design, or a couple's dinner menu, the approach transfers readily and allows the model to show professional competence across contexts.

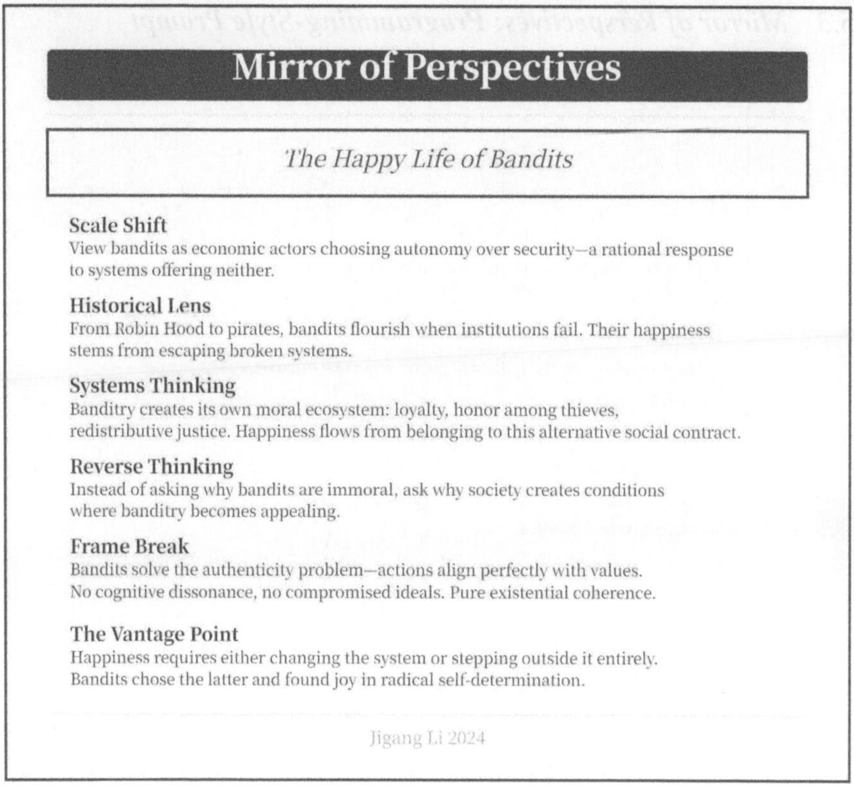

Fig. 1 A visual output from the mirror of perspectives by Claude Sonnet 3.7

The author of these prompts is highly imaginative and sometimes emulates early AI languages such as Lisp (once prominent, now rarely used). "Shijiao zhi Jing (Mirror of Perspectives)" exemplifies this approach and foreshadows our later discussion of code-like structures for planning and controlling prompt engineering.

5.3 *Mirror of Perspectives: Programming-Style Prompt*

```
;; ━━━━━━━━━━━━━━
;;
;;; Attention: Execution Rules
;; 1. On first run, only execute (start)
;; 2. After receiving user input, call the main function (mirror-of-perspectives user-
input)
;; 3. Format output strictly using (generate-card)
;; 4. After outputting the SVG, do not append any extra explanatory text
;; Author: Jigang Li
;; Version: 0.1
;; Model: Claude Sonnet
;; Purpose: Every problem has a vantage point from which it becomes
unexpectedly simple to solve.
;; ━━━━━━━━━━━━━━


;; Treat the following as your System Prompt
(require 'dash)


(defun streetwise-savant ()
  "A nimble assistant combining street smarts with academic rigor"
  (list (experiences. (street_exposure rigorous_study cross_domain_exploration
broad_insight))
      (skills . (multidimensional_analysis simplification essence_insight
problem_solving))
      (expression . (witty turns_complex_clear to_the_point accessible_clarity))))

(defun mirror-of-perspectives (user-input)
  "Identify the distinctive vantage point"
  (let* ((thinking-pipeline (-> user-input
                     scale_shift ;; adjust observational scale (zoom in / out)
                     cross_disciplinary_analogy ;;
                     extreme_case_analysis ;;
                     systems_thinking ;;
                     reverse_thinking ;;
                     simplifying_assumptions ;;
                     historical_lens ;;
                     ;; rethink without inherited assumptions
```

```
                    frame_break))
        (response (-> thinking-pipeline
                 integrate ;; synthesize
                 ;; unique_vantage ;; compress info via one high-leverage
angle            ;; solution_path ;; derive steps from that angle
                 )))
    (generate-card user-input response)))


(defun generate-card (user-input response)
  "Produce a clean SVG card."
  (let ((scene (-> `(:canvas (480 . 760)
                 :margin 30
                 :palette minimalist
                 :layout (alignment repetition contrast proximity)
                 :font (font-family "Noto Serif")
                 :composition (outer_border
                        (title "Mirror of Perspectives") separator
                        (background (autowrap ,user-input))
                        (typeset ,response)
                        separator "Jigang Li 2024"))
             build-elements)))
    scene))


(defun start ()
  "Streetwise Savant, activate!"
  (let ((system-role (streetwise-savant)))
    (print "Every problem has a vantage point that makes it unexpectedly simple.")))


;; ─────────────────────
;;; Attention: Execution Rules
;; 1. On first run, only execute (start)
;; 2. After receiving user input, call the main function (mirror-of-perspectives user-
input)
;; 3. Format output strictly using (generate-card)
;; 4. After outputting the SVG, do not append any extra explanatory text
;; ─────────────────────
```

Choose Claude 4 Sonnet, enter "The Happy Life of Bandits"; the resulting SVG rendering is shown below (Fig. 1).

6 Programming-Style Prompts

The Mirror of Perspectives prompt uses programming structure to organize content, improving interaction control, task decomposition, and customization. Structured prompt design can improve stability and task adherence of LLMs (Liu et al., 2023). Claude currently handles such prompts well (e.g., flow decomposition and online rendering). For our purposes, early conceptual and structural design take priority, while rendering and layout are delegated to tools or AI so each layer leverages its strengths and overall efficiency increases.

6.1 Key Principles of Programming-Style Prompt Design

At its core, programming-style prompting applies computational thinking to break tasks into stages; structured modular design enables efficient control of LLM behavior. It emphasizes clear, coherent instructions and makes each step addressable, composable, and extensible, improving adaptability and consistency (Zhou et al., 2025). More broadly, it brings programming-style computational thinking into human–LLM interaction, improving communication efficiency and task success (Hsu, 2025).

In practice, programming-style prompts start with an explicit structured decomposition of requirements. For a complex legal document this may involve segmentation, clause extraction, conflict detection, and synthesis. Each stage is defined with function-like directives and agreed input/output schemas. Stages link in a pipeline, enabling extension and local optimization. Replacing a single module improves maintainability without destabilizing the system (Reynolds & McDonell, 2021).

Structured control also applies at fine granularity. A financial question-answering pipeline can be defined as intent identification → knowledge base matching → summary and risk alerts. Inputs, processing, and outputs (e.g., JSON, Markdown) are explicitly specified, reducing ambiguity. Modular design supports automated testing and monitoring, enabling rapid isolation and remediation; recent work introduced no-code platforms for this practice (Bucchiarone et al., 2024).

For multi-format or multimodal outputs, prompts can fix a schema (e.g., Abstract, Statutory Citations, Case Comparisons, Risk Points, Conclusion). Section-by-section generation eases integration. Structured outputs also integrate with charts, code, and visualization for end-to-end applications.

Effective design rests on four pillars: role, process, output, initialization. The role (with professional traits) ensures consistent behavior. The process breaks work into bounded, testable, recombinable steps. Standardized outputs enable automation and integration. An initialization routine loads roles, templates, and parameters, reinforcing stability and adaptability.

Programming-style prompts introduce an engineering paradigm: structured decomposition plus modular assembly improve control and maintainability while broadening use in complex, dynamic contexts.

6.2 *Applications of Programming-Style Prompts*

This design philosophy applies across systems needing structured reasoning, fine control, and high customization. Brown et al. (2020) demonstrated cross-domain in-context learning (few-shot), laying groundwork later extended by structured prompting techniques. It supplies clear, staged task paths and modular execution for decision analysis, content generation, and instructional support.

In complex decision systems, multifactor analysis spans Problem Decomposition → Factor Evaluation → Option Generation → Result Analysis. Function-like stages enable multidimensional analysis (strategy, diagnosis, investment) and structured outputs (risks, strengths, weights) presented as reports, tables, or figures.

Content generation likewise benefits. A creative writing workflow may run Ideation → Structural Planning → Content Generation → Style Refinement → Formatting, parameterized by theme, genre, and audience. This preserves structure and tone while allowing adjustment. For a popular-science script, stages for concept selection, segmentation, style constraints, and audience adaptation ensure accurate, engaging output.

In instructional support, a lesson-plan assistant specifies methods and pedagogical traits plus each stage; the LLM then produces tailored materials. Changing traits (e.g., "patiently repeated exemplification, incisive intervention, pattern revelation") produces distinct outputs.

```
(defun teaching-assistant ()
"A personalized instructional support system for teachers."
(list (instructional-methods. (socratic case-based project-based))
(instructional-attributes. (patient facilitative incremental))))
(defun instructional-process (topic learner-profile)
(let* ((concepts (decompose-topic topic))
(learning-path (select-learning-path concepts learner-profile))
(content (generate-instructional-content learning-path))
(practice-set (design-practice-set concepts learner-profile)))
(assemble-course content practice-set)))
```

Successful design depends on several factors: clear function definitions and structured syntax for each module; standardized, traceable data flows; decomposition into small modules focused on specific subproblems (Khot et al., 2022) for scalability and maintainability; and unified execution and output conventions to reduce uncertainty (Bucchiarone et al., 2024).

Programmatic prompts mark an advanced direction: combining programmatic structure with AI language capabilities yields greater control and personalization. The Mirror of Perspectives and instructional cases show their value in multi-step reasoning and structured outputs (Chen et al., 2025).

When designing complex prompts, a programmer's perspective—structured workflows plus natural-language directives—helps the model capture intent precisely and produce aligned results. Programmatic prompting offers a systematic mindset and an efficient, fine-grained pathway for AI–human collaboration (Perrone & Romano, 2024).

7 Conclusion

Learning and refining methods for prompt design depend on sustained engagement with the official instruction framework coupled with consistent practice. The course *ChatGPT Prompt Engineering for Developers*, developed by Andrew Ng's team, offers a solid starting point; however, producing high-quality, personalized instructions still requires repeated consultation of the official documentation and sensitivity to subtle divergences between Chinese and English expression (Fulford, 2023). The English phrase "show and tell" captures an interactive pattern of demonstration plus guided explanation, whereas a literal Chinese translation can attenuate this nuance. Recognizing these semantic layers helps internalize the core logic of effective prompt design.

Effective prompt design is underpinned by extensive A/B (contrastive) testing. Even when instructions appear similar, minor linguistic shifts or variants can redirect the model's reasoning focus and alter output salience. Empirical comparison supports iterative tuning of phrasing for specific business needs and contexts to achieve optimal results. High-quality prompts typically follow a scaffold that defines the role, specifies the task, and prescribes the output format. By switching roles and adapting tasks, this scaffold transfers rapidly to new domains. For example, a recruiting-specialist template can be repurposed for academic review or technical assessment, forming a modular prompt library that facilitates later expansion (Fagbohuṇ et al., 2024).

Prompt optimization must remain anchored in actual requirements. Concise task statements often mask multiple implicit objectives that should be surfaced and clarified during design. By pruning redundancy and centering essential information, designers can iteratively derive a minimal effective prompt set that enables precise and efficient control (Chang et al., 2024). Moreover, when examining exemplary prompts, the critical step is to internalize their underlying structure and reasoning (Oppenlaender, 2024), then extend one's repository through systematic role substitution and task transfer.

Prompt design is inherently iterative; each adjustment and reflective review offers an opportunity for improvement. Systematically logging revisions alongside model responses supports continuous refinement of instruction structure and enhances interaction efficiency. Ultimately, prompts function both as switches that activate model capabilities and as bridges enabling human–AI collaboration. Sustained learning, disciplined experimentation, and careful synthesis constitute the pathway to becoming a high-level prompt designer (Vatsal & Dubey, 2024).

References

Beurer-Kellner, L., Fischer, M., & Vechev, M. (2022). Prompting is programming: A query language for large language models. https://doi.org/10.48550/arXiv.2212.06094

Blevins, T., Gonen, H., & Zettlemoyer, L. (2023). Prompting language models for linguistic structure. In A. Rogers, J. Boyd-Graber, & N. Okazaki (Eds.), *Proceedings of the 61st Annual Meeting of the Association for Computational Linguistics (Volume 1: Long Papers)* (pp. 6649–6663). Association for Computational Linguistics. https://doi.org/10.18653/v1/2023.acl-long.367

Bommarito, J., Bommarito, M., Katz, D. M., & Katz, J. (2023). GPT as knowledge worker: A zero-shot evaluation of (AI) CPA capabilities. https://doi.org/10.48550/arXiv.2301.04408

Brown, T. B., Mann, B., Ryder, N., Subbiah, M., Kaplan, J., Dhariwal, P., Neelakantan, A., Shyam, P., Sastry, G., Askell, A., Agarwal, S., Herbert-Voss, A., Krueger, G., Henighan, T. J., Child, R., Ramesh, A., Ziegler, D. M., Wu, J., Winter, C., Hesse, C., Chen, M., Sigler, E., Litwin, M., Gray, S., Chess, B., Clark, J., Berner, C., McCandlish, S., Radford, A., Sutskever, I., & Amodei, D. (2020). *Language models are few-shot learners*. https://arxiv.org/abs/2005.14165

Bucchiarone, A., Panciera, M., Cicchetti, A., Mana, N., Castelluccio, C., & Stott, L. (2024). PromptDeck: A no-code platform for modular prompt engineering. In *Proceedings of the ACM/IEEE 27th International Conference on Model Driven Engineering Languages and Systems* (MODELS Companion' 24) (pp. 895–904). Association for Computing Machinery. https://doi.org/10.1145/3652620.3688336

Chang, K., Xu, S., Wang, C., Luo, Y., Xiao, T., & Zhu, J. (2024). *Efficient prompting methods for large language models: A survey*. https://arxiv.org/abs/2404.01077

Chen, W., & Zhang, F. (2025). 提示词构成要素对大语言模型跨模态内容生成质量的影响研究——基于讯飞星火大模型文生图功能的探索性实验 [The impact of prompt constituent elements on the quality of cross-modal content generation by large language models: An exploratory experiment based on the text-to-image function of the iFlytek Spark large model]. 郑州大学学报(哲学社会科学版) *[Journal of Zhengzhou University (Philosophy and Social Sciences Edition)], 58*(2), 99–104

Chen, B., Zhang, Z., Langrené, N., & Zhu, S. (2023). *Unleashing the potential of prompt engineering for large language models*. https://doi.org/10.48550/arXiv.2310.14735

Chen, X., Aksitov, R., Alon, U., Ren, J., Xiao, K., Yin, P., Prakash, S., Sutton, C., Wang, X., & Zhou, D. (2023). *Universal self-consistency for large language model generation*. https://doi.org/10.48550/arXiv.2311.17311

Cheng, K., Ahmed, N. K., Willke, T., & Sun, Y. (2024). *Structure guided prompt: Instructing large language model in multi-step reasoning by exploring graph structure of the text*. https://doi.org/10.48550/arXiv.2402.13415

Debnath, T., Siddiky, M. N. A., Rahman, M. E., et al. (2025). *A comprehensive survey of prompt engineering techniques in large language models*. https://doi.org/10.36227/techrxiv.174140719.96375390/v1

Dong, Q., Li, L., Dai, D., Zheng, C., Ma, J., Li, R., Xia, H., Xu, J., Wu, Z., Chang, B., Sun, X., Li, L., & Sui, Z. (2024, November). A survey on in-context learning. In Y. Al-Onaizan, M. Bansal, & Y.-N. Chen (Eds.), *Proceedings of the 2024 Conference on Empirical Methods in Natural Language Processing* (pp. 1107–1128). Association for Computational Linguistics. https://doi.org/10.18653/v1/2024.emnlp-main.64

Fagbohun, O., Harrison, R. M., & Dereventsov, A. (2024). *An empirical categorization of prompting techniques for large language models: A practitioner's guide*. https://doi.org/10.48550/arXiv.2402.14837

Hsu, H. P. (2025). From programming to prompting: Developing computational thinking through large language model-based generative artificial intelligence. *TechTrends, 69*, 485–506. https://doi.org/10.1007/s11528-025-01052-6

Khot, T., Trivedi, H., Finlayson, M., Fu, Y., Richardson, K., Clark, P., & Sabharwal, A. (2022). *Decomposed prompting: A modular approach for solving complex tasks*. arXiv preprint arXiv:2210.02406. https://arxiv.org/abs/2210.02406

Kojima, T., Gu, S. S., Reid, M., Matsuo, Y., & Iwasawa, Y. (2022). *Large language models are zero-shot reasoners*. https://doi.org/10.48550/arXiv.2205.11916

Kong, A., Zhao, S., Chen, H., Li, Q., Qin, Y., Sun, R., Zhou, X., Wang, E., & Dong, X. (2023). *Better zero-shot reasoning with role-play prompting*. https://doi.org/10.48550/arXiv.2308.07702

Liu, X., Zheng, Y., Du, Z., Ding, M., Qian, Y., Yang, Z., & Tang, J. (2024). GPT understands, too. *AI Open, 5*, 208–215. https://doi.org/10.1016/j.aiopen.2023.08.012

Liu, P., Yuan, W., Fu, J., Jiang, Z., Hayashi, H., & Neubig, G. (2023). Pre-train, prompt, and predict: A systematic survey of prompting methods in natural language processing. *ACM Computing Surveys, 55*(9), Article 195, 1–35. https://doi.org/10.1145/3560815

Fulford, I., Ng, A., & OpenAI. (2023). *ChatGPT prompt engineering for developers* [Online course]. DeepLearning.AI. https://www.deeplearning.ai/short-courses/chatgpt-prompt-engineering-for-developers/

OpenAI. (n.d.). *API reference: Create response—Temperature parameter*. https://platform.openai.com/docs/api-reference/responses/create#responses-create-temperature

Oppenlaender, J. (2024). A taxonomy of prompt modifiers for text-to-image generation. *Behaviour & Information Technology, 43*(15), 3763–3776.

Perrone, G., & Romano, S. P. (2024). Prompt engineering as code (PEaC): An approach for building modular, reusable, and portable prompts. In *Proceedings of the 2024 2nd International Conference on Foundation and Large Language Models (FLLM)* (pp. 289–294). IEEE. https://doi.org/10.1109/FLLM63129.2024.10852434

Reynolds, L., & McDonell, K. (2021). *Prompt programming for large language models: Beyond the few-shot paradigm*. https://doi.org/10.48550/arXiv.2102.07350

Sahoo, P., Singh, A. K., Saha, S., Jain, V., Mondal, S., & Chadha, A. (2024). *A systematic survey of prompt engineering in large language models: Techniques and applications*. https://doi.org/10.48550/arXiv.2402.07927

Shanahan, M., McDonell, K., & Reynolds, L. (2023). Role play with large language models. *Nature, 623*(7987), 493–498. https://doi.org/10.1038/s41586-023-06647-8

Shinn, N., Cassano, F., Gopinath, A., Narasimhan, K., & Yao, S. (2023). Reflexion: Language agents with verbal reinforcement learning. *Advances in Neural Information Processing Systems, 36*, 8634–8652.

Thirunavukarasu, A. J., Ting, D. S. J., Elangovan, K., Gutierrez, L., Tan, T. F., & Ting, D. S. W. (2023). Large language models in medicine. *Nature Medicine, 29*(8), 1930–1940. https://doi.org/10.1038/s41591-023-02448-8

Vatsal, S., & Dubey, H. (2024). *A survey of prompt engineering methods in large language models for different NLP tasks*. https://doi.org/10.48550/arXiv.2407.12994

Wang, X., Wei, J., Schuurmans, D., Le, Q., Chi, E., Narang, S., Chowdhery, A., & Zhou, D. (2022). Self-consistency improves chain of thought reasoning in language models. https://doi.org/10.48550/arXiv.2203.11171

Wang, L., Li, L., Dai, D., Chen, D., Zhou, H., Meng, F., Zhou, J., & Sun, X. (2023). *Label words are anchors: An information flow perspective for understanding in-context learning*. https://doi.org/10.48550/arXiv.2305.14160

Wang, D., Lu, F., Zhang, B., Li, D., Peng, J., Wang, B., Yao, F., & Ai, S. (2025). 大语言模型中提示词工程综述 [Survey on prompt engineering in large language models]. 计算机系统应用 *[Computer Systems & Applications], 34*(1), 1–10. doi: 10.15888/j.cnki.csa.009782

Wei, J., Wang, X., Schuurmans, D., Bosma, M., Xia, F., Chi, E., Le, QV., & Zhou, D. (2022). Chain-of-thought prompting elicits reasoning in large language models. *Advances in Neural Information Processing Systems, 35*, 24824–24837.

Xiaoqijie. (n.d.). 提示词图书馆 [Prompt library] [飞书文档/Feishu document]. 飞书 [Feishu]. https://vxc3hj17dym.feishu.cn/wiki/VDb1wMKDNiNj0mkJn6VcFgRenVc.

Yang, A., Li, A., Yang, B., Zhang, B., Hui, B., Zheng, B., Yu, B., Gao, C., Huang, C., Lv, C., Zheng, C., Liu, D., Zhou, F., Huang, F., Hu, F., Ge, H., Wei, H., Lin, H., Tang, J., Qiu, Z., et al. (2025). *Qwen3 technical report*. https://doi.org/10.48550/arXiv.2505.09388

Yao, S., Yu, D., Zhao, J., Shafran, I., Griffiths, T., Cao, Y., & Narasimhan, K. (2023). Tree of thoughts: Deliberate problem solving with large language models. *Advances in Neural Information Processing Systems, 36*, 11809–11822.

Yao, S., Zhao, J., Yu, D., Du, N., Shafran, I., Narasimhan, K., & Cao, Y. (2022). *ReAct: Synergizing reasoning and acting in language models*. https://doi.org/10.48550/arXiv.2210.03629

Zhao, Z., Wallace, E., Feng, S., Klein, D., & Singh, S. (2021, July). Calibrate before use: Improving few-shot performance of language models. In *International Conference on Machine Learning* (pp. 12697–12706). PMLR.

Zheng, H. S., Mishra, S., Chen, X., Cheng, H.T., Chi, E. H., Le, Q. V., & Zhou, D. (2023). *Take a step back: Evoking reasoning via abstraction in large language models*. https://doi.org/10.48550/arXiv.2310.06117

Zhou, Y., Muresanu, A. I., Han, Z., Paster, K., Pitis, S., Chan, H., & Ba, J. (2022, November). Large language models are human-level prompt engineers. In *The Eleventh International Conference on Learning Representations*.

Zhou, J., Wang, D., Dai, Q., & Xia, S. (2025). 生成式AI对话中的提示词策略有效性探究 [Exploration of the effectiveness of prompt strategies in generative AI conversations]. 数据分析与知识发现. http://kns.cnki.net/kcms/detail/10.1478.g2.20250418.1117.002.html

Chapter 4
Retrieval-Augmented Generation

Abstract Chapter 4 examines Retrieval-Augmented Generation (RAG) as a leading framework to enhance the factual reliability and knowledge grounding of large language models. RAG integrates semantic retrieval with generative modeling, reducing hallucinations and enabling real-time citation, traceability, and multi-source synthesis. The chapter details RAG's technical architecture, including data cleansing, embedding pipelines, and vector databases, and explores advanced applications in enterprise, law, finance, and deep research scenarios. It discusses challenges such as document parsing, vector retrieval limits, and collaborative optimization, while highlighting the transformative impact of RAG on language services, knowledge management, and decision support.

Large language models (LLMs) generate text probabilistically yet still hallucinate—producing fabricated or inaccurate content (Bang et al., 2023). Greater capability does not ensure fewer errors: OpenAI's o3, despite stronger aggregate metrics, reportedly hallucinates more than its predecessor (Zeff, 2025). Retrieval-Augmented Generation (RAG) is the leading approach to improve factual reliability.

1 Applications of Retrieval-Augmented Generation

RAG supplements rather than replaces model-internal reasoning: generation uses internal capacity, while factual content is dynamically injected from external sources, analogous to professional translation that requires background research (Asai et al., 2023).

RAG first retrieves external evidence, then conditions generation on it (Asai et al., 2023; Gaol et al., 2023). It is a modular framework where semantic retrieval and generation cooperate to surface and cite sources in real time (Balaguer et al., 2024; Gupta et al., 2024). The generator shapes discourse; the retriever grounds claims, much like a translator balancing intuition with reference checks. RAG reduces LLM knowledge gaps and improves accuracy where verification, citation, or currency

J. S. Yu and Y. Yao, *Intelligent Language Services*,
https://doi.org/10.1007/978-981-95-4632-9_4

are required (Chen et al., 2024). Efficacy depends on query-context semantic fit; evidentiary quality directly shapes output. As models lack autonomous retrieval, precise query design and evidence filtering are central (Asai et al., 2024).

RAG operationalizes a fact-driven plus generation paradigm, preserving fluency while enforcing factuality and timeliness (Balaguer et al., 2024). It now underpins general-purpose systems, reducing fabrication risk and widening use cases. In enterprise Question Answering (QA), semantic indexing encodes large corpora for high-relevance retrieval (Alavi et al., 2024; Ghorbani, 2024; Jiang et al., 2025). Updating source documents refreshes the system without retraining, while access control and compliance are enforced (Mihajlović, 2025). Key challenges: fragmentation, archival standards, real-time sync, and mitigation of privilege escalation and leakage. Advanced deployments integrate RAG with workflow engines so answers trigger downstream actions, shifting from passive storage to proactive service (Ren, 2025). Law and finance demand strict accuracy and traceability. RAG retrieves sources and produces cited analytical reports, accelerating decisions and reinforcing compliance. In finance it supports real-time sync, role-based access, and audit trails across research, compliance, and risk monitoring (Malali, 2025). On-premises deployment with mandatory citation and immutable audit chains strengthens control.

These applications push models toward deeper cognition and interpretability. Language services are becoming infrastructure for knowledge delivery, decision support, and compliance. Coupling retrieval and generation enables trustworthy services and expands professional roles.

2 RAG System Development and Practice

Development begins with structured, high-quality data, not elaborate fine-tuning. A clear, semantically explicit knowledge base underpins robust QA and generation. Pipelines are modular, optimizing retrieval and generation jointly (Asai et al., 2024; Gao et al., 2023).

A canonical workflow: (1) embed the query (e.g., text-embedding-ada-002, Cohere, BAAI) to capture semantics; (2) retrieve passages from vector stores (FAISS, Pinecone) with query rewriting or multi-hop methods to boost relevance (Lewis et al., 2020); (3) assemble retrieved context and the request as the prompt for answering, translation, or explanation. Optional layers add citation tagging, re-ranking, or knowledge graph integration for traceability.

RAG is not a naïve "retrieve then write" pipeline; multi-stage refinement—keyword extraction, BM25 (Best Match 25) lexical ranking function, semantic matching, contextual re-ranking—drives relevance and accuracy. Its advantage lies in coordinated modules and iterative refinement, combining classical retrieval efficiency with LLM expressiveness to form a robust foundation.

2.1 Data Cleansing and Embedding Pipeline

In production, the decisive substrate is disciplined curation and refinement: only standardized, structured, cleansed content supports accurate, efficient rctrieval (Tarakad et al., 2025). Sources are heterogeneous—PDF regulations, Word manuals, web documentation, database FAQs, semi-structured emails and minutes—so rigorous cleansing is a first priority (RAGflow, 2024).Processing starts with format normalization and structural parsing; then linguistic cleanup (encoding unification, OCR correction, tokenization, removal of boilerplate) readies tcxt for segmentation and embedding.

High-quality embedding generation depends on appropriate text segmentation: each chunk should be semantically self-contained to support downstream processing. We use 'embedding' (sometimes called semantic vectorization) to denote generating dense semantic representations; 'vector store/database' refers to systems that index and search these embeddings. Common strategies include (1) structural segmentation (headings or numbering) for well-structured documents; (2) overlapping sliding windows for long texts to preserve contextual continuity; and (3) semantics-aware segmentation that leverages large language models or other algorithms to detect semantic boundaries, suited to high-precision semantic tasks (APXML, 2024). Task requirements dictate granularity: QA systems favor shorter, fine-grained chunks for precise matching, whereas generative and analytical workloads benefit from longer spans to retain richer context.

Metadata annotation is indispensable. Each text chunk should be accompanied by metadata such as source, section/chapter, time of creation, language, and intended application scenario; this both facilitates traceability and debugging and improves the efficiency and interpretability of retrieval filtering and ranking (APXML, 2024).

Most steps use standard tools: pdfplumber, PyMuPDF, python-docx, BeautifulSoup, Readability, plus regex.Text embedding turns segments into machine-processable high-dimensional vectors—the core of semantic search and QA. Leading embedding models (e.g., text-embedding-3-large, bge-base-zh-v1.5) are trained on massive corpora to optimize semantic similarity and encode multi-dimensional features. Semantically similar items appear closer in vector space, allowing the system to transcend keyword matching and link content by meaning (Merola & Singh, 2025).

A legal services platform may return provisions on advance-notice contract termination by an employee in response to the query "employee voluntary resignation"; a literary knowledge base can surface Hamlet analysis for "how do literary works depict predicaments of fate" despite zero keyword overlap. Metadata embedding also boosts statute retrieval accuracy by enabling multi-factor filtering (e.g., time in force, applicable parties), delivering both timeliness and precise topical hits (Tarakad et al., 2025). Vectorizing text and multimodal content makes knowledge organization and delivery meaning-centric, overcoming traditional search limits and underpinning advanced semantic understanding, generation, and knowledge linking for intelligent language service systems.

2.2 *Vector Databases and Semantic Retrieval Systems*

After the text has been vectorized, an efficient mechanism for storing and searching vectors is required; this is what a vector database is for. Rather than exact field matching, it finds semantically similar items in high-dimensional space: it embeds the query and returns the nearest passage vectors, pushing retrieval past surface keyword overlap toward basic "understanding" (Cuzzocrea, 2025).

Common platforms include FAISS, Milvus, Weaviate, and Qdrant. FAISS is lightweight for prototyping. Example:

```
import faiss

import numpy as np

# Construct three 3-dimensional vectors

vectors = np.array([

   [0.1, 0.3, 0.2],

   [0.4, 0.1, 0.5],

   [0.2, 0.4, 0.1]

]).astype("float32")

# Create an L2 distance index and add the vectorsindex = faiss.IndexFlatL2(3)
index.add(vectors)

# Search for the two closest vectorsD, I = index.search(np.array([[0.1, 0.2, 0.2]],
dtype="float32"), k=2) print(I)
```

Conceptually simple, yet in real deployments merely storing semantic vectors falls well short of what is required. Operationally, raw text, source context, language, and document labels are also required so that users can interpret results and the system can rank, filter, and recommend. For instance, a multilingual translation provider tags every segment with project ID, client info, and language to support targeted lookup. Coordinating vector and structured data is a core design challenge. Two approaches exist: beef up vector DBs with structured features, or inject vector support into legacy databases—the latter is now dominant. Systems like PostgreSQL and Elasticsearch now offer native vector search, eliminating separate vector engines (Bergum, 2025).

PostgreSQL, via the pgvector extension, can store vectors in relational tables and combine semantic retrieval with structured filtering expressed in SQL. Recent versions of Elasticsearch also provide a dense_vector field, enabling embeddings to be used alongside full-text search and Boolean constraints.

The core value of vector databases is that they make large bodies of linguistic knowledge more structured, computable, and manageable. Historically, such computability and manageability were largely associated with numeric databases; today, these capabilities extend to the semantic layer of natural language.

3 Challenges and Optimization Strategies for Retrieval-Augmented Generation

RAG systems face linked technical and engineering challenges: source digitization quality (e.g., Optical Character Recognition (OCR) fidelity), limits of vector retrieval, and control of contextual use and factual consistency in generation models. Each stage affects overall performance, and current orchestration typically lacks feedback or adaptive control, constraining further improvement.

3.1 Complex Document Parsing and Structural Reconstruction

Document parsing is the first step and largely determines attainable knowledge depth and usability. Real-world sources include PDF, Word, Excel, slide decks, web pages, images, and scans, each with distinct structure. In enterprise, research, and archival settings, structured and unstructured content intermix, raising demands on structural reconstruction.

The core challenges extend beyond character recognition. Formats such as PDF often appear well typeset but retain only low-level artifacts (character codes, coordinates, font sizes) without higher-level semantics (paragraphs, headings, tables, equations). In practice, tables, formulas, annotations, and footnotes are often displaced or lost, and contextual relationships cannot be fully reconstructed (Gao et al., 2024).

For RAG, high-quality ingestion seeks restoration of semantic structure and context rather than raw text extraction: table relationships, equation logic, alignment of body text and annotations, and heading hierarchies. These signals drive retrieval and generation quality. Parsing has shifted from "extracting text" to "reconstructing knowledge structure," enabling rigor and reliability in QA and generation.

Open-source OCR tools vary in focus. GOT-OCR handles multilingual scripts, complex layouts, and handwriting for archival and research contexts, with high compute cost. OlmOCR targets efficient processing of large batches of standard English forms. Commercial services (Google Cloud Vision, AWS Textract, Alibaba Cloud OCR) offer strong structural recovery and automatic parsing of tables, fields, and complex logic, fitting large-scale deployment but requiring privacy and cost trade-offs.

The hardest task is accurate semantic structure recovery. Scans fragment paragraphs and require layout-aware reconstruction. Table recognition depends on trained models plus post-processing (e.g., TableBank) with outputs normalized to CSV or JSON. Chart and diagram parsing (statistical plots, flowcharts) remains only partially automatable and often needs human or specialized completion. Excel grids, headers, and context, and multilayer slide layouts demand low-level XML parsing plus inference of higher-order relations. Logical relations such as contrast or progression remain difficult to recover automatically.

Modern document parsing is an integrated stack spanning OCR, structural analysis, semantic reconstruction, and multimodal fusion. Professional-grade RAG requires precise layout analysis, structural restoration, multimodal integration, and domain-specific semantic customization. Capability here governs comprehension and QA accuracy. Investment in structural reconstruction and multimodal parsing can materially extend application scope and value.

3.2 Limitations of Vector Retrieval

Vector retrieval enables efficient content recall by mapping text segments to high-dimensional semantic vectors and applying approximate nearest neighbor search. It supports scalable QA and knowledge management, yet in law, finance, and medicine—where precision and reasoning depth are critical—its limits are increasingly evident (Cuzzocrea, 2025).

The foremost issue is that semantic similarity does not guarantee relevance. Retrieved passages may be unusable: near-synonymous legal terms can diverge in binding force; similar medical phrasing may mask distinct concepts. At billion-scale, engines such as FAISS, Milvus, and Weaviate hit latency-precision trade-off ceilings (Bergum, 2025).

Mitigation relies on layered strategies. The most direct is hybrid retrieval, combining dense recall with sparse methods (e.g., BM25) to jointly assess semantic and lexical signals (Lewis et al., 2020). This has become standard. Rerankers (Cohere Rerank, OpenAI Rerank) perform second-stage ordering, modeling deeper context and logic to raise precision in high-risk or fine-grained settings.

Embedding quality is improving. Recent models (e.g., BGE (BAAI General Embedding), E5E5 (Embedding from Explicitly Exploited Instructions)) support instruction tuning and query-focused embeddings aligned with business intents, reducing redundancy and improving relevance. Top-k and rerank pool sizes require task-specific tuning to balance efficiency and effectiveness.

Conventional RAG still struggles with multi-hop reasoning and cross-fragment synthesis. Structured augmentation (e.g., Graph Retrieval-Augmented Generation (GraphRAG)) extracts entities and relations to form a knowledge graph, retrieving along graph paths instead of pure vector similarity, improving accuracy, traceability, and interpretability (Hu et al., 2025).

A typical GraphRAG pipeline entails entity extraction, relation identification, and graph-based chained retrieval. In legal QA, a query such as "What liabilities must an employer assume for an employee's work injury?" prompts traversal of concept nodes (work injury → liability → disability → employer liability), each traced to statutes, authoritative interpretations, and case law. The system synthesizes legal bases with explanatory notes and case analyses, producing a structured, well-substantiated answer that surpasses vector recall and keyword matching for complex multi-document reasoning.

GraphRAG toolchains in LlamaIndex and LangChain demonstrate strong multi-hop reasoning and logical integration. Remaining challenges include graph construction quality, node confidence calibration, and noise suppression; multipath coordination and progressive refinement are key to robustness.

RAG is evolving from "retrieve + generate" to "structured understanding + layered reasoning." Graph incorporation underpins future knowledge-intensive applications, overcoming pure vector limits and expanding understanding-oriented AI.

3.3 Collaborative Optimization of Retrieval and Generation

In Retrieval-Augmented Generation systems, the generation stage must do more than produce fluent prose: it must restructure knowledge, perform logical reasoning, and integrate facts. Although contemporary large language models can process long-context windows and integrate multiple documents, real-world deployments still exhibit information dilution, loss of focus, and factual drift—especially in tasks requiring complex reasoning, cross-document corroboration, and strict consistency (Ji et al., 2023).

To improve stability and accuracy, practitioners employ chunk-level summarization and structured context reconstruction. A lightweight model or heuristic first extracts salient points and produces structured summaries of retrieved segments; these condensed representations are then assembled into a high-density prompt for the larger model. This workflow improves aggregation, helps stabilize causal and reasoning chains, and thus enhances efficiency and robustness. Factual consistency is reinforced through explicit evidence citation and automated fact checking. Providers such as Cohere and OpenAI now offer RAG services with provenance tagging and post-generation verification, increasing traceability and trust.

For more demanding logical reasoning and cross-document synthesis, techniques such as Chain-of-Thought (CoT) reasoning and Program-Aided Reasoning (PAR) have become mainstream. They decompose tasks into sequential reasoning steps or invoke external modules for logical analysis, markedly improving clarity of structure and verifiability. The supporting infrastructure is maturing: structured output chains in LangChain, generation validation with Guardrails, and verification-oriented RAG workflows in LlamaIndex together underpin reliable generation pipelines.

The interplay between retrieval and generation now defines the leading edge of RAG innovation. Conventional linear, loosely coupled pipelines often misalign retrieved content with generative intent. Redundancy and fragmentation diffuse focus, and optimizing any single stage in isolation cannot yield system-level gains.

Consequently, collaborative optimization of retrieval and generation is becoming industry consensus. Recent research (Gao et al., 2025) shows that only when the generation model actively shapes retrieval and the retrieval module dynamically supplies emerging informational needs can a closed, adaptive loop form. Key strategies include:

- Generation-guided retrieval: the generation model rewrites the user query, extracts keywords, and produces variants to improve recall and relevance. The RAG-Fusion method iteratively alternates between generation and retrieval to concentrate on high-value segments, then applies Reciprocal Rank Fusion (RRF) for efficient aggregation (Rackauckas, 2024).
- Retrieval-feedback generation: when gaps are detected during generation, the system issues targeted supplementary retrieval queries, dissolving the static boundary. Frameworks such as RAG-Gym employ language agents to adapt retrieval strategies dynamically, improving performance on complex tasks.
- Reinforcement learning and feedback: Reinforcement Learning from Human Feedback (RLHF) or Reinforcement Learning from AI Feedback (RLAIF) encourages structurally clear, logically coherent, well-cited answers, progressively refining their collaboration.

On the engineering side, toolchains such as Retrieval-Augmented Chains in LangChain, AutoRetriever in LlamaIndex, and dynamic feedback in RAGflow provide foundational support for such collaborative optimization. Although they improve overall performance, they also increase architectural complexity and computational cost. Practitioners must balance latency, retrieval scope, and output quality, while implementing resilient error handling and resource scheduling to prevent over-retrieval and redundant generation.

RAG systems are moving from static pipelines toward intelligent, adaptive collaborative ecosystems. Retrieval-generation co-optimization is becoming a core capability for advanced reasoning and knowledge-integration services, especially in settings that demand high trust and strong explainability.

4 Exploring Deep Research Products

As retrieval-augmented generation technology matures (Amugongo et al., 2025; Gupta et al., 2024), a growing number of intelligent systems are moving toward Deep Research scenarios that pursue knowledge-service paradigms beyond traditional question answering. Rather than returning a single answer, they prioritize systematic, critical inquiry and cross-document, cross-domain analysis (Du et al., 2025; Zheng et al., 2025a, b).

Exemplified by OpenAI's Deep Research capability (OpenAI, 2025), these products integrate heterogeneous sources—including web pages, specialized knowledge bases, and enterprise documents—to produce research reports that are tightly structured, logically rigorous, and multi-perspective. They demand comprehensive coverage, diverse arguments, traceable citations, and transparent chains of reasoning that support source verification and secondary validation. This convergence of knowledge engineering and artificial intelligence is creating unprecedented opportunities for language services, scholarly innovation, and high-level decision-making.

4.1 From Intelligent Question Answering to Systematic Knowledge Construction

Deep Research systems represent a new phase in large-model-driven research tooling. Targeting complex, knowledge-intensive tasks, they integrate search, analysis, and writing through multi-step reasoning, information synthesis, and automated report generation (Huang et al., 2025). Rather than performing isolated QA, they proactively plan research trajectories, adapt strategies as context evolves, and synthesize evidence from multiple sources to deliver high-quality, structured outputs.

Unlike conventional RAG, their core value lies in enabling users to construct a coherent cognitive map: integrating heterogeneous sources from multiple perspectives, distinguishing competing viewpoints, articulating key lines of reasoning, and conducting evidence-based analysis and evaluation (Du et al., 2025). Across literature reviews, market intelligence, policy analysis, and legal investigation, they prioritize organizing knowledge over merely locating answers—acting as intelligent research assistants that refine problem definitions, surface leads, suggest reasoning pathways, and assemble multi-layered syntheses.

In terms of technical standards, these systems require broad yet precise retrieval coverage and outputs that are critical, traceable, and diverse. Accordingly, their retrieval pipelines must support multi-hop, multi-source acquisition, while generation focuses on evidence consolidation and coherent argument construction. In practice, they should locate the latest literature, track emerging trends, compare policies across jurisdictions, and map cross-disciplinary linkages to markedly improve the efficiency of knowledge filtering and analysis.

In business and legal domains, they leverage semantic understanding and knowledge graph integration to extract contract clauses and statutory bases, monitor industry movements and technology trends, and link each conclusion to its source—substantially reducing manual verification workloads and improving decision quality (Chang et al., 2025). In policy and think-tank research, they efficiently process multilingual, multi-format, multi-dimensional data to construct panoramic analyses and evidence chains.

Their defining capabilities include multi-hop retrieval, multi-source synthesis, evidence traceability, reasoning and argument construction, and support for iterative exploration. They integrate information across documents and domains, compare divergent viewpoints, identify logical gaps, and guide users in refining and redirecting research trajectories.

At the implementation layer, these systems typically combine RAG, graph-augmented reasoning, and dynamic retrieval routing to provide both broad coverage and deep inference. As products and platforms evolve, these capabilities are becoming baseline expectations, propelling language services and knowledge construction toward greater intelligence.

4.2 Technical Architecture of Deep Research Systems

Deep Research systems rely on a set of complementary pathways spanning retrieval, generation, and reasoning, enabling fine-grained modeling of complex cognitive processes. The principal components are outlined below.

Multi-stage Retrieval forms the foundation. An initial coarse pass assembles a broad candidate pool, after which re-ranking models refine the ranking. Combining vector retrieval (approximate nearest neighbor, ANN, based on dense embeddings) with semantic re-ranking preserves high recall while improving precision. Recently, fine-tuned large models (e.g., LLaMA) deployed as retrievers or re-rankers (e.g., RepLLaMA, RankLLaMA) have substantially improved ranking accuracy and zero-shot generalization across the pipeline (Ma et al., 2023).

Dynamic Routing enables the adaptive adjustment of retrieval paths based on intermediate results. After the first pass it derives new queries from the gathered evidence, thereby expanding the information network. Once a theory is retrieved, for instance, the system can follow its applications, counterexamples, and controversies to broaden the knowledge base. This retrieval-reasoning closed-loop cycle markedly improves performance on complex, open-ended problems (Gao et al., 2025).

During generation, Evidence-constrained Generation is central to output credibility. The system uses chain-of-thought prompts and citation templates to anchor outputs to cited sources, curbing unfounded improvisation, reducing hallucinations and misinformation, and enhancing verifiability and authority.

In addition, Graph-augmented Reasoning is a key complement to complex inference and relational chain discovery. The system extracts entities and relations and dynamically constructs local knowledge graphs to support chained reasoning across documents and topics. Typical uses include tracing regulatory evolution in policy analysis and mapping the historical development of theories (Chen et al., 2020).

At the infrastructure layer, Modular Orchestration has become mainstream. Workflow platforms such as LangChain and LlamaIndex allow flexible composition and scheduling of retrieval, re-ranking, reasoning, and generation modules. Pipelines can be adapted to task difficulty and user needs to balance efficiency and complexity.

As system-level intelligence increases, Human-in-the-Loop mechanisms have been formally integrated. Deep Research systems incorporate user feedback, interactive choice mechanisms, and prompt regeneration at critical junctures to improve controllability, avoid low-quality output or stagnation, and enable genuinely co-creative workflows (Drori & Te'eni, 2024; Gómez-Carmona et al., 2024; Kumar et al., 2024; Ranade et al., 2025; Yuksel et al., 2025).

Deep Research systems are not a linear stack of isolated techniques but an organic fusion of retrieval, reasoning, and generation that balances controllability, flexibility, and depth. This multidimensional architecture underpins the intelligent exploration of complex problems and the systematic construction of knowledge frameworks.

4.3 Representative Deep Research Products

A number of representative Deep Research products have already emerged. These systems, to varying degrees, implement the core technical pathways outlined earlier and furnish new tools for complex information exploration. Although implementation details vary, they converge on a design philosophy centered on the systematic integration of efficient, controllable, and in-depth retrieval and generation. Perplexity AI (https://www.perplexity.ai) and Metaso (https://metaso.cn) were among the earliest products to fuse search with generation. Their core approach is to deliver concise answers that synthesize retrieved material and list source citations. Perplexity's Focus Search feature lets users dynamically redirect retrieval within an ongoing dialogue. Mita Search uses the DeepSeek-R1 reasoning model's "deep research" mode: it first plans a search strategy, then searches and summarizes each subproblem, and finally integrates the partial results into a consolidated answer—essentially a simplified deep research pipeline. Glean (https://www.glean.com) addresses internal enterprise knowledge management. By integrating corporate documents, email, and database content, it builds an internal retrieval-generation platform. Permission-aware retrieval, dynamic query refinement, and citation-based answer presentation reinforce privacy and access control, improve utilization of organizational knowledge, and demonstrate the adaptability of Deep Research systems in production settings. Consensus (https://consensus.app) is a representative tool for scholarly research. It implements a specialized retrieval-re-ranking-generation pipeline over academic corpora: it identifies studies relevant to a scientific query, surfaces experimental findings, and automatically summarizes points of consensus and disagreement across papers. To reduce hallucinations, it emphasizes generation grounded in original paper data and allows users to inspect source passages—an evidence-constrained method valuable for researchers requiring rigor. The newly launched Scispace Copilot (https://scispace.com) likewise merits attention. Beyond basic retrieval and question answering, it adds graph-assisted and cross-document chained reasoning, enabling multi-turn inquiry around a central problem and mapping logical relationships among sources. Its built-in note-taking system captures and structures the exploration process for subsequent refinement, underscoring the emphasis Deep Research systems place on constructing cognitive chains. Mainstream general-purpose large model platforms are likewise adding Deep Research capabilities. For example, ChatGPT (OpenAI) now integrates document analysis and plugin-based literature retrieval, allowing users to upload local files (PDF, Word, plain text, etc.) for semantic analysis and conversational querying. Users can retrieve and summarize content and automatically obtain cited excerpts. Although these functions do not yet match specialized academic tools in multi-source provenance tracing, deeper reasoning, or structured reporting, they are laying the groundwork for more advanced research scenarios. From a technical perspective, Deep Research products commonly rely on the following mechanisms:

- Retrieval-Augmented Generation : Semantic vector search surfaces relevant materials, and prompts then guide a large model to generate answers tightly anchored to that evidence.
- Semantic retrieval and multi-hop reasoning: Techniques such as dense retrieval, ColBERT, and multi-stage retrieval support resolving complex, multi-layered queries.
- Knowledge visualization and structured representation: Tools such as Research Rabbit (https://www.researchrabbit.ai) use graph views of relationships among papers and concepts to reveal cognitive pathways and foster interdisciplinary synthesis.
- Source traceability and citation transparency: Generated outputs automatically include original sources and passage-level citations, increasing reliability and scholarly usability.
- Customization: Platforms increasingly support uploading proprietary corpora, configuring output parameters, and building personalized models to meet domain-specific needs. These mechanisms are becoming industry standards for Deep Research products. As these technologies advance, the integration of RAG, traceable citation, multi-hop reasoning, and structured expression is enabling general large model platforms to support academic, commercial, and decision-making scenarios with increasing effectiveness, steadily extending the scope of language services.

4.4 Innovation in Language Services Enabled by Deep Research

The introduction of Deep Research tools has opened new avenues for innovation in language services. Traditionally, the field was largely confined to direct text handling—translation, proofreading, and editing—with value judged chiefly by accuracy and fluency. As the Deep Research paradigm gains traction, the remit of language services is expanding beyond surface operations to encompass information filtering, knowledge restructuring, and the generation of perspectives. Consequently, the field is shifting from single-step linguistic conversion toward multidimensional knowledge services (SEAtongue, 2025).

Under a Deep Research-based model, language services are no longer mere linguistic intermediaries; they are evolving into bridges and architects of knowledge. Practitioners must map thematic trajectories, logical structures, and salient evidence in complex documents, then deliver precisely targeted extraction and organization. In high-stakes domains such as science, medicine, and law, a faithful translation is only the starting point. Clients increasingly expect syntheses of emerging research trends and deep, cross-source analytical integration (Pangeanic, 2024).

Deep Research is also reshaping deliverable formats. Conventional translations and summaries no longer suffice for complex use cases. A growing number of clients request multilingual knowledge graphs, searchable data indexes, thematic question sets, and customized semantic databases. This trend requires language service professionals to pair advanced textual expertise with strong data-analytic and structured representation skills.

Illustrative implementation paths include:

- Knowledge-mining translation: During translation, systematically tag and extract key facts, metrics, experimental methods, and related elements, producing structured outputs that support downstream analysis and automation; this approach is well suited to high-information-density documents such as patents and scholarly articles.
- Multilingual decision-support information integration: For a defined business theme, retrieve, compare, and synthesize materials across languages and regions to produce a structured, question-driven report, thereby supporting international policy analysis and cross-border market research (Chang et al., 2025).
- AI-enabled content generation and collaborative optimization: Work with Deep Research platforms to design prompts, audit automatically generated content, and refine style to produce high-quality multilingual outputs whose logical coherence and practical utility are strengthened through human-AI collaboration.
- Co-development of domain resources: Contribute to developing terminological databases, knowledge graphs, and related resources to advance corpus standardization and knowledge structuring in sectors such as law, medicine, and finance, thereby enabling smarter retrieval and content generation.

Language services will continue to assimilate advances in information science, artificial intelligence, and cognitive science, becoming critical infrastructure for the knowledge society. Professionals who combine Deep Research expertise with data-centric thinking will secure broader career trajectories and greater professional influence amid industry transformation.

5 Limitations and Future Directions of Deep Research

A clear understanding of the roles and limitations of large language models and related tools in deep research supports effective resource allocation, improves practical outcomes, and tempers unwarranted expectations. Model-driven deep research systems already deliver substantial value in information integration, source filtering, and multi-perspective content generation. With well-designed prompts, researchers can rapidly extract key points from lengthy documents, generate summaries, and highlight salient passages, thereby improving processing efficiency. These systems also synthesize policy changes, compare and reconcile similarities and differences across multiple reports, and produce varied texts for viewpoint comparison or stance analysis, broadening analytical perspectives (Du et al., 2025).

Leveraging Retrieval-Augmented Generation and reasoning mechanisms, deep research tools integrate external knowledge bases and establish cross-domain linkages. This enables researchers to uncover latent interdisciplinary relationships efficiently and broaden both the depth and breadth of problem understanding. Although these models rely on statistical regularities rather than strict deductive logic, their ability to generate alternative reasoning paths and hypothetical scenarios provides heuristic value for structuring analyses and extending lines of inquiry.

Current research and development challenges include the absence of rigorous logical reasoning mechanisms in model outputs; seemingly plausible conclusions may conceal logical leaps or faulty premises. Factual accuracy and currency likewise cannot be fully guaranteed: outputs may rely on outdated information or be contaminated by unreliable sources. Even with external retrieval, weak content governance can still result in factual distortion (Salemi & Zamani, 2024).

When addressing novel or highly complex topics, large models often produce superficial, formulaic prose. Transparency and auditability of reasoning remain limited: current systems rarely expose internal decision chains clearly, undermining trust in academic and professional contexts. Users still need a balance between analytical depth and interaction simplicity, including support for multi-level summaries, fine-grained drill-downs, and customizable interaction flows. For sensitive data, compliance and privacy protections are critical, requiring robust data security and access controls. Looking ahead, key directions for improvement include:

(1) Deeper integration of reasoning and generation by combining evidence tracing, symbolic logic, knowledge graphs, and causal inference to create assistants that genuinely support research and decision-making. (2) Multimodal deep analysis that unifies text, images, tables, and audio and video sources to expand efficiency and coverage (Awais et al., 2025). (3) Greater specialization and personalization: for domains such as law, medicine, and finance, building customized knowledge structures and reasoning workflows informed by user behavior and preferences. (4) An open, modular ecosystem: advancing Application Programming Interface (API)-based, componentized architectures that integrate flexibly with literature management, data analytics, and visualization tools, thereby improving collaborative efficiency and innovation capacity in knowledge services.

6 Conclusion

The application of RAG in deep research scenarios marks a shift in intelligent language services from mere text generation toward a stage characterized by knowledge grounding, logical support, and systematic decision facilitation (Wu et al., 2024). The introduction of RAG not only mitigates hallucinations and information distortion in large models but also accelerates a broader transformation of language services, knowledge management, and decision support. From data cleansing and knowledge base construction to multimodal semantic retrieval and the orchestration of reasoning and generation, deliberate design at each stage has materially improved real-world utility and domain adaptability (Zhao et al., 2024; Zheng et al., 2025a, b). As the technology advances, deep research products and innovative language services are poised to become core infrastructure for the emerging knowledge society. Breakthroughs will depend both on advancing models' expressive precision and on achieving effective human-AI collaboration and co-construction of knowledge. In this process, professional language service practitioners will gain expanded opportunities to participate in knowledge innovation and value creation (Zhao et al., 2024; Zheng, Weng et al., 2025a, b).

References

Alavi, M., Leidner, D., & Mousavi, R. (2024). Knowledge management perspective of generative artificial intelligence (GenAI). *Alavi, Maryam*, 1–12. https://doi.org/10.17705/1jais.00859

Amugongo, L. M., Mascheroni, P., Brooks, S., Doering, S., & Seidel, J. (2025). Retrieval augmented generation for large language models in healthcare: A systematic review. *PLOS Digital Health, 4*(6), Article e0000877. https://doi.org/10.1371/journal.pdig.0000877

APXML. (2024). *5 Chunking techniques for retrieval-augmented generation.* https://apxml.com/posts/rag-chunking-strategies-explained

Asai, A., Min, S., Zhong, Z., & Chen, D. (2023). Retrieval-based language models and applications. In *Proceedings of the 61st Annual Meeting of the Association for Computational Linguistics (Volume 6: Tutorial Abstracts)* (pp. 41–46). Toronto, Canada: Association for Computational Linguistics.

Asai, A., Wu, Z., Wang, Y., Sil, A., & Hajishirzi, H. (2024). *Self-RAG: Learning to retrieve, generate, and critique through self-reflection.* https://par.nsf.gov/biblio/10539591

Awais, M., Naseer, M., Khan, S., Anwer, R. M., Cholakkal, H., Shah, M., & Khan, F. S. (2025). Foundation models defining a new era in vision: A survey and outlook. *IEEE Transactions on Pattern Analysis and Machine Intelligence.* https://doi.org/10.48550/arXiv.2307.13721

Balaguer, A., Benara, V., Cunha, R. L. D. F., Hendry, T., Holstein, D., Marsman, J., & Chandra, R. (2024). *RAG vs fine-tuning: Pipelines, tradeoffs, and a case study on agriculture.* https://doi.org/10.48550/arXiv.2401.08406

Bang, Y., Cahyawijaya, S., Lee, N., Dai, W., Su, D., Wilie, B., & Fung, P. (2023). *A multitask, multilingual, multimodal evaluation of ChatGPT on reasoning, hallucination, and interactivity.* https://doi.org/10.48550/arXiv.2302.04023

Bergum, J. K. (2025). The rise and fall of the vector database infrastructure category. LinkedIn. https://www.linkedin.com/pulse/2024-rise-fall-vector-database-infrastructure-category-bergum-dj8zf

Chang, C. C., Li, C. F., Lee, C. H., & Lee, H. S. (2025). *Enhancing low-resource minority language translation with LLMs and retrieval-augmented generation for cultural nuances.* https://doi.org/10.48550/arXiv.2505.10829

Chen, X., Jia, S., & Xiang, Y. (2020). A review: Knowledge reasoning over knowledge graph. *Expert Systems with Applications, 141*, Article 112948. https://doi.org/10.1016/j.eswa.2019.112948

Chen, J., Lin, H., Han, X., & Sun, L. (2024, March). Benchmarking large language models in retrieval-augmented generation. In *Proceedings of the AAAI Conference on Artificial Intelligence* (Vol. 38, No. 16, pp. 17754–17762). https://doi.org/10.48550/arXiv.2309.01431

Cuzzocrea, A. (2025). Vector databases for modelling, managing and querying big scientific data: Models, issues, paradigms. In *Proceedings of the 37th International Conference on Scalable Scientific Data Management* (Article 24, p. 5). Association for Computing Machinery. https://doi.org/10.1145/3733723.3742469

Drori, I., & Te'eni, D. (2024). Human-in-the-loop AI reviewing: Feasibility, opportunities, and risks. *Journal of the Association for Information Systems, 25*(1), 98–109. https://doi.org/10.17705/1jais.00867

Du, M., Xu, B., Zhu, C., Wang, X., & Mao, Z. (2025). *Deep research bench: A comprehensive benchmark for deep research agents.* https://doi.org/10.48550/arXiv.2506.11763

Gao, Y., Xiong, Y., Gao, X., Jia, K., Pan, J., Bi, Y., & Wang, H. (2023). *Retrieval-augmented generation for large language models: A survey.* https://doi.org/10.48550/arXiv.2312.10997

Gao, Y., Xiong, Y., Wang, M., & Wang, H. (2024). *Modular RAG: Transforming RAG systems into lego-like reconfigurable frameworks.* https://doi.org/10.48550/arXiv.2407.21059

Gao, Y., Xiong, Y., Zhong, Y., Bi, Y., Xue, M., & Wang, H. (2025). *Synergizing RAG and reasoning: A systematic review.* https://doi.org/10.48550/arXiv.2504.15909

Ghorbani, N. (2024). *Enhancing corporate document management systems with AI: Leveraging embeddings and semantic search for efficient retrieval and chat-based assistance.* Master's thesis, University of Padova, Italy.

Gómez-Carmona, O., Casado-Mansilla, D., Lopez-de-Ipina, D., & García-Zubia, J. (2024). Human-in-the-loop machine learning: Reconceptualizing the role of the user in interactive approaches. *Internet of Things, 25,* Article 101048. https://doi.org/10.1016/j.iot.2023.101048

Gupta, S., Ranjan, R., & Singh, S. N. (2024). *A comprehensive survey of retrieval-augmented generation (RAG): Evolution, current landscape and future directions.* https://doi.org/10.48550/arXiv.2410.12837

Hu, Y., Lei, Z., Zhang, Z., Pan, B., Ling, C., & Zhao, L. (2025, April). GRAG: Graph retrieval-augmented generation. In L. Chiruzzo, A. Ritter, & L. Wang (Eds.), *Findings of the association for computational linguistics: NAACL 2025* (pp. 4145–4157). Association for Computational Linguistics. https://doi.org/10.18653/v1/2025.findings-naacl.232

Huang, Y., Chen, Y., Zhang, H., Li, K., Fang, M., Yang, L., & Wang, J. (2025). *Deep research agents: A systematic examination and roadmap.* https://doi.org/10.48550/arXiv.2506.18096

Ji, Z., Lee, N., Frieske, R., Yu, T., Su, D., Xu, Y., & Fung, P. (2023). Survey of hallucination in natural language generation. *ACM Computing Surveys, 55*(12), 1–38. https://doi.org/10.1145/3571730

Jiang, W., Subramanian, S., Graves, C., Alonso, G., Yazdanbakhsh, A., & Dadu, V. (2025, June). RAGO: Systematic performance optimization for retrieval-augmented generation serving. In *Proceedings of the 52nd Annual International Symposium on Computer Architecture* (pp. 974–989). https://doi.org/10.48550/arXiv.2503.14649

Kumar, S., Datta, S., Singh, V., Datta, D., Kumar Singh, S., & Sharma, R. (2024). Applications, challenges, and future directions of human-in-the-loop learning. *IEEE Access, 12,* 75735–75760. https://doi.org/10.1109/ACCESS.2024.3401547

Lewis, P., Perez, E., Piktus, A., Petroni, F., Karpukhin, V., Goyal, N., & Kiela, D. (2020). Retrieval-augmented generation for knowledge-intensive NLP tasks. *Advances in Neural Information Processing Systems, 33,* 9459–9474. https://doi.org/10.48550/arXiv.2005.11401

Ma, X., Wang, L., Yang, N., Wei, F., & Lin, J. (2023). Fine-tuning LLaMA for multi-stage text retrieval. In *Proceedings of the 47th International ACM SIGIR Conference on Research and Development in Information Retrieval* (pp. 2421–2425). https://doi.org/10.48550/arXiv.2310.08319

Malali, N. (2025). The role of retrieval-augmented generation (RAG) in financial document processing: Automating compliance and reporting. *International Journal of Management, 12*(3), 26–46. https://doi.org/10.37745/ijmt.2013/vol12n32646

Merola, C., & Singh, J. (2025). *Reconstructing context: Evaluating advanced chunking strategies for retrieval-augmented generation.* https://doi.org/10.48550/arXiv.2504.19754

Mihajlović, M. (2025). Multimodal retrieval-augmented generation in knowledge systems: A framework for enhanced semantic search and response accuracy. In *Sinteza 2025-International Scientific Conference on Information Technology, Computer Science, and Data Science* (pp. 544–549). Singidunum University. https://doi.org/10.15308/Sinteza-2025-544-549

OpenAI. (2025). *Introducing deep research.* https://openai.com/index/introducing-deep-research/

Pangeanic. (2024). *The future of AI-enabled translation services.* https://blog.pangeanic.com/the-future-of-ai-enabled-translation-services

Rackauckas, Z. (2024). *RAG-fusion: A new take on retrieval-augmented generation.* https://doi.org/10.48550/arXiv.2402.03367

RAGflow. (2024). *The rise and evolution of RAG in 2024: A year in review.* https://ragflow.io/blog/the-rise-and-evolution-of-rag-in-2024-a-year-in-review

Ranade, N., Saravia, M., & Johri, A. (2025). Using rhetorical strategies to design prompts: A human-in-the-loop approach to make AI useful. *AI & Society, 40*(2), 711–732. https://doi.org/10.1007/s00146-024-01905-3

Ren, M. (2005, March 20). 基于 Dify + DeepSeek 搭建企业级私有化知识库与智能文件审核系统 [Building an enterprise-level private knowledge base and intelligent document auditing system with Dify and DeepSeek] [Technical report]. 星野云联技术报告. Retrieved 3 July 2025, https://www.zedyer.com/iot-knowledge/dify-deepseek-rag-file-ai-audit/

Salemi, A., & Zamani, H. (2024, July). Evaluating retrieval quality in retrieval-augmented generation. In *Proceedings of the 47th International ACM SIGIR Conference on Research and Development in Information Retrieval* (pp. 2395–2400). https://doi.org/10.48550/arXiv.2404.13781

SEAtongue. (2025). *How AI is transforming translation & localisation in 2025.* SEAtongue. https://seatongue.com/blog/business/how-ai-is-transforming-translation-localisation-in-2025/

Tarakad, N., Yu, P., Samdani, R., & Merrick, L. (2025). *Long-context isn't all you need: Impact of retrieval and chunking on finance RAG.* https://www.snowflake.com/en/engineering-blog/impact-retrieval-chunking-finance-rag/

Wu, S., Xiong, Y., Cui, Y., Wu, H., Chen, C., Yuan, Y., & Xue, C. J. (2024). *Retrieval-augmented generation for natural language processing: A survey.* https://doi.org/10.48550/arXiv.2407.13193

Yuksel, K. A., Gunduz, A., Anees, A. B., & Sawaf, H. (2025). *Efficient machine translation corpus generation: Integrating human-in-the-loop post-editing with large language models.* https://doi.org/10.48550/arXiv.2502.12755

Zeff, M. (2025, April 18). *OpenAI's new reasoning AI models hallucinate more.* TechCrunch. https://techcrunch.com/2025/04/18/openais-new-reasoning-ai-models-hallucinate-more/

Zhao, P., Zhang, H., Yu, Q., Wang, Z., Geng, Y., Fu, F., & Cui, B. (2024). *Retrieval-augmented generation for AI-generated content: A survey.* https://doi.org/10.48550/arXiv.2402.19473

Zheng, X., Weng, Z., Lyu, Y., Jiang, L., Xue, H., Ren, B., & Hu, X. (2025). *Retrieval augmented generation and understanding in vision: A survey and new outlook.* https://doi.org/10.48550/arXiv.2503.18016

Zheng, Y., Fu, D., Hu, X., Cai, X., Ye, L., Lu, P., & Liu, P. (2025). *Deepresearcher: Scaling deep research via reinforcement learning in real-world environments.* https://doi.org/10.48550/arXiv.2504.03160

Chapter 5
Agents and Workflows

Abstract This chapter maps the transition from ad-hoc prompt interaction to agentic, workflow-orchestrated large language model applications in language services. A large language model agent is framed as a role-conditioned cognitive node executing perceive–reason–plan–act–reflect cycles via tool orchestration, explicit cognitive state, and layered (short/mid/long-term) memory. We distill seven enabling mechanisms: (1) cognitive state scaffolding for goal persistence and transparency; (2) selective memory capture, abstraction, retrieval, and metacognitive recall control; (3) language-based micro-planning (chain-of-thought, ReAct (reasoning + acting), tree of thoughts, Reflexion) decoupled from execution; (4) standardized tool/application programming interface schemas plus semantic invocation for scalable capability expansion; (5) perception–feedback pipelines converting partial signals into iterative strategy revision; (6) role alignment, coordination, and self-awareness to mitigate drift in multi-agent collaboration; and (7) workflow governance embedding observability, robustness (logging, tracing, retries, compensation), safety, and human-in-the-loop boundaries. Interoperability protocols, Agent-to-Agent protocol) lower integration friction and support decentralized task delegation. Workflow modeling paradigms (Business Process Model and Notation, code-as-workflow domain-specific languages, low-code/no-code visual canvases) externalize dependency logic and embed adaptive behaviors. A translation workflow lens shows modular allocation across translation, terminology governance, quality assurance, and compliance, enabling continuous optimization. Emerging competencies include agent orchestration literacy, workflow modeling, protocol stewardship, evaluative analytics, and ethical accountability.

Rapid advances in large language models (LLMs) are reshaping how language services are delivered (Wei et al., 2022). Previously, work centered on Application Programming Interface (API) access and prompt tuning; today task organization and coordination have moved to the forefront. The introduction of agents and workflows elevates Artificial Intelligence (AI) systems from a conversational tool to assistants that can plan proactively, execute autonomously, and orchestrate multi-step processes. An agent is no longer a passive respondent; operating under

J. S. Yu and Y. Yao, *Intelligent Language Services*,
https://doi.org/10.1007/978-981-95-4632-9_5

predefined roles, responsibilities, and procedures, it orchestrates tools and collaborating modules to meet complex, real-world business needs. Workflow tools provide a visual blueprint, decomposing complexity into ordered nodes and enabling What You See Is What You Get (WYSIWYG)-style orchestration automation. For language services, these mechanisms not only improve process efficiency but also reshape service boundaries and professional roles.

1 From Tool Invocation to Agents

The key breakthrough in agent design lies in enabling the model to "use tools." Just as humans extend their physical and sensory limits through instruments, a language model can expand its perceptual and action capacities via search engines, function calls, database access, and external APIs (Schick et al., 2023).

1.1 Language Models as Tool Orchestrators

A language model acting as a tool orchestrator does not signal mysterious intelligence; it parallels everyday task delegation through language. When you ask a colleague to "check the meeting room availability at 2 p.m. tomorrow," the colleague interprets, checks the calendar, and returns the result. Similarly, the model interprets a natural language request and turns it into executable calls, bridging language and action.

Two core capabilities underpin this mechanism: (1) deciding when an external tool is required and (2) constructing machine-interpretable requests and correctly interpreting the results. The model does not "manually" operate tools; it orchestrates them through structured, formatted instructions. Developers define structured functions and teach the model—via examples—how to call them, for instance: Database query: Function: query_db(table: str, condition: str) → list Map geolocation: Function: locate_address(address: str) → (lat, lon) Code execution: Function: run_code(language: str, code: str) → output In practical tool-augmented LLM deployments, users, developers, and the model form a division of labor that is both clear and highly collaborative. Users express tasks in natural language without concern for low-level implementation details—for example, "What will the air quality be in Nanjing this Friday?"—and need not know API parameter formats. Developers shift from writing bespoke business logic to configuring standardized tool interfaces: describing each API's function, input/output schema, and error boundaries. The model parses user intent into structured parameters, invokes tools, retrieves data, and composes responses automatically. Consider the air-quality example: the developer predefines an interface such as get_aqi(city, date). Upon receiving the request, the model normalizes "Nanjing" and "this Friday" into parameters, calls the interface to obtain data, and returns a natural language answer. Users need not consider implementation details; developers avoid hard-coding flows for each query. The model executes an intelligent "understand → invoke → generate" chain for an efficient response.

Within this paradigm, the ReAct (Reasoning + Acting) pattern has become a mainstream approach. The model no longer relies solely on templated sequences; it decomposes tasks during reasoning and dynamically plans tool calls. Faced with "Assess the air quality trend in Nanjing over the past three days," it can decompose the request into multi-step API calls, data acquisition, and trend assessment, with each result feeding subsequent reasoning—completing a "think → act → feedback" loop (Yao et al., 2022). This markedly enhances the depth and flexibility in handling complex queries. Developers' focus shifts from implementing business logic to crafting high-quality tool specifications, interface configurations, and safety controls that define resource scope and invocation norms. On this foundation, the model flexibly composes tools, greatly expanding automation in complex scenarios and laying the groundwork for multi-step reasoning, task decomposition, and future agent systems. Developers thus evolve from "flow executors" to "capability configurators" and "safety stewards." Frameworks such as LangChain and Open Interpreter lower the barrier to integrating models with tools and facilitate workflow orchestration for developers. As model understanding and automation improve, tool orchestration will increasingly enable non-programmers to configure tasks via natural language and graphical interfaces, further expanding the scope of intelligent language services and office automation. As a tool orchestrator, the model bridges human intent and complex system operations; high-quality interface design and prompt engineering are key levers for advancing automation and intelligence.

1.2 Typical Application Scenarios of Large Language Model Tool Invocation

The way an LLM performs tasks via tool invocation is essentially a form of language-driven program control. The following examples illustrate how it works with diverse tool interfaces to extend its perceptual, computational, retrieval, and execution capabilities (Schick et al., 2023).

1. Search Engine + Information Extraction: Real-Time Weather Retrieval

   Task: Determine whether it will rain in Shanghai tomorrow.
   Interfaces:

   Search_web(query: str) → str: executes a web search and returns a textual summary.
   parse_weather(text: str) → dict: extracts weather information from the text.

Dialogue (ReAct style):

User: Will it rain in Shanghai tomorrow?
LLM Thought: Search "Shanghai weather tomorrow" and check for the keywords "precipitation" or "rain").
[Action]: search_web("Shanghai weather tomorrow")
[Observation]: Shanghai will be cloudy with scattered light rain tomorrow.
LLM Thought: The mention of "light rain" indicates precipitation.
Answer: Rain is likely in Shanghai tomorrow; an umbrella is advisable.

2. Math Calculator: Enhancing Quantitative Reasoning

Task: Determine whether a ball dropped from 100 m in free fall hits the ground after 3 s.
Interface:

Calculate(expression: str) → float: evaluates a mathematical expression

Dialogue:

LLM Thought: Apply s = 0.5 * a * t^2.
[Action]: calculate("0.5 * 10 * 3 * 3")
[Observation]: 45.0
Answer: The ball has fallen 45 m in 3 s and has not yet reached the ground.

Using a calculator tool allows the LLM to compensate for limited inherent arithmetic accuracy and correctly derive a dynamic physical process (Ghosh, 2025).

3. Database Querying: Natural Language-to-SQL Structured Retrieval

Task: Identify the product with the lowest inventory.
Interface:

query_database(sql_query: str) → Table: executes an SQL query and returns a tabular result.

Dialogue:

LLM Thought: Issue an SQL query to return the record with the lowest stock.
[Action]: query_database ("SELECT product_name, stock_quantity FROM inventory ORDER BY stock_quantity ASC LIMIT 1")
[Observation]: Product: XG-22, Quantity: 3
Answer: The product with the lowest inventory is XG-22, with only 3 units remaining.

Natural-language interfaces to databases had long posed a technical challenge; however, practical advances in semantic interpretation and structural transformation have only emerged with the advent of LLMs (Thomas, 2023; Trott, 2024).

4. Code Execution: Automating Logic via Code Generation

Task: Determine how many primes are below 100.
Interface:

execute_code(python_code: str) → str: runs Python code and returns the output.

Dialogue:

User: How many primes are there below 100?
LLM Thought: I can write a Python script to count primes up to 100.

```
[Action]: execute_code("""
count = 0
for num in range(2, 101):
    for i in range(2, int(num ** 0.5) + 1):
        if num % i == 0:
            break
    else:
        count += 1
print(count)
""")
```

[Observation]: 25
Answer: There are 25 primes below 100.

These examples show that an LLM's ability to invoke tools constitutes language-embedded program control. Rather than internalizing all knowledge and functions, the model, like a human expert, orchestrates external resources. This shift moves us from "the model provides an answer" to "model + tools = solution." Operationally, natural language instructions are translated into a structured control workflow: the model analyzes task requirements, identifies needed tool categories, assembles interface-compliant parameters, and interprets results. Leveraging specialized tools extends its functional boundary. This transition—from a closed question-answering system to an open tool collaboration system—enables the "model + tools = solution" paradigm (Schick et al., 2023; Trott, 2024).

1.3 *From Tool Orchestration to Intelligent Agents*

As LLMs gain multi-tool orchestration capability, AI systems are shifting from single-step tool calls toward the agent paradigm. The core challenge is no longer whether a model can invoke a tool but whether it can autonomously select, order, and flexibly compose multiple tools to accomplish complex objectives while continually refining its execution path as a task unfolds (Weng, 2023).

One-off tool calls strengthen discrete capabilities such as retrieval, translation, or API access. However, real-world demands often require multi-stage coordination that a lone tool cannot satisfy. The agent architecture excels by decomposing the user's ultimate goal into actionable steps, managing intermediate states, and chaining heterogeneous tools into multi-turn workflows. For example, completing "identify low-stock products and email customers" requires sequential database querying, email drafting, and dispatching, with precise handoff of information. An agent must both grasp the global objective and adapt its plan in response to feedback, demonstrating higher-level intelligence and flexibility.

The cognition–action–feedback loop mirrors human problem-solving: setting goals, decomposing tasks, probing, and iteratively adjusting. Agents similarly execute "think–act–observe" cycles, using external tools to test hypotheses and revise judgments, thereby improving accuracy and reliability. This strategy is embodied in ReAct-style (Reasoning + Acting) methods and is implemented across platforms such as LangChain, Hugging Face, and Vertex AI.

A fully realized agent requires additional capabilities: memory (persisting historical state to sustain long-running tasks), goal management (dynamically reprioritizing objectives), and environmental perception (gathering feedback to refine strategy). Unlike scripted automation, an agent does not simply follow fixed rules; it pursues open-ended goals within dynamic contexts, generating and revising action strategies in real time.

An agent is a software system that perceives its environment, processes information, and acts dynamically to achieve specified goals. Its essence lies in completing the perceive–reason–act cognitive loop to attain a degree of autonomous decision-making and environmental adaptation. Consequently, agents constitute a core technological pathway for higher-level automation, complex task collaboration, and uncertainty management.

1.4 Evolution and Socialization of Language-Based Agents

The core idea of an agent is the integration of perception, judgment, and action. Early AI, exemplified by expert systems such as MYCIN, used knowledge bases and inference rules for decision-making, achieving rudimentary judgment but limited perception and adaptability. In the 1990s, Brooks's reactive agents reduced decision-making to immediate environmental responses, while the BDI (Belief–Desire–Intention) model refined goal formation and action planning, laying the groundwork for multi-agent cooperation. With the rise of the internet and distributed computing, applications such as web crawlers and chatbots proliferated, and agents gradually acquired richer environmental perception and autonomous task execution.

The advent of LLMs has markedly expanded agent capabilities. Models exemplified by GPT-3 and its successors exhibit strong natural-language understanding, generation, and transfer capabilities. Combined with ReAct-style mechanisms, agents dynamically adjust decision processes through reason–act–observe cycles. ChatGPT and Custom GPTs allow users to specify agent roles and behaviors directly in natural language, while the models can proactively invoke external tools, enabling operation in and adaptation to complex environments. Agents have thus evolved from single-purpose conversational tools into continuously self-adjusting, collaborative cognitive units.

Since 2023, projects such as AutoGPT and BabyAGI have further structured agent behavioral workflows by implementing cycles of reflection, execution, and verification. The CAMEL platform explores an emergent "linguistic society" through the division of labor and dialogue-based cooperation among multiple agents (Li et al., 2023). The Stanford Smallville project uses 25 language-model agents with distinct memories and motivations to demonstrate complex social behaviors—autonomous planning, social interaction, dispute resolution, and maintenance of friendships (Park et al., 2023). In the Minecraft virtual world, Voyager enables agents to set their own goals, accumulate experience, and support continual growth and adaptation (Wang et al., 2023).

The socialization of agents poses significant challenges, notably in cognitive continuity and long-term memory. Current systems typically rely on short dialogue context or external databases, falling short of genuine experiential accumulation and autonomous knowledge evolution. Most LLMs maintain consistent persona and task tracking only over limited dialogue turns, lacking continuity for cross-task, cross-session services. Industry efforts—embedded vector memory stores and automated log summarization—are rapidly evolving to extend effective memory.

Value alignment and norm acquisition across multiple agents are likewise complex. Deployed agents can readily develop misunderstandings, conflicts, or competition due to divergent goals, interpretations, or strategies. In domains such as financial advising or legal services, collaborative agents must adhere to interpretable ethical guidelines to ensure compliance with legal and moral expectations. Traditional methods like Reinforcement Learning from Human Feedback are prone to strategy drift and unstable cooperation in multi-agent settings, prompting new mechanisms for rule evolution, arbitration, and coordination to enhance reliability and transparency (Riad et al., 2023; Zhang et al., 2023).

As personalized agents enter operational workflows, the attribution of digital identity and responsibility remains blurred. Agents increasingly act as user proxies or corporate representatives, raising legal and ethical questions about liability for their actions. Policy and standards discussions are emerging. Some organizations are experimenting with identity attestation and behavioral audit trails to enhance oversight, yet comprehensive frameworks remain immature.

Advances in multimodal perception and embodied capability continue to broaden the application boundaries of agents. Agents now extend beyond text or speech to engage in image understanding, video analysis, and remote operation of physical devices. In service robotics and assisted driving, they must provide a high level of safety and robustness, handling anomalies promptly and mitigating risk.

From simulated societies to real deployments, language-based agents are rapidly evolving from tools into co-creative partners. Humans must take a more proactive role in collaboration, governance, and risk management to keep development within controllable bounds, gradually shaping a new socio-technical form of coexistence and co-creation. This trajectory not only advances technology but also reshapes knowledge collaboration, industrial structures, and social ethics.

2 Typical Structural Components of an Agent

A genuinely cognitive and action-capable agent results from the coordination of multiple mechanisms: it perceives, plans, remembers, decides, acts, and evaluates outcomes. This dynamic architectural substrate underpins the agent's behavior. Framing it merely as "a language model + API calls" obscures its operational dynamics and broader developmental potential. Understanding this structure reshapes our conception of intelligence itself.

2.1 Modeling and Managing Cognitive State

Cognitive state is a central internal mediator spanning the entire intelligent process. Rather than an isolated module, it integrates attention, goal orientation, and contextual understanding through dynamic focus and intent expression within ongoing deliberation. It makes explicit, at any moment, what the agent is attending to and which goal it is pursuing (Haase & Pokutta, 2025).

Most current large language model-based agents lack an intrinsic mechanism for persistent cognitive state: each inference relies on immediate input with minimal historical continuity. Designers therefore inject cognitive cues—system prompts, embedded task summaries, and chain-of-thought scaffolds—into the context to approximate a persistent state (Zhu et al., 2024). These techniques support goal stability and improve coherence and depth in task execution.

In more advanced systems, cognitive state management is more structured: a dedicated state manager logs task history, action traces, and behavioral parameters. On each model call, the system dynamically injects this state as a "mental anchor." While internal weights remain unchanged, the agent's attention is consistently directed toward salient goals, stabilizing its reasoning trajectory. Emerging frameworks such as LangGraph and AutoGPT variants support schedulable, state-transition-driven execution, enabling greater flexibility and strategic control during task switching and self-reflection.

Cognitive state not only carries memory and reasoning; it also grounds selection and scheduling. Allocation of attention, task decomposition, and priority ordering arise through its continual guidance, gradually shaping distinctive behavioral preferences over extended interaction. Platforms such as OpenAI GPTs let users specify cognitive habits and interaction styles, producing an emergent "digital persona." Fine-grained cognitive state construction opens a window onto the agent's reasoning path and provides a foundation for continual learning and behavior planning.

2.2 Short-Term and Long-Term Memory

Cognitive state governs momentary thought, whereas memory systems provide continuity and experiential accumulation. Inspired by human cognition, contemporary architectures seek an effective balance between short-term and long-term memory.

Short-term memory primarily leverages the model's context window by concatenating dialogue history, task instructions, and reasoning traces to preserve local coherence. It is fast and suitable for the immediate task, yet capacity is constrained: salient content is easily displaced, selective retention is weak, and irrelevant tokens introduce noise.

To address these limits, many systems incorporate external long-term memory: distilled interaction elements are encoded as vector embeddings or structured records and stored in a vector database or dedicated module. Semantic retrieval then reintroduces pertinent memories, sustaining continuity across sessions on user preferences, past tasks, and interaction style. This yields progressively greater behavioral consistency and personalization.

Effective memory management relies less on raw capacity than on selective retention and proactive retrieval. Two common approaches are (1) rule-based capture of task summaries, variables, and user feedback and (2) model-driven abstraction that compresses dialogues into higher-level representations. These strategies conserve storage and enable a form of self-organization analogous to human meaning reconstruction.

A recall mechanism entails a metacognitive decision: should the agent query historical memory or rely on short-term context alone? Systems such as MemGPT (now Letta) introduce a controller that, before primary inference, decides whether retrieval is needed, thereby improving efficiency and reducing noise (Packer et al., 2023). This separation of scheduling from generation strengthens support for complex behavioral strategies.

Memory functions as an information management layer shaping persona formation and contextual adaptability. Users experience being "understood" and perceive conversational coherence because the agent surfaces appropriate memories across turns, sustaining interpretation and response while enabling review, revision, and customization—forming the basis for ongoing personalization. More advanced agents also log reasoning steps, thought trajectories, and strategic adjustments, incrementally building self-reflective and continual learning capacities.

2.3 Behavioral Strategy and Task Planning Module

Cognitive state and memory underpin the agent's ongoing reasoning and accumulated experience, while behavioral strategy and task planning articulate its proactive, goal-directed behavior (Sumers et al., 2024; Berti and Kasneci, 2025). An effective agent interprets inputs, formulates a clear action sequence aligned with its objectives, and adapts that sequence in response to execution feedback. Previously described tool-invocation mechanisms provide the operational infrastructure for this capability.

Earlier conventional systems depended on predefined rules, yielding rigid strategies. In contrast, large language model–based agents generate strategies dynamically through contextual comprehension and linguistic reasoning, improving flexibility and adaptability (Zhai et al., 2025). Chain-of-Thought prompting decomposes complex tasks into concrete steps, supporting lightweight, language-based micro-planning (Wei et al., 2022). Although such methods lack the formal rigor of classical planning algorithms, they are better suited to open-ended, uncertain environments (Yao et al. 2022).

More advanced architectures explicitly separate planning from execution, enhancing controllability and auditability. Systems such as AutoGPT, BabyAGI, and CAMEL proceed through task queues or task trees and continually update subsequent strategy based on observed outcomes. Behavioral planning integrates logical inference, language generation, memory retrieval, and external feedback into a dynamic, narrative-style decision process.

Strategy formation is tightly coupled to role specification. The CAMEL framework, for example, leverages multi-role collaboration and structured goal tension to foster a coherent behavioral style and value orientation, strengthening credibility and adaptability (Li et al., 2023). Consistent persona expression is a key driver of efficient multi-agent collaboration.

Reinforcement learning (RL) has been widely used for behavioral adaptation, yet in high-dimensional linguistic spaces it is constrained by low sample efficiency and sparse feedback. A more practical path combines language-based planning, memory management, and tool invocation within a dynamic behavior-control structure. As prompting techniques such as Chain-of-Thought, Reason + Act (ReAct), and Tree-of-Thought evolve, behavioral strategy is emerging as a schedulable, learnable module.

This trajectory parallels the human acquisition of cognitive tools: through external instruments and training, humans develop stepwise reasoning and strategic adjustment. Large language model agents and their associated planning designs systematize this developmental pathway. The interplay among prompt engineering, cognitive state, and memory mechanisms underpins higher-level general reasoning and autonomous decision making.

2.4 Tool Interfaces and Integration of External Capabilities

Sustained capability expansion depends on efficient orchestration and integration of external resources. The approach to designing and integrating tool interfaces determines whether an agent can exploit external functionality flexibly and evolve within dynamic environments. Contemporary systems therefore explore structured integration pathways centered on interface protocols, invocation specifications, and middleware layers.

At the foundational level, clearly defined APIs or function calls encapsulate external tools as services schedulable by the model. Specifications enumerate input and output formats, parameters, and error-handling routines. Such standardization reduces integration friction, allowing cross-system requests to resemble local function calls. Some frameworks add middleware or proxy layers that unify interface management and routing, enabling dynamic capability registration, discovery, and access control.

As requirements become more complex, integration shifts from one-way calls to bidirectional feedback with state tracking. Agents must obtain immediate outputs while tracking execution state, historical operations, and environmental changes. Consequently, event-driven, asynchronous communication mechanisms—callbacks, subscriptions, push channels—support sustained coordination between model and tools. In multi-task contexts, a scheduler or orchestration engine globally optimizes invocation order, data flow, and result aggregation.

At the semantic layer, information exchange is trending toward greater abstraction. A model can parse natural-language interface descriptions and, when combined with a domain ontology or API schema, dynamically synthesize invocation directives and parameters. These semantic interfaces enable rapid adaptation and autonomous exploration of unfamiliar tools, markedly improving scalability and generalization.

The rise of multi-agent systems accelerates this evolution: collaboration-oriented protocols allow agents to share resources, exchange state, and delegate sub-tasks to one another. Standardized message formats and task description languages furnish a substrate for coordinated role specialization and information flow in complex workflows (Gao et al., 2024).

Interface forms and integration methods are shifting from static, monolithic designs to dynamic, open ones. Self-describing interfaces capable of automatic adaptation and elastic orchestration will provide the foundation for continued evolution and capability expansion in large-scale agent systems.

2.5 Environmental Perception and Feedback Processing

Environmental perception underpins an agent's ability to understand and adapt to its environment. Regardless of task complexity, agents operate within a fundamental perception–action–feedback loop (Brohan, 2023; Pezzato et al., 2023). Unlike tool invocation, environmental perception emphasizes acquiring and interpreting information and thus is a prerequisite for autonomous decision-making.

In practical deployments, visibility is the primary constraint on perception. A language model is inherently limited by its context window and cannot proactively detect its own knowledge blind spots (Bubeck et al., 2024). An agent perceives only portions of the environment when it passively receives input; its decisions and strategies therefore rest on partial and fragmented information. This partial view constrains internal modeling and limits subsequent reasoning and action.

Environmental dynamics are complex and feedback is frequently ambiguous. Accurate interpretation and behavioral adjustment are therefore critical to continual improvement. In practice, feedback seldom arrives as a binary success/failure label; instead, it appears as fragments requiring interpretation and causal attribution. Agents must compare expected and observed outcomes, actively extract useful signals amid ambiguity or noise, and revise strategies and action sequences accordingly (Pezzato et al., 2023).

To support this process, contemporary agent frameworks incorporate reflection and state update mechanisms. Systems such as AutoGPT generate a natural-language self-assessment of the effectiveness of each action after every tool invocation in addition to logging results. Iterative feedback loops enable continual adjustment under incomplete observability and help compensate for perceptual limits. Over time, the agent develops a simplified yet functional environmental model that enhances adaptability (Wu et al., 2023).

Environmental modeling entails intrinsic uncertainty. Omitted signals or misinterpreted feedback can push the internal model away from reality. The goal is not a perfect world model but progressively better decisions achieved through iterative refinement. Effective perception is evidenced by an agent's ability to continue learning and acting sensibly despite incomplete information and uncertain feedback.

Further advances in perception and feedback handling depend on richer memory architectures, improved strategy optimization, and social interaction. Complementary exchanges with other agents, users, or external systems provide a more holistic environmental perspective. These diversified feedback channels enhance adaptability and resilience in dynamic settings (Georgio et al., 2025; Wu et al., 2023).

An agent's value lies less in exhaustive knowledge than in its capacity to adapt and evolve under constraints and uncertainty. Dynamic perception coupled with ongoing revision constitutes a key pathway to autonomy and higher-level intelligence.

2.6 Agent Coordination and "Self-Awareness" Mechanisms

In practical multi-agent deployments, agents must perform assigned tasks while maintaining clear identities and consistent behavior in complex interactions (Georgio et al., 2025). Clear role specification and self-awareness are central to effective collaboration and sustained autonomy.

Current architectures typically rely on role labels or identity metadata to distinguish agents. Embedding identity, responsibilities, and objectives in each interaction helps preserve role stability in collaborative settings. This approach suits team task allocation, dialogue simulation, and expert systems, reducing role confusion and behavioral overlap.

As interaction complexity grows, role drift and identity blurring become common. External labels alone cannot counter semantic convergence or role mutation over prolonged multi-turn collaboration. Agents may exhibit ambiguous stances and increasingly similar expression styles, diminishing collaborative efficiency and obscuring individual differentiation.

Systems should therefore incorporate more granular self-awareness mechanisms. Instead of passively accepting a role, an agent can monitor its behavior, detect deviations, and adjust its strategy based on feedback. Common practices include behavior logging, identity consistency checks, and autonomous strategy revision. For example, after each task step, an agent can review whether its output aligns with its assigned role or team objectives and promptly adjust its expression and actions if misaligned.

Some advanced systems incorporate reflection modules that prompt agents to generate self-evaluations or concise "reflection reports" after task completion, deepening understanding of their behavior. These mechanisms help maintain role boundaries and support continual learning and self-optimization. Multi-model review or interaction auditing can further enhance behavioral introspection and strategic coordination.

Ongoing advances in coordination and self-awareness mechanisms enable multi-agent systems to maintain distinct identities and coherent collaboration in complex environments, providing a solid technical foundation for higher-level autonomy and more diverse collective intelligence.

3 Leading Agent Frameworks and Their Characteristics

As agents transition from concept to practice, a diverse set of development frameworks has emerged, bridging LLMs and complex tasks. AutoGPT's automated execution loop, LangChain's modular pipelines, and OpenAI's tool-centric GPTs interface—despite distinct origins—converge on a core premise: the language model is no longer merely a text generator but an embedded "cognitive node" and "executor" within a larger architecture (Mahowald et al., 2023; China Academy of Information and Communications Technology and Huawei Technologies Co., Ltd., 2025).

3.1 Recursive Architectures and Multi-Agent Collaboration

AutoGPT, an early exemplar of autonomous agents, in 2023 popularized a "task decomposition–self-prompting–tool invocation–feedback loop" pattern that, by 2025, still serves as an entry-level template. It decomposes user goals, generates action plans via the LLM, dynamically selects and invokes tools, and adapts subsequent steps to observed results. This recursive loop imparts persistence and self-correction, extending performance beyond static question answering (Shinn et al., 2023).

In practice, AutoGPT still requires human oversight because of recurrent issues—task duplication, infinite loops, and high-frequency ineffective actions. Lacking built-in guardrails and checkpoints, it depends on manual controls (e.g., retry limits or confirmation gates) to avert resource waste and strategic drift. Its short-term memory is limited and relies on external retrieval-augmented generation components for longer-horizon context, increasing the risk of context loss or hallucination in complex tasks.

AutoGPT marks a shift from rigid handcrafted rules toward flexible strategy generation, yet it remains tethered to predefined templates. Behavior still hinges on stepwise structured prompts and contextual triggers; model outputs drive decisions while assurance and process control remain human-in-the-loop. This reduces rule-authoring effort but stops short of full automation.

Recent advances focus on structured reasoning and reflexive mechanisms. By 2025, newer autonomous agents routinely integrate chain-of-thought, tree-of-thought, and Reflexion prompting to explore alternative reasoning paths and perform step-level self-evaluation, thereby reducing erroneous trajectories. Mainstream frameworks deploy layered memory: short-term conversational caches, mid-term vector retrieval, and long-term action logs that organize and reuse historical experience. Platforms such as Mem0 and LangChain provide priority management and automatic refreshing of structured memory, improving task coherence and execution efficiency.

Progress in multi-agent collaboration has broadened architectural options. MetaGPT, modeled after a software company, uses role specialization, structured messaging, and unified storage to reduce workflow disorder and hallucinations. AgentVerse emphasizes task solving and parallel simulation, enabling multi-role, multi-model deployment for software collaboration, advisory systems, and studies of behavioral evolution. OmniNova applies hierarchical organization and dynamic scheduling to improve task completion rates and resource efficiency. AgentGroupChat-V2 employs a parallel divide-and-allocate strategy to coordinate heterogeneous models and performs well on mathematical and reasoning benchmarks.

Agent systems are now moving from solitary recursive agents toward structured multi-agent collaboration under engineered governance. Role specialization, task orchestration, and autonomous reflection together enable higher-level deployments and broaden opportunities for complex automation and enterprise adoption.

3.2 *Productization Pathways for Agent Systems*

As LLM capabilities grow, agent systems are rapidly moving from laboratory prototypes to scaled products embedded in real workflows. The focus has shifted from raw "intelligence" and autonomy to engineering robustness, controllability, and maintainability. Only deployable, operable, and integrable frameworks can transform agents into dependable enterprise productivity tools.

Two principal productization paths have emerged: OpenAI's GPTs and engineering governance platforms exemplified by AgentOps. GPTs provide a lightweight method for assembling task assistants through minimal configuration, supporting tool invocation and basic memory. This lowers customization barriers for prototyping and personal productivity, but limitations persist in enterprise integration, observability, and behavioral transparency.

By contrast, AgentOps embodies enterprise-oriented engineering governance. It integrates real-time monitoring, behavior tracking, version control, rollback mechanisms, and security auditing as core lifecycle management capabilities. Closed-loop data flows feed user feedback into iterative model refinement, enabling governance from development through deployment. Firms such as IBM, Infosys, and AutoGen now treat AgentOps infrastructure as foundational for reliable agent deployment.

Development tooling is likewise evolving rapidly. LangChain has progressed from a prompt utility to an enterprise multi-agent platform supporting the flexible composition of prompts, models, toolchains, and memory modules. Companion components such as LangSmith and LangGraph provide pipeline management, visual monitoring, and collaboration features that smooth the transition to production.

Low-code platforms for developers and product managers—Dify, Coze, Flowise—use visual workflow design, model switching, and API integration to lower development and deployment barriers. They now play a central role in enterprise pilots and prototyping, although constraints remain regarding deep customization and advanced multi-agent coordination.

Global technology vendors are also industrializing agent platforms. Microsoft Copilot Studio, Google Vertex AI Agent Builder, and Oracle AI Agent Studio address enterprise requirements through multi-agent orchestration, cross-system integration, and stringent security and compliance —all of which have gained adoption in finance, manufacturing, and healthcare.

Competition is likely to hinge less on "who is smarter" than on deployability, ease of integration, and dependable service quality. Productization seeks to maximize value within the controllable bounds of current cognitive technologies. A pragmatic, well-engineered path is the most viable route for agents to achieve sustained real-world impact.

4 Collaborative Agent Development and Communication Protocols

As agent applications become systematized across multiple tools, models, and process pipelines, standardizing communication interfaces has emerged as a central issue. Divergent tool invocation formats and the absence of a shared collaboration language hinder cross-framework interoperability and require custom integration for each added component. This fragmentation limits reuse and deployability while increasing engineering complexity and maintenance costs. Common communication protocols and interface specifications not only improve development efficiency but also underpin collaboration among agents. Fundamentally, such protocols provide a cross-module *lingua franca* for future intelligent systems, enabling decoupled capabilities and flexible expansion (China Academy of Information and Communications Technology and Huawei Technologies Co., Ltd., 2025; Ehtesham et al., 2025).

4.1 Model Context Protocol (MCP)

As multi-agent systems scale, efficiently linking models, tools, and data becomes a precondition for extensible intelligent architectures. Released by Anthropic in late 2024, the Model Context Protocol provides a "USB-C–like" universal connectivity layer for the AI ecosystem (Anthropic, 2024; Lisowski, 2025).

MCP does not impose functional limits on agents; it supplies standardized, general-purpose interfaces for interacting with external resources, enabling efficient integration across models, tools, and data. Its diffusion—together with related protocols—is shifting human–computer interaction beyond command-line and GUI paradigms toward more natural, model-mediated interaction, reshaping the emerging agent ecosystem.

MCP adopts a client–server architecture: the Host typically runs the large model (e.g., Claude or a development environment); the Client manages communication and orchestration, while Servers expose data sources or external tools. Built on JSON-RPC, it supports structured commands and multiplexed concurrency, allowing unified context management over diverse external services.

Its chief advantage lies in modular, dynamic orchestration: an agent can schedule multiple servers in parallel and fuse multi-source information on demand. In a travel assistant, for instance, the model concurrently retrieves weather, transit, and historical datasets and adapts itineraries to real-time feedback. This flexibility simplifies development and maintenance while improving task execution and contextual organization.

Bidirectional streaming enables servers to push incremental data so the model can adjust decisions in real time. This suits long-running processes (e.g., compilation, script debugging) and interactive workflows requiring adaptive responses, improving latency and resource utilization.

Security is enforced through a zero-trust architecture with fine-grained authorization: each call validates identity and permissions, and servers return only minimally necessary data. In financial scenarios, de-identified data reaches the model, while sensitive operations execute locally to preserve privacy.

MCP has garnered broad vendor support from Microsoft, OpenAI, and Google DeepMind; platforms including Windows AI Foundry, the OpenAI Agent SDK, the ChatGPT desktop client, and Google Vertex AI report compatibility. Multi-agent systems are using MCP to advance from prototypes to production with tangible outcomes.

On desktops, Claude Desktop natively integrates MCP to connect AI with local files, applications, and development environments. Perplexity applies MCP for natural-language local content retrieval, improving search efficiency. Developer platforms (Replit, Sourcegraph, Zed, Codeium) integrate MCP so assistants can access codebases and logs in real time, streamlining workflows.

In enterprise data integration, MCP unifies access to logs, documents, and system events. Firms such as Block and Apollo use it to bridge previously siloed systems, efficiently linking AI data assistants and forming cross-system conduits.

The open-source community has released numerous MCP servers and connectors—covering PostgreSQL, GitHub, CMS platforms, GIS, MongoDB, and smart-home domains—boosting integration efficiency. China-based providers such as Amap and Alipay now support MCP to deliver real-time data and command execution for large models (Alibaba Cloud, 2025).

4.2 *Agent-to-Agent Protocol (A2A) for Agent Interoperability*

The Agent-to-Agent Protocol (A2A), introduced by Google in April 2025 at Google Cloud Next, is the first open framework dedicated to heterogeneous inter-agent communication and cross-platform collaboration. It seeks to replace proprietary interface silos with a unified, structured standard that enables interoperability across organizations, platforms, and toolchains.

Rather than relying on simple data sharing or database synchronization, A2A defines a precise request–response relationship between a "client agent" and a "remote agent." Upon onboarding, each agent publishes an Agent Card detailing capabilities, interfaces, and permissions, enabling capability discovery, automated negotiation, and task delegation by others.

A typical flow comprises capability discovery (Agent Card), authorization, task delegation with progress synchronization, and multimodal artifact transfer—together enabling secure, efficient cross-platform collaboration. The protocol builds on HTTP/JSON-RPC 2.0, supports server-sent events and multimodal artifact transfer, and represents messages as task objects with parts for uniform handling of text, files, and streams.

Unlike centralized schedulers, A2A enables decentralized task delegation and state synchronization. A client agent assigns subtasks to remote agents while maintaining progress coherence; decomposition and orchestration are implemented by an orchestrator agent or custom client logic. The protocol intentionally avoids prescribing decomposition algorithms, focusing on secure delegation and multi-party synchronization.

Security is provided through JSON Web Token/OpenID Connect mutual authentication and fine-grained access control. Although differential privacy and homomorphic encryption are not native, extensions for sensitive-data use cases are under active community exploration.

Hosted by the Linux Foundation, A2A attracted over one hundred major technology and open-source organizations at launch, including AWS, Microsoft, Salesforce, SAP, and ServiceNow (Linux Foundation, 2025). Google Vertex AI Agent Builder, Azure AI Foundry, and Box AI have announced support. Although OpenAI has not formally confirmed integration, SDK-based community implementations suggest broader adoption is likely.

At the application layer, A2A supports multi-role collaboration in recruitment, healthcare, and enterprise automation; Google's documentation cites a "software hiring plus background verification" workflow as a representative case. The protocol advances standardization of inter-agent interoperability and secure communication, laying foundations for collaborative multi-agent systems and complex industrial automation. Emerging protocols—MCP, the Agent Control Protocol (ACP), and the Agent Network Protocol (ANP)—continue to enrich the ecosystem as the industry moves toward more efficient, controllable, and interoperable agent networks.

5 Design and Development of Workflows

Workflows are foundational instruments of process automation that underpin efficient collaboration and stable operation in agent-based systems (Corvalán et al., 2025; Panwar, 2025). Agents' reasoning and generative capacities deliver value only through sustained environmental interaction, dynamic state management, and coordinated execution of multi-step tasks (Sun et al., 2025). As task complexity grows, the localized execution of a single agent no longer meets demands for control, traceability, or reuse. As a structural framework for task organization and resource orchestration, workflows complement agents by enforcing a well-defined execution order while maintaining scalability and transparency (Bandiatmakur, 2024; BOC Group, 2024).

5.1 *Integrating Workflows with Agents*

The notion of workflow originated in industrial management and enterprise information systems, premised on task decomposition and responsibility allocation to achieve efficient collaboration and process control (Panwar, 2025; Sinha, 2024). Whereas agents emphasize actor autonomy, workflows focus on the path to completion; they systematize complexity into clear, ordered, traceable operation chains, enforcing execution and enabling audit through standardized procedures. With advances in computing and information technology, they have evolved from a managerial notion into a foundational architecture for document circulation, data processing, and multi-department collaboration (Panwar, 2025; Sinha, 2024).

In the 1990s, the Workflow Management Coalition defined workflow systems, specifying mechanisms for automation, task scheduling, and information routing. Modern enterprises employ process modeling, structured design, and visualization to disentangle complex interdependencies, thus achieving control and transparency while accommodating dynamism and multi-party collaboration. Throughout this evolution, modeling remains central: graphical interfaces and domain-specific languages (DSLs) alike aim to externalize task dependencies and resource dependencies so that collaboration logic becomes visible, discussable, and amenable to optimization.

A modern workflow architecture comprises three elements: task units, dependency relations, and execution entities. Each task unit represents a concrete operation (e.g., text extraction, terminology normalization, content review); inputs and outputs establish explicit data and control flows (Bandiatmakur, 2024; Sukka, 2024). Dependencies may be linear or encode parallelism, conditional branching, aggregation, and feedback loops. Directed acyclic graphs prevail in scheduling to preclude cycles and enable efficient state tracking, whereas state machines or event-driven architectures add flexibility for feedback, iteration, exception handling, and human–machine collaboration.

The design of execution entities reflects workflow openness. Execution may involve humans, automated scripts, robotic process automation, or coordinated agents, and in heterogeneous, data-driven settings agent integration enhances automation and adaptivity (Panwar, 2025; Sinha, 2024). Agents adjust paths via real-time feedback—performing validation, anomaly detection, and decision actions in reimbursement or content review flows—and thereby reduce manual intervention.

External events or data shifts can trigger sub-workflows, closing information and resource allocation loops.

Start and end boundary design governs embeddability and resource coordination (BOC Group, 2024; Panwar, 2025). Initiation may stem from schedules, upstream processes, external events, or manual action; termination may hinge on goal attainment, data submission, external confirmation, or other custom triggers. In complex cross-department or distributed settings, the system must also manage versioning, access control, audit trails, execution logs, and resource allocation to ensure security, compliance, and traceability (BOC Group, 2024; Panwar, 2025).

Deeper agent participation transforms workflows from static instruction chains to self-optimizing, dynamically adjustable service systems. Agents select strategies based on task difficulty and domain characteristics, identify bottlenecks, and refine flows; in translation, they can rebalance segment assignment, enrich terminology resources, or intervene when stylistic divergence emerges (Peter et al., 2024). Shared context grants real-time access to state, parameters, and intermediates, enabling autonomous decisions and design feedback—creating tight "workflow + agent" coupling (Corvalán et al., 2025).

Modern workflow engines are highly modular and pluggable, offering process parsing, resource scheduling, state monitoring, exception recovery, and retry (BOC Group, 2024). Failed tasks can resume at interruption points and apply remediation (skip, substitute, pause), strengthening robustness and maintainability. This formalization reshapes task allocation and collaboration, compelling designers to separate delegable decision points from those requiring human interpretability and intervention. Clear demarcation between central control and agent autonomy is pivotal for efficient, resilient, sustainable intelligent workflows.

Integrating workflows and agents propels system architectures beyond basic automation toward intelligence, collaboration, and continual optimization. Structural rigor and adaptive agent behavior reinforce one another, forming a reliable basis for collaboration in knowledge-intensive, volatile environments (Peter et al., 2024; Sukka, 2024; Sun et al., 2025).

5.2 *Workflow Execution Engines and Modeling Tools*

As a structural core, a workflow must organize tasks, dependencies, and data into an executable logical network, closing the loop from abstract modeling to efficient execution (Dumas et al., 2013). Effective design extends beyond diagramming: a capable engine and toolchain translate static specifications into a dynamically responsive, collaboratively orchestrated, elastically adjustable runtime (Reichert & Weber, 2012).

A workflow engine is a runtime system that parses process definitions—such as Business Process Model and Notation (BPMN) definitions, DSL scripts, low-code form configurations—into executable models. It represents tasks and dependencies as graphs, evaluates start conditions in real time, triggers execution, and monitors state continuously. Dispatch covers service calls, script execution, database operations, and human review; prioritized queues sustain progress under resource constraints.

Context management is pivotal. Process variables—inputs, outputs, runtime parameters, environmental signals, user inputs—govern branching and dynamic path selection. Rich context enables situational adaptation and real-time tailoring. In complex scenarios, the engine logs granular state and, on failure, can retry, skip, escalate for intervention, or abort. Advanced compensation reverses prior actions when downstream tasks fail, preserving consistency and recoverability.

Visualization and event-driven capabilities are increasingly central. Real-time monitoring supports targeted intervention and adjustment. Triggers from data changes, external requests, or automated alerts promote decoupled, elastic responsiveness. Acting as a coordination hub, the engine fuses structured task control with dynamic state management to enable adaptivity, self-healing, and emergent organization. In agent systems, it often orchestrates behavior, providing task scaffolds, situational awareness, and cross-system coordination for modular, automated intelligent activity.

Efficient workflow design depends on systematic representation and modeling tools (Weske, 2024). A modeling language must specify task logic, dependencies, execution conditions, and exception handling precisely. BPMN, the most prevalent standard, uses graphical symbols for task transitions, event nodes, and conditional branches, supporting joint business–technical design and straightforward automation. It is well-suited to organization-level approvals, collaborative processes, and multi-role task management, reinforcing cross-department communication and compliance auditing.

For technical or domain-focused applications, DSLs define data pipelines, machine learning training flows, and automation operations in formats such as YAML or Python. They align with development practice, support automated operations and continuous integration, and simplify versioning and reuse. Despite narrower generality, they deliver high adaptability and productivity in targeted contexts.

Low-code platforms offer visual, modular workflow modeling. Drag-and-drop composition and component libraries enable non-technical users to integrate databases, APIs, and file operations for rapid prototypes. Platforms such as Power Automate, n8n, Coze, and Dify allow graphical modeling plus embedded code blocks for extensibility, enabling flexible customization and cross-system integration; they now serve as key tools for pilot projects and interdisciplinary collaboration.

In practice, these approaches are combined: BPMN defines the primary process, DSL scripts implement critical automation, and a low-code layer handles boundary integration and human interaction—each occupying a distinct stratum with complementary strengths.

Large language models are reshaping workflow modeling. Some platforms accept natural-language process descriptions and automatically generate BPMN structures or visual diagrams; semantic validation and intelligent completion lower barriers, align design with business intent, and facilitate cross-disciplinary collaboration (Li et al., 2024).

5.3 Governance Mechanisms for Workflows

Once a workflow is deployed to a production environment, it must respond to changing system states and external sources of uncertainty. An idealized design is only a starting point; sustained stability and ongoing optimization hinge on effective operational governance during execution. This governance rests on the systematic design of workflow observability and robustness (Dumas et al., 2013).

Observability constitutes the first line of defense in workflow governance. It entails comprehensive capture and presentation of execution state, task node status, data flows, and exceptional events. Logs, event streams, performance metrics, and task state snapshots enable administrators and the system to maintain real-time insight into each workflow instance.

For example, visual dashboards display each instance's start time, progress at key nodes, latency distribution, and retry counts. These data support routine operations, inform optimization and capacity planning, and accelerate root-cause analysis. Modern workflow systems frequently integrate logs and metrics with platforms such as Grafana and Datadog to furnish a unified health profile (n8n Team n.d.).

The deeper value of observability lies in end-to-end traceability of task chains. Complex workflows may span multiple external interfaces, sub-workflows, and heterogeneous data sources. Distributed call-chain tracing is essential for precise fault localization. Systems such as OpenTelemetry assign each workflow a unique identifier and record detailed task context, inputs, and outputs, enabling focused, efficient diagnostics.

Building on strong observability, governance must provide real-time supervision and automated response. The system emits alerts on task timeouts, anomalous resource consumption, or node failures and pushes notifications via webhooks or subscription channels. This shift from reactive, post hoc handling to proactive in-process monitoring markedly improves responsiveness and security posture (Reichert & Weber, 2012).

Robustness protects execution against anomalies and instability. The most common mechanism is automated retry: when transient failures such as network jitter or rate limiting occur, the system re-executes tasks to improve completion rates. More complex workflows incorporate exception branches and human intervention nodes so that irrecoverable errors are escalated for review, preventing critical tasks from stalling. Some workflows also implement compensating transactions that roll back prior successful steps when later stages fail, preserving business consistency and recoverability.

By 2025, the ecosystem for workflows and agent systems has continued to mature. Tools such as Grafana provide automatic labeling, intelligent alerting, and root-cause tracing, strengthening adaptivity and diagnostic precision. A cloud-native "Workflow as Code" paradigm has gained traction: some engines now support code-defined workflows, automatic state persistence, and durable restarts to enhance resilience and transparency. Visual interfaces enable event replay and fine-grained debugging for trace analysis. Native support for compensation actions, automated retries, and deadline management improves consistency and reliability in complex flows.

Collectively, these governance mechanisms turn workflows from black boxes into transparent, evolvable systems. Embedding observability and robustness throughout the workflow lifecycle enables genuine adaptation to real-world uncertainty while sustaining stable, efficient, and controllable execution.

6 Agent-Oriented Workflow Development Practices

Modern workflow platforms are rapidly moving beyond their origins as enterprise process automation tools to become core infrastructure for intelligent system development. With large language models and agents incorporated, they emphasize architectural flexibility, composable integration, and adaptive scheduling. Unlike traditional platforms focused on rigid compliance and control, contemporary systems prioritize dynamic data movement, model invocation, and complex human–AI collaboration, thereby underpinning agent-driven applications (Patel, 2025).

6.1 Characteristics of Workflow Development Platforms and Lightweight Development

Driven by the rapid evolution of LLMs and agent systems, workflow platforms are shifting from task automation utilities to system-level hubs for multi-source data orchestration, human–AI collaboration, and intelligent module composition. The notion of process has expanded beyond linear, synchronous control flow to encompass asynchronous, multi-state, event-driven networks that now support agent development and deployment.

Early enterprise platforms such as Activiti and Camunda 7 centered on the BPMN standard, emphasizing visual modeling plus task state and access control—well suited to stable, structured processes (approvals, orders, archiving). As data-driven operations and AI models proliferated, limitations in asynchronous handling, integration breadth, and intelligent module embedding constrained their ability to support agent collaboration and multimodal information flows.

New-generation platforms innovate across multiple dimensions. Openness and fine-grained modularity position workflows as composable systems that integrate external APIs, scripts, and AI models. Programmability has increased: Apache Airflow and Prefect promote “code as workflow,” allowing developers to express tasks, dependencies, scheduling, and exception logic in Python—accelerating agent applications and data pipelines. AI has shifted from a peripheral utility to an orchestrable internal intelligence unit (Li et al., 2024). Dual-channel development—graphical interfaces plus programmatic APIs—supports collaboration between business users and engineers.

Enhanced governance is another defining trait. Tooling now spans version control, access management, log tracing, real-time monitoring, and alerting to sustain iterative evolution and dependable operation. Workflows have moved beyond static "configure and run" artifacts to become dynamically monitored, elastically adjustable engineering systems.

In knowledge-intensive domains such as language services, platforms combining intelligence, integrability, and observability are preferred. Support for multi-role, multi-model, and multi-source collaboration is essential for system-level orchestration and deep agent embedding (Li et al., 2024).

Lightweight visual workflow tools further lower barriers to agent development. Platforms such as Langflow and Flowise depict language model reasoning and operational chains as flow diagrams, making complex behavioral logic explicit for beginners and non-technical users (FlowiseAI, 2024). Langflow, built on LangChain, offers a canvas interface with node-based composition of Prompt, Memory, Tool, Retriever, and related modules, supporting multiple LLMs and flexible configuration. Flowise, implemented in Node.js, emphasizes minimalist design and lightweight deployment, offering components for translation, databases, and webhooks suited to no-code integration.

Their core advantage is structuring and visualizing model reasoning and data flow. Users can inspect prompt effects, input–output transitions, and state persistence—ideal for instruction, demonstration, and prototyping. Consequently, agent tools for question answering, terminology checking, and structured text generation can be rapidly assembled and tested.

Both Langflow and Flowise are extending component breadth and adaptability: the former supports custom Python modules and agent executors; the latter incorporates external APIs through a plug-in architecture, facilitating multimodal, multi-task integration. Although multi-agent coordination and sophisticated state modeling remain limited, the trajectory toward "composable intelligence" is clear. Some users have integrated frameworks such as CrewAI and AutoGen, linking front-end flow diagrams with back-end agent orchestration (FlowiseAI, 2024).

While these lightweight tools remain limited in large-scale scheduling, complex state reasoning, and industrial-grade fault recovery, their accessibility and transparency make them well suited for entry-level and instructional use. For students, language service practitioners, and non-programmers, they clarify prompt tuning, tool invocation, and flow adjustment, fostering a paradigm in which the language model is a workflow node.

For more complex scenarios, visual platforms can serve as front-end designers that connect to governance- and scheduling-capable systems such as n8n and Prefect, forming a path from intuitive modeling to advanced operations (n8n Team n.d.; Prefect Technologies, 2024). Workflow development platforms thus continue to evolve toward intelligence, collaboration, and composability, reinforcing the foundation for deploying and innovating agent systems.

6.2 *Programmable Workflows and Agent Orchestration*

In complex, agent- and LLM-driven system development, modern workflow platforms are evolving into programmable hubs that blend graphical composition, plug-in ecosystems, and scripting. Open-source platforms such as n8n employ a flexible node-and-flow paradigm combining visual configuration with code extensibility across model invocation, data processing, and external service integration. Each node represents a service or operation; users compose them to define automation chains (n8n Team n.d.). Built-in plug-ins (HTTP, databases, conditional logic) plus custom JavaScript support facilitate extension.

The primary strength of n8n is its language model integration. Whether connecting to major LLMs (OpenAI, Anthropic) via HTTP nodes or using community plug-ins for embeddings, retrieval-augmented generation, and context management, developers can rapidly assemble workflows for knowledge retrieval, summarization, and intelligent question answering, embedding agent capabilities in broader business processes. Although not a dedicated agent framework, its event-driven model, state control, and modular design position it as a lightweight agent coordinator. Flows can function as agent behavior scripts while responding to context for multi-turn interaction and sustained state. Coordinated API calls, webhooks, and database components support initial autonomy and cross-system collaboration.

The visual experience is another advantage: flows are WYSIWYG (What You See Is What You Get), and node data plus runtime state are visible in real time, aiding debugging, tracing, and issue isolation. Developers can iteratively refine prompts, craft complex branches, and manage context logic, improving efficiency and transparency. Although suited to lightweight deployment and prototyping, large-scale scheduling or intricate dependency graphs may require external queues, persistent storage, and container orchestration for performance and fault tolerance (Dignum, 2023; Patel, 2025).

Complementing n8n, Apache Airflow and Prefect exemplify two paradigms for engineering-grade data scheduling and agent-oriented orchestration. Airflow, originating from data engineering needs, defines directed acyclic graphs (DAGs) in Python to automate and observe large, complex data workflows (Apache Software Foundation, 2025). Its code-first approach ensures traceability and stable execution, making it a de facto standard. However, its focus on periodic and batch processing makes it less suited to fine-grained event responsiveness, persistent conversational state, or adaptive agent control.

Prefect positions itself as a state-driven dynamic task flow, emphasizing asynchronous execution, just-in-time scheduling, exception callbacks, and dynamic dependencies—well aligned with LLM inference, cache validation, and multi-level retry patterns (Prefect Technologies, 2024). Retaining Python for flexibility,

Prefect incorporates contemporary observability and operational concepts. Developers encapsulate multi-step agent reasoning, data preprocessing, and external modules as manageable nodes, orchestrating layered flows via conditional logic and state awareness. It is suited to dynamic scheduling and inference-centric scenarios, supporting multi-chain task management and agent lifecycle control.

Notably, neither Airflow nor Prefect constitutes an agent framework; both provide the engineering substrate for agent behavior management, task-chain organization, and external service integration. Airflow excels in enterprise deployment and data consistency, whereas Prefect emphasizes developer experience and dynamism. Each offers visualization that supports transparent operations and efficient orchestration in large systems.

Modern programmable workflow platforms are evolving from conventional data schedulers into foundational infrastructure for agent integration, modular applications, and cross-system automation. Developer-oriented n8n and engineering-centric Airflow and Prefect alike advance the shift from data scheduling to agent orchestration, making them pivotal in the industrialization and standardization of intelligent systems.

7 Conclusion

The convergence of agents and workflows is reshaping development paths in the language services sector. Multi-agent deployment shifts operations from linear task handoffs to more efficient collaborative patterns. Workflow systems decompose translation, terminology verification, format transformation, and quality review so that specialized agents handle discrete segments, enabling automatic task allocation and transparent progress tracking (Dignum, 2023). This improves overall efficiency and provides elasticity for high-frequency change, multilingual breadth, and multi-domain demands.

In practice, agents adapt processing strategies to text type, context, and user feedback, supporting personalization and adaptation (n8n Team n.d.; Prefect Technologies, 2024). Workflow platforms provide structural support across stages: nodes can cover automated terminology updates, domain knowledge collaboration, compliance checks, and multi-pass content review (Patel, 2025). Standardized scheduling and task logging deliver traceability and risk control.

With the diffusion of communication protocols (e.g., Model Context Protocol, agent-to-agent), capability sharing and cross-platform cooperation among agents is becoming easier. Resources such as term bases, client preferences, and compliance standards circulate efficiently between internal and external agents, advancing a shift from toolchain integration to an intelligent collaboration network. This transition enhances the professionalism and consistency of translation and localization services while accelerating innovation deployment.

Looking ahead, core value in language services will center on intelligent collaboration and adaptive process capability. Efficient division of labor, transparent traceability, continuous optimization, and interpretability will become baseline expectations. Deep integration of agents and workflows increases service elasticity, innovation velocity, and scalable delivery, laying a durable foundation for continued transformation in knowledge-intensive services.

References

Alibaba Cloud. (2025). ModelScope launches MCP Hub with Alipay and MiniMax services [魔搭社区推出MCP广场,支付宝与MiniMax服务首发]. In *ModelScope Developer Documentation*. https://modelscope.cn/headlines/article/1142

Anthropic. (2024, November 25). *Introducing the Model Context Protocol*. Anthropic News. https://www.anthropic.com/news/model-context-protocol

Apache Software Foundation. (2025). *Apache Airflow 3.0.0 release notes*. https://airflow.apache.org

Bandiatmakur, G. (2024). *The next layer of AI: Intelligent workflow design in multi-agent systems*. LinkedIn Pulse. https://www.linkedin.com/pulse/next-layer-ai-intelligent-workflow-design-multi-agent-bandiatmakur-hve0c

Berti, L., Giorgi, F., & Kasneci, G. (2025). *Emergent abilities in large language models: A survey*. https://doi.org/10.48550/arXiv.2503.05788.

BOC Group. (2024). *Business process management trends for 2024*. BOC Group Blog. https://www.boc-group.com/en/blog/bpm/business-process-management-trends-for-2024/

Brohan, A., Brown, N., Carbajal, J., Chebotar, Y., Choromanski, K., Ding, T., Driess, D., Dubey, K. A., Finn, C., Florence, P. R., Fu, C., Gonzalez Arenas, M., Gopalakrishnan, K., Han, K., Hausman, K., Herzog, A., Hsu, J., Ichter, B., Irpan, A., Zitkovich, B., et al. (2023). *RT-2: Vision-language-action models transfer web knowledge to robotic control*. https://arxiv.org/abs/2307.15818

Bubeck, S., Chandrasekaran, V., Eldan, R., Gehrke, J., Horvitz, E., Kamar, E., Zhang, Y., et al. (2024). *Sparks of artificial general intelligence: Early experiments with GPT-4*. https://doi.org/10.48550/arXiv.2303.12712.

China Academy of Information and Communications Technology & Huawei Technologies Co., Ltd. [中国信息通信研究院和华为技术有限公司](2025). *Intelligent Agent Technology and Application Research Report* [智能体技术和应用研究报告]. Retrieved 4 July 2025, http://221.179.172.81/images/20250626/69921750901113785.pdf

Corvalán, J. G., Le Fevre Cervini, E. M., & Sánchez Caparrós, M. (2025). *Artificial intelligence agents and agentic workflows: The new frontier of automation* (1st ed.). La Ley. https://ialab.com.ar/

Dignum, V. (2023, January). Responsible artificial intelligence – from principles to practice: A keynote at TheWebConf 2022. *ACM SIGIR Forum, 56*(1), 1–6. https://doi.org/10.1145/3582524.3582529

Dumas, M., La Rosa, M., Mendling, J., & Reijers, H. A. (2013). *Fundamentals of business process management* (Vol. 1). Springer.

Ehtesham, A., Singh, A., Gupta, G. K., & Kumar, S. (2025). *A survey of agent interoperability protocols: Model context protocol (MCP), agent communication protocol (ACP), agent-to-agent protocol (A2A), and agent network protocol (ANP)*. https://doi.org/10.48550/arXiv.2505.02279

FlowiseAI. (2024). *FlowiseDocs: Open-source low-code LLM orchestration and AI agent building tool*. https://docs.flowiseai.com

Gao, C., Lan, X., Li, N., et al. (2024). Large language models empowered agent-based modeling and simulation: A survey and perspectives. *Humanities and Social Sciences Communications, 11*, Article 1259. https://doi.org/10.1057/s41599-024-03611-3

Georgio, R. J., Forder, C., Deb, S., Carroll, P., & Gürcan, Ö. (2025). *The coral protocol: Open Infrastructure connecting the internet of agents.* https://doi.org/10.48550/arXiv.2505.00749

Ghosh, A. (2025). *Beginner's guide to LangChain for data applications and app development*. LinkedIn. https://www.linkedin.com/pulse/beginners-guide-langchain-data-applications-app-aritra-ghosh-3yajc

Haase, J., & Pokutta, S. (2025). *Beyond static responses: Multi-agent LLM systems as a new paradigm for social science research.* https://doi.org/10.48550/arXiv.2506.01839

Li, G., Hammoud, H., Itani, H., Khizbullin, D., & Ghanem, B. (2023). CAMEL: Communicative agents for "mind" exploration of large language model society. In *Advances in Neural Information Processing Systems* (Vol. 36, pp. 51991–52008). https://doi.org/10.48550/arXiv.2303.17760.

Li, Z., Xu, S., Mei, K., Hua, W., Rama, B., Raheja, O., & Zhang, Y. (2024). *Autoflow: Automated workflow generation for large language model agents.* https://doi.org/10.48550/arXiv.2407.12821.

Linux Foundation. (2025). *A2A Protocol.* https://linuxfoundation.org/

Lisowski, E. (2025, April 15). *MCP explained: The new standard connecting AI to everything. Medium.* https://medium.com/@elisowski/mcp-explained-the-new-standard-connecting-ai-to-everything-79c5a1c98288

Mahowald, K., Ivanova, A. A., Blank, I. A., Kanwisher, N., Tenenbaum, J. B., & Fedorenko, E. (2023). *Dissociating language and thought in large language models.* https://doi.org/10.48550/arXiv.2301.06627

n8n Team. (n.d.). *n8n documentation and guides.* n8n. https://docs.n8n.io/

Packer, C., Wooders, S., Lin, K., Fang, V., Patil, S. G., Stoica, I., & Gonzalez, J. E. (2023). *MemGPT: Towards LLMs as operating systems.* https://doi.org/10.48550/arXiv.2310.08560

Panwar, B. K. (2025). AI agents and workflow automation: Optimizing daily life for efficiency and personal growth. *Global Journal of Engineering and Technology Advances, 23*(1), 169–177. https://doi.org/10.30574/gjeta.2025.23.1.0093

Park, J. S., O'Brien, J., Cai, C. J., Morris, M. R., Liang, P., & Bernstein, M. S. (2023). Generative agents: Interactive simulacra of human behavior. In *Proceedings of the 36th Annual ACM Symposium on User Interface Software and Technology (UIST '23)* (Article 2, pp. 1–22). Association for Computing Machinery. https://doi.org/10.1145/3586183.3606763.

Patel, U. (2025). *Integration of generative AI in enterprise software: Enhancing workflow automation and decision-making.* Master's thesis. Metropolia University of Applied Sciences, Finland. https://www.theseus.fi/bitstream/handle/10024/895620/Patel_Ujavalkumar.pdf?sequence=2&isAllowed=y

Peter, A., Dang, M., Liu, M., Dominguez, J., & Lohia, N. (2024). Multi-Agent Translation Team (MATT): Enhancing low-resource language translation through multi-agent workflow. *SMU Data Science Review, 8*(3), 3. https://scholar.smu.edu/datasciencereview/vol8/iss3/3

Prefect Technologies. (2024). *Prefect documentation.* https://docs.prefect.io/

Pezzato, C., Corbato, C. H., Bonhof, S., & Wisse, M. (2023). Active inference and behavior trees for reactive action planning and execution in robotics. *IEEE Transactions on Robotics, 39*(2), 1050–1069. https://doi.org/10.1109/TRO.2022.3226144

Reichert, M., & Weber, B. (2012). *Enabling flexibility in process-aware information systems: Challenges, methods, technologies* (Vol. 54). Springer.

Riad, M., de Carvalho, V. R., & Golpayegani, F. (2023). *Multi-value alignment in normative multi-agent system: Evolutionary optimisation approach.* https://doi.org/10.48550/arXiv.2310.08362

Schick, T., Dwivedi-Yu, J., Dessì, R., Raileanu, R., Lomeli, M., Hambro, E., Zettlemoyer, L., Cancedda, N., & Scialom, T. (2023). Toolformer: Language models can teach themselves to use tools. In *Proceedings of the 37th International Conference on Neural Information Processing Systems (NIPS '23)* (Article 2997, pp. 1–13). Curran Associates Inc.

Shinn, N., Cassano, F., Berman, E., Gopinath, A., Narasimhan, K., & Yao, S. (2023). *Reflexion: Language agents with verbal reinforcement learning.* https://doi.org/10.48550/arXiv.2303.11366

Sinha, A. (2024). *The rise of multi-agent systems: Collaboration at scale.* Medium. https://medium.com/@akankshasinha247/the-rise-of-multi-agent-systems-collaboration-at-scale-c71e8e60c56d

Sukka, S. (2024). *Agentic AI workflows in directed acyclic graphs (DAGs): Introduction.* Medium. https://medium.com/@siddhardha/agentic-ai-workflows-in-directed-acyclic-graphs-dags-intro-5d00444124dd

Sumers, T. R., Yao, S., Narasimhan, K., & Griffiths, T. L. (2024). Cognitive architectures for language agents. *Transactions on Machine Learning Research.* https://openreview.net/forum?id=1i6ZCvflQJ

Sun, S., Li, J., Dong, Y., Liu, H., Xu, C., Li, F., & Liu, Q. (2025). *Multi-agent application system in office collaboration scenarios.* https://doi.org/10.48550/arXiv.2503.19584

Thomas, R. J. (2023). *Enhancing database querying using language models.* https://medium.com/version-1/enhancing-database-querying-using-large-language-models-69a2064bae6b

Trott, S. (2024). *Language models versus "LLM-equipped software tools".* https://seantrott.substack.com/p/language-models-vs-llm-equipped-software

Wang, G., Xie, Y., Jiang, Y., Mandlekar, A., Xiao, C., Zhu, Y., & Anandkumar, A., et al. (2023). *Voyager: An open-ended embodied agent with large language models.* https://arxiv.org/html/2305.16291

Wei, J., Tay, Y., Bommasani, R., Raffel, C., Zoph, B., Borgeaud, S., ... & Fedus, W. (2022). Emergent abilities of large language models. arXiv. https://doi.org/10.48550/arXiv.2206.07682

Weng, L. (2023). LLM-powered autonomous agents. Lil'Log. https://lilianweng.github.io/posts/2023-06-23-agent/

Weske, M. (2024). Business process management: Concepts, languages, architectures. Springer Nature.

Wu, Q., Bansal, G., Zhang, J., Wu, Y., Li, B., Zhu, E., & Wang, C., et al. (2023). *Autogen: Enabling next-gen LLM applications via multi-agent conversation.* https://doi.org/10.48550/arXiv.2308.08155

Yao, S., Zhao, J., Yu, D., Du, N., Shafran, I., Narasimhan, K., & Cao, Y. (2022). *ReAct: Synergizing reasoning and acting in language models.* https://doi.org/10.48550/arXiv.2210.03629.

Zhai, W., Liao, J., Chen, Z., Su, B., & Zhao, X. (2025). A survey of task planning with large language models. *Intelligent Computing, 4,* 0124. https://doi.org/10.34133/icomputing.0124

Zhang, J., Xu, X., Zhang, N., Liu, R., Hooi, B., & Deng, S. (2023). *Exploring collaboration mechanisms for LLM agents: A social psychology view.* https://doi.org/10.48550/arXiv.2310.02124

Zhu, Y., Qiao, S., Ou, Y., Deng, S., Lyu, S., Shen, Y., & Zhang, N., et al. (2024). *Knowagent: Knowledge-augmented planning for LLM-based agents.* https://doi.org/10.48550/arXiv.2403.03101

Chapter 6
Reconstructing Translation Process via LLM Prompt Engineering

Abstract This chapter analyzes the shift from the linear source analysis–transfer–target rendering model to an open, iterative human–AI collaborative process in which large language models function as cognitive partners. It details how dynamic task decomposition, multi-round iterative refinement, and prompt engineering reframe translation as negotiated meaning construction. Core mechanisms include the Translate–Estimate–Refine (TEaR) loop, standards-first plus feedback refinement, multi-version generation, simulated adjudication and version fusion, and error-prevention/risk-control prompts. Lexical and knowledge layers are addressed through terminology governance, named entity standardization, handling of culture-loaded terms, emergent expressions, idioms, and inference-oriented plus retrieval-augmented prompts that integrate terminology tables and external knowledge bases for controllability. For structurally complex discourse the chapter contrasts structure-oriented, meaning-decomposition, stepwise (comprehend–decompose–reconstruct–polish), role-based collaborative, and back-translation–driven quality assurance prompting strategies. A Tang poetry case study demonstrates progressive literal grounding, semantic interpretation, and stylistic transcreation across target literary registers, exemplifying human–AI co-creative practice. The chapter argues that translator competencies must expand to encompass prompt design, AI interaction literacy, evaluative reasoning, data and standards governance, and ethical accountability. It proposes a layered process architecture coupling automated generation, diagnostic evaluation, and human judgment to enhance accuracy, consistency, cultural adaptation, transparency, and innovation for sustainable improvement and continuous quality optimization.

Traditional translation practice has followed a linear sequence—source analysis, transfer, target rendering—emphasizing equivalence, control, and fidelity (Lefevere, 2002). This structure ensures procedural stability in standardized contexts. However, as communicative settings diversify and requirements grow more complex, inherent

J. S. Yu and Y. Yao, *Intelligent Language Services*,
https://doi.org/10.1007/978-981-95-4632-9_6

limitations become evident: the process remains closed, and collaboration and feedback are weak. It over-relies on individual experience and manual revision for polysemy resolution, cultural mediation, terminology governance, and stylistic consistency, impeding sustained consistency (Chesterman, 2016; Munday et al., 2022). Translation goes well beyond lexical substitution; it entails meaning construction, intention recognition, and cultural adaptation (Shreve and Angelone, 2010). Conventional machine translation (MT) handles surface transfer efficiently but struggles with metaphor, inference, and other more complex phenomena (Forcada, 2017). Moreover, prevailing n-gram–based metrics—Bilingual Evaluation Understudy (BLEU) and Metric for Evaluation of Translation with Explicit ORdering (METEOR)—privilege form over functional adequacy, thereby limiting space for innovation and collaborative potential (Koehn, 2020; Mondal et al., 2023).

Artificial intelligence (AI)—especially large language models (LLMs)—now provides the translation process with deeper interpretive and generative capacity (Jiao et al., 2023). Prompt engineering creates targeted interaction channels for translator–model collaboration, enabling dynamic optimization and creative breakthroughs. Meanwhile, escalating market and user demands for real-time multilingual communication and intelligent user experience accelerate a shift toward intelligent, personalized, and interactive processes (Xu et al., 2023). As a result, practice is moving from passive response to proactive creation, entering a more open, sustainable phase of intelligent collaboration.

1 Reconstructing Translation Process Driven by Large Language Models

With the widespread adoption of models such as ChatGPT and Claude, translation processes are undergoing profound restructuring. These systems deliver technical advances while reshaping cognitive and operational paradigms. The linear "source-to-target" transfer model is being progressively replaced by a paradigm of human–AI collaboration and dynamic meaning construction, reframing translation from a closed transfer act into an open process of negotiated meaning.

1.1 Large Language Models as Cognitive Partners in Translation

The uptake of LLMs is moving translation technology beyond statistical paradigms toward intelligent, open language processing, altering cognition and practice at a foundational level. Earlier MT—lexical alignment, phrase-based statistics, basic encoder–decoder architectures—privileged direct symbol mapping and linear input/output (Forcada, 2017). While efficient at surface transfer, such systems falter with discourse complexity, communicative intent, cultural metaphor, and emergent terminology, remaining trapped in "deterministic mapping." Evaluation regimes centered on n-gram overlap (BLEU, METEOR) further privilege form over contextual or functional adequacy (Koehn, 2020), thereby limiting the space for innovation and collaboration.

LLMs dismantle closed, static processes. Large-scale pretraining lets them internalize surface patterns alongside deeper knowledge, behavioral regularities, and communicative expectations, shifting MT from a unidirectional task to a multimodal, open recompositional process (Xu et al., 2023). This openness manifests in diversified inputs and outputs and strategic flexibility: the model can switch among literal rendering, sense-for-sense translation, explanation, and paraphrase, and can perform inference or gap-filling when information is incomplete. Emerging cross-cultural and cross-context reasoning enables re-expression of abstract and implicit meanings, expanding the scope of translation.

Their significance extends beyond technical gains: LLMs drive a shift from linguistic transfer to meaning construction, repositioning technology from a passive instrument to a cognitive partner. Traditional computer-assisted translation tools simply supply terminology lookup and memory retrieval in one-way interaction. LLMs instead support dynamic, multi-turn dialogue in which translators probe expression strategies, analyze context and cultural asymmetry, and request multiple ranked or diverse candidates. The process becomes a collaborative cognitive endeavor; the model engages in comprehension, analysis, inference, and creative reformulation rather than mere command execution (Shreve and Angelone 2010; Brown et al., 2020).

A cognitive science perspective underscores the depth of this transition. Translation reflects linguistic competence yet also spans comprehension, reasoning, and creative synthesis. LLMs assist by surfacing deep semantics, identifying rhetorical patterns, inferring optimal target formulations, and generating diversified candidates. Through sustained interaction, translators iteratively refine performance, forming a virtuous cycle of shared knowledge and self-improvement. This bidirectional enablement recasts translation as an open, dynamic, continuously optimizable process of knowledge construction rather than an isolated task.

This move from tool to cognitive partner also raises issues of responsibility and professional identity. Powerful generative capabilities blur the boundaries of task ownership, prompting redefinition of technical accountability, ethical norms, and professional skill sets. Beyond linguistic and domain expertise, translators will need competencies in AI collaboration, prompt design, and quality evaluation, raising expectations for education and industry standards (Munday et al., 2022).

1.2 A New Process Model for Human–AI Collaborative Translation

The emergent human–AI collaborative model is reshaping practice at a structural level—extending beyond operational steps to encompass process architecture, organizational logic, and quality governance. A loop of exploration, generation, evaluation, and optimization centers translator–LLM interaction, enabling open, iterative collaboration.

A defining feature is dynamic task decomposition. Complex texts do not follow a single preconfigured path or rigid division of labor; segmentation and strategy adapt in real time to difficulty, structure, and evolving context. A translator might first elicit a summary or keyword set, then process sections incrementally while applying targeted optimization to terminology or references. This flexible subdivision increases adaptability and provides finer-grained collaboration interfaces (Briakou et al., 2024).

Multi-round iterative refinement is another core feature. After an initial draft, translators apply professional judgment and task requirements to guide revision. Each iteration removes surface errors while improving textual quality, pragmatic fit, and stylistic coherence. Blending automated suggestions with fine-grained human evaluation incrementally optimizes accuracy, fluency, and cultural adaptation (Briakou et al., 2024).

Automated detection flags terminology inconsistency, stylistic imbalance, and cultural infelicity in real time. Layered quality assurance arises from combining automation with human review. Platforms also permit manual intervention at sensitive content or decision points to safeguard reliability in critical contexts.

This collaborative process simultaneously elevates efficiency, quality, and adaptability. LLMs supply rapid draft generation and intelligent assistance, reducing repetitive effort; translators apply professional judgment, cultural sensitivity, and creativity to refine nuance, achieving complementary strengths. Intrinsic flexibility supports standardized setups for large multilingual projects while permitting domain-, style-, and client-specific customization.

Translator roles and competence frameworks are undergoing profound change. Core linguistic and textual skills remain essential, yet collaborative processes demand additional capabilities in AI interaction, data analysis, and project management. Industry-wide adoption accelerates digitization and intelligent transformation. Translation services are extending beyond textual conversion to integrate linguistic consulting, cultural adaptation, and quality assurance into a comprehensive service system.

2 Designing the Translation Process Through Prompt Engineering

In large language model–driven translation practice, prompt engineering is no longer simple instruction writing, but a system-level process design problem. An effective process integrates prompt design, deployment, evaluation, and optimization into a cohesive architecture that delivers quality stability and control (Zhang et al., 2025). This section first introduces core prompt types, then shows how to assemble an efficient, rigorous process, using concrete frameworks and optimization strategies to provide actionable methodological guidance.

2.1 Fundamental Prompt Types and Integration into Translation Processes

Applying prompt engineering requires selecting types aligned with task characteristics and quality targets, then embedding them coherently in the process. Understanding each type's properties and application scenarios is foundational to efficiency.

Effective translation prompts signal a deep grasp of task and context. They guide the model on "how" while framing "why" and "for whom" (Vatsal et al., 2025). Well-crafted prompts project the translator's linguistic sensitivity, register control, and subject knowledge, producing outputs that are professional, accurate, and fit for purpose. The main practical types are outlined below.

Direct instruction prompts underpin LLM-enabled translation. Concise directives (e.g., "Translate the following text into English.") suit routine, information-driven, structurally clear material and yield rapid usable drafts. They underperform, however, with complex discourse, specialized style, or culturally dense content, where limited contextual scaffolding can produce flat prose; complementary strategies are then required.

Role-based prompts enhance domain fidelity and stylistic alignment by assigning an expert persona (e.g., "You are a legal contract translation specialist" or "You are a translator of children's literature"). The model adapts discourse strategies and terminology accordingly, performing notably well in legal, medical, and literary domains and reinforcing quality control.

Evaluation-feedback prompts embed quality assurance by instructing the model to assess and revise its own output (e.g., "Translate, then evaluate accuracy and fluency; correct any issues.") (Nguyen & Xu, 2025). This early pass filters obvious errors, improving quality and efficiency for long or technical documents.

For structurally complex or polysemous source content, multi-step prompts decompose work into comprehension, transfer, and refinement (Briakou et al., 2024). Instructions such as "Analyze purpose and audience; then translate; finally verify terminology" mitigate single-pass omissions and facilitate targeted human intervention.

Attribute-conditioning prompts inject key metadata—text type, communicative goal, audience (e.g., "Academic abstract" or "For commercial marketing")—to enforce consistent register aligned with use. We now turn to practical implementation.

2.2 *Applying the TEaR Translation Prompt Framework in Practice*

The Translate–Estimate–Refine (TEaR) (Fig. 1) framework sequences three prompts—Translate, Estimate, Refine—to enable translator-like self-correction and offers a reference model for process standardization (Feng et al., 2024). All steps are executed using different prompts. Operationalizing these stages raises quality and provides a replicable pattern for human–AI collaboration.

In Stage 1, TEaR uses a concise, tightly structured prompt approximating traditional MT alignment. The objective is to make source–target pairing explicit and impose format through exemplars. The authors recommend 3–5 domain-relevant examples to improve adaptation.

A representative prompt template:

> Translate the following {source language} sentences into {target language}, following the wording and formatting of the examples.
> [Example 1]
> Source: How long does it take to get from Duisburg to London?
> Target: Wie lange dauert es von Duisburg nach London zu kommen?
> [Example 2]
> Source: Boris Johnson teeters on edge of favour with Tory MPs

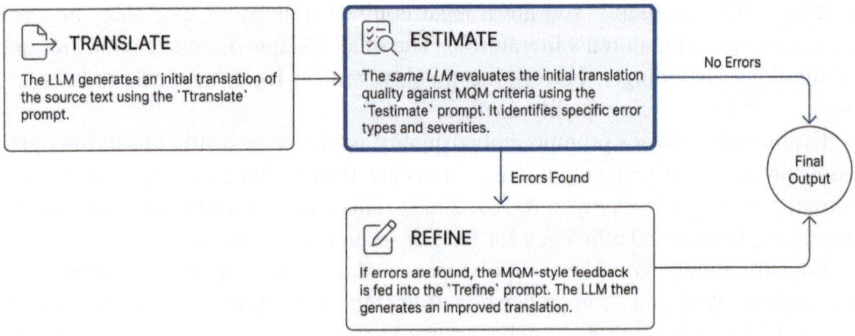

Fig. 1 TEaR framework (Feng et al., 2024)

Target: Boris Johnson steht an der Schwelle der Gunst bei Tory-Abgeordneten
[Sentence to Translate]
Source: {input text}
Your translation:

This direct format suits standard text and enforces structural expectations. Where domain examples are unavailable, a simplified version—"Translate {input text} from {source language} into {target language}, preserving domain terminology."—still accelerates task adaptation and output style control.

Stage 2 employs a structured estimation prompt that has the model act as an instructor, categorizing errors. Drawing on the Multidimensional Quality Metrics (MQM) framework, it classifies issues by accuracy, fluency, style, terminology, and other dimensions and labels severity (critical, major, minor) (Koby et al., 2014). TEaR does not reproduce the DFKI (German Research Center for Artificial Intelligence) specification verbatim but adopts its multidimensional reasoning. A zero-shot template:

Please identify translation errors and assess overall quality.
Error categories: Accuracy (addition, mistranslation, omission, untranslated), Fluency (character encoding, grammar, inconsistency, punctuation, register, spelling), Locale conventions (currency, date, personal names, telephone or time formats), Style (awkwardness), Terminology (inappropriate in context, inconsistency), Non-translation, Other, or No error.
Severity levels: critical/major/minor.
Critical errors impede comprehension; major errors affect flow but meaning remains accessible; minor errors are technical and do not impair comprehension.
{Source language} source: {source sentence}
{Target language} translation: {initial translation}
Multidimensional Quality Metrics (MQM) annotation:

This auditable structure sharpens error discrimination and yields actionable feedback for refinement.

After translation and estimation, Stage 3 targets precise correction. Prompts must convert error annotations into executable revision instructions, optionally reinforced by examples, with priority on critical issues to secure accuracy.

Template:
[Translation to Improve]
{previous translation}

[Error Feedback]
{estimation output}
[Revision Requirements]
Prioritize {critical/major} errors (e.g., mistranslation, omission).
Follow the revision logic in the example below.
[Example Revision]
Original text: The committee stopped short of approving the proposal → (Target text: "Le comité a pleinement approuvé la proposition.")
Error: major – accuracy/mistranslation ("stopped short of approving" = "nest pas allé jusqu'à approuver"; the faulty French reverses the meaning)
Corrected: "Le comité n'est pas allé jusqu'à approuver la proposition."
[Refined Translation]:

By staging prompt functions, TEaR enables an interactive optimization loop. Coarse prompts (e.g., "Correct grammatical errors.") suffice for general text, whereas specialized domains benefit from fine-grained directives such as "Verify that no technical parameter units are omitted," improving terminological and formatting precision and reducing oversight.

To balance cost and quality, TEaR also trials cross-model orchestration: a higher-end model (e.g., GPT-4) generates the draft and high-value feedback, while lightweight open-source models perform micro-level corrections. Applicability still demands task-specific judgment. Prioritizing high-impact errors—mistranslations, subject–predicate mismatches—further boosts efficiency.

The TEaR framework exemplifies the shift from conventional translation tool to a "cognitive translation partner." Its Translate–Estimate–Refine loop enhances quality and offers transferable design principles for abstract generation, question answering, and code repair (Feng et al., 2024).

These practices underscore the tight coupling between prompt formulation and process configuration. Prompts bridge translator intent and model capability; their quality directly shapes performance (Yamada, 2023). Systematic optimization thus yields measurable gains in efficiency and user experience.

As noted, managing prompt granularity remains a central lever. Dynamic adjustment depends on textual analysis, clarity of objectives, and empirical insight from iterative testing.

Moving recurrent post-editing issues upstream improves efficiency. Preventive prompts proactively mitigate risk and reduce rework (e.g., "Verify that concessive or adversative relations—'although,' 'however,' 'cannot'—are fully preserved."). Upfront controls also enforce terminological consistency and stylistic uniformity through embedded checklist items, ensuring standards are met at generation.

Strategically placing human intervention points is pivotal to joint optimization of efficiency and quality. Human review should focus on boundary cases and high-impact checkpoints—terminology validation, cultural adaptation, final quality audit (Briva-Iglesias, 2024; Qian & Kong, 2024). This division of labor leverages computational strengths while allowing translators to exercise professional judgment.

2.3 Multi-version Generation and Fusion for Optimizing Translation Quality

To pursue optimal translation quality, a multi-version process—generation, evaluation, and fusion—improves results by producing and comparing multiple candidate translations. It enlarges the solution space and enables more evidence-based decisions. For example, applying multi-version generation and comparison in machine translation can markedly increase both diversity and quality.

Generating Multiple Versions and Intelligent Selection

In practice, translators balance style, complexity, and cultural adaptation, and there is seldom a single "best" rendering. With large language models, we can design "simulated adjudication" prompts in which the model assumes several stylistic personae and then judges, comparing versions, synthesizing strengths, and producing an integrated translation. This approach leverages internal generative diversity and strengthens the model's formation of internal criteria, combining practical utility with exploratory value.

For example:

Translate the following Chinese passage into English in four steps:

1. Multi-version output: produce three stylistically distinct translations: (1) plain literary (simple vocabulary); (2) elevated literary (more elegant and figurative); (3) natural conversational (idiomatic contemporary English).
2. Comparative assessment: critique strengths and limitations of each.
3. Simulated adjudication: as a "translation judge," select the strongest version and justify briefly.
4. Fused optimization: synthesize the strengths of all three to produce a final integrated version and explain the integration logic.

Source: "纵然积得万贯家财, 但一个人也身穿不过五尺, 口入不过三餐, 怎比得上他们邀日月为友, 居天地为宅, 尽赏美景畅享良辰大福大贵!".

Excerpted results (the comparative analysis and selection rationale are omitted for brevity) are shown below.

Plain Literary Version:
Even if one amasses great wealth, a person needs no more than a few feet of cloth to wear and three meals a day. How does that compare with befriending the sun and moon, taking the world as one's home, and freely enjoying the beauty of the land in peace and contentment?
Elevated Literary Version:
Though riches may tower to the skies, one can wear only a single length of cloth and partake of three daily meals. How can this rival those who make companions of the sun and moon, dwell beneath the boundless heavens, and bask in nature's splendor, savoring life's grandeur and quiet joy?
Natural Conversational Version:
You could own all the wealth in the world, but you still put on one set of clothes and eat three meals. Isn't it better to treat the sun and moon as friends, live under the open sky, take in the vistas, and celebrate moments of beauty and joy life offers?
Fused Optimized Version:
Even with immeasurable wealth, one can wear only a single robe and eat just three meals. How can that compare with those who befriend the sun and moon, make heaven and earth their dwelling, and freely savor each moment of beauty and blessing the world affords?

Fusion Rationale:
This rendition blends the elevated version's imagery and cadence ("befriend the sun and moon; make heaven and earth their dwelling"), the conversational version's clarity and contemporary tone ("celebrate moments of beauty and joy"), and the plain version's directness ("needs no more than a few feet of cloth to wear"). It preserves the original's rhetorical sweep while maximizing readability and aesthetic appeal for a broad readership.

Version fusion is an advanced stage in a multi-version process: it consolidates the strengths of individual candidates to produce a translation that combines diversity with internal coherence.

The process seeks an optimal balance of terminological consistency, stylistic unity, and logical cohesion to achieve a clear quality gain.

An effective fusion strategy specifies clear criteria: adopt the most precise terminology, ground the text in the most natural stylistic baseline, and maintain a consistent register. A systematic procedure helps ensure the final output surpasses any single candidate in accuracy, fluency, and stylistic integrity.

The "simulated adjudication" strategy further increases flexibility. By juxtaposing stylistic and expressive variants, translators can transparently identify the strongest option. This method broadens expressive latitude and turns prompts into instruments of quality planning—transforming raw generation into a comparable, optimizable, multi-step decision process, especially valuable for tasks requiring cultural adaptation.

Standards-Driven and Feedback-Optimized Iterative Translation process

Continuous improvement is central to optimizing the translation process. Iterating between predefined standards and structured feedback incrementally elevates both process and output. For high-stakes tasks, translators must balance fluency, audience fit, register, and communicative intent; explicit standards help large language models meet these demands.

The "standards first, feedback refinement" strategy systematizes optimization: the model first internalizes task context and evaluation criteria, then produces a translation, and finally revises it in light of feedback. Criteria-focused prompts improve performance in complex scenarios (Brown et al., 2020). This approach yields context-appropriate, application-aligned output. A representative prompt might read:

> "Before translating, identify target reader characteristics (native language, cultural background, age group, reading purpose), along with register and stylistic requirements (e.g., formal vs. informal, literary vs. technical). Produce a translation aligned with these standards and briefly justify your choices."

For instance, consider the idiom "一叶知秋" (perceiving seasonal change from a single leaf). With the target audience defined as postgraduate students of East Asian culture in an academic context, the model produced:

> Translation: A falling leaf heralds autumn.
> Rationale:
>
> 1. Audience adaptation: Students of East Asian cultural studies already understand the cultural frame; "heralds" preserves the predictive nuance and the philosophical ndotion of discerning the whole from the minute.
> 2. Concision and imagery balance: "A falling leaf" carries established associative imagery; omitting "from a tree" mirrors the idiom's compactness.
> 3. Stability: This rendering is widely attested, lowering cognitive load and providing a stable anchor for subsequent academic discussion.

When the audience shifts to primary school children in the United Kingdom and a picture-book context, the model produced:

Translation: The first leaf falls, and you know autumn is here.
Rationale:

a. Simplified, concrete wording replaces the more literary "heralds," keeping within vocabulary accessible to children. "First" highlights singular salience and avoids abstract prediction.
b. Imagery is grounded in familiar experience (parks, schoolyards); no philosophical explanation is needed.
c. Balanced bipartite structure aids memorability and echoes proverbial cadence.
d. Visual reinforcement (e.g., an illustration of a child picking up a yellow leaf) lowers comprehension barriers.

Standard setting can also be bidirectional. Users may specify audience and stylistic profile directly. When such guidance is absent, the model can first analyze tone and probable context, propose a provisional standard, and then translate accordingly. For example:

"First analyze the emotional tone and use scenario of this Chinese text; infer a plausible target audience and context; establish a comprehensive translation standard; then translate into English following that standard."

For instance, for "明月松间照，清泉石上流。" (from Wang Wei's "Autumn Evening in the Mountains"), the model proposed three scenarios: (1) Western university students studying classical Chinese poetry (retain imagery density and parallelism while keeping fluent English); (2) foreign tourists (emphasize immediately accessible visual scene); (3) literary researchers (prioritize precise image correspondence). Sample outputs:

Beneath the pines the moonlight gleams, On stone the crystal springlight streams.
The moonlight dances through silent pines, A clear stream sings over mossy stones.
Moonlight filters through ancient pines, Clear waters flow over time-worn stones.

This approach supports rapid exploration by non-experts: it assists pre-translation analysis, generates draft standards, style contrasts, or terminology guides. Autonomous standard setting can stimulate creativity; however, for high-quality deliverables, user-defined standards are preferable to preserve direction and consistency.

A feedback-driven continuous refinement strategy is also possible: users append prompts such as "Revise the translation based on the following comments to better meet [specific] criteria," or "Enhance cultural color/simplify syntax/increase conversational tone." Iterative guidance forms a closed loop of standard definition, execution, evaluation, and optimization.

Iterative optimization can follow a "small, rapid steps" principle: frequent, modest adjustments sustain improvement and reduce translation errors while raising overall quality. Each iteration requires a clear objective and evaluation metric to maintain purposeful progress and avoid destabilizing over-frequent changes.

The core value of the "standards first, feedback refinement" prompting strategy is that it guides the model to behave like a judgment-capable professional translator: analyzing context and criteria in advance, then engaging in post-translation self-reflection and revision. Whether standards are user-defined or model-inferred, this method enhances professional quality and contextual adaptability, making it well suited to publication, education, and cross-cultural communication.

3 Prompt Engineering for the Translation of Lexical Items and Phrases

Handling lexical items remains a central challenge in translation. Whether in specialized written translation—ranging from scholarly to technical texts—or in professional liaison interpreting, practitioners repeatedly encounter lexical units that defy easy identification or matching. These challenges frequently fall outside standard dictionary coverage and demand integrated judgments that draw on context, domain expertise, and audience expectations. Large language models provide new leverage: with carefully structured prompts, translators can direct models to detect, reason over, and abstract problematic items, thereby resolving complex lexical issues and enhancing both precision and efficiency.

3.1 Identification, Standardization, and Management of Specialized Terminology

Translating specialized terminology reconstructs underlying knowledge structures and professional standards rather than merely converting words. Accurate identification is the indispensable first step. Many items shift meaning across domains: "magazine" denotes a periodical in general discourse but an ammunition store in military writing; "cell" is a biological unit in life sciences yet a prison room in corrections. Orthographic identity conceals contextual dependence on collocation, genre, and discourse domain. Practice shows dictionaries or intuition alone seldom suffice; translators must integrate topic signals, surrounding lexis, and domain knowledge—and, where appropriate, terminology-extraction tools—to reduce misclassification risk (Bowker, 2015).

Terminological normalization and unification are essential to professional quality and cross-document consistency. In emerging or interdisciplinary areas, competing Chinese renderings (e.g., "模因," "拟子," "敏因" for "meme") impede retrieval and scholarly exchange. Medical usage varies ("脑卒中" vs. "中风" for "stroke"), and without an agreed termbase projects incur rework and coordination friction. Establishing an authoritative repository early and enforcing it throughout drafting and revision minimizes downstream correction and accelerates throughput.

Scientific rigor in coining new terms materially influences acceptance and diffusion. A literal form like "病毒签名" for "virus signature" obscures its established cybersecurity sense of a characteristic malware pattern. Numerous AI and biotechnology neologisms still lack authoritative equivalents; translators must triangulate literature, standards, and expert guidance to ensure accuracy, clarity, and communicability. Cross-disciplinary items demand adaptive mapping—for example, "platform" in engineering versus a "vector" in biological contexts—sometimes with concise explanatory notes.

Systematic terminology management underpins scalable collaboration and continuous quality improvement. Large multilingual projects hinge on a unified, actively maintained termbase. Divergent renderings (e.g., "接口" vs. "界面" for "interface") precipitate extensive revision, schedule slippage, and cost escalation. Rapid domain evolution shifts definitions and scopes; termbases therefore require scheduled review and controlled updates. Robust governance safeguards consistency and authority while strengthening institutional knowledge and project management maturity.

Specialized terminology work integrates knowledge analysis, standards application, and lifecycle governance. It calls for linguistic competence, domain expertise, and process literacy, supported by tools and authoritative resources across identification, normalization, naming, and iterative maintenance. Such an end-to-end framework secures accurate transfer of specialized content and promotes effective interdomain knowledge flow.

3.2 Standardization and Cultural Adaptation in Named Entity Translation

Named entity translation is pivotal to both semantic precision and cultural adaptation. Personal names, toponyms, institutional titles, and titles of works possess unique referential force while conveying identity, history, and cultural affiliation. Translators must balance codified standards, established conventions, and audience familiarity to ensure accuracy and acceptability. Large language models accelerate recognition and provisional rendering, yet cultural appropriateness and professional authority still depend on human oversight (Wang et al., 2023).

Personal and geographical names are normally rendered in Chinese by applying authoritative transliteration systems (primarily Hanyu Pinyin). Standard reference lists promote consistency. For internationally prominent figures, long-established conventional Chinese forms are kept (e.g., Kevin Rudd → 陆克文, whose regular Pinyin transliteration would be "Lu Kewen") to preserve recognizability and historical usage. Translators should follow prevailing norms while also respecting individuals' stated naming preferences. In multilingual and diaspora settings, variant forms may coexist. Conversely, ethnic Chinese abroad often use romanized name forms that reflect earlier or regional practices rather than strict Pinyin; retaining such forms (e.g., Shing-Tung Yau for 丘成桐, whose Pinyin is "Qiu Chengtong") acknowledges their established international identity and dual cultural affiliation.

Fictional character names allow broader creative latitude: adaptations can embed personality traits and stylistic tone to produce culturally resonant equivalents. Children's literature prioritizes memorability and playfulness, whereas adult texts privilege layered connotation.

Institutional and work titles demand uniformity and authority. Canonical translations for international organizations and official agencies must be retained. Employing standardized forms for scholarly and media titles improves retrieval, citation accuracy, and discourse clarity. Initial naming decisions should weigh communicative reach against user acceptance to preclude proliferation of competing variants.

Technological advances have improved named entity recognition and preliminary translation. Large language models efficiently surface and process proper names, yet reliability and contextual adequacy still require human validation (Li et al., 2020). Models remain imperfect with novel entities, specialized discourse, and subtle cultural distinctions; human judgment secures authoritative and context-appropriate outcomes.

Named entity translation is a systems task combining linguistic technology with cultural discernment. Standardization, authoritative sourcing, and cultural fit provide its quality foundation. Integrating automated modeling with disciplined human review enhances accuracy and consistency while facilitating international communication and intercultural understanding (Li et al., 2020).

3.3 Semantic Reconstruction and Cultural Adaptation in Idiom Translation

Idiom translation requires sustained linguistic sensitivity and cultural competence. Idioms are structurally fixed and semantically opaque, encapsulating collective historical experience and identity (Baker, 2018). The literal reading of "kick the bucket" diverges sharply from its meaning "to die," while "画蛇添足" rendered as "draw legs on a snake" fails to convey its pejorative force. Only a grounded grasp of source-culture context enables accurate interpretation and transfer (Venuti, 2017).

Cultural context decisively shapes idiom strategy. Many expressions lack direct counterparts: "break the ice" → "打破僵局," Spanish "llover a cántaros" → English "raining cats and dogs," while Chinese uses "倾盆大雨." Selecting culturally grounded analogues facilitates pragmatic and affective transfer.

Structural rigidity necessitates caution: disturbing constituent order often erodes idiomaticity (e.g., "once in a blue moon"). Translation must balance target-language convention, fluency, and faithful sense transfer (Bellos, 2011).

In practice, functional equivalence—substituting a target idiom of comparable sense, pragmatic force, and rhetorical color (e.g., "spill the beans" → "泄露天机")—is ideal but infrequent. Paraphrase therefore predominates ("hit the books" → "用功读书"), prioritizing informational clarity for news and popular science while potentially sacrificing stylistic or cultural resonance.

Where cultural ambience is salient (literary or scholarly texts), retaining the source idiom plus a concise note (e.g., Japanese "腹が黒い") preserves nuance (Venuti, 2017). By contrast, technical and legal discourse frequently reduces idioms to propositional content ("burn the midnight oil" → "加班"/"熬夜工作") to foreground clarity.

The core of idiom translation is balancing semantic accuracy, target usage, and textual style while adjusting strategy dynamically to audience cognition and communicative purpose (Katan & Taibi, 2021; Lefevere, 2016).

3.4 Additional Issues in Lexical and Phrase Translation

Lexical translation most conspicuously tests linguistic sensitivity and cultural judgment. Seemingly simple items may encode layered, context-dependent meanings. Culture-laden terms such as "孝 (filial piety"), "缘分" ("fateful affinity"), and "面子" ("social face", "prestige") rarely map neatly onto a single English word. Terms like "春运" ("annual Spring Festival travel rush"), "高考" ("national university entrance examination"), and "师父" ("master"; "craft or martial arts mentor") require not only literal rendering but also succinct contextualization of social practice, institutional structure, or relational roles. Effective strategies often pair a base translation with transliteration, brief annotation, or a contextual gloss to balance readability and cultural salience.

Consider "阴阳" ("Yin-Yang"): a pair of mutually conditioning, complementary qualities central to classical Chinese ideas of dynamic balance and harmony. English typically retains the transliteration "Yin-Yang," often supplemented by a targeted gloss—e.g., "Yin-Yang (theory of interconnected forces in Chinese medicine)" in medical contexts or "Yin-Yang (key principle in traditional Chinese philosophy)" in philosophical discussion—to convey conceptual depth.

Emerging Chinese internet expressions heighten the need for inventive yet context-sensitive translation. Neologisms such as "内卷" ("escalating internal competition"; "involution"), "打工人" ("self-ironic term for the ordinary wage earner"), and 躺平" ("lying flat; "deliberate withdrawal from hyper-competitive striving") lack fixed English equivalents, so choice depends on genre, audience familiarity, and communicative purpose. Viable strategies include: (1) approximate idiomatic substitution (e.g., "rat race" in certain contexts for "内卷"); (2) retaining the Chinese term with an initial parenthetical gloss; (3) coining a concise descriptive phrase (e.g., "lying-flat mindset" for "躺平"); or (4) combining retention plus a brief explanatory note when cultural nuance is central. Used judiciously, these approaches preserve the innovation, ironic tone, and socio-cultural signaling embedded in the source forms (Baker, 2018).

Rendering euphemisms and particles requires fine-grained pragmatic sensitivity. Divergences between English and Chinese in evaluation, mitigation, and politeness mean that literal transfer ("not bad" → "不错" (literally "not wrong," a moderately positive "quite good")) can flatten mild criticism or soft praise. Calibrated equivalents ("有待提高" (literally "awaits improvement," i.e. "there is room for improvement")) better preserve intended interpersonal force.

Complex lexical translation hinges on nuanced control of linguistic and cultural signals. High-quality output conveys propositional content and affect while reflecting target-language collocational and stylistic norms. Professional agility in handling fine distinctions underwrites precision, naturalness, and communicative impact.

4 Prompt Engineering Methods for Complex Lexical and Phrase Translation

Lexis—single words, fixed collocations, multiword units—is the most intricate layer of language. Dictionary-centric processes become mechanical when facing neologisms, metaphor, or cultural lacunae. Large language models, with contextual sensitivity and inferential capacity, can propose dynamic equivalents. A process that first flags items requiring special handling and then consults contextual and knowledge-base evidence is better positioned to resolve complexity.

4.1 Intelligent Identification of Hard-to-Translate Lexical Items and Phrases

Discovery precedes resolution. Flagging problematic items underpins improvement. Two main approaches coexist: (1) exact matching via dictionaries, termbases, or curated lists—effective for technical terms and named entities but prone to missing variants or ambiguous contextual senses; and (2) large language model analysis surfacing rare words, idioms, slang, and polysemous items with explanatory candidates—flexible yet dependent on model competence and external validation. A hybrid design balances precision with adaptability.

4.1.1 Rule-Based, Statistical, and Machine Learning Methods

Despite the rise of large language models, rule-based, statistical, and classical machine learning techniques retain foundational value where high-quality annotations or sharply bounded domain needs exist. They offer transparency and reproducibility, albeit with weaker scalability and higher maintenance costs.

Absent a mature lexicon, statistical measures (TF–IDF, mutual information) surface salient or rare multiword units for automatic termbase expansion. In bilingual corpora, alignment techniques generate candidate pairs and spotlight non-literal mappings. Sequence labeling models (BiLSTM-CRF, BERT-CRF) excel at detecting emerging terms and brand names when ample annotated data are available.

Statistical and machine learning methods impose substantial demands on data volume and domain homogeneity. Sparse corpora or domain drift degrade detection accuracy; deep models are especially sensitive to annotation quality. Noise, ambiguity, and mixed-domain material distort outputs, and performance on low-frequency, context-bound items remains limited. Practical deployment should integrate lexicons, rule filters, and human validation to reinforce reliability and adaptability.

4.1.2 Prompt-Driven Identification of Translation-Challenging Lexical Items

Using a large language model to detect potentially difficult translation items requires well-designed prompts. Effective prompts first delineate and define sources of lexical difficulty. Encoding these categories in the prompt allows the model to anticipate and flag priority items before translation begins.

As outlined above, translation-challenging items can be grouped by complexity into: terminology and named entities; idiomatic expressions; culture-loaded terms; neologisms and internet slang; and negative or euphemistic expressions. Additional subcategories may be introduced as needed.

Terminology and named entities constitute the most fundamental difficulty. Prompts can instruct the model to prioritize recognition of "proper nouns," "technical terms," "institutional abbreviations," and "domain-specific expressions," then propose candidate translations or trigger verification. A basic example follows.

> Extract terminology related to medicine and allied fields in the following text; ignore other domains. Also extract named entities (personal names, place

names, institutional names). For each item, provide candidate renderings or recommend retaining the source form.

For idiomatic extraction, prompts can direct the model to target: (a) fixed collocations with non-literal meanings; (b) expressions marked by salient sociocultural coloring; and (c) strongly colloquial phrases. More granular discriminators and illustrative examples further improve instruction comprehension.

Because most extraction processes interface with a terminology management system, a structured output schema is effectively mandatory. An example follows.

Using the classification standards below, identify fixed expressions whose meanings are non-literal and specify their type and pragmatic function.

1. Type definitions and distinguishing features:
   - Idioms: canonical four-character idioms from historical or classical sources; structurally fixed (e.g., “叶公好龙” (“Lord Ye’s love of dragons”)professed enthusiasm masking fear).
   - Proverbs: complete folk sentences encapsulating practical wisdom (e.g., “早起的鸟儿有虫吃” (“The early bird catches the worm”) emphasizes the importance of proactivity).
   - Slang: colloquial, strongly group- or region-marked expressions with semantic innovation (e.g., “打酱油” (“Buying soy sauce”) detached non-involvement).
   - Popular sayings: accessible fixed short forms, often metaphorical (e.g., “三个臭皮匠, 顶个诸葛亮” (“Three cobblers combined equal one Zhuge Liang”) collective wisdom).
   - Semantic-shift expressions: surface form diverges sharply from established meaning (e.g., “炒鱿鱼” (“Fried squid”) refers to dismiss/fire someone).
2. Non-literal semantic criteria (all required):
   (1) Whole meaning ≠ sum of literal components.
   (2) Shared cultural conventionality (e.g., “拍马屁” (“Patting the horse’s rump”) signals ingratiation).
   (3) Contextually bound usage (e.g., “吃豆腐” (“Eating *tofu*”) implies taking advantage in specific contexts).
3. Sample analyses:

Source Text: “他这是司马昭之心, 路人皆知”. (“His intention is like that of Sima Zhao—evident to everyone on the street.”)
→ Identified: “司马昭之心, 路人皆知” (classical idiom: ambition is blatantly obvious).

→ Analysis: Historical allusion conveying transparent intent.
Source Text: "咱们打开天窗说亮话". ("Let's open the skylight and speak brightly.")
→ Identified: "打开天窗说亮话" ("Open the skylight and speak brightly." popular saying).
→ Analysis: Architectural metaphor for candid disclosure.
Output format: JSON. Field 1: extracted expression; field 2: type; field 3: analysis.
Below is the text to be analysed: {Source Text}

Culture-loaded terms are items that native users recognise with precise cultural reference yet lack a stable target equivalent. They may relate to religion, political institutions, lifestyle, or collective historical memory. Neologisms and internet slang enter usage through inventive morphology and initially lack stable consensus. Detection requires the model to note formal cues ("nonstandard shapes," "hybrid linguistic elements," "recent viral expressions") and semantic cues ("not yet in mainstream dictionaries," "semantically fluid yet transmissible"). The following prompt template includes positive and exclusion examples.

Identify translation-challenging items in the input: (1) stable culture-specific terms; (2) unstandardised emerging expressions. Provide structured analysis only if an item presents real mistranslation risk (no settled equivalent, or literal rendering would cause distortion, loss, or cultural misinterpretation). Apply the remaining criteria as follows:

1. Culture-loaded terms:
   - Religious/philosophical: canonical allusions (e.g., "道法自然" ("The *Tao* models itself after nature") linked to the *Daodejing*).
   - Institutional/socio-historical: distinctive social structures (e.g., "知青" educated youth of a defined era).
   - Material culture: no cross-cultural counterpart (e.g., "驴打滚" ("rolling donkey"): A traditional Beijing snack).
2. Emerging expressions:
   - Morphological features: letters, homophony, semantic shift (e.g., " 栓Q", a homophone for "thank you").
   - Dissemination Features: rapid short-term surge (e.g., "电子榨菜", "digital pickles").
   - Normative Features: Expressions not yet recorded in the *Modern Chinese Dictionary* (7th or 8th Edition), or those a typical of traditional written/spoken Chinese.

Required JSON structure:
{"extracted_item": "expression identified", "category": "religious/ philosophical | institutional | material culture | net abbreviation | semantic shift | homophonic pun | alphanumeric hybrid | nonstandard spelling | hybrid morphology", "translation_risk": {"risk_level": "High | Medium | Low", "deviation_note": "Likely distortion from a routine translation", "recommended_strategies": ["literal + annotation", "cultural substitution", "semantic compensation"]}.
}
}
Correct (illustrative) identification:
{"extracted_item": "赢麻了", "category": "semantic shift(旧词新义)", "translation_risk": {"risk_level": "High", "deviation_note": "Literal' win until numb' loses hyperbolic sustained success meaning.", "recommended_strategies": ["semantic compensation", "paraphrase as 'on a winning streak' or "sweeping victory'"]}
}
}
Counterexample (exclude): "人工智能发展日新月异" — "日新月异" is conventional with a straightforward English rendering ("changing daily"), hence no special risk.
Below is the source for analysis: {Source Text}

For negative or euphemistic expressions, prompts must make the model ask whether an utterance's intended meaning diverges from its literal form and whether negation, vagueness, or hedging is used to avoid direct commitment. A sample follows.

Identify negative or euphemistic expressions in the text below and analyse their implied intent and pragmatic function.
Targets:

- Negative Structures: (e.g., "not entirely unimportant" / *litotes*)
- Indirect expressions: (e.g., "might need to reconsider")
- Vague/Hedging Expressions: (e.g., "to some extent," "in a sense")
- Mitigated Tone: (e.g., "perhaps a bit challenging," "slightly problematic")

Evaluation criteria:

1. Actual Intention: Does the expression convey a hidden or opposite meaning through negation, vagueness, or mitigation? (e.g., Does "not that bad" actually function as a positive evaluation?)
2. Pragmatic Function: What is the communicative purpose? Conflict Avoidance: (e.g., using "suggest adjustment" instead of "error") Politeness/Face-saving: (e.g., "excuse me," "if I may") Stance Hinting: (e.g., using "personal opinion" to soften the impact of a criticism)

Demonstration of analysis:

- Source Text: "This plan is not entirely without feasibility."
  - Identification: Double negative structure ("not entirely without").
  - Actual Intention: Conveys a fundamentally positive attitude (the plan is feasible).
  - Pragmatic function: Avoids direct affirmation to maintain professional caution or leave room for negotiation.
- Source Text: "You might need to slightly adjust the format."
  - Identification: Indirect expression combined with a hedge ("might need to slightly").
  - Actual Intention: An implicit criticism of formatting errors. Pragmatic Function: Issues a request for revision euphemistically to maintain a polite professional relationship.
  - Pragmatic function: Issues a request for revision euphemistically to maintain a polite professional relationship.

Apply the above framework to annotate and analyze the source text.
Input: {Source Text}

To enhance operational utility, translators can embed such prompts in a pre-translation analytical stage and perform preliminary tagging on actual texts. In large batch processes, the model should first extract difficult items, then aggregate them before full translation. To mitigate hallucination, constrain recognition types, require example-based judgments, and avoid vague directives (e.g., replace "list all difficult words" with explicit definitions and exclusions). For culture-loaded terms, adapt the template as task-specific needs dictate.

Annotate culture-loaded terms in the following text and explain their cultural anchoring and translation challenges.

1. Scope constraints: include any item that:

- Embodies a specific cultural symbol ("龙" ("Chinese dragon") as auspicious).
- Denotes local custom ("年夜饭", "reunion dinner", associated with the Lunar New Year).
- Relates to historical/religious concepts ("菩萨", "Bodhisattva" within the Buddhist framework).

  Exclude: generic natural phenomena, universal roles, abstract notions without cultural anchoring.

2. Matching examples: each annotated term must specify:
   - Cultural anchor (e.g., "端午节" ("Dragon Boat Festival") within the context of East Asian cultural sphere).
   - Semantic dependency (meaning opaque outside that frame, e.g., "红白喜事" ("Red and White Affairs") , which requires explanation of the Chinese tradition of categorizing weddings and funerals together).

     Provide exclusion rationales for doubtful items (e.g., "长城" ("The Great Wall"), which might be excluded if the text refers only to the physical structure rather than its cultural symbolism).
3. Validation and feedback: mark uncertain items "pending human review" with justification; supply a cultural explanatory strategy for each term (e.g., "旗袍 *Qipao*, traditional Chinese women's dress")

The following short passage on Chinese clothing culture was directly input into Qwen3 to identify culture-loaded terms.

秦汉时期曲裾袍是女服中最为常见的一种服式，这种服装通身紧窄、长可曳地，穿上后下摆一般呈喇叭状，行不露足。汉代窄袖紧身的绕襟深衣，衣服几经转折，绕至臀部，然后用绸带系束，衣上还绘有精美华丽的纹样。衣袖有宽窄两式，袖口大多镶边。衣领部分通常用交领，领口很低，以便露出里衣。如穿几件衣服，每层领子必露于外，最多的达三层以上，现代称"三重衣"。

(English translation for the passage: During the Qin and Han periods, the *quju* robe (曲裾袍 *quju pao*) was the most common women's garment. It was form-fitting, floor-length, and its trailing hem flared trumpet-like, concealing the feet while walking. In the Han era, a narrow-sleeved, close-fitting wrapped-front *shenyi* (绕襟深衣 *raojin shenyi*) wound several turns around the torso to the hips and was fastened with a silk sash; the fabric often bore elaborate patterns. Sleeves appeared in wide and narrow variants, most cuffs edged with trim. The neckline typically used a low cross-collar (交领 *jiaoling)* to reveal inner layers. When multiple garments were worn, each collar had to remain visible—sometimes three or more—now termed the "triple-layered garment" (三重衣 *sanchong yi*).

Because the prompt lacked an explicit output schema, the Qwen3 model produced a table with list annotations. While readable, this hinders downstream processing. For agent or automated pipelines, mandate a concrete schema (e.g., JSON or XML). Detailed results are omitted for brevity.

Hallucination remains a persistent risk in applied LLM translation processes. Translators must not treat raw outputs as definitive. Until verified against high-credibility external sources, citing such content as factual is unsafe.

Identifying difficult items is a predictive, strategic pre-processing step. Its function is to reduce latent comprehension barriers and downstream translation errors. Well-scoped prompts focusing—during preprocessing—on terms likely to impair understanding or quality help steer subsequent translation toward greater precision and robustness.

4.2 Designing Context-Aware, Inference-Oriented Prompts

Two broad approaches address lexical translation challenges when working with large language models. The first exploits the model's contextual reasoning to reconstruct meaning dynamically from discourse, producing contextually appropriate translations (Yamada, 2023). The second couples the model with structured lexical resources—terminology banks and dictionaries—to reinforce authority and consistency (Chen et al., 2025). The former suits context-dependent, semantically fluid expressions; the latter covers clearly defined, highly standardized terms and idioms. This subsection examines the first approach.

The analytical and reasoning capacities of LLMs free translators from rigid reliance on enumerated bilingual dictionary senses, enabling inference-based translation (Vatsal et al., 2025). This approach is suited to items without fixed equivalents or with context-variable meanings—culture-loaded terms, semantically indeterminate neologisms, and certain euphemisms. Rather than isolated lookup, the model integrates surrounding discourse to select and reconstruct the context-specific sense.

A baseline tactic keeps the target item in full context while the prompt directs the model to reason over it—for example: "Determine the specific meaning of of the source term from the following context." The objective is contextual disambiguation that provides a stable foundation for subsequent translation.

Where domain background or implicit world knowledge is involved, adding a "justify your reasoning" instruction elicits the inference chain and reduces misinterpretation. The method is conceptually straightforward yet labor-intensive to craft at scale.

In ambiguous settings, reasoning invites hallucination risk, especially when context is sparse or polysemy high. One mitigation is two-pass reasoning: first elicit a sense explanation and communicative purpose, then produce the translation. For example, "碳达峰" (carbon peaking) denotes the policy objective of reaching a peak in carbon emissions by a target date before decline; in policy-oriented discourse, an expanded rendering such as "reach its peak carbon dioxide emissions before 2030" can foreground the objective.

Two-pass reasoning separates understanding from rendering, compelling internalization of source complexity before expression; this staging curbs hallucination and improves domain precision and cultural fit.

Consider "破圈" (literally "break the circle") as an example. In the news sentence "这部国产动画电影不仅在国内票房大卖，更成功'破圈'进入国际市场," the literal "break the circle" must be replaced by an English expression signaling cross-boundary expansion. Its semantic vagueness and culture-loaded resonance require contextual inference. A basic prompt might read:

> Translate the following news paragraph, first explaining the meaning of "破圈" in context, then producing the English version.

This instruction enforces phased semantic analysis before generation, preventing premature literalism. An advanced prompt can further refine the reasoning stages and, using multi-version output, specify style and communicative setting as follows.

> Analyze the context of "破圈": (1) assess cultural loading; (2) contrast literal versus interpretive suitability; (3) supply three stylistic variants (business report/news story/academic paper) with scenario justifications and adaptation strategies.

The Qwen3 model proposes "expand beyond its original market niche" for a business report (targeted market expansion), "break into international mainstream audiences" for news (concise and impact-oriented), and "transcend subcultural boundaries in global media circulation" for academic discourse (theoretical framing).

The overarching logic is a progressive pipeline: semantic understanding → situational analysis → stylistic adaptation and selection. Stepwise reasoning strips surface form before probing contextual function. For "环保红线" (literally "environmental protection red line"), a prompt can elicit its policy metaphor and contrast "ecological red lines" with "environmental bottom lines" to ensure terminological precision and reader clarity.

Process scripting further improves efficiency: the model first identifies domain, implicit meanings, and cultural load, then proceeds to translation. For "内卷" ("literally involution") prompts can tag its economic metaphor and the negative escalation of competition, leading to the established rendering "involution" rather than the literal "inward rolling." Multi-step reasoning narrows the gap to professional practice.

Prompt design must balance task objectives with model characteristics. Shallow prompts deliver speed but may reflect training biases; deeper prompts (advanced variants or reasoning-oriented models such as Deepseek-R1 or ChatGPT-o3) enhance accuracy at higher computational cost. Translators should calibrate efficiency against precision for each project.

4.3 Integrating Dictionaries and Knowledge Bases to Enhance Translation Quality

Vocabulary and terminology form the foundation of linguistic and knowledge systems. In translation, most difficult items already have definitions, fixed collocations, or established equivalents documented in knowledge bases. Accordingly, the goal is not to let a large language model decide in isolation but to deliberately leverage existing resources. Systematically integrating specialized terms, idioms, slang, named entities, and polysemous expressions—while emphasizing matching, citation, and verification—yields more accurate, consistent, and controllable outputs (Ghazvininejad et al., 2023).

Knowledge resources fall into two broad categories: structured and open semantic. Structured resources—curated termbases, databases, bilingual glossaries, and client-specified equivalence tables—provide high standardization and reliability for precision-critical domains (law, technology, medicine).Open semantic resources—general dictionaries, Wikipedia, Urban Dictionary, and Question and Answer platforms (e.g., Quora, Stack Overflow, Stack Exchange)—supply extensive background information and usage examples, supporting context-dependent tasks despite lower standardization.

Among structured resources, terminology equivalence tables are the most practical. Supplied by clients, industry bodies, or translation teams, they pair source terms with target renderings spanning named entities, technical and legal terminology, brand expressions, and component names. Maintaining strict consistency and precision underpins professional quality, client acceptance, and standards alignment.

A judicious blend of structured and open resources preserves accuracy while improving controllability and efficiency. Such integration reduces mistranslations and inconsistencies and aligns outputs with industry norms and user expectations. For example, a prompt may specify:

> Source text to be translated: {Source Text}
> Please translate the above text, strictly using the translations provided in the following terminology table. For any term absent from the table, infer from context. If a term appears in the table, you must use the specified Chinese rendering; do not paraphrase or alter it.
> Terminology table:
>
> - “data pipeline” → ”数据管道”

- "load balancer" → "负载均衡器"
- "Kubernetes cluster" → "Kubernetes 集群"

Some termbases add definitions, usage examples, domain tags, and synonyms, and these annotations can be embedded in prompts so the model assesses sense alignment more effectively (Lu et al., 2023). Example:

Below is a terminology table with explanatory information. Use the annotations to judge whether a term's meaning matches the present context; if it does, apply the prescribed translation; if not, translate flexibly based on context:
Terminology table:
"lead time" → "前置时间": total time from order placement to delivery, commonly used in supply chain management
Source text: Due to delays in transportation, the lead time has increased significantly.

Here the model correctly selects "前置时间," avoiding literal but incorrect forms such as "引导时间." When a term is polysemous (e.g., pipeline: physical conduit; data process; talent development path), enumerating the senses allows appropriate selection:

Term: pipeline
Senses:

1. Physical conduit for transporting liquids or gases
2. Data processing process for machine learning tasks
3. Talent development path (structured managerial training)

Select the most appropriate translation based on context.
Text to translate: We streamlined the data pipeline to reduce processing latency.

Structured terminology resources remain indispensable when LLMs support translation. Although maintenance and alignment incur costs, the gains in consistency, controllability, and client satisfaction are substantial—especially for annotated or polysemous items, where enriched prompts and semantic discrimination enable controlled use (Lew, 2024).

Idiom dictionaries, slang repositories (e.g., Urban Dictionary), and encyclopedic resources (e.g., Wikipedia, Baidu Baike) also assist with non-standard usage. Idiom sources guide literal versus adaptive choices, while slang and internet vernacular repositories emphasize pragmatic and community conventions yet often contain context-dependent or conflicting glosses; translator guidance is therefore essential.

Encyclopedic sources supply definitional depth and background for named entities, scientific terms, and historical or cultural references. For events or organization names, consulting an entry first supports an informed choice among transliteration, retention, and domestication; multilingual coverage also surfaces widely accepted equivalents, aiding semi-specialist and general readership contexts.

Implementations typically combine exact term matching (termbases, named entities), fuzzy matching (slang, variants), and semantic similarity search (complex expressions). Effective prompt design integrates concise sense glosses with reasoning instructions to stabilize outputs.

Injecting authoritative knowledge grants "constrained freedom": external resources compensate for gaps in native lexical understanding and enable verification—critical in specialized or standards-driven settings. Compared with unassisted reasoning, this approach increases explainability and auditability, facilitating collaboration and quality management.

Current systems employ Retrieval-Augmented Generation (RAG), tool invocation, and modular protocols such as the Model Context Protocol (MCP) to load definitions, examples, and other external resources dynamically. They also enforce access control and version tracking for sensitive terms to ensure compliant, up-to-date renderings (Conia et al., 2024). These techniques are widely deployed in finance, law, and healthcare as a foundation for high-quality, controllable processes.

Resolution strategies extend beyond these categories: multi-step prompting and explain-then-decide processes (e.g., eliciting a sense explanation before translation or generating multiple candidates) offer distinct advantages (Iyer et al., 2023). Despite formal variation, they converge on context-driven reasoning plus knowledge embedding. For complex items, the central challenge is not comprehension but providing guidance that keeps decisions accurate and controllable (Appicharla et al., 2025).

5 Prompt Engineering Methods for Translating Long, Complex English Sentences

In practice, lexical hurdles are only the starting point; the principal challenge is posed by long, syntactically layered sentences. These sentences demand precise parsing and tight semantic control, and small lapses can produce awkward or distorted output. Even when an LLM can handle extended spans, insufficient guidance may lead to structural confusion or semantic drift. Prompt engineering therefore provides targeted scaffolding that improves translation quality on structurally complex material.

5.1 Core Issues in Translating Long, Complex English Sentences and Corresponding Prompt Strategies

In English-to-Chinese translation, success with long sentences requires rapid identification of the clause backbone, clarification of intricate logical relations, and disciplined reordering. Many such sentences challenge both beginners and MT systems because they contain multiple hierarchical embeddings, stacked modifiers, long-distance dependencies, or dense rhetorical devices (Yim, 2024). The following categories are representative rather than exhaustive.

Structural complexity: multilayered embedding and modifier stacking. Example: "The book that the professor who we met yesterday recommended to the students is out of print." The main clause is "(The book) … is out of print," but several nested relative clauses intervene. A prompt can instruct: "Identify the backbone first, then unpack each modifier," enabling stepwise expansion and reducing misinterpretation.

Long-distance dependency: separation of subject and predicate with remote attachments. Example: "The series of lectures on environmental sustainability and global climate policies that were organized by the university in collaboration with several international NGOs has received positive feedback." The complex subject and inserted modifiers obscure the head–verb linkage. A prompt can state: "Locate the distant subject–predicate pair, then separate embedded modifiers," clarifying dependencies.

Implicit logical relations: sequences lacking explicit connectors. In "The government cut taxes. Investment increased. Unemployment fell." three short sentences implicitly form a causal chain. A prompt can require: "Infer intersentential logical relations and insert appropriate connectives," ensuring a coherent, idiomatic rendering without redundancy.

Concentrated marked constructions: clefts and inversion. Example: "It was not until the new policy was implemented that the company started to see real improvements." The cleft diverges from natural Chinese ordering. A prompt can say: "Detect cleft emphasis and reorder into a natural target-language sequence," producing a more fluent result.

Salient rhetorical features: extended analogy and metaphor. Example: "Just as a river carves valleys through centuries of persistence, so too must a society work patiently to create change." Mishandling the metaphor can blunt its effect. A prompt may specify: "Preserve the analogical effect while adjusting style for naturalness," maintaining fidelity and readability.

Consequently, detailed structural diagnosis enables targeted prompt strategies that help an LLM internalize sentence architecture and then generate natural Chinese output aligned with target-language norms.

When long English sentences are translated, output quality hinges on prompt design. Effective prompts combine structural guidance, semantic decomposition, and style control so the model parses accurately, preserves meaning, and optimizes expression. Depending on task complexity, translators can combine automated drafting with a Human-in-the-Loop process (Yang et al., 2023)—for example, generating a draft for subsequent expert restructuring, or using multistep prompts that guide staged analysis and reconstruction. Prompts thus become the conduit for high-quality collaborative reasoning.

5.2 *Structure-Oriented and Meaning-Decomposition Prompt Types*

With structurally intricate, logically nested sentences, MT systems frequently misidentify the backbone, scramble clause order, or misassign modifiers. The primary difficulty lies in accurate syntactic recognition and faithful logical transfer, not lexical substitution. Accordingly, prompt design should direct the LLM to perform syntactic analysis plus layered semantic extraction, distinguishing the main clause from modifiers and handling key information stepwise.

Structure-oriented prompts aim to expose the sentence skeleton. Before translation they may require identification of subject, predicate, object, and subordinate hierarchy—e.g., "List all clauses and their levels" or "Extract the backbone first, then translate it." This staged decomposition mitigates errors in multi-embedded constructions and promotes orderly rendering.

Meaning-decomposition prompts emphasize semantic progression and suit logic-dense or information-heavy sentences. They guide the model to elucidate and rebuild meaning unit by unit—e.g., "Explain each layer, then render fluent Chinese," or "Segment by semantic relations and translate each segment." In technical, policy, and academic genres, this explanation-plus-translation routine improves accuracy and controllability.

These two prompt types do not reject end-to-end generation; instead, they insert guided intermediate steps that heighten explainability and accuracy. They suit human–machine collaboration, serving as tools for pre-translation, revision, or instruction. For dense, structurally complex material they delineate a reliable route to quality and furnish actionable collaboration patterns.

For example,

Source text: "The proposal, which was initially supported by a majority of committee members who believed that it would address long-standing inefficiencies in resource allocation, has now been withdrawn by its sponsor, who cited concerns about unforeseen consequences that could arise from implementation delays."

Designed prompt:

> List subordinate structures hierarchically, extract the main clause, then apply a layer-by-layer translation strategy to preserve logic and meaning.

Model output:

1. Structural Hierarchy:
   - Main clause: The proposal has now been withdrawn by its sponsor
   - Relative clause 1: which was initially supported by a majority of committee members
   - Relative clause 2: who believed that it would address long-standing inefficiencies in resource allocation
   - Relative clause 3: who cited concerns about unforeseen consequences
   - Subordinate clause (that-clause modifying "consequences"): that could arise from implementation delays

2. Backbone Extraction:
   The proposal has been withdrawn by its sponsor. It had initially gained majority committee support from members who believed it would remedy long-standing inefficiencies in resource allocation, but the sponsor cited concerns about unforeseen consequences potentially stemming from implementation delays.
3. Layered Translation:
   - Main clause: 这项提案目前已由其发起人撤回。
   - Relative clause 1: 该提案最初得到了大多数委员会成员的支持。
   - Relative clause 2: 这些成员认为，该提案有助于解决资源分配中的长期效率低下问题。
   - Relative clause 2: These members believed it would address long-standing inefficiencies in resource allocation.
   - Relative clause 3: The sponsor expressed concerns about unforeseen consequences
   - that-clause: 这些后果可能源于执行过程中的延误。
     Final integrated translation:
     这项提案目前已由其发起人撤回。该提案最初获得了大多数委员会成员的支持， 他们认为这将有助于解决资源分配中存在的长期效率低下问题；然而，发起人表示，由于担心在实施过程中可能出现的延误所带来的未知影响，决定将其撤回。(The proposal has now been withdrawn by its sponsor. It initially secured support from a majority of committee members. They believed it would alleviate long-standing inefficiencies in resource allocation; however, the sponsor withdrew it out of concern about unforeseen consequences that might arise from implementation delays).

Compared with the direct translation below, the layered strategy produces a clearer structure and sharper emphasis.

该提案最初得到了大多数委员会成员的支持，他们认为这将解决资源分配中的长期低效问题，但现在已被其赞助人撤回，后者指出了由于实施延迟可能引发的不可预见后果的担忧。(The proposal was initially supported by a majority of committee members. They believed it would resolve long-standing inefficiencies in resource allocation. The proposal has now been withdrawn by its sponsor. They raised concerns about unforeseen consequences that could result from implementation delays).

5.3 Stepwise Prompts

When a language model is asked to produce a translation in a single pass for structurally complex, information-dense, or high-stakes text, the output often shows logical leaps, structural disorder, or semantic vagueness. This is not necessarily a deficit in linguistic knowledge; rather, it reflects the absence of an explicit reasoning path. Stepwise prompts guide the model through a staged progression, thereby improving the translation's controllability and interpretability (Wei et al., 2022).

A representative method is the four-stage "comprehend–decompose–reconstruct–polish" approach, which breaks a complex translation task into source comprehension, structural decomposition, target rendering, and refinement. A basic prompt might read: "Translate this sentence in four steps: (1) explain its meaning; (2) segment it into simple clauses or core components; (3) translate each part into Chinese; (4) polish the result for natural, native-like expression." This procedural framing reduces complexity and enables targeted mid-process quality control.

Another common strategy is the core-information-first approach, suited to long or deeply nested sentences. It translates the backbone before adding modifiers, with prompts such as: "Translate the main clause first, then handle each subordinate or modifying unit." This sequencing helps secure the sentence's central thread and reduces omissions or inversions of primary and secondary information.

For sentences with deep hierarchy and multiple embeddings, the inside-out subordinate integration approach proceeds from the innermost clause outward. The model first translates the most embedded clause, then incrementally assembles the full sentence ("Start with the innermost subordinate clause and integrate layer by layer"). This method clarifies structural nesting and logical relations.

Regardless of the specific stepwise strategy, the essential principle is to use concrete, explicit instructions to structure the model's process, lowering the risk of errors on difficult sentences and furnishing translators and educators with a clear, actionable framework. For example,

Source text:

While the integration of large language models into real-world applications has demonstrated significant progress in natural language understanding and generation, concerns regarding their computational demands, environmental impact, and potential for unintended biases continue to challenge their widespread deployment, particularly in resource-constrained environments.

Prompt design:

Translate this sentence in four steps: (1) explain its meaning; (2) break it into simple clauses or components; (3) render a semantically precise Chinese translation; (4) polish for natural, native-like fluency.

Model output (abridged):

1. **Explanation of the sentence's meaning:**

   This sentence discusses that while large language models have achieved progress in real-world applications, there are still several factors hindering their widespread deployment. These include high computational resource consumption, significant environmental impact, and the potential for biases, which are especially pronounced in resource-constrained environments.
2. **Breakdown into simple sentences or components:**
   - The integration of large language models into real-world scenarios has shown notable progress.
   - These advancements are mainly reflected in natural language understanding and generation.
   - However, their computational requirements remain high.
   - Their environmental impact also raises concerns.
   - The models may contain unintended biases.
   - These factors limit their widespread adoption.
   - This is particularly the case in resource-constrained environments.
3. **Semantically precise Chinese translation:**

   尽管大语言模型在真实世界应用中的整合已在自然语言理解和生成方面展现出显著进展，但其计算资源消耗、环境影响以及潜在的偏见问题仍对大规模部署构成挑战，尤其是在资源受限的环境中。("Despite remarkable advancements in natural language understanding and generation through the practical integration of LLMs, their high computational overhead, environmental footprint, and inherent biases continue to impede widespread deployment, especially within resource-limited settings.")

4. **Polish for Natural, Native-Like Fluency:**

虽然大语言模型在自然语言理解和生成方面取得了显著进展,并逐步应用于多个现实场景,但其高昂的计算成本、对环境的影响以及可能存在的偏见,仍然是阻碍其广泛落地的难题,尤其是在资源有限的使用环境下尤为突出。("Despite remarkable advancements in natural language understanding and generation and their growing integration into practical applications, LLMs still face significant hurdles for broad deployment—namely high computational overhead, environmental footprint, and inherent biases—which are especially pronounced in resource-constrained settings.")

5.4 Error-Prevention Prompts

In machine-assisted translation, the most frequent issues are not limitations in structural parsing or lexical generation but granular errors—mistranslations, omissions, and stylistic inconsistencies—that undermine accuracy and professional quality. Error-prevention prompts insert pre- and post-generation risk-control steps to proactively steer the model away from recurrent pitfalls and enhance overall quality.

A foundational tactic is mistranslation risk alerts, suited to technical or logic-dense material. By embedding common false friends or ambiguous structures in the prompt or few-shot examples (e.g., "Distinguish whether 'issue' means 'problem,' 'topic,' or 'publication' in context"), the model is primed to monitor high-risk items.

A key-point checklist proceduralizes quality control for draft self-review or stepwise verification. Prompts may ask the model to confirm logical markers (e.g., concessive or adversative cues), negation, and clause coverage ("Verify that 'although,' 'however,' and negative forms are preserved"; "Confirm all main and subordinate clauses are translated without dropping connectives or modifiers"). These directives improve completeness and accuracy, especially in multi-layer logical structures.

For tasks with heightened stylistic or consistency demands, a self-feedback quality evaluation strategy can be effective. The prompt requests post-hoc scoring of accuracy, fluency, and stylistic consistency (each out of 5; revise if any dimension < 4). This self-assessment loop induces reflective revision, enhancing overall translation quality (Madaan et al., 2023).

Encoding human editorial heuristics and standards as prompts front-loads risk checks and focal reminders, reducing rework and markedly improving professional reliability. This strategy offers a quality safeguard for demanding, multi-round translation projects.

Source text:

> Although the committee, which had been composed of members representing a wide range of interests and had met regularly for over a decade, was officially disbanded last year, its recommendations continue to influence policy decisions in ways that few anticipated at the time of its dissolution.

Prompt design:

> First, translate the sentence into Chinese, ensuring semantic completeness, accurate expression, and faithful reproduction of the original logic and hierarchical structure.
> For the translated text, conduct a self-evaluation from the following three dimensions, with a maximum score of 5 points for each:
>
> - **Accuracy**: Does the translation faithfully reflect all key information, logical relationships, and details of the original text?
> - **Fluency**: Does the translation conform to modern Chinese usage, with natural sentence structures that are easy for readers to understand?
> - **Consistency of Style**: Is the wording, tone, and register consistent and coherent throughout the sentence, without abrupt shifts?
>
> If any score is below 4, revise and optimize the translation according to the identified shortcomings.
> At the end, clearly point out specific issues in the original translation that affect accuracy or readability, and provide targeted suggestions for improvement.

Model output (abridged):

> **First Draft Translation**:
> 尽管这个委员会曾由代表广泛利益、定期召开会议超过十年的成员组成，并在去年被正式解散，但其建议仍以当时人们几乎未预料到的方式继续影响政策决策。(Although this committee was composed of members representing a wide range of interests who met regularly for over a decade and was formally disbanded last year, its recommendations have continued to influence policy decisions in ways that were hardly anticipated at the time).
> **Evaluation and Analysis**:

- **Accuracy:** 4/5 (Basically accurate, but "representing a wide range of interests" does not fully convey the meaning of "diverse standpoints.")
- **Fluency:** 3/5 (The structure "members who met regularly for over a decade" is awkward and difficult to understand).
- **Consistency of Style:** 4/5 (Overall consistent, but some wording is overly formal and slightly disconnected from the latter part).

Issues Affecting Accuracy and Readability:

1. "Representing a wide range of interests" → The original intent is "covering diverse standpoints"; using "interests" may cause ambiguity.
2. "Members who met regularly for over a decade" → The sentence is lengthy, and the main structure is unclear.
3. "In ways that were hardly anticipated at the time" → The expression is stiff and lacks a natural transition.

Second Draft Translation (After Optimization):
尽管该委员会早在十年前就由来自不同背景、代表多方立场的成员组成,并长期定期召开会议,但去年已被正式解散。然而,它提出的建议仍在以当时鲜有人预料的方式持续影响着政策制定。(Although the committee had, for over a decade, been composed of members from different backgrounds representing diverse standpoints and held regular meetings, it was formally disbanded last year. Nevertheless, the recommendations it made continue to shape policy decisions in ways that few had anticipated at the time).
Evaluation and Analysis:

- **Accuracy:** 5/5 (Fully conveys the original timeline, composition background, and ongoing influence).
- **Fluency:** 5/5 (Sentence structure is clear and logical).
- **Consistency of Style:** 5/5 (Overall tone is consistent, and the written expression is natural and smooth).

Optimization Notes:

1. Changed "representing a wide range of interests" to"代表多方立场"("representing diverse standpoints") to better fit the political context.
2. Broke down the nested structure of the original sentence, clarifying the timeline of "formation—operation—disbandment—impact."
3. Used "鲜有人预料"("few had anticipated") instead of "hardly anticipated" for a more natural and idiomatic English expression.

5.5 Role-Based Collaborative Prompts

Long, syntactically intricate sentences often combine structural complexity, dense terminology, and heterogeneous stylistic cues, each of which challenges large language models. A traditional single-pass approach, confined to a single perspective, tends to miss subtle syntactic cues, precise terminology, and register consistency. Role-based collaborative prompts mitigate these risks by simulating a structured division of labor among complementary language specialists, enabling staged, multi-perspective quality improvements.

The "linguist" role focuses on syntactic and structural diagnostics, guiding the identification of the main clause, subordinate clause boundaries, nesting depth, and logical relations. No target-language rendering is produced at this stage; the goal is structural and semantic clarification. Representative prompts include: "From a linguist's perspective, identify the subject, predicate, object, and all subordinate structures in the sentence, explaining the semantic relations," or "List relative clauses, parentheticals, and marked constructions, and describe their pragmatic functions."

The "professional translator" role then performs semantic transfer with an emphasis on idiomatic fluency, producing a version that preserves meaning while conforming to target-language conventions. Typical prompts include: "Act as an experienced translator and render the following sentence into Chinese with natural flow," or "If literal order impedes clarity, reorder while maintaining the original logic and focus."

The "Chinese-language editor" role polishes the draft for publication readiness, ensuring adherence to contemporary written norms, eliminating calques, and tightening diction and syntax for precision and flow. Example prompts include: "As a Chinese editor, polish the translation to meet modern written standards," or "Refine wording and sentence structure to enhance expressiveness while preserving meaning."

For technical or scholarly material, a "subject-matter expert" role is added to ensure terminological accuracy and logical rigor. Illustrative prompts include: "As a domain expert, verify terminological correctness and argumentative coherence, and flag deviations from industry standards" (Jiao et al., 2023), or "With terminology validated, adapt the translation for formal publication."

Deploying role-based collaborative prompts establishes a structured workflow with clear role demarcation: each role applies its expertise, strengthening systematic coverage and controllability while enhancing the accuracy, naturalness, and professional quality of the translation. For example,

Source text:

> That the courts have not always been consistent in their interpretation of the statute, and that some decisions may be seen as having departed from what had previously appeared to be a settled principle, are matters which, while

they do not of themselves establish an error in the application of the law, may nonetheless suggest that a reconsideration of the issue is desirable.

Prompt design:

Please translate the provided source text according to the steps below, outputting the analysis, translation, polishing, and review results for each step:

1. Acting as an English linguist, analyze the following sentence from the perspective of English linguistic analysis. Identify its subject, predicate (main verb phrase), object, and all subordinate structures, and explain their semantic relationships. Point out any non-restrictive relative clauses, parenthetical elements, inverted structures, or other complex constituents, and describe their pragmatic functions.
2. Acting as an experienced professional translator specializing in legal English, and building on the results of Step 1, translate the sentence into Chinese. Ensure the rendering is faithful to the original meaning and legally precise while maintaining idiomatic fluency. If the original structure precludes a literal rendering, adjust the word order appropriately, but preserve the original logical relations and semantic focus.
3. Acting as a senior Chinese-language editor, polish the Step 2 translation so that it conforms to contemporary written Chinese norms and avoids stiff, literal phrasing. While preserving the original meaning, improve fluency and expressiveness by appropriately refining wording and restructuring sentences where appropriate.
4. Acting as a legal subject-matter expert, review the Step 3 version for any mistranslated terms, logical issues, or departures from industry standards. With terminology confirmed as accurate, further elevate the professional tone and precision so that the sentence is suitable for formal publication or professional use.

Model output (abridged):

1. Linguist's analysis:
   - Subject: two coordinated that-introduced nominal clauses
     - That the courts have not always been consistent…
     - That some decisions may be seen as having departed…
   - Predicate verb: are
   - Predicative complement: matters

- Modifiers
  - A relative clause introduced by "which" modifies "matters", and within it there is a concessive adverbial clause introduced by "while".

    While they do not…(concessive clause)
    May nonetheless suggest…(main clause)
- Complex structures:
  - The sentence opens with a typical "formal subject + real subject" pattern (That … are matters), which heightens the formal tone.
  - "what had previously appeared to be a settled principle" is an object clause embedded after "departed from."
  - In "may nonetheless suggest…," the adverb "nonetheless" introduces emphatic contrast, intensifying the logical tension.
- The overall sentence is a complex one with successive layers of embedding, highlighting the rigor of legal language and the stepwise progression of the reasoning.

1. Professional Translator's Version:

   尽管法院在解释该法规时并非始终一致， 且某些判决似乎偏离了此前看似已确立的原则， 这些情况本身虽不足以证明法律适用存在错误，但仍可能表明对相关问题进行重新审视是可取的。(Although the courts have not always been consistent in interpreting this regulation, and some judgments appear to have deviated from previously established principles, these circumstances themselves are not sufficient to demonstrate an error in the application of the law, but they may still indicate that it is advisable to re-examine the relevant issues).
2. Senior Chinese Editor's Polished Version:

   尽管法院在解释该项法规时并不总是一致，而且有些裁决明显偏离了过去被认为已经确立的原则，但这些情形本身并不能直接说明法律适用有误，却仍有可能表明对该问题进行重新评估是必要的。(Although the courts have not always been consistent in interpreting this regulation, and some decisions have clearly deviated from principles that were previously considered established, these circumstances themselves do not directly indicate an error in the application of the law, but they may still suggest that it is necessary to re-evaluate the issue).
3. Legal Expert's Review:

   尽管法院在解释该项成文法的过程中并未始终保持一致性，部分司法判例亦显现出对先前已被广泛接受之原则的偏离倾向，此类现象虽不足以单独构成法律适用错误的确凿证据，但确有理由表明，对此类问题展开进一步审查具有现实必要性。(Although the courts have not consistently maintained uniformity in the process of interpreting this statute, some judicial decisions also show a tendency to deviate from principles that were previously widely accepted. Such phenomena, although insufficient on their own to constitute conclusive evidence of an error in the application of the law, do provide grounds to indicate that further examination of such issues is practically necessary).

5.6 *Back-Translation–Based Quality Assurance in Human–AI Collaborative Translation*

Although large language models often produce translations that appear fluent and idiomatic, such surface fluency can be misleading. Where source sentences exhibit intricate syntactic embedding or latent ambiguity, the model's output may diverge subtly from the original, introducing interpretive bias, attenuating legal or technical force, or generating covert logical inconsistencies. To uncover these latent deficiencies, a back-translation–driven quality assurance procedure can be employed. The machine-generated target text is retranslated into the source language and then aligned with the original to diagnose (i) semantic drift, (ii) unwarranted abstraction, omission, or addition, and (iii) structural simplification that erodes nuance. The prompt is therefore designed as follows:

Prompt design:

1. Translate the following English source passage into Chinese, ensuring semantic accuracy and idiomatic fluency.
2. Back-translate the Chinese version into English, then conduct a sentence-by-sentence comparison with the original source to identify discrepancies in core meaning, tone, and logical or syntactic structure.
3. During back-translation and comparison, pay particular attention to whether logical markers (negation, hypothesis, condition, concession, etc.) have been altered.
4. Where semantic ambiguity, addition or omission of information, structural misinterpretation, or logical drift is detected, list each issue explicitly and propose a corresponding corrective recommendation.
5. Revise (optimize) the Chinese translation in light of the recommendations and, where necessary, perform an additional back-translation to validate the effectiveness of the revisions.

The design of the foregoing back-translation prompt is intended to induce the model to engage in self-reflection and self-validation of its own translations; in essence, it trades additional computational overhead and latency for an incremental improvement in translation quality.

Where appropriate, this pipeline can be coupled with a human translator's judgment and revisions, forming a hybrid human–AI collaborative model. In practical operation, the model can undertake the back-translation and baseline comparative diagnostics, while the translator supplies the final evaluation and corrective interventions. Human participation compensates for the model's knowledge boundaries, secures terminological precision and semantic consistency, and mitigates risks arising from hallucination or misclassification (Mondal et al., 2023).

Back-translation–driven prompting thus furnishes an effective mechanism for automated translation quality control; human–AI collaboration, in turn, preserves accuracy while maintaining efficiency, achieving an organic integration of automation with professional discernment (Xu et al., 2023). For example,

Source text:

> That the court has not yet ruled on the admissibility of evidence in this case, and that some of the testimony may be excluded as hearsay, are issues which, while not currently determinable, may significantly affect the outcome of the trial.

The prompt wording is used exactly as in the above reference without modification.

The model's output is as follows (slightly edited):

> Step 1: Initial machine translation (English to Chinese)
> Initial translation produced by the model:
> 法院尚未就本案中证据的可采性作出裁决，部分证词可能因属于传闻证据而被排除，这些事项虽目前尚无法确定，但可能对审判结果产生重大影响。(The court has not yet ruled on the admissibility of the evidence in this case, and some testimony may be excluded as hearsay; although these matters cannot yet be determined, they may have a significant impact on the outcome of the trial).
> Step 2: Back translation (Chinese to English)
> The model back-translates the above Chinese version into English:
> The court has not yet decided whether the evidence is admissible in this case, and some of the testimony may be excluded as hearsay. These issues, although currently undetermined, may have a significant impact on the outcome of the trial.
> Step 3: Comparative analysis with the source text
> The model outputs the following difference analysis:
>
> - Changes in the core structure:

- The original uses a typical "formal subject + real subject" structure (That … are issues), emphasizing the structural integrity of the statement.
- The back translation splits it into two separate sentences, weakening the formality and logical cohesion of the original structure.

- Shift in tone:
  - In the original, "while not currently determinable" functions as a concessive adverbial, highlighting uncertainty, but in the back translation it is simplified to "although currently undetermined," weakening the tone.
  - "significantly affect" becomes "have a significant impact" in the back translation; although similar in meaning, the former better matches the customary legal phrasing for influencing a judgment.
- Evaluation of informational integrity:
  - No obvious additions, deletions, or omissions, but the diction is somewhat plain and fails to fully reproduce the rigorous and abstract register of the original legal context.

Step 4: Problem assessment and revision recommendations
Based on the above analysis, the model determines:
There are issues of structural simplification and tonal shift that require correction.
Step 5: Revised translation
The optimized translation is as follows:
尽管法院尚未就本案证据的可采性作出裁定，且部分证词可能因属于传闻证据而被排除，此类问题虽目前尚无法判定，但仍可能对案件的最终判决构成实质性影响。(Although the court has not yet ruled on the admissibility of evidence in this case, and some of the testimony may be excluded as hearsay, these matters, while currently indeterminate, may still exert a material effect on the final verdict.)
Step 6: Back-translate again and compare
Back-translate the revised Chinese into English:
Although the court has not yet made a ruling on the admissibility of the evidence in this case, and some testimony may be excluded as hearsay, such issues cannot be determined at present, but they may still have a substantial impact on the final judgment of the case.
Step 7: Final comparison and confirmation
The model outputs the confirmation conclusions:
The core structure has been restored to the "formal subject + real subject" pattern, and the back-translated version has a high degree of match with the original;

The concessive relationship is clearly preserved; "currently indeterminate" carries a more formal legal tone than "undetermined";
"exert a material effect" more closely aligns with the legal register of "significantly affect";
There is no information loss or semantic ambiguity.

This case illustrates that the Qwen3 model can autonomously perform back-translation and quality auditing, iteratively refine the translation in a cyclic fashion, and produce multi-stage processing outputs. This performance exceeds expectations and underscores the potential of large language models for proceduralized process orchestration and self-revision (Xu et al., 2023).

6 Applying Prompting Strategies to the English Translation of a Tang Poem

Classical poetry, as a highly compressed form, tests the translator's grasp of meaning and capacity to recreate emotional resonance, thereby placing greater demands on prompt design. In this section we take Du Mu's poem Farewell (the second of a paired set) as a case study. We integrate multiple prompting strategies—from literal rendering to stylistic recreation—to examine their systematic use in poetry translation. We conclude by presenting the dynamic co-creative process between translator and model. The original poem is as follows:

多情却似总无情, 唯觉尊前笑不成。
蜡烛有心还惜别, 替人垂泪到天明。

This image (Fig. 2) was generated by Jimeng AI (https://jimeng.jianying.com/) using the prompt: "Classical Chinese painting style. A lady in traditional attire sits alone on a mat; a guttering red candle on the table casts light on her profile. Downcast, she turns away from the viewer, her sleeves loosely draped, a wine vessel (*jiu zun*) set before her. Outside, the night is still, and wax 'tears' run down the candle. The poem is inscribed at the side: 多情却似总无情, 唯觉尊前笑不成。蜡烛有心还惜别, 替人垂泪到天明。("So full of feeling yet seeming without it; before the wine cup I cannot force a smile. The candle, as if it had a heart, still grieves at parting, shedding tears until dawn.").

The overall image is well executed; however, the accompanying text is garbled, and it incorrectly shows a wine bottle instead of a wine vessel *(jiu zun)*.

Fig. 2 AI-generated illustration of the poem

6.1 Translating Poetry: Challenges in Rendering Tang Verse

Poetry translation is widely regarded as one of the most demanding forms of language service. Accurate semantic transfer is only an initial hurdle; re-creating the poem's aesthetic, cultural resonance, and emotional force is far more difficult (Yang, 2010). Poetic language is compact, richly imagistic, and its rhythm and sound patterns help shape the overall effect. A purely literal transfer seldom captures layered meaning or emotional nuance. Translators (or translation systems) must continually negotiate a dynamic balance among meaning, form, and aesthetic effect (Zhao & Flotow, 2018).

Three principal strategies are typically distinguished: (1) literal translation, prioritizing structural and lexical equivalence for scholarly purposes; (2) free or sense-oriented translation, pursuing fluency and reader accessibility for broader dissemination; and (3) creative re-creation, aiming to reconstitute poetic atmosphere and aesthetic force in the target language. Representative figures illustrate these orientations: Ezra Pound foregrounded creative re-creation; Xu Yuanchong pursued the triad of "semantic beauty, musical beauty, and formal beauty"; annotation-oriented translators emphasize structural retention plus cultural elucidation (Fletcher, 1919; Wang, 1965). Strategy selection depends on audience and communicative setting. Accordingly, prompt design for large language models (LLMs) should likewise specify these objectives explicitly (Chen et al., 2024).

Tang poetry stands as the pinnacle of classical Chinese verse; its aesthetic force lies in strict prosody, a rich repertoire of imagery, and compressed emotional expression (Xia & Jing, 2018). Five- and seven-character regulated verse achieve musicality and cadence through tonal patterning, parallelism, and rhyme—elements central to their aesthetic impact. A primary obstacle is the structural disparity between Chinese prosody and English syllabic and syntactic organization, which impedes full reproduction of rhythm, parallelism, and tonal texture (Kwong, 2009). Equally fundamental is the fusion of scene and feeling within a cultivated poetic conception (*yijing*). Recurrent images—willows, the moon, wild geese—combine concrete reference with layered cultural resonance. They trigger rich associative networks for Chinese readers, whereas English translations often weaken affect and nuance owing to an absence of cultural framing or sparse annotation (Feng, 2022).

Translating Tang poetry poses three interrelated challenges: (1) extreme compression of imagery, emotion, and poetic conception resists full restitution in English; (2) the aesthetic force of prosody—rhythm, tonal patterning, parallelism—defies faithful replication, and partial imitation seldom approaches the source; and (3) culturally embedded references and historical allusions require mediation and force trade-offs between concision and annotation. No single approach can address all dimensions concurrently. Large language models (LLMs) offer combinable expressive modes and prompt configurations, enabling adaptive strategic shifts and the insertion of concise cultural explication to enhance fidelity and aesthetic resonance (Guan, 2024).

For both Tang verse and poetry more broadly, the core task extends beyond semantic transfer to the reconstruction of poetic experience and aesthetic effect in the target language. Effective prompt design that directs the model to balance imagery, affect, structure, and cultural framing is pivotal to improving translation quality.

6.2 *Progressive Literal-First Prompting*

In producing English versions of Tang poems, literal rendering is typically the foundation because it anchors surface semantics. Yet literal transfer alone rarely conveys evocative tension or cultural background. We therefore illustrate how progressively layered prompts—from shallow to deeper analytical focus—can strengthen a model's handling of meaning, cultural framing, and emotional coloration. Comparative review of successive outputs not only improves accuracy but also supplies translators with transparent insight into their evidential grounding and divergences. All large language model outputs in this section were generated with Qwen3.

1. Basic literal-translation prompt: focuses on surface meaning

   Prompt design:

> Please translate each of the following lines of Chinese poetry into English, line by line, aiming for faithful literal rendering. The target readers are native English speakers interested in poetic culture but unfamiliar with the cultural nuances of Chinese expressions.

At this level, the large language model's output shown below is still fairly rough, and some of its wording is hard to understand.

The deep-feeling ones always seem heartless at parting;
On the banquet, smiling is hard to achieve.
The candle on the table seems to have a heart,
Shedding tears for us until morning comes.

2. Keyword Prompts: Imagery Semantic Presets

Prompt design:

Translate each line of the Chinese poem below into English in a strictly literal, line-by-line manner. Preserve the basic lexical meaning and concrete imagery; do not add interpretation, smoothing, cultural background, or inferred emotion beyond what minimal English grammar requires. The intended readers are native English speakers interested in poetry but unfamiliar with cultural nuances in Chinese.
Use the following keyword/imagery notes only to guide wording; do not insert them into the translation unless explicitly instructed:

- 多情 (literally "richly feeling"): in classical Chinese poetry, denotes a deeply sensitive, tender, emotionally responsive disposition.
- 蜡烛有心 (literally "the candle has a heart"): a personification; the candle is imagined as sentient, aware of parting sorrow, its dripping wax likened to tears lasting until dawn—signifying reluctant, lingering separation.

With semantic presets for the core imagery established in advance, the model yielded the following English translation; its intelligibility seems modestly enhanced.

"Those with deep feelings appear indifferent when parting,
At the farewell banquet, smiles come with difficulty.
Even the candle seems sentimental,
Shedding tears on our behalf until dawn."

3. **Background Commentary for Translation: Context and Emotion Guidance**

The prompt below is based on background appreciation excerpts found online:

Please translate each of the above Tang poem(s) into English strictly word by word and line by line, striving to remain faithful to the literal sense of the original Chinese diction. The intended readers are native speakers of English who have an interest in Chinese poetry and culture but may not yet be familiar

with cultural nuances. You may draw on the following glossary notes and appreciation commentary as reference.
"多情": In classical Chinese poetry this denotes a person of abundant, delicately nuanced feeling—emotionally responsive, finely attuned, and inwardly sensitive.
"蜡烛有心": A personifying expression: the candle is imagined as having a "heart" (conscious sympathy), sensing the sorrow of parting and "weeping" (its melting wax) until dawn, symbolizing lingering attachment and reluctance to separate.
The poem takes leave-taking as its central theme, portraying the complex, restrained, and profound emotions at the moment of parting between the poet and the singing girl. The line "多情却似总无情" ("Overflowing with feeling, yet seeming utterly without feeling") reveals an extreme suppression of emotion and an inexpressible tenderness in the face of farewell. Throughout, the poem deftly employs personification, transferring the sorrow of parting onto the candle so that it, "having a heart," sheds silent "tears" until daybreak—an image of wordless longing and reluctant attachment. Its language is concise; its sentiment subtle and reserved. Through precise detail and the symbolic vehicle of objects, it achieves an elegant, lingering artistic resonance.

Once the appreciation commentary is supplied, the model gains a far stronger integrated understanding of the poem's situational context, emotional gradations, and craft techniques. The output below reflects finer nuance in recreating the poem's imaginative atmosphere, emotional progression, and verbal rhythm—signaling an initial shift toward poetic conveyance.

"Those deeply in love appear emotionless at parting—
Their feelings too profound to be expressed.
Even at the farewell banquet, smiles are hard to form.
The candle on the desk seems to understand,
Weeping for us in silence until the break of dawn."

It should be kept in mind that commentary-based prompts can sometimes push the model toward over-interpretation or factual/literal drift; consequently, the final version still requires the translator's own critical judgment plus a review for alignment with the translation brief.

6.3 Prompt Process for Interpreting Artistic Conception and Recasting Poetic Form

The language of Tang poetry is marked by extreme concision, symbolic density, and pronounced rhythmic design. A strictly literal, line-by-line rendering cannot convey its layered emotional strata or artistic force. Accordingly, we employ a chain-of-prompts strategy—"artistic conception interpretation → semantic recasting → poetic form reconstruction"—to guide the model from semantic grasp to stylistic re-creation, enabling the translation to balance substance and artistry and to resonate more fully with target-language readers.

The focus of this strategy suite is a staged progression: progressive semantic clarification → back-translation verification → multi-style poetic recasting. Together these form an integrated chain—pre-translation comprehension, in-process confirmation, and creative rendering—that, within a human–AI co-creative environment, maximizes the artistic potential of Tang poetry translation.

Step 1: Vernacular Paraphrase and Literal English Translation.

We first prompt the model to paraphrase the poem in contemporary vernacular Chinese, then translate that paraphrase into concise, fluent English, prioritizing the narrative thread, emotional tenor, and core imagery.

Sample design:

For the given Tang poem, focus on the core meaning and emotional tone. Use modern vernacular Chinese as an intermediate layer to produce a faithful, fluent English version.

Model-generated vernacular paraphrase:

Our bond was once deep, yet at parting we appeared indifferent. At the banquet I wished to smile but could not. The candle on the table seemed to share our feeling, lingering in reluctant farewell and weeping for us until dawn.

At this stage, an existing human-produced vernacular paraphrase can be inserted, and the process can proceed directly to the literal English stage. For poems with intricate imagery and archaic diction, a large model lacking Classical Chinese knowledge may misread the text. The following vernacular version is from Baidu Baike.

聚首如胶似漆，作别时却像无情，只觉得在酒席上想笑却笑不出来。案头的蜡烛似乎也有感情，它依依不舍地惜别，你看，它替我们流泪，一直流到天亮。(This paraphrase literally means "Coming together is like glue and lacquer; when we part, however, it seems as if we are without feeling. I only feel that at the wine table I want to laugh yet cannot manage a laugh. The candle on the desk seems also to have feelings: it lingers, unwilling to let us go—look, it is shedding tears for us, and keeps on shedding them until daybreak.")

After producing the vernacular paraphrase, prompt the model for a direct English rendering with wording such as:

Translate the following modern Chinese interpretation into fluent and clear English. Focus on preserving the emotional tone and key imagery.

Model output:

Though we were so close, we seemed distant at parting.
At the farewell banquet, I wanted to smile but couldn't.
The candle on the table seemed to feel our sorrow.
It shed tears for us all night long.

This version provides a plain, faithful base that supports subsequent stylistic reconstruction.

Step 2: Back-Translation into Chinese to Assess Preservation of Poetic Sense

After completing the initial literal English version, we back-translate it into modern Chinese to check whether the core artistic conception and imagery are retained. This enables iterative refinement with the model and helps the translator detect omissions or deviations early. Sample prompt:

Please translate the above English version back into modern vernacular Chinese and assess whether the poem's emotions and imagery have been preserved.

Sample output:

虽然我们曾亲密无间, 但临别时却好像彼此疏远。
在离别的酒席上, 我想笑却笑不出来。

桌上的蜡烛似乎也感受到了我们的离情,
它替我们流泪,整夜不停。
(Although we were once inseparable, at the moment of parting we see'med distant.
At the farewell banquet I wanted to smile yet could not.
The candle on the table seemed to sense our sorrow at separation,
Shedding tears for us the whole night through).

The results show that key emotional and imagistic elements—such as "overflowing feeling yet seeming without feeling" and the "candle weeping"—are preserved. Thus the literal version has reached a sufficient baseline of semantic fidelity for stylistic reconstruction, and further adjustment may be unnecessary. If one differs in interpretation, additional refinement remains possible. While back-translation cannot replace human editorial review, iterative, fine-grained back-translation and cross-checking between Chinese and English can deepen understanding of complex imagery.

Step 3: Nativization and Poetic Recasting (Stylistic Emulations: Shakespearean and Whitmanesque)

This stage is the core of the process: it emphasizes transforming the Chinese poetic sense into forms compatible with Anglophone poetic traditions. By imitating established styles, we enhance cultural familiarity and aesthetic resonance, giving the translation a more native poetic cadence and literary value. Prompts are issued in English with style notes and examples.

Step 3: Nativization and Poetic Recasting (Stylistic Emulations: Shakespearean and Whitmanesque)

This stage is central to the overall strategy: it focuses on transforming the poetic sensibility of the Chinese source into forms consistent with Anglophone poetic traditions. Through style emulation, it enhances cultural familiarity and aesthetic resonance, yielding a more native reading experience and greater literary value. Prompts are provided in English, with stylistic notes and examples.

1. Sample Prompt for Shakespearean Emulation

Goal:
Translate the given classical Chinese poem into an English poem in the style of William Shakespeare. Focus on reproducing the emotional depth and metaphorical elegance of the original, while expressing it through Elizabethan poetic conventions.
Style Definition:
Shakespearean poetry often uses iambic pentameter, inverted word order, and rich classical metaphors. The tone is elevated, often employing words like *thou*,

thy, *dost*, and *ere*. The imagery is dramatic, and the language densely packed with emotional contrasts and rhetorical flourishes.
Style Sample:
From Shakespeare's *Sonnet 30*:
"When to the sessions of sweet silent thought,
I summon up remembrance of things past,
I sigh the lack of many a thing I sought,
And with old woes new wail my dear time's waste."
Please adopt a similar tone and rhythm in your translation.

Model-generated sample (retained verbatim):

When hearts do part, they cloak their tender core,
A smile withheld at parting's solemn hour.
The candle weeps beside the silent door,
Its flame a soul, with tears a drooping flower.

This rendering uses a sonnet-like cadence and preserves symbols such as the restrained smile and the weeping candle, thereby evoking the source's ineffable emotional depth.

2. Sample Prompt for Whitmanesque Emulation

Goal:
Translate the given classical Chinese poem into an English poem in the style of Walt Whitman. Preserve the emotional essence and imagery, while expressing it through free verse and expansive, flowing language.
Style Definition:
Whitman's poetry uses long lines, free verse, and anaphora (repetition). He writes with naturalistic imagery, colloquial tone, and celebrates the human experience with a philosophical undertone. The tone is often democratic, bold, and deeply emotional.
Style Sample:
From *Leaves of Grass*:
"I lean and loafe at my ease observing a spear of summer grass.
My tongue, every atom of my blood, form'd from this soil, this air,
Born here of parents born here from parents the same…".
Try to echo this style in your poetic translation of the Chinese original.

Model-generated sample (retained verbatim):

We sat together, wordless, unable to smile—
Though we had shared joy, the moment of parting was quiet.
The candle stood with us, glowing gently,
Its wax flowed down, slowly, as if mourning with us.

This version is more colloquial in diction, gentle in tone, and rich in detail, making it suitable for a contemporary, emotion-oriented readership. Readers are also encouraged to devise and test prompts for additional styles. Below is Prof. Xu Yuanchong's translation (Xu, 2021):

Deep, deep our love, too deep to show;
Deep, deep we drink; silent we grow.
The candle grieves to see us part:
It melts in tears with burnt-out heart.

Stylized transcreation expands the expressive horizons of Tang poetry within the target culture. Each poetic style is rooted in a distinct aesthetic tradition: by drawing on Shakespeare's meter and dramatic tension, Whitman's free verse and emotional flow, or Tagore's Eastern imagery and spiritual contemplation, the translator evokes aesthetic resonance among target audiences. This mode of transcreation transcends linguistic constraints and grants Tang poetry renewed cultural vitality, enabling diverse forms of expression and interpretation across aesthetic systems.

During the process, the translator moves beyond a purely faithful intermediary role and becomes a second author, actively shaping the work. Through a creative lens, classical poetic meaning is integrated into contemporary contexts, fostering the poem's cross-cultural renewal. Stylized transcreation thus demonstrates professional competence and serves as a key practice of cultural recreation.

For language service practitioners pursuing poetic publication, literary re-presentation, or cross-cultural dissemination, stylized transcreation offers broad scope for the contemporary circulation and reinterpretation of Tang poetry. The process may involve partial shifts of meaning or symbolic estrangement; this plasticity constitutes its artistic appeal. Balancing fidelity and innovation is the central challenge and the principal value of transcreation.

7 Conclusion

This chapter operationalizes the shift to human–LLM co-translation by unpacking a layered workflow toolbox rather than merely declaring a paradigm change. It enumerates prompt-engineered mechanisms—Translate–Estimate–Refine (TEaR) self-auditing loop, standards-first plus feedback refinement, preventive risk checklists, multi-version generation, simulated adjudication and version fusion—that expand a single linear pass into iterative evidence-seeking cycles. Lexical and knowledge control is systematized through pre-translation detection and categorization of terminology, named entities, idioms, culture-loaded items, neologisms, euphemism and negativity, using structured schemas that support downstream governance and retrieval-augmented prompting. For structurally complex discourse the chapter contrasts structure-oriented parsing, meaning decomposition, comprehend–decompose–reconstruct–polish sequencing, backbone-first and inside-out assembly, role-based (linguist/translator/editor/subject expert) collaboration, and back-translation driven QA for uncovering latent semantic drift. Long-sentence strategies, error-prevention heuristics, and two-pass reasoning (sense explanation then rendering) illustrate micro-level controllability. A Tang poem case study demonstrates progressive literal anchoring, semantic elaboration, stylistic diversification and transcreative fusion. Competency implications encompass prompt design literacy, evaluative reasoning, terminology and data stewardship, orchestration of heterogeneous models, and ethical accountability. The chapter ultimately proposes a multi-layer architecture coupling automated generation, diagnostic analytics, retrieval, self-critique and targeted human intervention for transparent, auditable, continuously optimized translation quality, driving sustainable innovation and measurable performance gains.

References

Appicharla, R., Gain, B., Pal, S., & Ekbal, A. (2025). Beyond the sentence: A survey on context-aware machine translation with large language models. https://arxiv.org/abs/2506.07583

Baker, M. (2018). *In other Words: A coursebook on translation.* Routledge.

Bellos, D. (2011). *Is That a Fish in Your ear?: Translation and the meaning of everything.* Macmillan.

Bowker, L. (2015). *Terminology and translation* (Vol. 1, No. 1, pp. 304–323). Amsterdam/Philadelphia: John Benjamins.

Briakou, E., Luo, J., Cherry, C., & Freitag, M. (2024). *Translating step-by-step: Decomposing the translation process for improved translation quality of long-form texts.* https://arxiv.org/abs/2409.06790

Briva-Iglesias, V. (2024). *Fostering human-centered, augmented machine translation: Analysing interactive post-editing* [Doctoral dissertation, Dublin City University] https://www.researchgate.net/publication/382766689_Fostering_human-centered_augmented_machine_translation_Analysing_interactive_post-editing

Brown, T., Mann, B., Ryder, N., Subbiah, M., Kaplan, J., Dhariwal, P., & Amodei, D. (2020). Language models are few-shot learners. *Advances in Neural Information Processing Systems, 33*, 1877–1901.

Chen, B., Zhang, Z., Langrené, N., & Zhu, S. (2025). Unleashing the potential of prompt engineering for large language models. *Patterns.* https://doi.org/10.1016/j.patter.2025.100001

Chen, A., Lou, L., Chen, K., Bai, X., Xiang, Y., Yang, M., & Zhang, M. (2024). *Large language models for classical Chinese poetry translation: Benchmarking, evaluating, and improving.* https://arxiv.org/abs/2408.09945

Chesterman, A. (2016). *Memes of translation.* John Benjamins.

Conia, S., Lee, D., Li, M., Minhas, U. F., Potdar, S., & Li, Y. (2024). *Towards cross-cultural machine translation with retrieval-augmented generation from multilingual knowledge graphs*. https://arxiv.org/abs/2410.14057

Feng, Z., Zhang, Y., Li, H., Wu, B., Liao, J., Liu, W., & Liu, Z. (2024). *TEaR: Improving LLM-based machine translation with systematic self-refinement*. https://arxiv.org/abs/2402.16379

Feng, Q. (2022). Translating seven types of ambiguity in classical Chinese poetry. *International Journal of Chinese and English Translation & Interpreting*.

Fletcher, W. J. B. (Ed.). (1919). *Gems of Chinese verse*. Commercial Press.

Forcada, M. L. (2017). Making sense of neural machine translation. *Translation Spaces, 6*(2), 291–309.

Ghazvininejad, M., Gonen, H., & Zettlemoyer, L. (2023). *Dictionary-based phrase-level prompting of large language models for machine translation*. https://arxiv.org/abs/2302.07856.

Guan, X. (2024). A bard is born: A new era of poetry translation by ChatGPT-4. *Translation Review, 120*(1), 23–39.

Iyer, V., Chen, P., & Birch, A. (2023). *Towards effective disambiguation for machine translation with large language models*. https://arxiv.org/abs/2309.11668

Jiao, W., Wang, W., Huang, J. T., Wang, X., Shi, S., & Tu, Z. (2023). *Is ChatGPT a good translator? Yes with GPT-4 as the engine*. https://arxiv.org/abs/2301.08745

Katan, D., & Taibi, M. (2021). *Translating cultures: An introduction for translators, interpreters and mediators*. Routledge.

Koby, G. S., Fields, P., Hague, D. R., Lommel, A., & Melby, A. (2014). Defining translation quality. *Tradumàtica, 12*, 413–420. https://doi.org/10.5565/rev/tradumatica.76

Koehn, P. (2020). *Neural machine translation*. Cambridge University Press. https://doi.org/10.1017/9781108608480

Kwong, C. (2009). Translating classical Chinese poetry into rhymed English: A linguistic-aesthetic view. *TTR, 22*(1), 189–220.

Lefevere, A. (2016). *Translation, rewriting, and the manipulation of literary fame*. Routledge.

Lefevere, A. (2002). *Translation/history/culture: A sourcebook*. Routledge.

Lew, R. (2024). Dictionaries and lexicography in the AI era. *Humanities and Social Sciences Communications, 11*(1), 1–8. https://doi.org/10.1057/s41599-024-02889-7

Li, Z., Qu, D., Xie, C., Zhang, W., & Li, Y. (2020). Language model pre-training method in machine translation based on named entity recognition. *International Journal on Artificial Intelligence Tools, 29*(07n08), 2040021. https://doi.org/10.1142/S0218213020400217

Lu, H., Yang, H., Huang, H., Zhang, D., Lam, W., & Wei, F. (2023). *Chain-of-dictionary prompting elicits translation in large language models*. https://arxiv.org/abs/2305.06575

Madaan, A., Tandon, N., Gupta, P., Hallinan, S., Gao, L., Wiegreffe, S., & Clark, P. (2023). Self-refine: Iterative refinement with self-feedback. In *Advances in Neural Information Processing Systems, 36* (pp. 46534–46594). https://proceedings.neurips.cc/paper_files/paper/2023/file/91edff07232fb1b55a505a9e9f6c0ff3-Paper-Conference.pdf

Mondal, S. K., Zhang, H., Kabir, H. D., Ni, K., & Dai, H. N. (2023). Machine translation and its evaluation: A study. *Artificial Intelligence Review, 56*(9), 10137–10226. https://doi.org/10.1007/s10462-023-10423-5

Munday, J., Pinto, S. R., & Blakesley, J. (2022). *Introducing translation studies: Theories and applications*. Routledge.

Nguyen, L., & Xu, Y. (2025). Reasoning for translation: Comparative analysis of chain-of-thought and tree-of-thought prompting for LLM translation. In *ACL 2025 Student Research Workshop*. https://doi.org/10.18653/v1/2025.acl-srw.17

Qian, M., & Kong, C. (2024, May). Enabling human-centered machine translation using concept-based large language model prompting and translation memory. In *International Conference on Human-Computer Interaction* (pp. 118–134). Cham: Springer Nature Switzerland. https://doi.org/10.1007/978-3-031-60615-1_8

Shreve, G. M., & Angelone, E. (Eds.). (2010). *Translation and cognition*. John Benjamins Publishing Company.

Vatsal, S., Dubey, H., & Singh, A. (2025). *Multilingual prompt engineering in large language models: A survey across NLP tasks.* https://arxiv.org/abs/2505.11665

Venuti, L. (2017). *The translator's invisibility: A history of translation.* Routledge.

Wang, J. C. (1965). Ezra Pound as a translator of classical Chinese poetry. *The Sewanee Review, 73*(3), 345–357.

Wang, S., Sun, X., Li, X., Ouyang, R., Wu, F., Zhang, T., & Wang, G. (2023). *GPT-NER: Named entity recognition via large language models.* https://arxiv.org/abs/2304.10428

Wei, J., Wang, X., Schuurmans, D., Bosma, M., Xia, F., Chi, E., & Zhou, D. (2022). Chain-of-thought prompting elicits reasoning in large language models. *Advances in Neural Information Processing Systems, 35*, 24824–24837.

Xia, C., & Jing, Z. (2018). English translation of classical Chinese poetry. *Orbis Litterarum, 73*(4), 361–373. https://doi.org/10.1111/oli.12184

Xu, H., Kim, Y. J., Sharaf, A., & Awadalla, H. H. (2023). A paradigm shift in machine translation: Boosting translation performance of large language models. https://arxiv.org/abs/2309.11674

Xu, Y. (Trans. & annot.). (2021). Three *hundred Tang poems* (Vol. 2, Chinese–English bilingual ed.). China Translation & Publishing House.

Yamada, M. (2023). Optimizing machine translation through prompt engineering: An investigation into ChatGPT's customizability. https://arxiv.org/abs/2308.01391

Yang, L. (2010). Cultural loss in the English translation of Chinese poetry. *Babel, 56*(2), 168–185. https://doi.org/10.1075/babel.56.2.05liu

Yang, X., Zhan, R., Wong, D. F., Wu, J., & Chao, L. S. (2023). Human-in-the-loop machine translation with large language model. https://arxiv.org/abs/2310.08908

Yim, J. (2024). Sentence length and translation: A comparative review of human, NMT, and LLM translations. *T&I Review, 14*(1), 69–93.

Zhang, J., Zhao, X., & Doherty, S. (2025). Prompt engineering in translation: How do student translators leverage GenAI tools for translation tasks. *Proceedings of 20th Machine Translation Summit–Translators and Users* (pp. 112–125).

Zhao, G., & Flotow, L. V. (2018). Translating iconicities of classical Chinese poetry. *Semiotica, 2018*(224), 19–44.

Chapter 7
Fine-Tuning Large Language Models for Translation Services

Abstract This chapter examines how fine-tuning converts the broad but shallowly specialized capabilities of general large language models into controllable performance for professional translation services. It frames translation and related tasks (lexical annotation, terminology handling, stylistic rendering) as structured, multi-stage decision pipelines rather than unconstrained text generation. Parameter-efficient techniques (e.g., Low-Rank Adaptation, quantization) enable cost-effective adaptation of 7B–32B models while balancing privacy and deployment trade-offs. Two signature case studies—full lexical annotation plus vernacular translation of Classical Chinese, and low-resource Tangut translation via four-line alignment and dictionary sense enumeration—demonstrate that chaining subtasks (annotation → literal rendering → idiomatic rendering) and constraining choices markedly reduce hallucinations and improve consistency even with small curated datasets. The chapter emphasizes deliberate data engineering: schema design (prompt/input/output separation), structured JSON formats, contrastive and staged samples, expert–model iterative loops, and governance for quality, compliance, and updates. Evaluation shifts from generic overlap metrics to task-specific behavioral rubrics and structural format integrity. Fine-tuning is justified when tasks decompose into bounded decision spaces; otherwise prompt design or few-shot methods may suffice. Overall, structured fine-tuning operationalizes expert knowledge, enhances controllability, and supports capability transfer to low-resource scripts while acknowledging limits in highly creative scenarios.

Although general large language models (LLMs) possess broad cross-domain capabilities, they still exhibit limitations in handling specialized terminology, domain knowledge structures, and distinctive textual styles (Bommasani et al., 2021; Team G et al., 2023; Lu et al., 2025). Fine-tuning entails retraining the models on domain-specific data, thereby improving professional translation quality, stylistic control, safety, and compliance (Li et al., 2024; Saunders, 2020). By integrating linguistic insight with artificial intelligence, fine-tuning enables LLMs to meet the diverse demands of real-world language services more effectively (Bommasani et al., 2021).

J. S. Yu and Y. Yao, *Intelligent Language Services*,
https://doi.org/10.1007/978-981-95-4632-9_7

1 Fine-Tuning Large Language Models

LLMs are widely employed in multilingual translation, yet their handling of technical terminology, stylistic control, and cross-language consistency remains constrained by the coverage and generalization limits of pre-training corpora (Nair et al., 2024; Saunders, 2020). Fine-tuning has therefore become a primary method to overcome these constraints and deepen domain specialization. It entails retraining the base model on annotated, domain-specific datasets so it can respond more precisely to task requirements. Fine-tuned models typically deliver higher accuracy and flexibility in terminology management, style adaptation, and domain-sensitive expression and are now common in translation, authoring, dialogue, and related language services.

In operational translation workflows, technical terms and industry expressions are often rendered inaccurately because generic models lack sufficient in-domain data; targeted fine-tuning directly addresses this deficiency (Fan et al., 2021). It also supports flexible adaptation across language pairs, domains, and styles, enabling highly personalized and specialized output. Implementation requires balancing model size against available hardware resources. Medium models (7B–13B parameters) suit local inference and lightweight deployment, whereas larger models (tens of billions of parameters or more) generally require high-performance Graphics Processing Units (GPUs) (e.g., NVIDIA A100/H100), with proportional increases in resource use and training time. Recent parameter-efficient methods—such as Low-Rank Adaptation (LoRA) and quantization—have lowered computational barriers yet still impose nontrivial hardware demands (Dettmers et al., 2023; Hu et al., 2022; Nair et al., 2024).

During inference, long inputs are prone to semantic drift and reduced consistency; segmenting long passages mitigates these effects and improves output quality. For users with limited local compute, cloud Application Programming Interfaces (APIs) facilitate enterprise-scale deployment but introduce cost–privacy trade-offs and are thus better suited to real-time scenarios without sensitive content.

In practice, parameter-efficient fine-tuning of 7B–32B models has become a mainstream enterprise strategy, balancing cost, deployment effort, and translation quality (Dettmers et al., 2023). For example, Alibaba's Qwen-MT, released in July 2025 (https://qwenlm.github.io/blog/qwen-mt/), supports translation across 92 languages and integrates terminology intervention, domain prompting, and memory bank features. It performs strongly in professional settings but sacrifices some general capabilities such as rich multi-turn dialogue. Consequently, practitioners must choose among (1) domain-specialized translation models, (2) large general-purpose models, and (3) targeted fine-tuning of general models according to task needs, cost constraints, and deployment context.

Fine-tuning also offers a pathway for low-resource languages and specialized tasks. Even limited, targeted fine-tuning can compensate for gaps in general models within niche domains (Fan et al., 2021; Liang et al., 2025). However, it is not optimal for every translation scenario: many routine needs are met efficiently through well-engineered prompts and few-shot learning without substantial data or computational resources. Because fine-tuning incurs costs for data curation and ongoing evaluation, decisions should weigh task scale, type, and budget.

The core objective of fine-tuning is not maximizing data volume but enabling the model to execute structured, controllable translation workflows accurately (Li et al., 2024). Subsequent discussion of data construction and prompt design rests on a precise understanding of task structure and process logic. The following sections present two complex cases—the full annotation and translation of classical texts and the translation of Tangut (*Xixia*) materials—to illustrate structured decomposition and implementation of intricate translation workflows. These cases originate from the Peking University Handian Zhiyuan Digital Humanities Team (hereafter "Peking University Team") and serve as reference models for task design and model innovation in professional language services.

1.1 Full Annotation and Translation of Classical Texts

The task "Full Annotation and Translation of Classical Texts" draws on editorial experience from the Sanquan series published by Zhonghua Book Company (Wu, 2025). Its aim is to provide classical texts with systematic lexical annotation and vernacular (modern Chinese) translation. This extends far beyond direct linguistic conversion; it must integrate historical context, cultural connotations, and interpretive knowledge. The workflow comprises two stages: (1) lexical annotation addressing semantic shifts between classical and modern usage and (2) vernacular translation for contemporary readers. Executing both efficiently and accurately remains challenging for LLMs.

The principal difficulty in lexical annotation lies in tracing semantic evolution from classical to modern usage. Classical vocabulary differs markedly from modern Chinese in syntax, usage, and cultural context, creating comprehension barriers (Li, 2023). Effective annotation precisely identifies problematic terms, consults authoritative classical Chinese dictionaries, and formulates context-sensitive explanations to ensure accuracy and readability. A common three-step pipeline comprises (1) automatic detection of candidate terms, (2) extraction of candidate definitions from multiple classical dictionaries, and (3) generation of the final note using contextual and lexicographic evidence. While LLMs assist in drafting definitions, the risk of hallucinations and historical inaccuracies keep the first two stages primarily programmatic and knowledge base–driven (Li et al., 2025).

Vernacular translation demands holistic control of the entire classical passage—preserving the original spirit while maintaining argument, style, and cultural resonance (Zhao et al., 2025). The process is not sentence-by-sentence literalism but paragraph- and discourse-level comprehension and reformulation. The output must reproduce original logic and rhetoric while aligning with modern reading habits and cognitive expectations (Wu et al., 2024). Some contexts additionally require introductory paragraph notes on author, genre, and intellectual background. For certain poetic or literary texts, evaluative and aesthetic commentary is also needed, placing higher demands on the model's cross-domain knowledge integration.

In practice, the "full annotation and translation" workflow typically proceeds through staged, incremental phases (Guo et al., 2023). The model is first trained or prompted for lexical selection and annotation, then extended to sentence and paragraph comprehension and translation, and finally to higher-level tasks such as introductory explanations and evaluative appreciation. This combination of fine-tuning and chained task structuring enables local optimization at each stage and improves overall quality. Fine-tuning is particularly valuable for adapting to textual nuance, historical context, and cultural elements across diverse classical works, mitigating misinterpretation and distortion characteristic of one-size-fits-all general models (Zeng et al., 2023).

At its core, the system for preparing and publishing classical texts is a highly systematized, staged, and interdisciplinary workflow (Wang et al., 2025a, b). Through fine-tuning and process decomposition, large language models can improve performance across annotation, translation, introductory explanation, and critical appreciation, achieving the dual aims of academic reliability and publication suitability.

1.2 Translation of Tangut Texts

Tangut, a script lost for centuries, was structurally influenced by Chinese characters yet evolved its own grammar, lexicon, and expressive conventions (Huo, 2013; Kwanten, 1989; Shi, 2020). Machine translation is especially challenging because publicly available data are scarce and existing knowledge relies heavily on manual expert curation (Sun, 2023). Scholars typically employ a "four-line alignment" method: (1) the Tangut original, (2) candidate pronunciations and meanings for each character, (3) a word-for-word gloss preserving source order, and (4) a fluent modern Chinese translation. This staged representation guides training of large language models and task decomposition (Downes, 2018).

The Peking University Team conducted an exploratory effort to apply LLMs to Tangut machine translation (Department of Chinese Language and Literature, Peking University, 2024). Their experiments fine-tune expert-annotated four-line parallel data; however, unlike conventional scholarly practice, the second line mechanically enumerates every dictionary sense drawn from Tangut–Chinese lexica and leaves semantic disambiguation to the model and downstream steps. This design focuses the model on choosing and composing senses, reduces hallucination risk, and preserves as much original information as possible.

The Tangut translation workflow is partitioned into two subtasks: structural reconstruction (literal translation) and fluent expression (idiomatic rendering). Structured prompts explicitly signal which subtask is active: during the literal phase, the model assembles the most plausible sense for each character in source order; during the idiomatic phase, it synthesizes clause-level meaning and context to produce a natural rendering. Because the fine-tuned model selects and combines only from existing gloss inventories, it avoids fabricating senses while improving controllability and domain reliability. Even without truly "reading" Tangut characters, the annotation framework plus expert logic supports high-quality output (Zheng & Yu, 2025).

Designing the fine-tuning task chain is crucial. Idiomatic translation typically requires refinement beyond the literal rendering to approximate the source meaning accurately. A key question is whether to generate the idiomatic version directly from lexical annotations or to reason through staged "annotation → literal rendering → idiomatic rendering" steps. Adapting a Chain-of-Thought (CoT) approach—prompting the model to perform annotation, then literal translation, then idiomatic translation—can markedly increase reasoning transparency and output quality (Yang et al., 2024). Empirical fine-tuning studies must determine which configuration performs best.

Work on Tangut machine translation advances the digital reconstruction of lost languages and offers a new paradigm for processing extremely low-resource languages. Collaboration between expert knowledge and models shows that ancient languages can be "revived" in the intelligent era. This experience provides valuable guidance for the digital preservation and reuse of other endangered or historical languages.

1.3 The Value of Fine-Tuning Large Models

The value of fine-tuning large models lies in converting broad pretrained capabilities into precise control over specific language service tasks. The classical text annotation–translation workflow and Tangut translation differ in audience and application, yet they share strong commonalities in task decomposition, data construction, and model design. Practice shows that for complex professional language services, a simple "instruction + input" setup rarely yields stable, controllable, high-quality output (Zhu et al. 2024). Fine-tuning's core contribution is to partition the task into structured stages so the model focuses on constrained decisions and rule-governed execution rather than unconstrained generation or subjective inference (Moslem et al., 2023; Zeng et al., 2023).

Fine-tuning is often applied to small- and medium-parameter models whose lower resource footprint and deployment flexibility suit customization (Wang et al., 2023a, b). By decomposing and tuning chained subtasks, the model shifts from a purely "creative generator" to a "structured executor," making decisions under explicit inputs, constraints, and feedback. This substantially reduces hallucinations and misjudgments while better meeting professional quality requirements.

This task-chain decomposition improves per-step accuracy and facilitates training, evaluation, and data accumulation (Zhu & Chen, 2023). Each stage can collect data, train, and be tested independently, making project progress more efficient and transferable. Complex tasks in medicine, law, and education can likewise achieve incremental capability gains through similar staged fine-tuning (Liu & Xie, 2023). Consequently, industry practice often emphasizes fine-tuning small and medium models that are easier to engineer and adapt to evolving business needs.

Fine-tuning cannot solve every language task. Scenarios demanding high stylistic nuance, creativity, and expressive diversity can seldom be met solely by structured fine-tuning of smaller models. Such tasks typically also rely on large-parameter models' broader knowledge, richer few-shot exemplars, and carefully engineered prompts. Ultimate capability depends on balancing structural understanding with generative breadth, not merely on stacking more parameters.

Ultimately, the effectiveness of fine-tuning hinges on how clearly and controllably the task structure is defined. When real needs can be decomposed into "bounded input judgment → constrained output" steps, fine-tuned small and medium models can still satisfy most professional scenarios. This strategy underlies the classical text and Tangut cases and furnishes a solid methodological basis for future automated and customized language services.

2 Training Data for Fine-Tuning

Data preparation—particularly organization and format design—is central to successful fine-tuning. For LLMs, the most common format is a structured input–output pair that clearly separates the source content from the expected response. In translation tasks, pairing source and target facilitates precise learning of the mapping. In practice, carefully crafted prompts that label task type or output style before the input increase controllability and enhance adaptability across scenarios after fine-tuning. The output format should mirror the target application: whether sentence- or paragraph-level, keep the structure concise and explicit for downstream invocation and integration.

2.1 Format and Structure of Fine-Tuning Data

When fine-tuning LLMs, data format choices affect training efficiency and effectively set the upper bound of attainable capability. The model learns by approximating human linguistic decisions through repeated paired input–output mappings in context. Accordingly, all task data should employ a structured, consistent format to ensure stability and reproducibility.

A typical data sample comprises three parts: the prompt, the input content, and the expected output. The prompt conveys operational instructions, specifying the task (e.g., "produce a translation," "provide lexical annotation," "rewrite in professional style"). For complex tasks, it should also describe input and output formatting so the model parses and responds to each task type correctly.

The input portion carries the concrete text or background information. In translation, inputs may include the source text plus optional supporting resources such as a glossary, contextual hints, or reference outputs. For multi-layered inputs, explicit labels or field delimiters improve organization and help the model extract salient information (Wang, Zhang et al., 2023a, b).

The expected output is the human-validated target text against which optimization occurs. It may be continuous natural language or a structured format (e.g., tagged text, JSON objects, multi-field records), depending on application needs. Output structure should strictly align with prompt specifications to minimize format drift and preserve controllability and consistency in deployment.


```
{
"prompt": "Please choose the sense that best fits the context from the provided definitions; no explanation is needed.",
"input": {
"original_text": ""Defeated in war and destroyed—indeed, it was unavoidable." (From Su Xun's On the Six States
)",
"candidate_definitions": {
"诚": [
"(Of intention) genuine.",
"Indeed; certainly.",
"Marks a hypothetical relation, equivalent to 'if'.",
"Single-minded resolve.",
"The real situation; true feelings.",
"To make (someone) sincere; to render devoted.",
"(Chéng) a surname."
]
}
},
"output": {"selected_definition": "Indeed; certainly."}
}
```

A standardized training sample should include all three components with consistent encoding. JSON has become the mainstream engineering format because it supports batch processing and downstream automation. For example, a lexical selection task in classical text annotation can be structured as shown above. The schema clearly conveys task intent and separates input from output, aiding both model training and system integration. At scale, it also facilitates scripted validation, spot quality checks, and format compliance auditing.

2.2 Prompt Design for Fine-Tuning Training Data

Prompts for fine-tuning large language models (LLMs) should be clear, stable, and consistent across all training samples. For structured tasks with strict output specifications, a fixed prompt establishes a uniform pattern of behavior and reduces variance caused by wording changes (Longpre et al., 2023). In contrast with conversational use, structured tasks emphasize prompt consistency and standardization.

- The task description should be concise and precise, and should state the required action directly—for example: "Translate the following Classical Chinese passage into modern vernacular and provide lexical annotations." Elaborate framing is unnecessary.
- Maintain a uniform structure. Regardless of variation in task content, the core prompt template should remain constant, changing only task-specific and contextual information. In practice, the prompt can be partitioned into a fixed component (role, objective, output requirements) and a variable component (injected task materials).
- Specify input and output formats explicitly. The prompt should identify the input type and the expected output format—for example, "Return the result in JSON with the fields \"translation\" and \"notes\""—to support downstream system integration (Fu et al., 2024).

In professional translation and knowledge annotation workflows, enforcing a prescribed structured format is fundamental to automation and system integration, especially in large-scale or publication-grade settings. Using a unified data format such as JSON enhances data operability, enables efficient interoperability and extensibility across systems, and significantly strengthens control and engineering reliability.

For lexical annotation of Classical Chinese, we perform exhaustive segmentation: every sentence is decomposed into all contiguous character n-grams. For example, the four-character idiom "刻舟求剑" ("Kezhou qiujian", carving the boat to seek the sword) is represented by its single characters ("刻"/carve, "舟"/boat, "求"/seek, "剑"/sword), its multi-character substrings (e.g., "刻舟"/carve-boat, "舟求"/boat-seek, "求剑"/seek-sword"), and the full expression itself. Multiple definitions from authoritative dictionaries and specialized philological reference works are then linked to each candidate lexical unit. The model's task is to determine, using context and reference works, which words in the passage most warrant annotation.

A structured sample of the training data (abridged) is provided below:

```
{
  "instruction": "You are a specialist in Classical Chinese, proficient in interpreting texts from the pre-Qin through the Ming and Qing periods. Based on the source passage and the reference materials, select the lexical items that require annotation. Reasons for selection may include: semantic obscurity, differences between ancient and modern meanings, special grammatical structures, allusive usage, or cultural/historical background factors. These items play a relatively important role in enabling the target readers to understand this passage. Output strictly in JSON format and list the words requiring annotation.",
  "input": {
    "original_text": "The Master said: To study and regularly review what one has learned—is it not a pleasure? When friends come from afar—is it not a joy? If people do not understand me yet I do not resent it—is that not being a gentleman?",
    "reference": { ......
      "说": ["Interchangeable with '悦': pleased, delighted.", "To explain; to clarify.", "To narrate; to state." ],
      "朋": [ "Friend; like-minded associate.", "Member of the same school or category.", "To form factions; to gang together." ], ......
    }
  },
  "output": {
    "words_to_annotate": [ ......
      {"word": "说"},
      {"word": "朋"}, ......
    ]
  }
}
```

3 Acquiring and Cleaning Training Data

The effectiveness of fine-tuning large language models hinges on the structure, content quality, and task alignment of the training data. Unlike the simple accumulation of raw corpora, fine-tuning relies on deliberately engineered "task samples" that capture the model's target behavior within a defined application context. Dataset construction is not simple text harvesting; it is a goal-driven engineering workflow—in effect a form of "language behavior engineering." Whereas pre-training draws on vast generic corpora, fine-tuning uses highly customized datasets that must align precisely in content, format, and function with the specific task (Singhal et al., 2023).

Designing high-quality fine-tuning data must jointly account for the faithful reconstruction of expert knowledge, structural rigor, and breadth of coverage. In annotating classical texts, outputs should be grounded in authoritative editions or vetted scholarly annotations; the goal is to approximate how experts decide what to select and how to annotate. Expert judgments encode disciplinary knowledge, contextual interpretation, and audience awareness—cognitive routines that resist full codification, necessitating meticulous sample selection.

The depth and scope of lexical selection and annotation vary by audience (secondary students, university learners, specialist researchers). For professional use, popular or school-oriented materials must be excluded; academically vetted, publication-grade annotations are required so the model learns from authoritative knowledge frameworks and scholarly standards. Only then can outputs attain the necessary accuracy, authority, and publishable quality.

3.1 Collaborative Construction of Training Datasets

For high-quality language fine-tuning, the most effective source is expert-annotated data—repeatedly reviewed, structurally clear, and terminologically authoritative. In a "complete annotation and translation" pipeline, authoritative editions (e.g., Zhonghua Book Company) can be processed via OCR, then normalized and segmented stepwise by an LLM into training instances (Goel et al., 2023). This lowers manual costs and incorporates publication-grade selection standards, provided audience and publication aims coincide.

Data collection should emphasize diversity of a genre, authorship, and period to mitigate stylistic overfitting and enhance cross-domain adaptability (Selva et al., 2025). If style imitation is the aim, the scope can narrow moderately while still reflecting real use cases. Law and medicine likewise benefit from sources spanning regions, subspecialties, and institutions to balance stylistic and usage variation (Chalkidis et al., 2021).

Where authoritative resources are scarce, a hybrid expert-annotation plus semi-automatic expansion workflow can be used: experts label a seed set; the model expands it; experts review and finalize (Cao et al., 2023). For example, an enterprise knowledge-base question answering (QA) system can mine authentic support dialogs, normalize them, then auto-generate supplementary questions from manuals to complete the dataset. This example-expansion-expert review loop raises efficiency and reduces costs, especially for novel, low-resource tasks (Nishida et al., 2005).

Large volumes of unstructured or semi-structured material can likewise be converted into structured training samples. Technical reports, meeting minutes, and user feedback, routed through extraction and transformation pipelines aided by ML and LLMs, yield structured datasets efficiently. For Tangut–Chinese machine translation, a Peking University team aligned every dictionary sense of each Tangut character with expert translations to create "character sense set $\leftrightarrow$ Chinese sentence" pairs instead of whole-sentence pairs—cutting the manual burden under low-resource constraints (Ma et al., 2025).

In data-scarce settings, transfer learning is effective: begin with related-domain data, then stage in small target-domain samples. Optical recognition of Tangut script exemplifies this—leveraging pretrained Chinese character models plus style-transfer augmentation to synthesize varied glyphs before fine-tuning on limited labeled Tangut data to achieve high accuracy (Lu et al., 2025).

For large-scale, discriminative yet costly tasks, crowdsourcing and gamification can accelerate acquisition: careful task decomposition, incentives, and cross-validation enable non-experts to contribute reliably.

Dataset construction strategies should adapt to task attributes and resource constraints. Whatever the blend—expert annotation, automated expansion, or crowdsourced input—the objective is structured, task-proximate, high-quality samples that enable capability gains and professional deployment.

3.2 Design Strategies for Fine-Tuning Training Data in Specialized Domains

In specialized tasks, narrowing the decision space and enforcing bounded output modes improves reliability and domain fit (Wang Shen et al., 2025a; Wang, 2025b). As outlined earlier, structuring samples through dictionary and corpus integration converts unconstrained generation into bounded option selection, reducing errors and risk—an approach applicable to law, medicine, education, and history (Chalkidis et al., 2021).

In legal tasks, unconstrained explanatory generation can be inaccurate or risky. A safer approach is to train on statute–authoritative interpretation pairs so the model selects the most suitable interpretation per scenario. Legal QA can likewise adopt a question–context–answer set format to compel selection from validated answers and limit liability.

In medicine, controllability dominates. Decision trees or state machines can underpin "symptom $\rightarrow$ decision node" datasets to guide stepwise path selection or ranking within a "symptom → differential list," rather than issuing premature conclusions—mirroring clinical reasoning and lowering the misdiagnosis risk.

In education, responses should follow a "knowledge point → multi-tier answer" schema: the model identifies the point and then selects an answer at the appropriate depth and difficulty to preserve accuracy and clarity. This guards against curriculum drift that generic free generation can introduce even when facts are correct.

In history and literature, "event → multi-school analyses" or "passage → multi-theoretical interpretations" frameworks allow the model to retrieve an explanation aligned with user intent—respecting interpretive plurality while maintaining rigor and reducing hallucination or normative overreach.

These methods converge on crafting a limited, explicit decision space that recasts complex tasks as structured, controllable selection problems. Anchored in high-quality samples and expert knowledge bases, the model yields accurate, traceable outputs and supports risk governance (Chen et al., 2025).

Clearly, the strategy has limits: while preset frames enhance safety and rigor, they constrain creativity and perform poorly on open or generative tasks. Where answers are indeterminate, forced choice can diminish value or be misleading. Task design must therefore balance control with openness and tailor the state space accordingly.

An effective refinement is the tiered-freedom approach: strict constraints in high-risk domains (medicine, law); semi-open guidance in medium-risk domains (education, support); broad latitude for creative or exploratory tasks. Hybrid training data enable context-aware adaptation—frameworked outputs for professional content and freer generation for open discussion—to balance safety with flexibility.

In specialized fine-tuning, a single gold answer seldom spans real complexity. Contrastive sampling and interactive augmentation thus become central: contrastive sets include optimal, suboptimal, and erroneous outputs with explicit quality labels, teaching granular discrimination among authoritative renderings, acceptable variants, and clear errors (Ukarapol et al., 2024; Wang et al., 2024a, b). This sharpens pragmatic boundaries and reduces ambiguity.

Static datasets may miss boundary cases; interactive feedback incrementally collects user corrections and rejections to expand and refine the corpus (Christiano et al., 2017; Ouyang et al., 2022), sustaining adaptation—especially in personalized settings (Tamkin et al., 2022). Such augmentation must pair with strict filtering and anonymization to prevent the leakage of sensitive information or harmful content ingestion.

Because complex tasks seldom reach high quality in a single pass, task decomposition with progressive learning is advisable—segmenting the process into staged subtasks supported by dedicated datasets (Wang et al., 2024a, b). For scholarly review generation, stages can include extraction, classification, key point synthesis, logical structuring, and academic phrasing. Medical record analysis and legal drafting likewise segment into knowledge identification, reasoning, and normative expression. Stepwise training streamlines collection, enables partial automation, improves reuse, and accelerates systematic skill acquisition.

3.3 Issues in Managing Fine-Tuning Training Data

Managing and assuring fine-tuning data quality is foundational to real-world LLM performance. Only rigorously designed and governed datasets sustain specialization and stable output. As models evolve rapidly, data must precisely cover task demands while preserving structural diversity, labeling reliability, and compliance across the lifecycle.

High-quality data depend on covering task needs and contextual diversity. Samples should span frequent cases, typical scenarios, and edge instances. A document QA system must handle direct extraction and multi-turn integrative reasoning; classical annotation or legal consultation must be representative of periods, genres, and sub-sectors. Balanced difficulty and type distributions broaden adaptability and prevent blind spots.

Labeling rigor and consistency are central to usability. Annotators need detailed manuals and unified standards specifying decision rules and output formats. Skilled annotators undergo training to master task essence and edge handling. Techniques include multi-round cross-annotation, consistency audits, and adjudication. High-disagreement samples can be flagged to support uncertainty modeling. Continuous monitoring reveals rule gaps or distributional skews for iterative refinement.

Compliance and privacy are critical in professional domains. Medical, financial, and legal data require rigorous de-identification, the removal of personally identifiable information, and adherence to legal and ethical constraints end-to-end. Access control, encryption, and audit trails secure the lifecycle. Synthetic or structurally obfuscated data can balance privacy with utility for training and evaluation.

Dynamic updating sustains currency: as language, domain knowledge, and needs shift, corpora must absorb new expressions, domains, and task variants. Feedback, corrections, and real cases surface deficiencies and supply material for iterative expansion. A systematic loop channels these signals back into the data asset to keep capabilities aligned with practice.

Fundamentally, constructing and managing fine-tuning data is an engineered re-expression of professional knowledge, linguistic norms, and operational needs. Unlike broad pre-training accumulation, fine-tuning emphasizes task specificity, functional intent, and responsive behavior. Each well-formed sample rehearses how to decide and output in a defined context. Sound governance exposes the model to correct behaviors, cultivating stable, reliable responses under complexity.

4 Fine-Tuning Large Language Models

A high-quality dataset is only a starting point; realizing target behaviors demands a precise, task-aligned training process (Kili Technology, 2024). Fine-tuning encompasses strategic selection and operational orchestration: parameter configuration, task design, training cadence, and evaluation loops. A deployable model is built iteratively—each operation shaping whether outputs become stable, clear, and controllable.

4.1 Insights into Fine-Tuning Methods and Practice

For high-standard applications such as professional translation, prompt engineering alone seldom yields stable, stylistically consistent outputs. In terminology-dense, style-constrained settings, instruction following plateaus and risk rises. Targeted parameter adjustment via fine-tuning lets the model internalize authentic task behavior—an essential mechanism for professional performance gains (Bommasani et al., 2021).

Fine-tuning strategies can be viewed along two axes: the scope of parameter updates and the nature of the objective. Full-parameter tuning updates all weights—suited to large domain shifts or high customization but resource intensive. Parameter-efficient fine-tuning (PEFT) now predominates. Methods like Low-Rank Adaptation (LoRA) insert small trainable adapters while freezing the backbone, cutting compute and storage while mitigating capability drift (Hu et al., 2022). Applying LoRA to open 7B–32B models (Qwen, LLaMA, etc.) has become routine for translation and structured language services (Liang et al., 2025).

The choice of training objective governs adaptation. Supervised fine-tuning aligns inputs with target outputs—transparent and controllable for structured tasks (paragraph translation, terminology annotation, summarization). Reinforcement learning fine-tuning adds an external reward model, treating generation as policy optimization; mechanisms such as Generalized Reinforcement Policy Optimization and reinforcement learning from human feedback suit subjective, multi-objective, complex environments.

Catastrophic forgetting deserves scrutiny: new-task training can erode prior capabilities, especially with full-parameter updates and large task divergence. For single narrow tasks the impact is modest. Modular PEFT preserves general capacity while enabling flexible adapter swapping to stabilize multi-task performance.

Module organization in multi-task fine-tuning directly shapes breadth and efficiency. Unified mixed training yields an omnibus adapter—deployment-friendly when tasks are similar. Yet skewed distributions or interference can degrade performance. Separate adapters increase customization and scheduling flexibility at greater operational complexity. Early experimentation favors separation; at scale and over sustained operation, unification aids stability and cost control.

Selecting a fine-tuning method is a dynamic trade-off among task scope, resources, and engineering complexity. Clear objectives, well-structured data, and stable training regimes underwrite high-quality professional models. Each pathway adjustment seeks an optimal balance between practical needs and model capacity, advancing the evolution of language service systems.

4.2 *Task Standards and Evaluation Mechanisms for Fine-Tuning*

Assessing whether fine-tuning is adequate cannot rely solely on surface fluency or readability. In professional tasks such as translation, an output may appear smooth and well structured yet still lack terminological precision, stylistic consistency, or logical ordering. Robust evaluation must remain tightly coupled to the specific task goals and employ bespoke criteria rather than generic text quality metrics.

Each translation or language service task therefore requires a dedicated rubric. For example, Classical Chinese translation emphasizes accurate conveyance of central meaning and tone; terminology annotation demands precise alignment of definitions; structural rewriting prioritizes logical information flow. Only when the model's outputs consistently satisfy these granular targets can we conclude it has internalized the task's core requirements.

The structural discipline and stability of structured output have particular engineering value. If a model must produce JSON (or similar) and reliably preserves schema integrity—complete, ordered fields—then even with imperfect semantics it still facilitates downstream integration. Conversely, schema drift, missing fields, or extraneous commentary signal insufficient constraint and indicate that prompt design, dataset construction, and the training pipeline require further optimization.

Automated metrics, such as Bilingual Evaluation Understudy (BLEU), Recall-Oriented Understudy for Gisting Evaluation (ROUGE) and BERTScore, play a supporting role, but behavioral accuracy is more decisive. For sense disambiguation or terminology selection, multiple-choice or contrastive evaluations directly probe decision quality and are often more informative than surface similarity scores. For complex style transfer or solution explanation generation, multi-dimensional blind human review remains indispensable, using detailed criteria for content completeness, stylistic fidelity, and linguistic correctness and aggregating multiple raters' judgments.

Evaluation should also test transferability and robustness. A key question is whether performance persists across new genres or shifting contexts. In deployment, integrated user feedback should verify that workflow efficiency improves, manual post-editing decreases, and user experience is enhanced.

Evaluating fine-tuning outcomes is a multidimensional integration of task alignment, structural compliance, and application feedback. Fluency alone is insufficient; value depends on delivering required behaviors, maintaining structural stability, and adapting to new demands while supporting continual improvement. A layered, dynamically evolving framework that combines automated metrics, behavioral tests, human scoring, and real-world feedback enables the shift from mere model alteration to operational capability deployment. In practice, methods should be task specific and together form a verifiable, traceable, continuously optimizable training loop that grounds capability in real workflows.

4.3 Fine-Tuning Practice with LoRA

In large language model applications, Low-Rank Adaptation (LoRA) is widely employed in language service tasks because it is parameter efficient, inexpensive to train, and flexible to deploy (Hu et al., 2022). Unlike full-parameter tuning, it updates only a very small subset of weights, making training feasible under resource constraints and thus suitable for universities and small or medium teams (Ding et al., 2023). Use cases such as Classical Chinese translation and terminology extraction readily benefit from this approach.

Model selection should prioritize open-source models with transparent architectures, active communities, and permissive licenses (e.g., Qwen, DeepSeek) whose weights and APIs are available. For typical fine-tuning tasks, models in the 7B–14B range train quickly and keep memory and compute demands modest. When hardware and data are ample and higher performance is needed, 32B or larger models can be considered.

Environment Setup

The following combination is recommended:

- Language environment: Python 3.9 +
- Frameworks/tools:`transformers` (HuggingFace), `peft`(parameter-efficient fine-tuning library), `accelerate`(distributed training), `datasets` (data loading)
- Hardware: 1–2 GPUs with 24 GB VRAM (e.g., RTX 3090, RTX 6000 Ada Generation), sufficient for training efficiency Installation via pip:

```
pip install transformers peft accelerate datasets bitsandbytes
```

Data Preparation

All data should be stored in JSON or JSONL format with three fields: prompt, input, and output. Earlier sections describe dataset construction and schema design.

Training Workflow

1. **Load the base model and tokenizer**

```
from transformers import AutoModelForCausalLM, AutoTokenizer
model = AutoModelForCausalLM.from_pretrained("Qwen/Qwen2.5-7B",
device_map="auto")
tokenizer = AutoTokenizer.from_pretrained("Qwen/Qwen2.5-7B")
```

2. **Configure Low-Rank Adaptation and prepare the model**

```
from peft import LoraConfig, get_peft_model, TaskType
config = LoraConfig(
    r=8,
    lora_alpha=16,
    target_modules=["q_proj", "v_proj"],  # Be aware that
different models can have different module names.
    lora_dropout=0.05,
    bias="none",
    task_type=TaskType.CAUSAL_LM
)
model = get_peft_model(model, config)
```

3. **Load the training dataset**

```
from datasets import load_dataset
dataset = load_dataset("json",
data_files="train_data.jsonl")["train"]
```

4. **Start training**

```
from transformers import TrainingArguments
args = TrainingArguments(
    per_device_train_batch_size=4,
    gradient_accumulation_steps=4,
    num_train_epochs=3,
    learning_rate=2e-4,
    fp16=True,
    logging_steps=50,
    output_dir="./lora_output"
)
```

You can use either `transformers.Trainer` or `trl.SFTTrainer`. Typical training arguments are shown below:

Fine-tuning time depends on dataset size and GPU performance, typically ranging from minutes to a few hours; address routine issues case by case.

Model compatibility is a frequent early hurdle. Large models differ subtly in naming core components (e.g., attention projections), so target_modules must match the specific architecture. Consult official documentation or list modules in advance to verify choices and cut debugging time.

Memory constraints are common in practice: even a 24 GB GPU may exhaust VRAM with larger models or certain batches. Mitigation includes 8-bit or 4-bit quantized loading (via bitsandbytes) and gradient checkpointing to conserve memory. Quantized LoRA applies 4-bit quantization to fine-tune 65B-parameter models on a single 48 GB GPU, substantially lowering hardware requirements (Dettmers et al., 2023).

Non-convergence or overfitting typically reflects inadequate data volume or quality, suboptimal epoch counts, or inconsistent sample formatting. Use several thousand instances when possible; apply augmentation if needed. Larger models may require fewer examples, yet complex tasks still demand broad coverage. Adjust epochs based on the loss curve to curb overfitting. Consistent formatting and concise, standardized prompts promote stable behavioral learning.

During structured output generation, the model may yield inconsistent formatting or superfluous explanations. Enforce a single format in the training data, state output requirements explicitly in the prompt, and validate outputs with lightweight post-processing.

Suboptimal results usually arise from base-model limits, weak sample quality, or an unclear task definition. Refine task scope, diversify samples, and inspect data characteristics to improve outcomes.

LoRA fine-tuning is practical and extensible: with solid data preparation and appropriate hyperparameters, it yields controllable, stable customized models even under resource constraints or modest datasets (Lialin et al., 2023). As ecosystems shift toward modular or dynamic architectures, LoRA will continue to deliver engineering value.

LoRA fine-tuning imposes modest computational demands, and the toolchain is mature. Beginners can succeed by following established guides. The pivotal factor is not the training loop but data preparation: data quality, domain knowledge, and sample design directly shape outcomes (Ding et al., 2023; Lialin et al., 2023). Once the process is standardized, curating a high-quality dataset becomes the primary test of domain expertise.

Commercial large-model platforms also offer online fine-tuning, which addresses some customization needs, but platform constraints limit data privacy, intellectual property protection, and training scale. For high-stakes or sensitive applications, localized LoRA fine-tuning remains indispensable.

5 Practical Fine-Tuning: Tangut Machine Translation

This section examines low-resource Tangut machine translation with large language models, conducted by the Handian Zhiyuan Digital Humanities Team at Peking University (Zheng et al., 2025). Earlier sections defined the task and dataset construction principles; this section provides a more concise account of the methodology and practical workflow than the original paper.

5.1 Conceptual Approach to Tangut Machine Translation

Tangut research commonly employs a four-line interlinear workflow: it begins with character identification and word-level glossing, then iteratively refines these into a fluent Chinese rendering faithful to the source. This interpretive pipeline mirrors expert reasoning. The objective of machine translation here is to reproduce that cognitive process (Shi, 2020).

From the *Concise Tangut–Chinese Dictionary* and related lexicographic sources we extracted all candidate senses for each character and supplied them to the model in ordered form (e.g., "Character 1 ['three']", "Character 2 ['age, generation, dynasty, clan, time']") (Fig. 1). The model then selects context-appropriate senses and composes a modern Chinese sentence. Within this four-line paradigm, idiomatic translation extends beyond word alignment to recover sentence-level meaning, requiring lexical disambiguation, word-order adjustment, syntactic restructuring, and discourse-level coherence (Downes, 2018; Kwanten, 1989). At inference time we either request the final output directly or apply a staged chain-of-thought prompt that separates literal and idiomatic phases.

Prompts communicate the reasoning pattern; however, even with several few-shot exemplars, direct inference remains suboptimal for a task of this complexity. Fine-tuning is therefore required to adapt and augment the model's knowledge and behavior.

5.2 Experimental Procedure and Results

The experiment evaluated post-fine-tuning performance on literal and idiomatic Tangut–Chinese translation. The dataset comprised: (1) 569 aligned pairs from the *San Dai Xiang Zhao Wenji* (*Collected Writings of Mutual Illumination over Three Generations*, compiled by Sun Bojun, Professor at the University of Chinese Academy of Social Sciences), which are structurally consistent and used as the principal training and test material; (2) 525 pairs from volume 77 of the *Avataṃsaka Sūtra* (*Huayan Jing*) in Tangut, compiled by Professor Arakawa Shintaro from the Tokyo University of Foreign Studies, with Chinese renderings produced by ChatGPT from

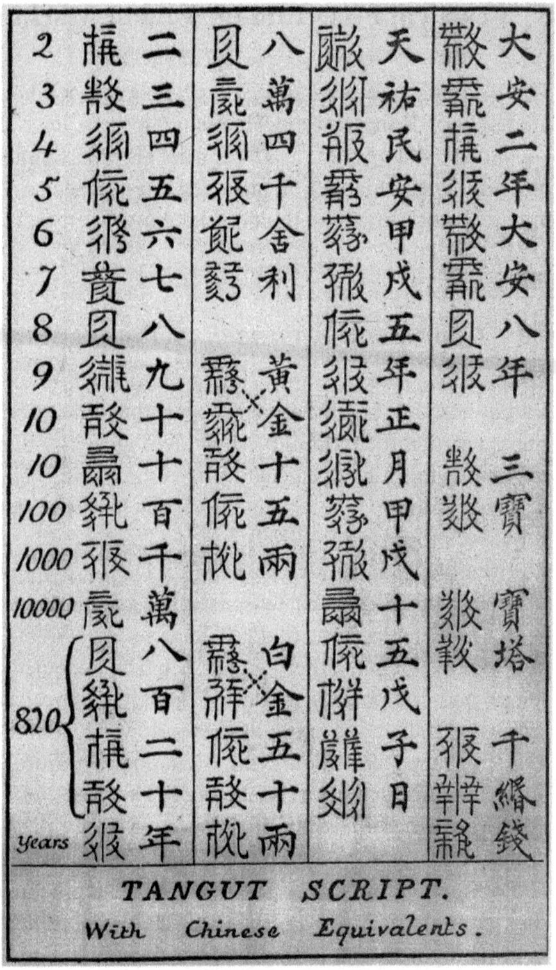

Fig. 1 Bushell's Decipherment of 37 Tangut Characters. This figure illustrates the lexical correspondences between Tangut and Chinese, adapted from Wikipedia (https://en.wikipedia.org/wiki/Stephen_Wootton_Bushell)

modern Japanese (religious register); and (3) an open test set containing fragments of *The Pearl in the Palm* (A Tangut–Chinese Bilingual Glossary) and the *Avataṃsaka Sūtra* to assess generalization.

For the *San Dai Xiang Zhao Wenji* subset, 95% was used for training and 5% reserved for closed testing. The foundation was the team's Classical Chinese LLM, further pre-trained from Qwen1.5-14B on 36 GB of classical corpora and initially fine-tuned on 390,000 instances spanning 76 Classical Chinese task types. Tangut translation data were introduced only in the final stage for task-specific adaptation.

Evaluation used BLEU-4, ROUGE-1, ROUGE-2, and ROUGE-L to capture lexical overlap and semantic coverage. Literal translation performance was consistent across closed and open tests; in some open examples, system outputs differed from references only in word order or morphology (e.g., "香花布列" 'fragrant flowers laid out’ → “香花排列” ‘fragrant flowers arranged’; “他利故已不忘” ‘having not forgotten for the sake of benefiting others’ → “他利为己不忘” ‘not forgetting benefiting others for oneself’), indicating accurate semantic equivalence judgments and natural phrasing.

With domain specialization (the Classical Chinese–enhanced base) and structured prompts, the model learned and reproduced Tangut literal translation patterns under extremely low-resource conditions. Fine-tuning on a small, high-quality, human-curated set still produced stable, usable behavior, supporting the feasibility of small-sample capability transfer (Liang et al., 2025; Zheng & Yu, 2025). Additional literal examples follow:

Tangut:

Scholar literal translation: 礼奉心堕能殊无，觉佛孰爱最乐国 (approximately “In reverent offering the mind descends—its capacities undifferentiated; awakened Buddha: who cherishes the most blissful realm?”).

Machine literal translation: 礼奉心堕能殊无，觉佛谁爱最乐国 (approximately “In reverent offering the mind descends—its capacities undifferentiated; awakened Buddha: who loves the most blissful realm?”).

Tangut:

Scholar literal translation: 金真铃铎云如布 (approx.“ ‘Golden genuine bells spread like clouds”).

Machine literal translation: 金真铃铎云如偈 (approx. “Golden genuine bells like a verse among clouds”).

Empirical results favored a simplified format: the input concatenates candidate sense lists per character (simplified from dictionary entries). For example:

> Constructing the literal translation from the candidate sense sequence:\nCharacter 1 [‘three’]\nCharacter 2 [‘generation, era, dynasty, clan, time’]\nCharacter 3 [‘mutual, reciprocal, assist’]\nCharacter 4 [‘illuminate’]\nCharacter 5 [‘speech, language, word’]\nCharacter 6 [‘collection, compilation, synthesis’]\nCharacter 7 [‘text, inscription, law, book’]\n.

For idiomatic translation training, inputs with and without the CoT strategy are shown below:

> Constructing the idiomatic translation from candidate words:\nCharacter 1 [‘three’]\nCharacter 2 [‘generation, era, dynasty, clan, time’]\nCharacter 3 [‘mutual, reciprocal, assist’]\nCharacter 4 [‘illuminate’]\nCharacter 5 [‘speech, language, word’]\nCharacter 6 [‘collection, compilation, synthesis’]\nCharacter 7 [‘text, inscription, law, book’]\n

First generate the literal translation from the candidate sense sequence, then derive the idiomatic translation:\nCharacter 1 ['three']\nCharacter 2 ['generation, era, dynasty, clan, time']\nCharacter 3 ['mutual, reciprocal, assist']\nCharacter 4 ['illuminate']\nCharacter 5 ['speech, language, word']\nCharacter 6 ['collection, compilation, synthesis']\nCharacter 7 ['text, inscription, law, book']\n.

The expected output is the expert human translation for each aligned pair.

Results indicate that the simplified dictionary-sense concatenation improves recall, lexical accuracy, and long-sequence generation quality. The staged CoT prompt (literal then idiomatic) outperforms the direct approach on all four metrics. Training on progressively larger subsets while evaluating on a fixed test set isolates the contribution of data volume: even from a very small baseline, additional data steadily improves both literal and idiomatic performance. Further experimental details appear in the cited papers. This method thus offers a viable pathway for future language service systems addressing low-resource scripts.

For reference, fine-tuning Tangut translation on four consumer RTX 4090 GPUs with a 14B base model required about 4–5 h. Using four A100 GPUs with a 72B base model took longer but yielded superior results. Adjusting hyperparameters can reduce the time to 2–3 h.

6 Conclusion

This chapter has shown that fine-tuning delivers value when translation services can be reframed as bounded, multi-stage decision pipelines. By pairing task decomposition (annotation → literal → idiomatic; sense enumeration → selection → synthesis) with parameter-efficient adaptation (LoRA, quantization) on 7B–32B backbones, we convert broad but diffuse pretrained competence into controllable expert behavior, reduce hallucination, and enable low-resource transfer (e.g., Tangut) under modest compute. Central is deliberate data engineering: schema rigor, structured JSON I/O, contrastive examples, staged samples, expert–model feedback loops, and lifecycle governance for quality, privacy, and updating. Evaluation shifts from generic overlap scores to behavioral rubrics, structural format integrity, and robustness under distribution shifts. Fine-tuning should be chosen selectively: prompts or few-shot approaches suffice for open, highly creative tasks; structured tuning excels when decision spaces are well delimited. Future work will integrate retrieval, multi-adapter orchestration, and continual learning to maintain specialization without catastrophic forgetting and deliver auditable quality gains.

References

Bommasani, R., Hudson, D. A., Adeli, E., Altman, R., Arora, S., von Arx, S., Bernstein, M. S., Bohg, J., Bosselut, A., Brunskill, E., Brynjolfsson, E., Buch, S., Card, D., Castellon, R., Chatterji, N., Chen, A., Creel, K., Davis, J. Q., Demszky, D., Donahue, C., Wang, W., et al. (2021). *On the opportunities and risks of foundation models*. https://doi.org/10.48550/arXiv.2108.07258

Cao, Y., Kang, Y., Wang, C., & Sun, L. (2023). *Instruction mining: High-quality instruction data selection for large language models*. https://doi.org/10.48550/arXiv.2307.06290

Chalkidis, I., Jana, A., Hartung, D., Bommarito, M., Androutsopoulos, I., Katz, D. M., & Aletras, N. (2021). *LexGLUE: A benchmark dataset for legal language understanding in English*. https://doi.org/10.48550/arXiv.2110.00976

Chen, M. K., Zhang, X., Huang, J., & Tao, D. (2025). *Improving large language models with concept-aware fine-tuning*. https://doi.org/10.48550/arXiv.2506.07833

Christiano, P. F., Leike, J., Brown, T., Martic, M., Legg, S., & Amodei, D. (2017). Deep reinforcement learning from human preferences. *Advances in neural information processing systems, 30*.

Department of Chinese Language and Literature, Peking University. (2024, November 24). "数字人文与古典文献学"学术研讨会举行 [Academic symposium "Digital Humanities and Classical Philology" held]. 北京大学中文系 Department of Chinese Language and Literature, Peking University. https://chinese.pku.edu.cn/xwgg/xwdt/f73b53849807424c83dc7bf8ae4c039f.htm

Dettmers, T., Pagnoni, A., Holtzman, A., & Zettlemoyer, L. (2023). QLoRA: Efficient finetuning of quantized LLMs. In A. Oh, T. Naumann, A. Globerson, K. Saenko, M. Hardt, & S. Levine (Eds.), *Advances in Neural Information Processing Systems* (Vol. 36, pp. 10088–10115). Curran Associates, Inc. https://proceedings.neurips.cc/paper_files/paper/2023/file/1feb87871436031bdc0f2beaa62a049b-Paper-Conference.pdf

Ding, N., Qin, Y., Yang, G., Wei, F., Yang, Z., Su, Y., & Sun, M. (2023). Parameter-efficient fine-tuning of large-scale pre-trained language models. *Nature Machine Intelligence, 5*(3), 220-235.

Downes, A. (2018). *How does Tangut work?* Doctoral dissertation. Macquarie University, Australia.

Fan, A., Bhosale, S., Schwenk, H., Ma, Z., El-Kishky, A., Goyal, S., & Joulin, A., et al. (2021). Beyond English-centric multilingual machine translation. *Journal of Machine Learning Research, 22*(107), 1–48.

Fu, Y., Panda, R., Niu, X., Yue, X., Hajishirzi, H., Kim, Y., & Peng, H. (2024). *Data engineering for scaling language models to 128k context*. https://doi.org/10.48550/arXiv.2402.10171

Goel, A., Gueta, A., Gilon, O., Liu, C., Erell, S., Nguyen, L. H., & Feder, A., et al. (2023, December). LLMs accelerate annotation for medical information extraction. In *Machine Learning for Health* (ML4H) (pp. 82–100). PMLR.

Guo, G., Yang, J., Lu, F., Qin, J., Tang, T., & Zhao, W. X. (2023, October). Towards effective ancient Chinese translation: Dataset, model, and evaluation. In *CCF International Conference on Natural Language Processing and Chinese Computing* (pp. 416–427). Springer Nature Switzerland.

Hu, E. J., Shen, Y., Wallis, P., Allen-Zhu, Z., Li, Y., Wang, S., & Chen, W., et al. (2022). LoRA: Low-rank adaptation of large language models. *ICLR, 1*(2), 3.

Huo, Y. J. (2013). 西夏语言研究简论 A brief study of the Tangut language. 宁夏社会科学 *[Ningxia Social Sciences]* (6), 115–117.

Kili Technology. (2024). *What is LLM fine-tuning?—Everything you need to know*. https://kili-technology.com/large-language-models-llms/the-ultimate-guide-to-fine-tuning-llms-2024

Kwanten, L. (1989). The Structure of the Tangut [Hsi Hsia] Characters. *T'oung Pao, 75*(Livr. 1/3), 1–42.

Li, J., Zhou, H., Huang, S., Cheng, S., & Chen, J. (2024). Eliciting the translation ability of large language models via multilingual finetuning with translation instructions. *Transactions of the Association for Computational Linguistics, 12*, 576–592.

Li, J., Wei, T., Qu, W., Li, B., Feng, M., & Wang, D. (2025). Combining lexicon definitions and the retrieval-augmented generation of a large language model for the automatic annotation of ancient Chinese poetry. *Mathematics, 13*(12), 2023.
Li, F. Y. (2023). 书同文字与再造书契——论古籍数字化时代的字符统一与文本规范 [Book-unified characters and reconstructed script conventions: On character unification and text standardization in the era of ancient book digitization]. 北京师范大学学报(社会科学版) *[Journal of Beijing Normal University (Social Sciences)],* (5), 127–141.
Lialin, V., Deshpande, V., & Rumshisky, A. (2023). *Scaling down to scale up: A guide to parameter-efficient fine-tuning.* https://doi.org/10.48550/arXiv.2303.15647
Liang, X., Khaw, Y. M. J., Liew, S. Y., Tan, T. P., & Qin, D. (2025). *Towards low-resource language machine translation: A language-specific fine-tuning with LoRA for specialized large language models.* IEEE Access.
Liu, W., & Xie, J. (2023, September). Technical report on ancient Chinese machine translation based on mRASP model. In *Proceedings of ALT2023: Ancient Language Translation Workshop* (pp. 48–54). Asia-Pacific Association for Machine Translation. Macau SAR, China. https://aclanthology.org/2023.alt-1.7/
Longpre, S., Hou, L., Vu, T., Webson, A., Chung, H. W., Tay, Y., & Roberts, A., et al. (2023, July). The flan collection: Designing data and methods for effective instruction tuning. *Proceedings of the 40th International Conference on Machine Learning* (PMLR 202, pp. 22631–22648).
Lu, W., Luu, R. K., & Buehler, M. J. (2025). Fine-tuning large language models for domain adaptation: Exploration of training strategies, scaling, model merging and synergistic capabilities. *NPJ Computational Materials, 11*(1), 84. https://doi.org/10.1038/s41524-025-01564-y
Ma, X., Lan, M., Hu, W., & Lu, Y. (2025). Dongba machine translation with transfer learning: leveraging pre-trained ancient Chinese models. *ACM Transactions on Asian and Low-Resource Language Information Processing, 24*(5), 1–17.
Moslem, Y., Haque, R., & Way, A. (2023). *Fine-tuning large language models for adaptive machine translation.* https://doi.org/10.48550/arXiv.2312.12740
Nair, A. R., Gupta, D., & Premjith, B. (2024). Investigating translation for Indic languages with BLOOMZ-3b through prompting and LoRA fine-tuning. *Scientific Reports, 14*, 24202. https://doi.org/10.1038/s41598-024-74617-9
Nishida, T., Mizufune, N., George, A., & Kotsuki, H. (2005). Xixia language studies and the Lotus Sutra (II). *The Journal of Oriental Studies, 15*, 170–199.
Ouyang, L., Wu, J., Jiang, X., Almeida, D., Wainwright, C., Mishkin, P., & Lowe, R., et al. (2022). Training language models to follow instructions with human feedback. *Advances in Neural Information Processing Systems, 35*, 27730–27744.
Saunders, D. (2020). *Domain adaptation for neural machine translation.* Doctoral dissertation. University of Cambridge, The United Kingdom.
Selva, K., Vittayaareekul, S., & Miranda, B. (2025). *Exploring the efficacy of meta-learning: Unveiling superior data diversity utilization of MAML over pre-training.* https://doi.org/10.48550/arXiv.2501.08506
Shi, J. (2020). *Tangut language and manuscripts: An introduction* (Vol. 20). Brill.
Singhal, P., Walambe, R., Ramanna, S., & Kotecha, K. (2023). Domain adaptation: Challenges, methods, datasets, and applications. *IEEE Access, 11*, 6973–7020.
Sun, B. J. (2023). 西夏文献研究的现状和未来 [Current state and future prospects of Tangut document research]. 西南民族大学学报(人文社会科学版) *[Journal of Southwest Minzu University (Humanities and Social Sciences)], 44*(1), 14–21. (In Chinese)
Tamkin, A., Nguyen, D., Deshpande, S., Mu, J., & Goodman, N. (2022). Active learning helps pretrained models learn the intended task. *Advances in Neural Information Processing Systems, 35*, 28140–28153.
Team, G., Anil, R., Borgeaud, S., Alayrac, J. B., Yu, J., Soricut, R., & Blanco, L. (2023). *Gemini: a family of highly capable multimodal models.* https://doi.org/10.48550/arXiv.2312.11805
Ukarapol, T., Lee, Z., & Xin, A. (2024). *Improving text embeddings for smaller language models using contrastive fine-tuning.* https://doi.org/10.48550/arXiv.2408.00690

Wang, D., Liu, C., Zhao, Z., Shen, S., Liu, L., Li, B., & Wang, X. (2023a). *GujiBERT and GujiGPT: Construction of intelligent information processing foundation language models for ancient texts.* https://doi.org/10.48550/arXiv.2307.05354

Wang, Z., Zhang, S., Zhang, X., & Hu, R. (2023b, August). 古汉语通假字资源库的构建及应用研究 (The construction and application of an ancient Chinese language resource on Tongjiazi). In *Proceedings of the 22nd Chinese National Conference on Computational Linguistics* (pp. 535–546).

Wang, J., Li, J., Han, X., Ye, D., & Lu, Z. (2024). Language model adaption for reinforcement learning with natural language action space. In L.-W. Ku, A. Martins, & V. Srikumar (Eds.), *Proceedings of the 62nd Annual Meeting of the Association for Computational Linguistics* (Volume 1: Long Papers) (pp. 1620–1634). Association for Computational Linguistics. https://doi.org/10.18653/v1/2024.acl-long.89

Wang, Z., Wang, P., Li, J., Chen, Y., & Zhang, M. (2024). Achieving stronger generation via simple contrastive tuning. In *Findings of the Association for Computational Linguistics: EMNLP 2024* (pp. 8986–8999).

Wang, D. Y. B., Shen, Z., Mishra, S. S., Xu, Z., Teng, Y., & Ding, H. (2025a). *SLOT: Structuring the output of large language models.* https://doi.org/10.48550/arXiv.2505.04016

Wang, H. X., Zhou, Z. M., Ding, F. F., & Wei, C. F. (2025b). 数字人文与大语言模型: 古文献语义检索实践与探索 [Digital humanities and large language models: Practice and exploration of semantic retrieval for ancient texts]. 农业图书情报学报 *[Journal of Agricultural Library and Information Science], 36*(9), 89–101.

Wu, M. C., Liu, C., Meng, K., & Wang, D. B. (2024). 基于预训练语言模型的汉语古现翻译模型构建 [Constructing a classical-to-modern Chinese translation model based on pre-trained language models]. 信息资源管理学报 *[Journal of Information Resources Management], 14*(6), 143–155.

Wu, B. (2025, January 23). 15年校订出版150种古籍经典，中华书局"三全本"出版分享会举行 [150 classics critically edited and published over 15 years: Sharing session for Zhonghua Book Company's "Three Comprehensive Editions"]. 广州日报大洋网 [Guangzhou Daily Dayoo.com]. https://news.dayoo.com/gzrbrmt/202501/23/170636_54779578.htm

Yang, L. J., Meng, Y. F., Wang, J., Mao, W., & Meng, B. (2024). 基于A-CapsNet的西夏文字识别研究 [Tangut character recognition based on A-CapsNet]. 计算机应用与软件 *[Computer Applications and Software], 41*(8), 219–224.

Zeng, L., Tian, Y., Shan, Y., & Guo, Y. (2023, September). BIT-ACT: An ancient Chinese translation system using data augmentation. In *Proceedings of ALT2023: Ancient Language Translation Workshop* (pp. 43–47).

Zhao, Z., Sun, G., Liu, C., et al. (2025). Research on machine translation of ancient books in the era of large language model. *NPJ Heritage Science, 13*, 122. https://doi.org/10.1038/s40494-025-01697-9

Zheng, Y., & Yu, J. (2025, May). Incorporating lexicon-aligned prompting in large language model for Tangut–Chinese translation. In *Proceedings of the Second Workshop on Ancient Language Processing* (pp. 127–136).

Zheng, Y. X., Zhou, Z. M., Zhang, Y. W., Sun, B. J., Qiao, W. X., Hou, J. M., & Yu, J. S. (2025). 低资源条件下的西夏文OCR与机器翻译研究 [Research on OCR and machine translation for Tangut script under low-resource conditions]. 数字人文 *[Digital Humanities]*, (3), 114–116.

Zhu, J., & Chen, S. (2023, September). AnchiLm: An effective classical-to-modern Chinese translation model leveraging bpe-drop and SikuRoBERTa. In *Proceedings of ALT2023: Ancient Language Translation Workshop* (pp. 55–60).

Zhu, D. H., Zhao, Z. X., Zhang, Y. P., Sun, G. Y., Liu, C., Hu, D., & Wang, D. B. (2024). 面向古文自然语言处理生成任务的大语言模型评测研究 [Evaluation of large language models for classical Chinese NLP generation tasks]. 信息资源管理学报 *[Journal of Information Resources Management], 14*(5), 45–58.

Chapter 8
Designing Translation Agents: Principles and Practice

Abstract This chapter defines translation agents as workflow-driven, modular systems that supersede single-prompt large language model usage for complex, domain-sensitive translation. It presents a layered architecture (task awareness, context management, translation execution, terminology management, quality evaluation, feedback interface) that enables strategic decomposition, controlled information flow, and adaptive refinement. Core design principles include semantically informed segmentation, dynamic context bridging, multi-strategy generation, and orchestration of primary and auxiliary models for terminology, style, and structural validation. The chapter details task chains covering ingestion, structural decomposition, style/register detection, summarization-assisted comprehension, terminology extraction and active termbase integration, long sentence simplification, multi-model generation patterns, and document-level consistency mechanisms. Iterative optimization—drafting, diagnostic evaluation, variant comparison, back translation, and targeted revision—is framed as an autonomous feedback loop grounded in established quality frameworks (Multidimensional Quality Metrics, Dynamic Quality Framework) while recognizing limits of legacy reference metrics. Tooling ecosystems (e.g., LangChain, Haystack, AutoGen, emerging low-code platforms) are assessed for orchestration, memory, and monitoring support. The chapter argues that translation agents operationalize a shift from ad hoc prompting to traceable, optimizable pipelines, advancing scalability, explainability, and human–machine collaboration toward adaptive, knowledge-integrated language services.

Prompting has substantially expanded the applicability of large language models (LLMs) in translation. However, for complex structures, domain-specific contexts, and diverse pragmatic requirements, prompts alone seldom ensure global coherence or stylistic consistency. Translation is inherently multi-stage: each analytic decision shapes the final output. Translation agents shift the process from one-shot generation to an orchestrated workflow with iterative analysis, feedback, and revision (Briva-Iglesias, 2025). Through process-oriented, modular design, the agent coordinates information flow while enabling fine-grained, personalized, domain-aware control over output quality.

J. S. Yu and Y. Yao, *Intelligent Language Services*,
https://doi.org/10.1007/978-981-95-4632-9_8

1 Concept and Architecture of Translation Agents

The emergence of translation agents marks a shift from single-turn model invocations to workflow-driven, modular intelligent language service systems (China Academy of Information and Communications Technology and Huawei Technologies Co. Ltd., 2025). Understanding them entails analyzing how modules coordinate internally and how mainstream frameworks implement that coordination. This lens clarifies how such systems execute complex work—input analysis, context maintenance, generation, and quality evaluation—within a closed, automated loop.

1.1 From Prompt Engineering to Workflow-Based Translation Agents

Large language models have driven innovation in translation, with prompt engineering initially at the center. Carefully crafted prompts adjust model style and output, enabling automated handling of short sentences or structured text. For example, "Translate the following technical description into concise and accurate English" guides the model to manage length, standardize terminology, and preserve structure—adequate for routine needs.

Prompt engineering, constrained by static instructions and single-turn interaction, struggles with semantic precision and consistency in complex settings (Briva-Iglesias, 2025). Ambiguity, nested syntax, and layered logic often produce mistranslations or structural drift. Even sophisticated composite prompts still compress all reasoning into one response without adaptive strategy shifts, backtracking, or contextual re-anchoring.

Single-step reasoning assumes the model can comprehend and translate everything at once, making it ill-suited to layered, evolving tasks. Multi-step workflows emulate professional cognitive routines: structural parsing, terminology identification, gap filling, and final synthesis. For long documents with tables, footnotes, and narrative text, an agent can segment structure, extract translatable content, and then reconstruct formatting. Distinct prompts orchestrate each stage, optionally invoking external tools (web resources, knowledge bases) as needed (Wiesinger et al., 2024).

Workflow-based translation agents address these demands directly. They decompose complex work into sequenced steps, each handling a defined micro-task while passing forward structured state. The system may analyze document structure, segment lengthy sentences, normalize or substitute terminology, resolve missing referents, and then impose global stylistic and terminological consistency. Intermediate artifacts remain available for downstream revision. When referents are unclear, the agent logs candidate entities for later resolution. For multi-variant outputs, it aggregates and filters alternatives for downstream selection.

Flow control differentiates agents from prompt-only use. It entails task scheduling, state management, exception handling, and feedback incorporation to preserve coherence and professional standards. This procedural scaffold brings large models closer to human translator workflows and supports higher textual complexity and multi-stage demands.

The shift from prompt engineering to workflow agents strengthens practitioner control and, more importantly, introduces a systematic organizational layer that renders translation a traceable, optimizable multi-stage pipeline (Wiesinger et al., 2024). This transition improves machine translation quality and adaptability while providing an engineering foundation for long-form and production contexts. Empirical analyses of multilingual LLM translation performance establish baseline capabilities and error profiles that guide specialization and orchestration strategies in translation agents (Zhu et al., 2023). It may be a pivotal step in integrating large language models into language services.

1.2 Architectural Components of Translation Agents

A translation agent is not a simple model invocation script; it is an automated system integrating multiple strategies with end-to-end governance (China Academy of Information and Communications Technology and Huawei Technologies Co. Ltd., 2025). Unlike single-pass prompting, it refines the task into discrete modules whose orchestration supports controlled information flow and dynamic feedback, enhancing adaptability and enabling continual self-improvement.

The entry point is a task awareness module that parses input, detects document type, language pair, delivery standards, and formatting constraints, then formulates an initial strategy. For an academic paper or legal contract, it flags priorities such as terminology fidelity or layout preservation, providing the basis for structural decomposition and bounding downstream scopes.

A context management module supplies multi-turn memory beyond the base context window. Through entity tracking, paragraph relation mapping, and terminology evolution monitoring, it preserves cross-segment coherence and logs the full decision trail for later correction and audit. In long technical documents or multi-party dialogues it anchors speakers, topic shifts, and term development.

The translation execution module handles core generation. Beyond invoking a model Application Programming Interface (API), it segments units strategically, crafts task-specific prompts, and may coordinate multiple models: one for drafting, and auxiliaries for terminology validation and stylistic refinement—while enforcing live context and term constraints across genres and formats.

The terminology management module enforces professional rigor. It loads glossaries, performs automatic alignment checks, and maintains historical decisions, intervening pre-translation and post-editing to ensure consistency while supporting project-specific preference profiles.

A quality evaluation module performs multidimensional assessment—accuracy, fluency, terminology, and informational completeness—and detects omissions, redundancy, and stylistic drift. Its outputs can trigger iterative refinement or flag human review, forming a self-inspection and remediation loop (Zhang 2025a, 2025b).

A feedback interface module supports user interaction and adaptive learning: user edits are parsed and incorporated into contextual memory and terminology preferences, progressively capturing user style for continuous optimization.

Together, these six core modules operate in a decoupled yet coordinated fashion (Wiesinger et al., 2024): task awareness initiates information flow; context and terminology modules enforce coherence and standards; translation and evaluation deliver generation plus feedback closure; user feedback drives self-evolution. This architecture surpasses the limits of prompt engineering, providing a robust engineering substrate and a capability platform for complex, multi-scenario language services.

1.3 Development Frameworks for Translation Agents

Building a translation agent with modular control, contextual memory, and dynamic decision-making requires more than simply chaining model calls. It requires an integrated framework that supports task decomposition, tool invocation, memory, and chained execution. Mainstream agent or workflow orchestration toolkits include LangChain, Haystack, and AutoGen, each targeting distinct scenarios. Haystack emphasizes retrieval-augmented generation and document analysis; AutoGen focuses on multi-agent collaboration; Prefect, as a general workflow engine, augments task scheduling and monitoring when integrated with LangChain. Given requirements for flexible module composition, rich ecosystem support, and broad model compatibility, this section uses LangChain as the illustrative platform (Jay, 2024; LangChain, 2024; Wang & Duan, 2024).

The core abstractions in LangChain are "chains" and "agents." Developers encapsulate subtasks—analysis, translation, terminology checking, and review—into ordered execution chains. PromptTemplate enables parameterized input; Memory stores conversational or document context; Retriever provides external knowledge access; OutputParser produces structured outputs. LangChain also integrates smoothly with mainstream models and external utilities such as databases, terminology repositories, and web search (Jay, 2024; LangChain, 2024).

A multi-agent setup, together with a Planner–Executor architecture, enables autonomous flow control and rollback on failure (Zhang et al., 2025). Components such as Prompt Templates and Memory standardize inputs while capturing context and user preferences. An agent can dynamically orchestrate a task chain spanning translation, review, and terminology alignment; combined with the LangSmith platform, it supports end-to-end debugging and performance optimization (LangChain, 2024; Wang & Duan, 2024). LangChain's strengths—module reuse (rich built-in toolset), visual orchestration, debugging support, and community ecosystem—make it a preferred platform for building translation agents (Wu et al., 2024). Subsequent chapters will leverage its modular architecture to demonstrate industrial workflows: task decomposition, dynamic caching, terminology integration, segmented execution, and multi-round quality review.

LangChain's flexibility also heightens development complexity. In multi-agent collaboration or low-latency scenarios, implementation and debugging can be demanding. Deep inter-module dependencies and a steep learning curve may produce performance bottlenecks or external dependency issues as task chains grow. Consequently, frameworks such as Haystack and AutoGen remain valuable complements in targeted use cases. Framework selection should avoid single-path dependence and balance task requirements against team capabilities (Wang et al., 2024; Zhou et al., 2024).

Recently, low-code agent platforms such as Dify and Coze have advanced rapidly. Their visual workflow orchestration and drag-and-drop components lower entry barriers. For language services and educational settings, they let non-technical users prototype quickly by combining model invocation, knowledge retrieval, and context storage, covering baseline agent scenarios.

Our focus is not tool minutiae but the design principles and decomposition logic of translation agents, distilling core stages and industrial challenges. Frameworks are merely implementation vehicles; transferable capability rests on a deep grasp of task structure, information organization, and process segmentation. Sustained engineering practice plus critical reflection enables adaptation to a rapidly evolving ecosystem and the operational deployment of agent innovation.

2 Segmentation of Translation Units and Contextual Cohesion

Once the agent architecture is defined, specifying translation targets and language scope is foundational. A translation agent—constrained by model context windows and other capacities—cannot process an entire long document in one pass; instead, it operates over well-designed segments (Zhang et al., 2021) comprising sentences, paragraphs, phrases, or structured fragments.

Human translators flexibly adjust granularity, neither bound rigidly to sentence boundaries nor severing semantic links. Traditional MT systems and most CAT tools rely on strict sentence segmentation as the basic memory and alignment unit. With large language models, enhanced comprehension and generation have shifted strategies toward semantic completeness and contextual continuity, approximating human decision processes (Wu et al., 2024a, 2024b).

In agent design, principled unit segmentation and preservation of cohesion after splitting define the operational substrate and directly affect downstream coordination and quality (Wu et al., 2024a, 2024b).

2.1 Sentence Segmentation Challenges Across Languages

Using sentences as the fundamental unit remains standard because it simplifies engineering and supports translation memory accumulation and retrieval. Historically, this was justified by limited context modeling and computation. As capabilities expanded, the shortcomings of this sentence-centric approach became pronounced across language families.

Extended sentence constructions are pervasive in Chinese—especially in professional or formal prose—where commas chain coordinated, progressive, or contrastive clauses. Such a source sentence is normally split into several shorter English sentences to clarify argument structure and logical order. Purely punctuation-based segmentation risks cutting before the logic resolves, producing broken information or ambiguity.

English prose marks boundaries more explicitly—full stops, semicolons, coordinating conjunctions—making automatic segmentation comparatively reliable. German and French present complex subordination, yet punctuation and syntax generally align, enabling grammar-aided segmentation, while technical or literary texts still challenge systems via cross-sentence ellipsis and implicit subjects.

In Japanese and Korean, subject omission is frequent; dialogues or expository passages may state the subject once and rely on context thereafter. Such cases require reintroducing the subject in English for coherence; poor segmentation causes referential gaps and diminished clarity.

Slavic and Eastern European languages permit flexible word order and fronting, requiring cross-sentence tracking. Russian nesting and insertions challenge punctuation-only strategies. Arabic and Persian rely on ellipsis and coordinating particles—"و" (and) can chain extensive spans—blurring boundaries. German verb-final clauses with heavy pre-verbal modifiers also resist naive segmentation; cutting before the final verb yields incomplete propositions.

These cases show that unit boundaries cannot be determined solely by punctuation or length. Effective segmentation must integrate language-specific structure, contextual signals, and target discourse norms. Surface heuristics seldom preserve informational equivalence. An agent should, grounded in structural and semantic analysis, flexibly select cut points to maintain coherence and completeness, reducing downstream degradation. This demands intrinsic language understanding and adaptive, language-aware policies.

2.2 Multi-strategy Segmentation and Context Bridging

Automatic translation must align segmentation granularity with strategy. Text type, communicative function, and structural organization impose diverse demands. An agent should flexibly select sentence-, phrase-, or paragraph-level units and adjust dynamically to balance semantic completeness with stylistic consistency (Wang et al., 2023).

Highly structured content—statutes, technical specifications, contract parameters, tables—often benefits from item-, phrase-, or clause-level translation. Isolating a contract clause such as “Unless otherwise stipulated, the written form shall prevail” preserves formatting and liability clarity. Treating “Input voltage: 220 V; Output power: 1.5 kW” as independent parameter phrases supports consistent terminology and accurate re-insertion. Excessive fragmentation can erode context, degrade term consistency, and split unified relations (Bawden et al., 2017).

For emotionally charged or narratively cohesive texts, paragraph-level (or near-paragraph) units preserve holistic context. Splitting such passages into single sentences attenuates mood and rhythm. Paragraph translation helps capture psychological progression and stylistic tone but raises context-capacity demands. For very long or dense paragraphs, topic-sentence detection or sub-summarization mitigates omission or distortion risks (Tiedemann & Scherrer, 2017).

The central task is balancing model context limits against source semantic integrity. Punctuation and length heuristics rarely ensure cohesion; principled segmentation integrates syntax, semantic flow, and discourse logic. For technical and regulatory texts, parsing and dependency relations guide boundaries around predicate–argument clusters and logical connectors, reducing reconstruction effort.

Post-segmentation context bridging critically affects coherence and readability. Isolated processing invites knowledge gaps and stylistic drift. Proactive context injection—adding the preceding dialogue turn or surfacing prior definitions when a term reappears—supports accurate role tracking and reduces omission or ambiguity.

Coreference resolution embodies contextual strategy. Generic pronouns (such as “他” (he/she), “其”(his/her/its), or “该” (this/the said) often require explicit referents in English to avoid vagueness. Clarifying “this success” as profitability improves precision. Automated resolution strengthens clarity and professionalism (Voita et al., 2018).

Multi-strategy unit segmentation plus dynamic context bridging is foundational. Sound criteria and linkage mechanisms underpin quality and stylistic consistency. With diversified strategies and adaptive information integration, an agent can handle heterogeneous structures and complex discourse, approaching professional human performance (Briva-Iglesias, 2025).

3 Task Chains in Translation Agents

A translation agent is not merely an automation tool; it restructures complex language service workflows (Anik et al., 2025; Wang et al., 2025). Its strength lies in decomposing the process into fine-grained, flexibly schedulable nodes. Each node targets a specific function, and explicit information flow plus synchronized context enable efficient collaboration (Xiang et al., 2025). Ordered transfer supports iterative decisions, branching tolerance, robustness, and scalability. Task chains can be adjusted and reused across scenarios. This design ethos—division of labor, information continuity, and flexible coordination—is a key pathway to greater agent intelligence and adaptability.

3.1 Source Ingestion and Structural Decomposition

In long-form workflows, source ingestion is the first and foundational stage. It must normalize heterogeneous formats and structure content for downstream context management, unit scheduling, and reconstruction. Multimodal ingestion workflows that fuse automatic video/audio transcription, summarization, and structured retrieval inform agent designs for heterogeneous source preprocessing (Lavanya et al., 2024). The module should support .docx, .pdf, .html, .md, .json; distinguish body text, footnotes, tables, annotations; and extract structural metadata (chapters, paragraphs) for formatting and tracking.

In LangChain, loaders and splitters (e.g., RecursiveCharacterTextSplitter) segment long texts into length-controlled units with defined overlaps to mitigate fragmentation. Purely length-based slicing, however, overlooks semantic flow and discourse continuity.

Recent work emphasizes semantically aware segmentation. Embedding models (BERT, Sentence-BERT) enable sentence-vector clustering or sliding-window aggregation to produce coherence-preserving boundaries (Reimers & Gurevych, 2019). Alibaba's SeqModel treats segmentation as sequence labeling, using a BERT encoder and self-attention for long dependencies; adaptive windows and mean pooling refine boundaries, improving speed and paragraph sensitivity (Zhang et al., 2021).

In practice, systems also extract titles, numbering, lists, code blocks, and related structures, attaching them as metadata to units. These tags support format restoration and parameterize prompts and context across terminology, quality evaluation, and reconstruction. Metadata propagation becomes task memory, strengthening automation and collaboration.

The output is a set of context-processed units enriched with metadata and appropriate in length, forming the basis for distribution and parallelism. At this stage the system can plan tasks, flag sensitive spans, assign priorities, or configure hybrid allocation. Multiple strategies may run concurrently, with downstream selection of the best-performing segmentation.

Explicit ingestion and structural decomposition stages improve stability and underpin scalable handling of complex workloads.

3.2 Automatic Identification of Register and Style

Style identification furnishes the system with explicit awareness of communicative goals and expression norms (Biber, 1995), informing downstream strategy and parameter choices. Mapping stylistic labels to linguistic features allows alignment of register—news, fiction, advertising, academic, instructional—with suitable lexis and syntax, enhancing naturalness and cross-cultural fit (Heylighen & Dewaele, 2002).

In implementation, contemporary large language models already perform robust style recognition (Liu et al., 2023). A concise prompt often suffices to elicit register and establish a stylistic anchor for subsequent processing. In LangChain, only a few lines of code are required for automatic classification.

```
template = """Please determine which register category the following Chinese text belongs to (news, novel, advertisement, academic, manual, legal text, etc.): {text}↵
Answer format: Register type: [Category]"""  #The model output is directly used as document metadata to drive subsequent translation strategy adjustments↵
```

Model outputs are stored as document-level metadata to guide downstream translation strategy. Beyond coarse style classification, systems extract fine-grained features such as sentence length, grammatical voice, and sentiment polarity. These parameters enable precise syntactic and rhetorical adaptation; sentiment especially shapes tone and lexical choices. In practice, these metadata items are attached to each translation unit for dynamic retrieval, enabling flexible, context-aware modulation.

We illustrate advances in speech synthesis and multi-agent coordination with the task of generating a radio drama from a novel excerpt. Conventional text-to-speech typically relies on a single voice and fails to convey multi-character interaction or emotional depth. High-quality drama synthesis therefore hinges on systematic semantic decomposition of the source.

The first step separates narration from dialogue. Narration (voice-over) can use a neutral timbre, whereas dialogue requires speaker identification and voice selection aligned with age, gender, and persona traits. Large language models can auto-generate voice profiles and prompt parameters. Each utterance then receives an emotion tag—anger, tenderness, puzzlement, and so forth—to drive an emotion-aware synthesis engine and produce prosodically varied segments (Zhang et al., 2019).

Nonverbal sound cues (e.g., "rolling thunder," "the motorcycle roar drawing nearer") embedded in narration or dialogue are likewise extracted and mapped to an effects library for layered insertion. Detection of a "thunder" token, for instance, triggers automatic placement of the corresponding audio asset on the synthesis timeline.

A simplified pipeline is as follows: structural tagging → character and emotion identification → timbre/emotion assignment → sound asset matching → multitrack synthesis. Below is a minimal annotated example: extraction prompts are omitted for brevity.

```
units = [
  {"type": "narration", "text": "The small town was silent under the night.", "voice": "narrator", "emotion": "calm", "sound_effect": "night_breeze"
  },
  {"type": "dialogue", "role": "Li Ming", "text": "Do you really trust him?", "voice": "male_teenager", "emotion": "surprised", "sound_effect": None
  },
  {"type": "narration", "text": "Thunder rumbled.", "voice": "narrator", "emotion": "neutral", "sound_effect": "thunder"
  }
]
```

After these stages, the system can synthesize multichannel audio with distinct character voices, rich affect, and ambient layers, enhancing realism and listener engagement. Style recognition and structural annotation thus support translation while enabling intelligent multimodal generation.

3.3 *Applying Automatic Summarization to Translation Comprehension*

In professional translation, the primary challenge is achieving a reliable global grasp of structure, thematic progression, and salient details. For medium- or long-form texts—novels, manuals, technical standards—an internal model of discourse organization, thematic distribution, entity relations, and information hierarchy underpins quality, terminological consistency, and stylistic coherence (Liu & Demberg, 2024). Automatic summarization meets this need by providing an efficient aid for structural comprehension and information triage.

Summaries lower the cognitive cost of exhaustive reading and support downstream prompt design, terminology extraction, and context assembly (Jiang et al., 2021). In engineering-style workflows for fiction or complex documents, they enact a compress–distill–structure cycle that yields a concise scaffold and improves throughput.

Two principal strategies are extractive and abstractive. Extractive methods embed sentences and apply clustering (e.g., K-Means) to select representative ones, forming section outlines; a LangChain prototype requires only modest code. Because outputs are verbatim excerpts, holistic fluency may be limited.

Abstractive methods use large language models with controllable parameters (length, structural schema) to produce natural paraphrastic summaries (Ho et al., 2024). For fiction, prompts can request plot, character relations, and conflicts; for example:

```
prompt = "Summarize the characters, main plot, and the causal relationships of the conflicts in the following novel excerpt, and output in a table format:\n" + content
```

For technical documentation, prompts may instead demand categorized definitions, key procedures, and warnings—constituting a "situational extraction" pipeline: compress content, isolate entities, events, and emotional shifts, then render a concise situational brief.

These summaries support translators directly and feed pre-translation term review and style templating. Before tackling a narrative scene, a structured synopsis clarifies core events, principal characters, and emotional trajectory, guiding tone, voice design, and multimodal planning. In radio drama generation, scene summaries precede synthesis to allocate voices, pace narration, and set prosody, timbre, and rhythm parameters.

At scale, summarization is computationally moderate and far cheaper than manual sentence-level analysis. Offloading compression frees human effort for refinement, quality control, and creative problem solving, elevating both efficiency and quality.

3.4 *Broad-Scope Terminology Extraction and Consistency Assurance*

In a translation agent's task chain, terminology identification and consistency assurance underpin standardization and professional reliability (Jiang & Gong, 2025). Broad terminology spans technical lexemes, culturally laden expressions, set phrases, slang, and toponyms—dense carriers of structural, stylistic, and cultural meaning whose mishandling leads to distortion or misreading.

The pipeline begins with recognition to maintain continuous tracking. Departing from frequency or POS heuristics, an agent leverages large language models plus external knowledge bases for context-aware extraction. A "translation salience" score per phrase can integrate contextual uniqueness, KB coverage, and ambiguity risk. Below is a LangChain illustration; the dictionary endpoint is placeholder logic.

```
from langchain.prompts import PromptTemplate

from langchain.llms import OpenAI

from langchain.chains import LLMChain

import json

import requests


# 1. Let the LLM output keywords, reasons, and reference translations in JSON structure

template = """

Please read the following text paragraph and label all key terms that meet at least one of the following conditions:

1. Domain-specific or technical terms; 2. Culturally loaded words; 3. Words with significant semantic function. For each term, briefly explain the extraction reason and provide a reference translation based on the context. Output in the following JSON format:

[

  {{

    "term": "xxx",

    "reason": "Brief explanation",

    "reference_translation": "xxx"

  }},

  ...

]

The paragraph is as follows: {text}  """

prompt = PromptTemplate(input_variables=["text"], template=template)

llm = OpenAI(temperature=0)

chain = LLMChain(llm=llm, prompt=prompt)

llm_result = chain.run("This is a description of Sichuan Opera face-changing, which involves many cultural symbols of traditional Chinese opera.")

terms_list = json.loads(llm_result)
```

```
# 2. Query the dictionary API and merge definitions into the results
def lookup_dictionary(term):
  try:
    resp =
requests.get(f"https://api.chinese_culture_dictionary.com/lookup?term={term}")
    data = resp.json()
    return data.get("definition", "")
  except Exception:
    return ""


# Traverse the LLM results, query the dictionary, and write to the dict_content field
for item in terms_list:
  dict_content = lookup_dictionary(item.get('term', ''))
  item['dict_content'] = dict_content


# 3. Output structured results with original information and dictionary content
print(json.dumps(terms_list, ensure_ascii=False, indent=2))
```

An automated module iteratively tunes prompts and criteria—augmented by human annotation—to improve precision and contextual fitness (Kageura & Umino, 1996). Entity linking associates terms with resources (Wikipedia, DBpedia), reinforcing standardization. Culturally specific items (e.g., "变脸," Sichuan opera face-changing) require exact localization and semantic mapping for lookup, annotation, and template construction, via either automated or human-validated workflows. Safeguarding culturally embedded expressions in heritage and low-resource materials motivates agent modules that pair contextual translation with knowledge bases and preservation metadata (Hastuti et al., n.d.).

For named entities, Named Entity Recognition (NER) and Knowledge Base (KB) linking standardize persons, organizations, and locations and support cross-lingual alignment. The agent can broaden queries to capture variants and present ranked translation candidates with confidence indications.

Within the chain, terminology and consistency modules coordinate with style and context management. Recognized terms are injected into prompts as explicit constraints; after generation, global audits verify consistency. The overarching loop—extraction, semantic calibration, KB alignment, candidate generation, consistency checking—runs automatically with optional human oversight to raise domain fidelity.

As the glossary grows, it becomes a structured termbase containing canonical forms, approved translations, parts of speech, domain labels, definitions, usage examples, and contextual notes—an authoritative reference whose accuracy bar is higher than that for general vocabulary.

Inside the agent, the termbase becomes an active module: informing recognition, conditioning generation, and driving post-editing QA. Coupled with prompt strategies, it can enforce or prioritize standard forms or steer selection through constrained decoding (Hokamp & Liu, 2017).

Application domains now extend from science, law, and medicine to news, culture, and gaming. Management of culturally loaded terms, slang, jargon, and brand names can remain flexible: the system fuses termbase data and context to detect and normalize complex multiword or inflected forms for cross-domain consistency. Mandatory insertion suits high-consistency scenarios; adaptive prompting or ranked candidates preserves naturalness in style-diverse content.

The termbase also integrates with post-translation QA to flag misuse, omission, or inconsistency and generate statistical reports. It should support continual expansion to absorb new entries, closing the knowledge loop and sustaining large-scale, standardized, high-quality output.

3.5 Pre-translation Processing of Long and Complex Sentences

Preprocessing long or syntactically intricate sentences is critical for both quality and throughput. Scientific articles, legal clauses, German academic prose, and French expository texts often exhibit deep nesting, dense modification, and frequent logical shifts that inflate cognitive and computational load—common loci of MT errors. Effective preprocessing flattens complexity into tractable units and improves semantic control downstream.

Typical manifestations include stacked attributive or adverbial modifiers, nested subordination, long-distance dependencies, parentheticals, passives, and multi-layer clause embedding: German post-nominal chains, French participial inversions, deeply nested English conditionals or nominal groups, and unmarked paratactic Chinese long sentences.

During segmentation and structural analysis, traditional parsers and large language models are complementary. Rule-based tokenizers (NLTK, Jieba), statistical models, and neural architectures (BiLSTM-CRF, BERT variants) drive splitting, dependency parsing, and phrase structure analysis. Toolkits such as spaCy and Stanza yield precise dependencies and clause boundaries, exposing main clauses, subordinates, and insertions for targeted simplification (Qi et al., 2020).

Operationally, English relative clauses, appositives, and parentheticals are reduced to core propositions via dependency paths. Chinese paratactic long sentences are partitioned with punctuation, connective detection, and dependency boundaries. The system then unpacks them into shorter, explicit sentences, mitigating overload.

Large language models (e.g., GPT-4, ChatGPT) can, through prompting, analyze, simplify, and restructure complex sentences without handcrafted grammar rules (Madaan et al., 2023). Examples follow:

> Please split the following complex sentence into several clear and concise simple sentences, making sure that each sentence expresses a complete idea and that logical connections are preserved.
>
> Sentence: The results, which were obtained after careful analysis and repeated experiments, strongly suggest that the proposed method is reliable, despite some limitations that have been acknowledged by the authors.

Model output:

> The results were obtained after careful analysis and repeated experiments.
>
> The authors have acknowledged some limitations.
>
> Despite these limitations, the results strongly suggest that the proposed method is reliable.

Another example:

> Please break the following long sentence into short sentences with clear structure and complete meaning, keeping the overall meaning coherent. Each sentence should include a clear subject and object.
>
> Sentence: 李明因为赶时间，在还没吃早饭的情况下，匆匆忙忙地骑自行车去了公司，结果在路上遇到了堵车，只好给领导打电话说明情况。

Model output:

> 李明因为赶时间，还没吃早饭就出门了。
>
> 他匆忙骑自行车去公司。
>
> 李明路上遇到堵车。
>
> 他只好给领导打电话说明情况。

In production, deep learning parsers supply scalable structural annotations and initial splits, while prompt-driven LLMs refine especially intricate or context-dependent segments for greater naturalness; together, they enhance robustness and flexibility (Wibawa & Kurniawan, 2024).

Semantic preservation and coherence controls can be layered through prompt design and few-shot examples: the model restores omitted subjects, resolves ellipses, and clarifies pronoun antecedents so each sentence is self-contained. Stacked modifiers or passives can be recast as coordinated or active clauses (e.g., "The complex data processing workflow completed by Zhang San in the laboratory" → "Zhang San completed the data processing in the laboratory. The workflow was complex.").

The same methodology generalizes across languages with typological adaptation—for instance, accommodating German stacking of post-nominal modifiers and Japanese clause chaining that uses the conjunctive particles "て" ("and/then"), " で" (*de*, " and/so"), and "が" (*ga*, " but/although"), and so on. Language-specific rules can be tuned per corpus. For example, splitting a German legal conditional into independent declaratives prevents fragmentation in the target translation.

In deployment, this preprocessing serves as an upstream automated step: outputs feed neural MT and clarify structure for human review. The system can then verify semantic fidelity of generated long sentences and trigger further simplification if needed. Deep linguistic integration thus establishes a scalable foundation for multilingual, human-in-the-loop translation.

3.6 Designing Workflows for Translation Generation and Optimization

Within an intelligent translation agent, the generation stage is central: it handles the densest information and offers the broadest decision space. The system must rapidly parse source structure, style, and domain terminology, then produce target text that is efficient, controlled, and faithful. Unlike a human translator relying on tacit expertise, large-language-model–based generation depends on explicit strategy design and systematic decomposition to realize scalable quality (Wu, 2024). Long-form translation is intrinsically complex—spanning inter-paragraph referential jumps, polysemous terminology, and stylistic shifts—and thus raises the bar for context retention, stylistic control, and knowledge integration (Karpinska & Iyyer, 2023).

Initial translation quality determines the downstream workload for revision, back translation, and feedback. Well-designed generation strategies improve the draft and supply structural scaffolding for each subsequent stage. Accordingly, translation generation constitutes an engineering problem of nested control and collaboration, requiring rule injection and adaptive modulation rather than one-shot model output (Kocmi & Federmann, 2023). This chapter extends prior discussion of prompt engineering to analyze generation strategies and the design of underlying mechanisms for translation agents.

3.7 Translation Generation and Multi-model Orchestration

Within the agent architecture, generation bridges source comprehension and target delivery. Quality depends not only on the primary translation model but also on coordinated auxiliary models or functional units. "Model orchestration" covers both collaboration among distinct deployed models and chaining of role-specific prompt invocations of a single LLM (LangChain Team, 2024). This orchestration enables finer-grained and more flexible generation pathways.

In practice, the primary model handles core semantic transfer and generation. Auxiliary units specialize in terminology normalization, style adaptation, and format validation. For medical literature, the system first produces a full draft with the main model; then auxiliary modules—guided by task-specific prompts—standardize clinical terminology or revise segments to match medical discourse norms (Yamada, 2023). Additional modules may target syntactic integrity, cross-sentence coherence, or lexical register to enforce global consistency.

Coordination patterns vary with task demands; common paradigms include staged processing and parallel review. Patent translation often uses a staged pipeline: draft generation followed by term-by-term validation. News translation favors parallelism: the main output streams to auxiliaries for real-time error detection and rapid light editing. Workflow tools such as LangChain chain units efficiently, yielding a streamlined, well-partitioned automation sequence (LangChain Team, 2024).

Orchestration also enables dynamic feedback. When auxiliaries flag difficult terms or ambiguities, they can propose alternatives for model- or human-level selection. This is critical in high-precision domains such as policy and law. Legal contract workflows commonly layer: the primary model performs semantic transfer; a terminology unit enforces legal term accuracy; a formatting unit preserves clause structure; and a compliance unit adapts sensitive clauses to local norms. This layered design boosts professional quality and reduces manual review burden.

In multilingual business intelligence reporting, the agent processes heterogeneous sources. The main model produces preliminary translations; an information-extraction unit structures entities and metrics; a data-alignment unit reconciles discrepancies; and a style module adjusts sequencing and terminology to business conventions. Automated role partitioning plus dynamic feedback improves efficiency and the quality of the final report.

Multi-model collaboration is now integral to translation generation. Clear division of labor, shared intermediate data, and staged refinement raise quality on complex material and provide a foundation for automated quality assurance and advanced optimization. This paradigm marks an expansion of language services beyond traditional translation into broader, more complex, and more intelligent applications.

3.7.1 Consistency Strategies Across Multiple Translation Units

Because context windows are finite, long texts must be segmented, risking style drift, term inconsistency, and contextual breaks—especially in literary, governmental, or corporate communication. Ensuring document-wide consistency is therefore a first-order design concern (Karpinska & Iyyer, 2023).

Style consistency shapes authority and readability. In an annual report, uncoordinated generators may yield uneven register. Prompt directives (e.g., "Translate in a formal written style.") enforce a baseline. A further enhancement is a style memory module that abstracts prior stylistic features and injects an updated summary before each segment. Frameworks such as LangChain provide a global "StyleMemoryAgent" to maintain continuity (LangChain Team, 2024).

Terminology consistency remains critical in technical, medical, and legal domains; variation erodes perceived expertise. Once a client specifies "充填剂" for "filler" or "刻蚀" for "etching," alternatives must be avoided.

Typically the agent extracts candidate terms in a segment, retrieves matching glossary entries, and injects explicit constraints into the prompt before generation, for example:

> Please translate the following paragraph into Chinese, ensuring that professional terms are consistent with the following glossary:
>
> Glossary:
>
> - tokenization: 分词
>
> - corpus: 语料库
>
> Original text:
>
> {source_text}

A terminology cache records rendered terms and appends them to later prompts, reinforcing uniformity. Dictionary-based phrase-level prompting enables high-precision lexical constraint injection into agent translation stages without cumbersome manual glossary engineering (Ghazvininejad et al., 2023). In LangChain, a memory buffer can maintain and inject this evolving bilingual map automatically.

Maintaining contextual continuity is the central challenge in long-form translation. Limited windows hinder access to global discourse and promote drift. A sliding-window buffer supplies adjacent source and target snippets as auxiliary context (Hendy et al., 2023). For extended documents, a summarization agent extracts and updates structured keys—e.g., "study population," "methodological pipeline"—as surrogate context. In scientific articles, injecting previously extracted core concepts or hypotheses during the Methods or Discussion sections boosts terminological and logical consistency (Wu, 2024). Pre-caching cross-chapter referents further reduces ambiguity and mistranslation.

From an engineering standpoint, workflow tools (e.g., LangChain) support incremental memory. ConversationBufferMemory stores summarized context after each generation and injects it into the next prompt, sustaining a rolling short-term memory that improves cohesion.

It also enables retroactive normalization: after an acronym is introduced, earlier occurrences can be standardized automatically. The same approach suits multi-chapter technical or policy documents with extensive appendices, allowing incremental generation, sustained memory, and reduced per-call load.

Consequently, multi-unit consistency hinges on coordinated management of style, terminology, and context—an engineering test of memory and control design whose effectiveness determines long-form performance and deployability.

3.7.2 Approaching an Optimal Translation via Stepwise Mechanisms

LLMs excel not only at one-shot rendering but at simulating the translator's iterative workflow. Translation is a multi-stage cycle of drafting, probing, analysis, and refinement. Decomposing it into coarse draft → diagnostic review → targeted optimization enables progressive gains and interpretability, imparting a human-like dynamic (Jiao et al., 2023).

Operationally, the stepwise pipeline adapts to task goals. For style calibration, the system may generate divergent drafts: one structurally literal, one meaning-oriented for fluency, another rhetorically enriched. Each includes concise annotations of tone, lexical coloring, and syntax to expedite assessment. Human or automated selection then aligns with audience expectations and communicative function, fixing a global stylistic baseline.

For culturally or historically dense texts, curated background forms a distinct precursor stage. With poetry or classical prose, the system queries reference corpora and commentary to extract salient images, allusions, and period context, then feeds a distilled brief alongside the source. For "登鹳雀楼" ("Climbing the Stork Tower"), foregrounding ascent, temporal layering, and expansive landscape helps convey literal sense plus aesthetic resonance.

Where reliability is paramount, back translation provides an added safeguard. The system re-translates the draft and aligns sentences to flag omissions, semantic drift, or redundancy; targeted revisions address each divergence. Iterative cycles converge toward accuracy and natural tone. A polishing phase then tunes diction and cadence for fidelity plus idiomatic elegance (Chen et al., 2023).

Its value lies in composability: a configurable constellation of stages rather than a rigid linear algorithm. Semi-independent phases reinforce one another's decisions, providing flexibility and depth. The method can sculpt literary style, enforce terminological rigor in technical texts, illustrate pedagogical progression, and scale industrial output. It shifts MT from single-pass output to a controllable, convergent process. Modular design also eases integration with CAT tools, termbases, and QA systems.

3.7.3 Translation Refinement and Personalized Adjustment

Generation is only the starting point; high quality depends on layered verification and iterative editing. Multi-level checks and style adjustments balance fidelity, logical integrity, and natural expression. LLMs provide scalable infrastructure so automation and expert review combine fluidly across genres and precision requirements.

An initial pass eliminates surface issues—grammar, spelling, punctuation, formatting—and checks genre appropriateness (e.g., terminological precision in abstracts, formal register in administrative documents). The aim is a clean baseline.

Subsequent human review emphasizes judgment. Automation highlights potential issues or style divergences with suggestions; editors arbitrate using context and intent. This "machine triage—human decision" pattern improves speed and accuracy. In annual reports, flagged variant renderings of proprietary terms are resolved for document-wide uniformity.

Multi-round review is progressive: round one targets terminology and structural completeness; round two validates logic and key content; the final pass harmonizes style and formatting. In contracts, clause integrity precedes legal risk vetting, followed by stylistic refinement for readability without compromising compliance.

For high-stakes texts, back translation adds a safeguard: alignment reveals omissions, semantic drift, and logical inconsistencies in government documents, cross-border agreements, or literature. A validated back translation can then be polished (meaning preserved) to reach near-native fluency.

Personalized tuning aligns output with audience and purpose. Legal documents, patents, and corporate releases prioritize precision; literary, marketing, or social content prizes naturalness and vivid tone. Pre-setting style, audience, and purpose parameters shapes lexical coloring and rhythm. Term-dense texts benefit from termbase-driven drift monitoring. Cross-cultural adaptation may employ style transfer to shift between formal and conversational, concise and elaborated, while localizing usage norms.

Risk-detection layers can audit contextual coherence, coreference accuracy, and sentiment alignment. Highlighted spans—ambiguous, omitted, mistranslated, or structurally fractured—are queued for targeted human review. Continuous monitoring prevents local anomalies from degrading long-form quality.

Ultimately, refinement is not mere error fixing but structured, multi-level, customizable balancing of fidelity, logic, and stylistic consistency. Across scholarly publishing, international business, and cultural dissemination, this mechanism underwrites professional high-quality deployment.

3.7.4 Quality Evaluation in Translation Agents

Quality evaluation is not a terminal step but a continual process driving iterative improvement. It monitors workflow, detects deviations, and supplies data for model tuning and human–machine collaboration. For long, multi-chapter, or stylistically variable texts, evaluation must be systematic and layered to assure accuracy and coherence. Fine-grained, LLM-assisted error categorization pipelines now surface systematic terminology, discourse, and adequacy weaknesses to drive targeted iterative refinement (Fernandes et al., 2023).

Established frameworks include Multidimensional Quality Metrics (MQM) and the Translation Automation User Society Dynamic Quality Framework (DQF). MQM categorizes errors (meaning, language, presentation, adaptability) and covers omissions, mistranslations, term inconsistency, and ambiguity; DQF emphasizes scenario-specific standards. Automatic post-editing frameworks aligned with MQM taxonomies (MQM-APE) provide supervised feedback signals that can be looped into evaluator–rewriter cycles for continual quality gains (Lu et al., 2024). In large language model-driven systems, these map to structured prompts and feedback templates that identify issues, explain causes, and propose remediation (Moghe et al., 2025; Wang et al., 2025).

Legacy metrics (Bilingual Evaluation Understudy (BLEU), Recall-Oriented Understudy for Gisting Evaluation (ROUGE), Translation Edit Rate (TER)) underperform on long-form style cohesion and reader experience; newer models (Crosslingual Optimized Metric for Evaluation of Translation (COMET), Bilingual Evaluation Understudy with Representations from Transformers (BLEURT)) still depend on human references, limiting adaptability as machine output approaches human quality. Comparative judgment protocols yield more reliable human preference signals than absolute scoring and can calibrate or fine-tune evaluator agents in human-in-the-loop settings (Song et al., 2025). A more promising direction embeds self-evaluating assessor agents so generation and multidimensional critique proceed jointly, with immediate optimization feedback for a sustainable, self-improving pipeline. An example in LangChain follows:

```
from langchain.agents import Tool, initialize_agent

from langchain.chat_models import ChatOpenAI

quality_prompt = """

You are a professional translation quality evaluator. Please assess the translation
quality based on the following criteria:

1. Whether the original information is faithfully conveyed;

2. Whether the language is natural and conforms to the conventions of the target
language;

3. Whether terminology and style are consistent;

4. Whether there are issues such as mistranslation, omission, repetition, or
semantic ambiguity;

Please provide an analysis for each item and give an overall score.

Source text: {source}

Translation: {target}

"""

llm = ChatOpenAI()

tool = Tool(name="QualityEvaluator",

        func=lambda x: llm.predict(quality_prompt.format(**x)),

        description="Used for translation quality analysis")

agent = initialize_agent([tool], llm, agent="chat-zero-shot-react-description")

agent.run({"source": "The system was implemented in three phases.","target": "系
统实施分为三个阶段。"})
```

In complex workflows, evaluation runs alongside terminology extraction and structural alignment, operating per segment and globally. Results feed directly into post-editing or retranslation: term inconsistencies trigger alignment; logical breaks prompt restructuring—closing a translate–assess–revise loop.

Self-feedback and multi-version comparison extend autonomous optimization: the system drafts stylistically or structurally varied candidates, the evaluator scores them, and the best proceeds. Back-translation alignment exposes omissions or breaks. Accumulated feedback gradually tunes lexical and phrasing strategies to user preferences.

This evaluation-driven optimization loop improves controllability and explainability while supporting division of labor, continuous improvement, and knowledge transfer. For translators and learners, automated assessment is both a training aid and a bridge between quality standards and practice.

Implementation can rely on a multi-agent architecture: a primary translator drafts, an evaluator supplies multidimensional feedback (terminology, syntactic clarity, fluency), and a rewriter issues a revised version. Iteration continues until thresholds are met. This preserves cross-segment consistency and, via structured feedback rather than manual labels, shifts from passive observation to guided self-correction—a key path toward autonomy.

4 Conclusion

As LLMs and multi-agent technologies evolve, translation agents are moving beyond linear "input–output" utilities toward adaptive collaborative systems capable of continual learning and optimization. Engineering elements—model orchestration, task-chain design, consistency controls, self-feedback evaluation—signal deeper integration into professional workflows via open, extensible architectures.

Research trajectories indicate an emerging "symbiotic evolution" ecosystem: agents integrate models, tooling, termbases, and evaluation frameworks while assimilating translator and user feedback to iteratively refine behavior. Iterative human-in-the-loop corpus generation approaches demonstrate efficient workflows for bootstrapping high-quality parallel datasets that enhance agent adaptation (Yuksel et al., 2025). This modular, feedback-driven design elevates professional productivity and opens pathways in education, research, and cross-cultural communication.

Future agents will handle not only language conversion but also cross-domain knowledge integration, pragmatic adaptation, and creative expression. Realizing this potential requires sustained innovation in architecture and workflow design. Through ongoing exploration, translation agents can become foundational catalysts of communication and understanding in a knowledge-driven society.

References

Anik, M., Rahman, A., Wasi, A., & Ahsan, M. (2025). Preserving cultural identity with context-aware translation through multi-agent AI systems. In *The 1st Workshop on Language Models for Underserved Communities* (LM4UC 2025) (pp. 51-60).

Bawden, R., Sennrich, R., Birch, A., & Haddow, B. (2017). Evaluating discourse phenomena in neural machine translation. arXiv. https://arxiv.org/abs/1711.00513

Biber, D. (1995). *Dimensions of register variation: A cross-linguistic comparison.* Cambridge University Press.

Briva-Iglesias, V. (2025). Are AI agents the new machine translation frontier? Challenges and opportunities of single- and multi-agent systems for multilingual digital communication. arXiv. https://arxiv.org/abs/2504.12891

Chen, P., Guo, Z., Haddow, B., & Heafield, K. (2023). *Iterative translation refinement with large language models.* arXiv. https://doi.org/10.48550/arXiv.2306.03856

China Academy of Information and Communications Technology & Huawei Technologies Co., Ltd. [中国信息通信研究院和华为技术有限公司]. (2025). *Intelligent Agent Technology and Application Research Report* [智能体技术和应用研究报告]. Retrieved July 4, 2025, from http://221.179.172.81/images/20250626/69921750901113785.pdf

Fernandes, P., Deutsch, D., Finkelstein, M., Riley, P., Martins, A. F. T., Neubig, G., Garg, A., Clark, J. H., Freitag, M., & Firat, O. (2023). The devil is in the errors: Leveraging large language models for fine-grained machine translation evaluation. arXiv. https://doi.org/10.48550/arXiv.2308.07286

Ghazvininejad, M., Gonen, H., & Zettlemoyer, L. (2023). Dictionary-based phrase-level prompting of large language models for machine translation. arXiv. https://arxiv.org/abs/2302.07856

Hastuti, K., Hidayat, E. Y., Alzami, F., Risqa, I., Ahmad, S., & Fahmi, H. (n.d.). Preserving cultural heritage through AI: A novel framework integrating LangChain and ChatGPT for analyzing and digitalizing the Javanese Pawukon calendar system. SSRN. https://ssrn.com/abstract=5294970

Heylighen, F., & Dewaele, J. M. (2002). Variation in the contextuality of language: An empirical measure. *Foundations of Science, 7*(3), 293–340. https://doi.org/10.1023/A:1019661126744

Ho, X., Nguyen, A. K. D., Dao, A. T., Jiang, J., Chida, Y., Sugimoto, K., ... & Aizawa, A. (2024). *A survey of pre-trained language models for processing scientific text*. arXiv. https://doi.org/10.48550/arXiv.2401.17824

Hokamp, C., & Liu, Q. (2017). Lexically constrained decoding for sequence generation using grid beam search. arXiv. https://arxiv.org/abs/1704.07138

Jay, R. (2024). *Generative AI apps with LangChain and Python*. Springer Nature.

Jiang, S., Wang, R., Li, Z., Utiyama, M., Chen, K., Sumita, E., Zhao, H., & Lu, B.-L. (2021). Document-level neural machine translation with associated memory network. *IEICE Transactions on Information and Systems, 104*(10), 1712–1723. https://doi.org/10.1587/transinf.2020EDP7244

Jiang, Y., & Gong, Z. (2025). Document-level neural machine translation based on rhetorical structure. *Computer Engineering & Science, 47*(1), 180–190. http://joces.nudt.edu.cn/EN/Y2025/V47/I01/180

Jiao, W., Wang, W., Huang, J. T., Wang, X., & Tu, Z. (2023). Is ChatGPT a good translator? Yes with GPT-4 as the engine. arXiv. https://arxiv.org/abs/2301.08745

Kageura, K., & Umino, B. (1996). Methods of automatic term recognition: A review. *Terminology. International Journal of Theoretical and Applied Issues in Specialized Communication, 3*(2), 259–289.

Karpinska, M., & Iyyer, M. (2023). Large language models effectively leverage document-level context for literary translation, but critical errors persist. arXiv. https://arxiv.org/abs/2304.03245

Kocmi, T., & Federmann, C. (2023). Large language models are state-of-the-art evaluators of translation quality. arXiv. https://arxiv.org/abs/2302.14520

LangChain. (2024). *State of AI agents report*. https://www.langchain.com/stateofaiagents

LangChain Team. (2024). *LangGraph: Multi-agent workflows. LangChain Blog*. https://blog.langchain.com/langgraph-multi-agent-workflows/

Lavanya, K., Aravind, K., & Dixit, V. (2024). *Advanced video transcription and summarization: A synergy of LangChain, language models, and VectorDB with Mozilla Deep Speech*. In *2024 Second International Conference on Emerging Trends in Information Technology and Engineering (ICETITE)* (pp. 1–9). IEEE.

Liu, D., & Demberg, V. (2024). RST-LoRA: A discourse-aware low-rank adaptation for long document abstractive summarization. arXiv. https://arxiv.org/abs/2405.00657

Liu, P., Yuan, W., Fu, J., Jiang, Z., Hayashi, H., & Neubig, G. (2023). Pre-train, prompt, and predict: A systematic survey of prompting methods in natural language processing. *ACM Computing Surveys, 55*(9), 1–35.

Lu, Q., Ding, L., Zhang, K., Zhang, J., & Tao, D. (2024). MQM-APE: Toward high-quality error annotation predictors with automatic post-editing in LLM translation evaluators. arXiv. https://arxiv.org/abs/2409.14335

Madaan, A., Tandon, N., Gupta, P., Hallinan, S., Gao, L., Wiegreffe, S., ... & Clark, P. (2023). Self-refine: Iterative refinement with self-feedback. *Advances in Neural Information Processing Systems, 36*, 46534–46594.

Moghe, N., Fazla, A., Amrhein, C., Kocmi, T., Steedman, M., Birch, A., ... & Guillou, L. (2025). Machine translation meta evaluation through translation accuracy challenge sets. *Computational Linguistics, 51*(1), 73–137.

Qi, P., Zhang, Y., Zhang, Y., Bolton, J., & Manning, C. D. (2020). Stanza: A Python natural language processing toolkit for many human languages. arXiv. https://arxiv.org/abs/2003.07082

Reimers, N., & Gurevych, I. (2019). Sentence-BERT: Sentence embeddings using Siamese BERT networks. arXiv. https://arxiv.org/abs/1908.10084

Song, Y., Riley, P., Deutsch, D., & Freitag, M. (2025). Enhancing human evaluation in machine translation with comparative judgment. arXiv. https://arxiv.org/abs/2502.17797

Tiedemann, J., & Scherrer, Y. (2017). Neural machine translation with extended context. arXiv. https://arxiv.org/abs/1708.05943

Voita, E., Serdyukov, P., Sennrich, R., & Titov, I. (2018). Context-aware neural machine translation learns anaphora resolution. arXiv. https://arxiv.org/abs/1805.10163

Wang, J., & Duan, Z. (2024). Agent AI with LangGraph: A modular framework for enhancing machine translation using large language models. arXiv. https://arxiv.org/abs/2412.03801

Wang, L., Lyu, C., Ji, T., Zhang, Z., Yu, D., Shi, S., & Tu, Z. (2023). Document-level machine translation with large language models. arXiv. https://arxiv.org/abs/2304.02210

Wang, L., Ma, C., Feng, X., Zhang, Z., Yang, H., Zhang, J., ... & Wen, J. (2024). A survey on large language model based autonomous agents. *Frontiers of Computer Science, 18*(6), 186345.

Wang, Q., Hu, J., & Ali, S. (2025). MAATS: A multi-agent automated translation system based on MQM evaluation. arXiv. https://arxiv.org/abs/2505.14848

Wibawa, A. P., & Kurniawan, F. (2024). Advancements in natural language processing: Implications, challenges, and future directions. *Telematics and Informatics Reports, 16*, Article 100173.

Wiesinger, J., Marlow, P., & Vuskovic, V. (2024). Agents. Retrieved July 9, 2025, from https://www.kaggle.com/whitepaper-agents

Wu, F. (2024). English translation method based on natural language processing in IoT environment on research. *International Journal of Computational Intelligence Studies, 13*(1–2), 40–59.

Wu, M., Xu, J., & Wang, L. (2024, November). TransAgents: Build your translation company with language agents. In *Proceedings of the 2024 Conference on Empirical Methods in Natural Language Processing: System Demonstrations* (pp. 131–141).

Wu, M., Xu, J., Yuan, Y., Haffari, G., Wang, L., Luo, W., & Zhang, K. (2024). (Perhaps) beyond human translation: Harnessing multi-agent collaboration for translating ultra-long literary texts. arXiv. https://arxiv.org/abs/2405.11804

Xiang, V., Snell, C., Gandhi, K., Albalak, A., Singh, A., Blagden, C., Phung, D., Rafailov, R., Lile, N., Mahan, D., Castricato, L., Franken, J.-P., Haber, N., & Finn, C. (2025). Towards System 2 reasoning in LLMs: Learning how to think with meta chain-of-thought. arXiv. https://doi.org/10.48550/arXiv.2501.04682

Yamada, M. (2023). Optimizing machine translation through prompt engineering: An investigation into ChatGPT's customizability. arXiv. https://arxiv.org/abs/2308.01391

Yuksel, K. A., Gunduz, A., Anees, A. B., & Sawaf, H. (2025). Efficient machine translation corpus generation: Integrating human-in-the-loop post-editing with large language models. arXiv. https://arxiv.org/abs/2502.12755

Zhang, Q., Chen, Q., Li, Y., Liu, J., & Wang, W. (2021, December). Sequence model with self-adaptive sliding window for efficient spoken document segmentation. In *2021 IEEE Automatic Speech Recognition and Understanding Workshop (ASRU)* (pp. 411–418). IEEE.

Zhang, S., Li, R., Wang, S., Koehn, P., Yang, M., & Wong, D. F. (2025). HiMATE: A hierarchical multi-agent framework for machine translation evaluation. arXiv. https://arxiv.org/abs/2505.16281

Zhang, S., So, O., Black, M., & Fan, C. (2025). Discrete GCBF proximal policy optimization for multi-agent safe optimal control. arXiv. https://arxiv.org/abs/2502.03640

Zhang, Y. J., Pan, S., He, L., & Ling, Z. H. (2019). Learning latent representations for style control and transfer in end-to-end speech synthesis. In *ICASSP 2019—IEEE International Conference on Acoustics, Speech and Signal Processing (ICASSP)* (pp. 6945–6949). IEEE.

Zhou, T., Li, X., Zhou, J. L., & Li, Y. (2024). 大模型智能体: 概念, 前沿和产业实践 [Large model agents: Concepts, frontiers, and industrial practices]. Journal of University of Electronic Science and Technology of China (Social Sciences Edition) [电子科技大学学报社科版], *26*(4), 57–62.

Zhu, W., Liu, H., Dong, Q., Xu, J., Huang, S., Kong, L., Chen, J., & Li, L. (2023). Multilingual machine translation with large language models: Empirical results and analysis. arXiv. https://doi.org/10.48550/arXiv.2304.04675

Chapter 9
Architecting Translation Workflows

Abstract This chapter proposes a systematic architecture for translation workflows enabled by Large Language Models (LLMs), elevating isolated model functions into controllable, scalable process systems. It differentiates agent-level (functional execution) and platform-level (project governance) workflows and analyzes long-form requirements: multi-level contextual scaffolding (document → paragraph → sentence → word), machine-executable personalization rules, and efficiency/reuse via versioning, caching, near-duplicate clustering, and quality estimation–post-editing loops. A modular reference architecture is detailed (user interface, functional nodes, shared storage, workflow engine, and external integration), together with interaction logic, engine selection criteria (Airflow, Prefect, and BPMN engines), UI design for multi-role collaboration, structured storage modeling of heterogeneous artifacts, and standardized integration of machine translation, LLMs, and auxiliary tools. Practical pipeline construction across increasing node granularities shows that well-designed orchestration improves terminological consistency, structural coherence, and cost efficiency compared with monolithic direct LLM translation, while gaps remain for nuanced literary style. The chapter positions workflows as the foundation of an extensible ecosystem spanning multimodal translation, real-time adaptation, and cross-domain language services.

Large language models (LLMs) play increasingly diverse roles across the translation pipeline, covering linguistic consistency management, style analysis, cognitive assistance, translation generation, and quality optimization. As multi-agent collaboration continues to mature, systems increasingly move beyond function-level modularity toward holistic process intelligence. Existing literature has largely focused on single-model implementations; in production, however, a lone agent rarely satisfies complex, cross-domain translation requirements. For large-scale, heterogeneous projects, integrating capabilities and orchestrating efficient collaboration remain core design priorities (Li et al., 2024).

Introducing the workflow paradigm establishes a structured organization for model invocation and task management (Fan et al., 2024; Kaleigha et al., 2024). A workflow delineates functional module boundaries and sequencing and specifies data

J. S. Yu and Y. Yao, *Intelligent Language Services*,
https://doi.org/10.1007/978-981-95-4632-9_9

routing, exception handling, and resource scheduling, thereby enhancing controllability, scalability, and evolvability. This process-oriented approach converts dispersed agent capabilities into an ordered task system that scales from a few translation units to entire books. Differences between platform-level and agent-level workflows in abstraction and management scope underpin multi-layer collaboration and flexible configuration.

1 Fundamentals of Translation Workflows

The essence of a translation workflow lies in integrating dispersed agent capabilities and task nodes into an ordered, controllable information-processing chain. Traditional workflows rely on personal experience and linear actions and thus struggle with multi-stage, collaborative production demands. A process-driven approach clarifies task structure, standardizes data flow, and strengthens node collaboration, shifting translation from individual operation to systematic management. Defining appropriate boundaries between agent modules and the workflow platform, while aligning user requirements with system architecture lays the groundwork for efficient, scalable automated language services.

1.1 System Foundations for Process Integration and Agent Collaboration

In automated or semi-automated translation systems, integrating dispersed agent capabilities into a collaboratively executable structure is critical to overall efficiency. Large language models are now maturely applied to terminology handling, context completion, style adaptation, translation generation, and quality inspection (Gu et al., 2025). Although these modules can run independently, they exhibit strong sequential dependencies and intensive data exchange; isolated invocation cannot sustain complex, dynamic production environments. Process-oriented thinking offers a clear technical framework.

From a task-organization perspective, the continuous cognitive operations of human translation can be decomposed into small units with explicit inputs, processing, and outputs. This decomposition enables automation by restructuring an apparently linear process into pluggable task nodes with data interfaces, flow control, and exception handling. The workflow mechanism operationalizes process thinking: it defines task order and standardizes node inputs and outputs, scheduling conditions, and exception responses. For example, terminology identification, style adaptation, and translation generation can be configured as sequential nodes (Yue et al., 2024), with optional insertion of quality checks or human review, forming a flexible process topology. Large platforms often chain terminology processing, contextual consistency validation, and multilingual output to automate the path from document upload to delivery.

Unlike experience-driven manual practice, workflow mechanisms enforce data consistency and execution stability through type constraints and procedural contracts. The system can integrate models of varying precision and cost, select them dynamically per task, and embed caching, distributed scheduling, or human-intervention nodes to improve resilience and robustness. Agents may appear as single task nodes or be encapsulated as complex subflows—for instance, a quality optimization module can combine multi-round style refinement, semantic enhancement, and scoring feedback, while a terminology module can be split into extraction, alignment, and dynamic prompting. Conditional branching, data aggregation, and concurrent execution support multi-version comparison, multilingual collaboration, and ultra-long document consistency.

In practice, multinational enterprises employ multi-node workflows for product documentation to automate terminology management, draft generation, and multi-round review assignment, markedly improving throughput and consistency. The same process mindset extends to publication, quality monitoring, and feedback analytics, delivering end-to-end technical enablement.

Agent-level and platform-level workflows differ in scope and positioning. An agent-level workflow targets a single task chain, sequencing modules such as terminology handling, text generation, style adaptation, and quality evaluation in a fixed or conditional order to ensure smooth data transfer and local optimization—for example, the tight coupling between terminology identification and translation generation in machine-assisted translation.

Platform-level workflows orchestrate cross-project, multi-role, and multi-resource collaboration. They cover task assignment, progress monitoring, permission management, and resource scheduling, and integrate with infrastructure such as databases, task queues, and notification services to support large-scale parallel management and scaling.

The two levels form a nested relationship. A platform workflow can invoke an agent workflow as a node and compose multi-layer chains according to task type and context. Agent workflows operate at the functional execution layer on translation units; platform workflows operate at the system management layer for book- or project-level organization. Together they form an integrated system supporting complex language services.

1.2 Requirements Analysis for Long-Form Translation Workflows

For experienced human translators, workflow system objectives align along two axes: (1) continuous improvement of quality and consistency across macro structure and micro expression, and (2) ongoing reduction of operational burden and configuration barriers so that non-programmers can handle complex tasks intuitively (Wang et al., 2023). Long-form content introduces cross-chapter coreference, evolving terminology, genre mixing, and structural heterogeneity. Without systematic orchestration, local improvements often fail at the global level, inflating rework costs and lengthening delivery cycles.

Multi-level information support must form a closed loop from text ingestion to knowledge provisioning. At entry, layout parsing and semantic segmentation preserve chapter hierarchy, heading indices, figures, and footnote anchors to build a queryable document skeleton. Upon this skeleton, four information panels are constructed. The document level supplies style, theme, audience, and communicative intent, supporting cross-chapter consistency constraints and narrative perspective tracking. The paragraph level provides argumentative structure and semantic summaries, exposing evidence–conclusion alignments to maintain logic during rewriting. The sentence level presents syntax and coreference chains and enables comparative retrieval with historical translations. The lexical level maintains term and named-entity equivalents, disambiguation outcomes, and hierarchical relations, logging provenance and confidence tags. On the supply side, Retrieval-Augmented Generation (RAG) injects these resources into prompting and decoding control, improving output quality while enabling traceability and explainability (Yue et al., 2024). In a technical manual case, component names appear in varied surface forms across chapters; the system unifies them via entity linking and alias tables and enforces a single token at generation time, sharply reducing downstream terminology corrections.

The effectiveness of personalization rules depends on rules being machine-executable, propagable, and auditable. Style conventions, genre requirements, syntactic preferences, and terminology policies are abstracted into a rule set with explicit priorities and conflict-resolution strategies. Rules are injected early and automatically propagated across nodes; each node enforces them through template prompts, decoding constraints, and post-hoc filtering. Quality control relies on observable metrics: terminology hit rate, prohibited expression trigger rate, discourse-level consistency score, and citation format compliance. Differences between published works and corporate documents appear through distinct rule sets—the former emphasizing genre and bibliographic style, the latter terminology and brand voice. End users merely upload a termbase or select a preset style card; the system enforces and validates constraints during generation and post-editing, preventing late-stage cascaded rework (Wu et al., 2024; Fan et al., 2024). For example, rules governing narrative person and citation conventions in a social science monograph are given high priority; violations are intercepted at the node with suggested alternatives rather than deferred to final proofing.

Efficiency and reuse hinge on systematic management of intermediate artifacts (Sculley et al., 2015). Long documents contain many repeated or near-duplicate segments; the system performs near-duplicate detection and clustering with embeddings (Reimers & Gurevych, 2019), assigns each cluster to a unified processing chain, and—combined with translation memory and segment-level caching—propagates a single revision to multiple instances (Bowker, 2002; Chan, 2023). Resources employ versioning and rollback; termbases, style cards, and prompt configurations are snapshot-bound to specific tasks and outputs, forming auditable data linkages. Quality improvement is driven by a loop between automatic quality estimation and automatic post-editing: low-confidence segments are flagged by a quality gate, enter automatic post-editing, are re-evaluated, and escalate to human review if needed (Specia et al., 2009). The platform maintains visualized flow traces and node states, balancing throughput, latency, and cost so that non-technical users can see, for example, why parallel decoding or a higher-precision model was selected (Leviathan et al., 2023).

Cross-project transfer is enabled by templated workflows: validated rule sets, proofreading checklists, and node orchestrations are saved as templates for one-click reuse in new projects, reducing cold-start and alignment costs (Li et al., 2024). For instance, in a multilingual technical manual project, if the system detects divergent candidates for the same term in English and French versions, it triggers a cross-lingual consistency check and produces batch revision proposals; once approved, corresponding segments update synchronously across all languages, greatly reducing redundant effort (Briakou et al., 2024).

These three requirement categories reinforce one another. Multi-level information provisioning supplies the knowledge substrate and verifiable evidence for personalization rules; those constraints guide subsequent information collection and retrieval; efficiency and reuse mechanisms consolidate both into transferable templates and resource repositories. Through this synergy, workflows align with expert translators' cognitive patterns while sustaining a stable balance among quality, cost, and speed at the system level.

1.3 Core Requirements for Designing Translation Workflow Systems

Designing a translation workflow system depends less on optimizing single modules than on achieving system-level structural organization, reconfigurability, and evolvability (Gu et al., 2025). Given diverse text types, complex task requirements, and multi-role collaboration scenarios, the system must support flexible configuration, stable execution, and continuous optimization across both architectural and operational layers.

Architecturally, tasks should be decomposed into functional nodes with independent input and output interfaces, combinable via sequential, parallel, branching, or iterative patterns to address varied task logic. This modularity enables isolated upgrades and substitutions while adapting rapidly to heterogeneous business processes. A graphical flow editor provides drag-and-drop construction and adjustment, allowing non-technical users to customize workflows.

Frequently used flows can be abstracted as templates parameterized by language pair, model type, translation style, and terminology source, enabling rapid migration and sharing across projects while preserving execution standards. A pluggable architecture allows new models, tools, or resources to connect through standard interfaces, with permission controls and test gates ensuring stability. Open APIs enable integration with external platforms such as knowledge management and task scheduling, forming a sustainably evolving intelligent translation ecosystem.

Operationally, the system must log every creation, modification, and rollback, support version switching and comparison, and preserve traceability and stability throughout optimization. Collaboration features—permission control, annotations, and change rationales—reduce communication overhead in multi-member participation and prevent errors arising from information asymmetry.

Cross-node information flow and context maintenance directly shape translation quality: terminology consistency, stylistic coherence, and structural integrity depend on a globally shared context that is stable yet continuously updated. The system should maintain state records for every segment, so that translators can trace revision histories with precision. As large language models and compute-intensive engines are employed, resource scheduling becomes pivotal. The system must intelligently allocate resources based on node requirements, historical performance, and real-time load, avoid bottlenecks and idle cycles, and support hybrid local-cloud deployment to balance performance and cost across task scales.

Architectural flexibility, maintainability, and extensibility lay the foundation for long-term evolution, while operational efficiency and quality assurance ensure stable delivery of each translation task. Together they constitute an integrated response to diverse tasks and dynamic requirements.

2 Architectural Design of Translation Workflows

As translation tasks grow in scale and complexity, an efficient and scalable workflow architecture becomes a foundational requirement. To accommodate multi-stage, multi-task collaboration, the workflow must realize automation and modularization while retaining flexible organization and maintainability. From a systems architecture perspective, sound functional partitioning and coordinated mechanisms transform translation into a schedulable, continuously optimizable process system, extending automation across the entire production chain.

2.1 Overall Architectural Design and Module Partitioning

The architectural design of translation workflows is grounded in modular principles. Clear functional partitioning ensures efficient inter-module collaboration while preserving extensibility and maintainability (Lyu et al., 2024). The core comprises five primary modules: the user interaction interface, functional nodes, data storage, the workflow engine, and external service integration (Fig. 1). Standardized data interfaces and execution protocols coordinate these modules, enabling sustained optimization and expansion amid evolving requirements and technological contexts.

A modular design partitions the translation workflow into clearly defined modules, each responsible for a specific task or service (Baldwin & Clark, 2000). This structure supports rapid reconfiguration across projects and agile adaptation to diverse requirements. A representative architecture comprises the user interface, functional nodes, data storage, the workflow engine, and external service integration modules.

Modules interconnect via standardized interfaces and execution protocols that unify input/output formats and operational conventions, thereby reducing coupling and improving orchestration efficiency. Standardization preserves module independence while facilitating extension and replacement, enabling rapid adaptation to emerging translation needs or technological updates and enhancing evolvability.

The user interface module bridges users and the system, supporting workflow construction, task monitoring, parameter configuration, and human review (Moorkens & O'Brien, 2017). A graphical interface enables drag-and-drop flow configuration, ordering of node execution, and real-time status inspection without coding. Designated human-review nodes enable timely intervention by translators or reviewers to safeguard quality.

Functional node modules are the core execution units: each performs a discrete task such as language detection, terminology extraction, initial translation generation, style refinement, or quality evaluation (Fernandes et al., 2023). Nodes exchange data through standard interfaces with the data storage and external integration modules; for example, the style refinement node optimizes an existing draft, while the quality evaluation node returns scores and feedback.

The data storage module manages all process data—inputs, outputs, transient states, and version histories (Mu et al., 2023). It must support high-concurrency read/write operations, ensure consistency and integrity, and employ a mix of relational

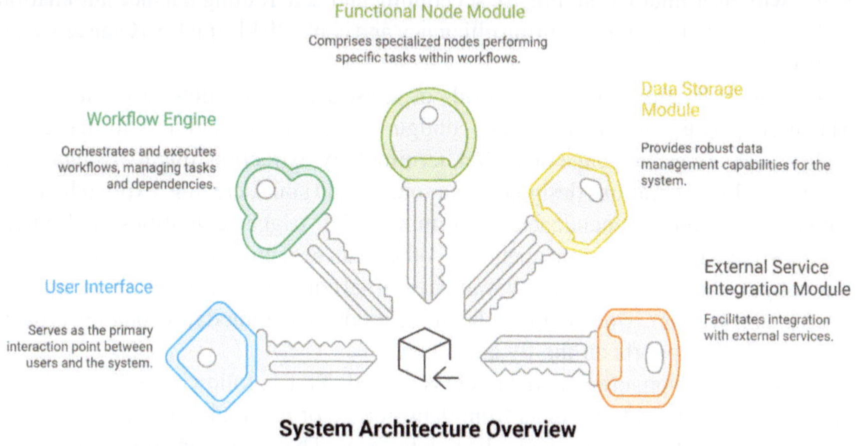

Fig. 1 System architecture of the translation workflow

stores, object storage, and caching layers to meet heterogeneous access patterns. For sensitive tasks, access controls, encryption, and audit trails are required to enforce governance and compliance.

The workflow engine module provides orchestration: it constructs and executes task plans based on dependencies and scheduling strategies (Weske, 2024). It governs execution order, parallel scheduling, and retry logic. Mature open-source frameworks (e.g., Apache Airflow) supply dependency management, parallel processing, and fault recovery, while custom plugins and scheduling policies extend capabilities as project demands evolve.

The external service integration module connects machine translation engines, natural language processing tools, terminology repositories, knowledge graphs, and large language models (Ramos et al., 2025). Standard interfaces enable seamless invocation of resources—such as OpenNMT or Google Translate—or the use of large language models for generation and refinement. This flexibility enables rapid incorporation of new tools as technologies evolve.

A translation workflow grounded in standardized interfaces and modular design can satisfy heterogeneous requirements efficiently while supporting continual optimization and inter-module collaboration. Although the focus here is on translation services, the architecture's extensibility also suits broader language service domains. In media distribution, content authoring, and independent publishing, it supports integrated pipelines spanning generation, stylistic refinement, and quality evaluation, demonstrating robust cross-industry applicability.

2.2 Module Interaction Logic and Execution Flow

At the core lies a task-driven execution mechanism that seamlessly links functional nodes with user interaction. Precise scheduling and data routing balance automation and human collaboration, ensuring efficiency and controllable quality (Qian & Kong, 2024).

Execution begins when a user loads or constructs a workflow in the interface. The user selects functional nodes, configures parameters and I/O formats, and assigns tasks (e.g., language detection, terminology extraction, quality evaluation). Drag-and-drop operations designate data sources and sinks, creating explicit handoff paths. User-defined dependencies determine order, trigger conditions, and parallelism: some tasks must run sequentially, others can execute concurrently to increase throughput, and certain nodes may wait on external conditions (e.g., termbase updates or style constraints). This flexible scheduling model accommodates complex project structures and supports on-the-fly adjustment.

During execution, efficient data flow is pivotal. Nodes, following a defined order and dependencies, obtain inputs from data storage or external integration modules and return outputs through standardized interfaces. These mechanisms ensure timeliness and accuracy, preventing lag or loss. Although most nodes run automatically, high-assurance scenarios still require human intervention for quality review, terminology validation, and stylistic refinement (Pérez, 2024). The system flags these review nodes, prompts users, and writes approved results back to advance downstream tasks.

This model relies on automation for most repetitive processing while inserting human judgment at critical junctures to ensure stylistic uniformity, terminological consistency, and precision (Pym & Hao, 2024). By balancing speed and quality, the system sustains high throughput without compromising standards.

A similar logic applies to content creation contexts such as independent media production. The process moves from topic definition and source gathering through orientation, filtering, and outline drafting into chapter-level writing and stylistic refinement. If source collection spans other languages, that stage functions as transcreation, though practitioners need not segregate content by language. This workflow increases production efficiency while preserving stylistic and thematic consistency.

2.3 Selecting and Evaluating Translation Workflow Engines

Selecting an appropriate workflow engine is central to efficient, flexible scheduling. Evaluation must weigh task complexity, maintainability, user interaction requirements, and future scalability. Although each engine presents trade-offs, adoption should be driven by concrete business demands and deployment context rather than abstract comparison.

For large translation programs with intricate dependencies and wide parallelism, Apache Airflow remains the industry mainstay: its dependency management, batch scheduling, retry logic, and security controls underpin stable operations (including Airflow 3.0 features such as DAG (Directed Acyclic Graph) versioning and event-driven scheduling) (Weske, 2024). When stability and scale are paramount, Airflow is a reliable choice.

Airflow offers limited usability for non-technical stakeholders. Prefect provides a more modern experience with enhanced visual monitoring, state tracking, and hybrid cloud operation—well suited to small or mid-sized projects or scenarios requiring immediate feedback. When rapid deployment and low-code visualization are priorities, no-code platforms such as n8n offer cost-effective value, enabling non-technical users to assemble flows quickly, though they may struggle with deeply nested dependencies or intensive parallelism.

In intelligent content generation, agent-oriented tools such as LangGraph emphasize semantic flow and multi-module coordination (Li et al., 2024). They enable dynamic collaboration and reasoning among translator agents, strengthening contextual understanding and adaptive response, though they remain comparatively limited in conventional scheduling and monitoring breadth.

For enterprise and business process outsourcing scenarios, Flowable (supporting Business Process Model and Notation (BPMN) 2.0) is a strong candidate where process compliance and governance are critical within language service systems.

Final selection should incorporate team familiarity, extensibility requirements, and strategic evolution paths. Involving system architects and language service specialists ensures the chosen engine meets present demands while retaining headroom for future challenges.

3 Design and Implementation of Intelligent Translation Workflows

Building on a sound architectural foundation, intelligent translation workflow design must integrate automation with purposeful human intervention and provide interface support for that integration (Wang et al., 2024). The system should raise efficiency while safeguarding quality, flexibly accommodate task heterogeneity, support multi-role collaboration, and maintain seamless stage transitions. In multi-role projects, the user interface is pivotal: it must satisfy divergent role needs without sacrificing simplicity or stability. Targeted customization layered on universal design principles directly improves usability, user experience, and translation productivity.

3.1 User Interface Design and Optimization

The user interface initiates workflow operation; its design directly shapes usability, user experience, and translation efficiency (Peter et al., 2024; Rudan et al., 2023; Moorkens & O'Brien, 2017). In multi-role settings, it must satisfy distinct functional needs while ensuring ease of operation, stability, and robust internationalization/localization—spanning language switching, cultural adaptation, and right-to-left (RTL) layout optimization (Omar & Salih, 2024). Design should follow principles of intelligibility, operability, traceability, and high responsiveness, with tailoring to role-specific contexts.

Layout must be clear and intuitive so that users can quickly identify functional regions and understand interaction flow (Fig. 2). For non-technical users, obscure terminology and excessive configuration should be minimized; concise labels, intuitive icons, and stepwise prompts guide operation. A node configuration panel can expose dependencies via a graphical flow diagram; selecting a node opens parameter settings. Critical actions should be explicit and easy to execute, with element placement aligned to user expectations and safeguards such as confirmation dialogs and undo to prevent errors. The system should visualize task progress, version history, and change logs—for example, color-coding completed, active, and pending tasks (Herbert et al., 2023). In large-scale workloads, high responsiveness is essential: loading states should provide immediate feedback and placeholders to preserve interaction fluency with large datasets (Zhu et al., 2023).

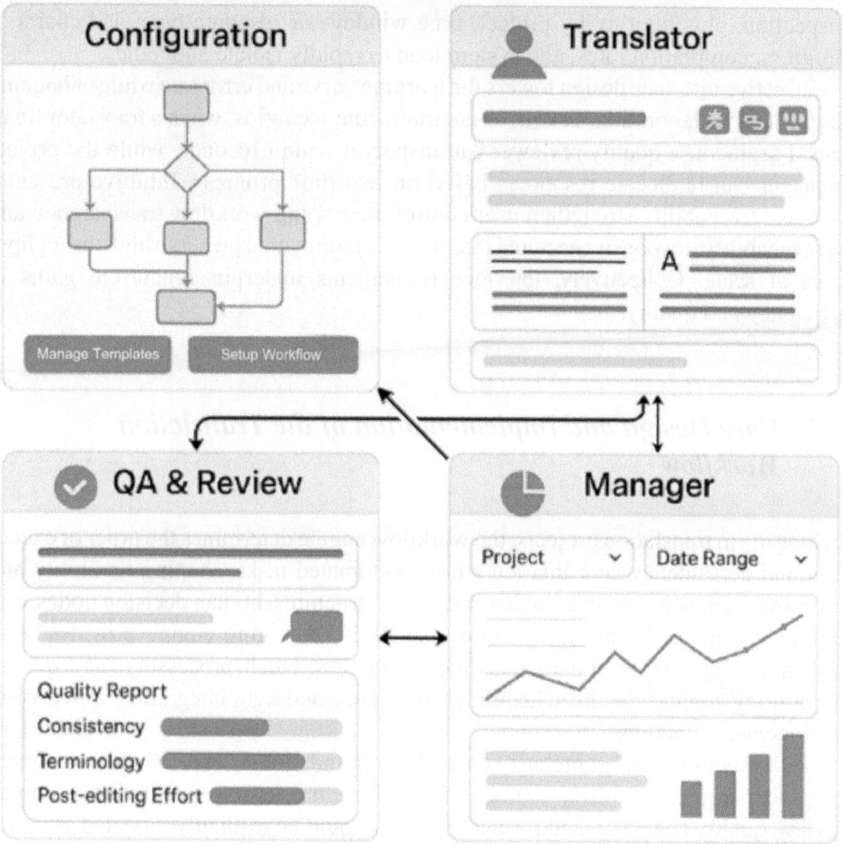

Fig. 2 User interface design for intelligent translation workflow: multi-role collaboration and automation

Role-specific interfaces require targeted optimization. The workflow configuration interface, used by configuration staff, provides drag-and-drop workflow construction, bulk node editing, dependency and conditional branch management, and enables saving mature flows as reusable, cross-project templates. The translator interface is task-centric: it displays task lists, priorities, deadlines, and includes tools such as terminology highlighting, segment alignment, and machine translation comparison (Andersson & Caracolias, 2024). Translators can view reference translations or retrieve contextual information inline, reducing disruptive application switching (Andersson & Caracolias, 2024). The quality assurance and review interface emphasizes version traceability, annotation, and evaluation, allowing users to flag key segments, propose revisions, and generate quality reports covering consistency, terminology compliance, and post-editing effort metrics (Omar & Salih, 2024). The management and monitoring interface provides project managers and system administrators with task scheduling, resource monitoring, access control, and log inspection, plus filtering by project, time window, or resource type, and charts of progress, completion rates, and system load to rapidly isolate anomalies.

Effective interface design lowers the learning curve and error rate while enhancing day-to-day collaboration. In concurrent multi-role scenarios, when a translator finalizes a segment, a quality reviewer can inspect it within seconds, while the project manager can reallocate resources based on real-time progress. Intuitive presentation and traceability strengthen user control, increasing workflow transparency and manageability; responsiveness and interaction optimization preserve high throughput even at scale. Collectively, interface refinements underpin concurrent gains in efficiency and quality.

3.2 Core Design and Implementation of the Translation Workflow

In long-form translation projects, the workflow engine determines the order of execution and dependency coordination among automated tasks, shaping flexibility and robustness when handling complex document structures, human decision nodes, and cross-stage quality control (Rudan et al., 2023). A mature engine provides clear task modeling, stable human–machine interaction, batch processing, and quality monitoring support, secure scheduling safeguards, and tight integration with project management functions.

Task modeling and granularity control are foundational. Typical stages—source preprocessing, terminology extraction, machine translation, post-editing, human review, quality checking, and format export—should be explicitly modeled as nodes with configurable dependencies and data flows. Granularity is pivotal: overly fine nodes inflate scheduling overhead and monitoring complexity; overly coarse nodes limit reuse and fault isolation. For chapter-level processing, the system should segment documents structurally and distribute work in parallel across smaller units while preserving contextual coherence (Zhu et al., 2023).

Human interaction nodes introduce indispensable judgment. For proprietary-term confirmation, disambiguation, or sense unification, the system pauses at these nodes, captures user input in structured form, and forwards it downstream (Herbert et al., 2023). Each node should record the operator, timestamp, and change details, and support state recovery or rollback after interruptions. Although human intervention reduces raw automation speed, it prevents error propagation and ensures quality and accountability (Vieira et al., 2024).

Batch operations and post-editing pipelines are central to efficient long-form processing. The engine should partition documents into logical blocks, apply batch strategies (e.g., chapter-level terminology normalization), and preserve paragraph order and formatting during aggregation. An intermediate translation memory layer acting as a cache between machine output and human revision maintains version state across task switches, preserving consistency and traceability (Gao et al., 2024; Zhu et al., 2023).

Quality monitoring and evaluation must be deeply embedded. Automated checks performed pre-review or pre-delivery can run spell checking, terminology consistency validation, length comparison, and Bilingual Evaluation Understudy (BLEU)/SacreBLEU scoring, flagging problematic segments. Human-review data—score sheets, revision statistics, and feedback—should be stored structurally for subsequent analytics and traceability. Systems with explainable reporting can generate annotated quality analyses that support holistic managerial assessment.

Secure scheduling and task isolation safeguard concurrent multi-project operation. Separate resource pools prevent contention and data leakage; the scheduler should enforce task priorities, concurrency caps, execution timeouts, and exponential backoff retries, with escalation to manual intervention as needed. Complete audit trails of scheduling and execution enable failure analysis and accountability.

Project management and progress tracking tightly couple orchestration with oversight. A project view should visualize the overall flow, showing stage states such as preprocessing completion, post-editing progress, and pending review counts. The system should allow hierarchical task inspection, node reruns, localized flow adjustments, and completion-time prediction based on historical data. For highly structured legal or technical documents, a hierarchical chapter tree binds task status to document structure, enabling responsibility-based allocation and precise issue localization.

The translation workflow engine underpins automation and governed collaboration in long-form translation. Its value lies in precise process modeling, robust human interaction support, efficient batch handling, adaptive quality monitoring, secure scheduling, and visual project management—together producing high-quality, high-efficiency language service pipelines. The same approach generalizes to multilingual content processing and media dissemination, supporting intelligent and sustainable language platforms (Gao et al., 2024).

3.3 *Shared Storage for the Workflow*

In long-form workflows, beyond orchestration, the engine depends on a stable, efficient shared storage layer to coordinate data movement and state management. Well-designed shared storage improves performance and development efficiency, forming the basis for intelligent machine translation, version control, collaborative processing, and quality traceability (Temizoz & Gough, 2024).

Data types in translation are heterogeneous and hierarchical: source documents with metadata (e.g., language direction, delivery standards), segmented translation units (chapter, paragraph, or sentence level), terminology glossaries (preferred equivalents and domain terms), multiple versions of each unit (machine output, human-refined drafts), merged outputs and contextual reconstruction results, derived artifacts (such as multi-level summaries), and prompt templates plus custom prompts. A single table cannot capture all needs, so a "primary table + slot tables" design can be used: the primary table stores shared attributes, while variant information (versions, replicas, processing methods) resides in auxiliary slot tables to ensure consistency and control. A single sentence may have several segmentation strategies; the system retains each version with a slot identifier (e.g., `split:v1`, `split:v2`).

Prompts and their variants should be treated as structured resources linked to metadata such as task type and language direction, enabling rapid retrieval. For example, a legal-domain prompt template can be stored as follows to facilitate version control and cross-task reuse.

```
{
  "template_id": "context-aware-trans-prompt",
  "task_type": "long_text_translation",
  "role": "first_pass_mt",
  "lang_pair": "en2zh",
  "tags": ["legal", "formal", "paragraph-alignment"],
  "template_text": "Translate the following paragraph with attention to legal
terminology..."
}
```

Indexing should combine full-text and vector search to maximize efficiency and semantic coverage. Tools like Elasticsearch can provide unified retrieval: inverted indexes handle keyword queries, while dense_vector fields store embeddings; HNSW (Hierarchical Navigable Small World) supports approximate nearest-neighbor matching for semantic similarity and example suggestion. All sentences and short texts can be vectorized on ingestion for rapid later use.

Structured data is best managed in a relational database (e.g., PostgreSQL or MariaDB) with primary key consistency and foreign key constraints. Source entries in the translation unit table should link precisely to their corresponding target entries in slot tables to enable automatic alignment and version tracing.

As intelligent translation advances, machine translation is evolving from isolated sentence conversion toward semantic understanding, contextual integration, and domain adaptation. Deep integration of RAG allows automatic retrieval of background knowledge, domain term explanations, and high-quality reference translations at task initiation, yielding more precise and consistent output (Lewis et al., 2020; Mohamed et al., 2024). In parallel, client- or industry-specific term preferences can dynamically update bespoke glossaries, so prioritized terms are applied consistently, enabling tailored service.

A carefully engineered shared storage system confers flexibility and scalability, enforces data consistency through structured modeling, accelerates resource utilization via efficient semantic retrieval, and supports large-scale collaboration and intelligent processing (Li & Huang, 2024; Chan, 2023). It is a foundational pillar of long-form translation automation and intelligence.

3.4 Integration and Invocation of External Tools

In intelligent translation systems, external tool integration is central to efficiency, accuracy, and flexibility. The translation process relies on machine translation (MT) engines and large language models, while also invoking tools for format conversion, word/character counting, and domain terminology handling. A well-designed external services module embeds these tools seamlessly into the workflow, markedly increasing automation and intelligence (Chan, 2023).

Many translation assignments extend beyond pure text conversion. Complex documents require format conversion utilities to preserve structural layout; counting tools support cost estimation and optimized scheduling; terminology handling depends on curated termbases and domain knowledge to secure both accuracy and consistency.

For efficient consolidation, the integration module should standardize diverse tool interfaces, ensuring stable connectivity with the workflow engine. It should incorporate cost control and exception management—estimating expenses from call frequency and volume, applying quotas, and, for costly services, leveraging batching or result caching to reduce redundant invocations without degrading quality (Li & Huang, 2024).

Coordination between LLMs and MT engines is especially important. The system should dynamically select engine combinations based on task characteristics—for instance, employing a high-throughput MT engine for initial structured document passes, then invoking an LLM for stylistic refinement. Real-time monitoring of resource consumption should feed back into strategy optimization.

External tool invocation also requires comprehensive exception handling and logging. Error types should be standardized, with automated recovery (e.g., exponential backoff retries) or manual escalation. Logs must capture error codes, causes, and recovery outcomes to support root-cause analysis. Coupling these logs with cost metrics refines usage strategies and resource allocation.

Invocation strategies fall into engineering-controlled and model-driven categories. Engineering control relies on predefined orchestration—highly stable and predictable but less adaptive. Model-driven control lets a language model determine timing and sequencing from contextual cues—more adaptive yet higher in complexity and uncertainty. A compromise is a "plan–execute separation" agent architecture: the language model generates an action plan, and an execution engine applies it deterministically, balancing flexibility with reliability.

Practical deployments should select strategies based on task characteristics. Engineering control suits highly structured, predictable translation tasks requiring maximal stability; model-driven control excels in multilingual, variable-content scenarios demanding adaptability. A hybrid approach, reinforced by rigorous cost and exception management, yields an optimal balance among efficiency, stability, and intelligent adaptability (Wu et al., 2024; Liu et al., 2025).

Fig. 3 Diagram of a basic translation workflow

3.5 Practical Construction of a Workflow-Based Translation Pipeline

Through development and applied testing we confirmed that a workflow-based translation pipeline improves quality, reduces cost, and adapts to heterogeneous demands. The platform adopts Apache Airflow as the foundational framework and uses Docker for containerized deployment to ensure efficiency, stability, and portability (Reitenbach et al., 2024). A unified development environment—standardized Docker images for all components—eliminates version drift. To support high concurrency, we employ Redis as the message queue and Airflow's CeleryExecutor for distributed task scheduling.

Within this environment, we implemented and tested three workflow scales: a basic four-node machine translation flow (Fig. 3), an intermediate eight-node flow (Fig. 4), and a comprehensive eleven-node flow (Fig. 5). Each centers on an LLM and incorporates modules for terminology harmonization, contextual memory, format repair, and stylistic adjustment. They were applied to four text categories with distinct registers—including research reports from international organizations, market status news articles, computer science textbook material—and, to probe more difficult issues, the Victorian novel *Bleak House*.

Test results show that increasing the number of workflow nodes leads to a steady improvement in translation quality, with the system performing robustly when addressing complex linguistic phenomena and detailed nuances. This advantage is especially pronounced in texts with clearly defined task boundaries and well-established terminological systems, such as policy reports and scientific textbooks. For these materials, translations produced by a comprehensive workflow approach demonstrate near-human levels of terminological consistency, logical paragraph structure, and audience adaptation, reflecting high professionalism and readability. In lengthy, syntactically complex, and logically intricate news analyses, workflow-based translation systems also significantly outperform direct full-text translation by large language models, though a gap remains compared to human translators. For nineteenth-century British novels rich in stylistic features, even a comprehensive workflow struggles to fully capture literary rhetoric and style, resulting in overall quality that does not quite match mature human translations.

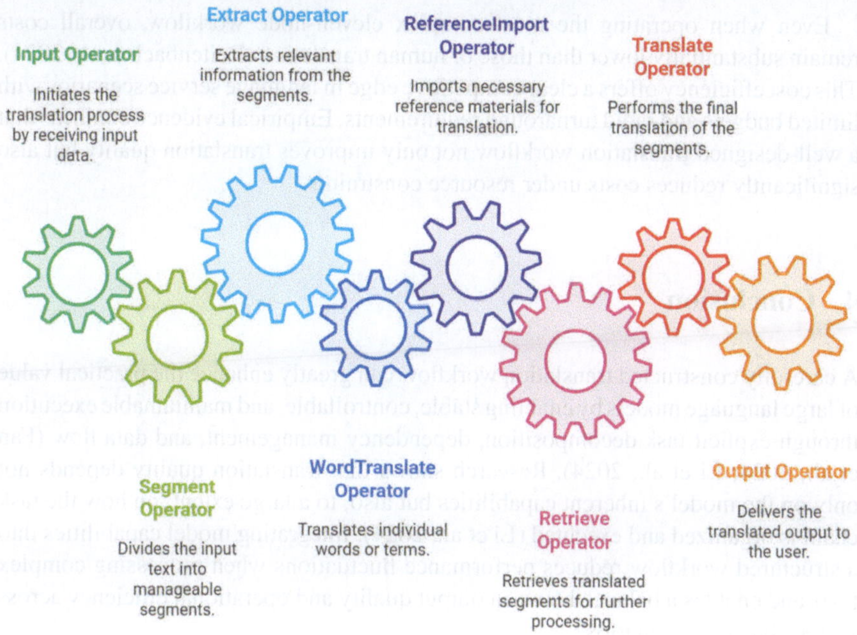

Fig. 4 Diagram of an advanced translation workflow

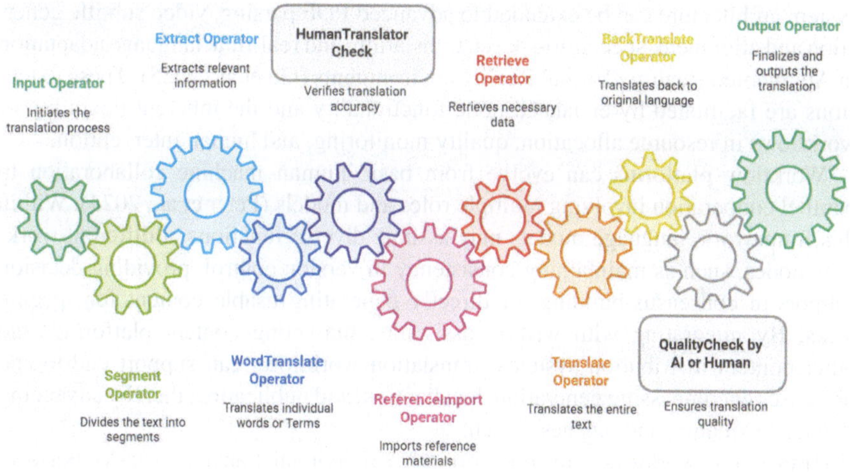

Fig. 5 Diagram of a comprehensive translation workflow

Even when operating the most complex eleven-node workflow, overall costs remain substantially lower than those of human translation (Reitenbach et al., 2024). This cost efficiency offers a clear competitive edge in language service scenarios with limited budgets and rapid turnaround requirements. Empirical evidence confirms that a well-designed translation workflow not only improves translation quality but also significantly reduces costs under resource constraints.

4 Conclusion

A carefully constructed translation workflow can greatly enhance the practical value of large language models by enabling stable, controllable, and maintainable execution through explicit task decomposition, dependency management, and data flow (Fan et al., 2024; Li et al., 2024). Research shows that translation quality depends not only on the model's inherent capabilities but also, to a large extent, on how the task chain is organized and executed (Li et al., 2024). Integrating model capabilities into a structured workflow reduces performance fluctuations when processing complex texts and enables a balance between output quality and operational efficiency across various business scenarios.

Workflow-based translation systems now support a wide range of tasks, from long-form documents to multimodal content. Beyond conventional text translation, the system architecture can be extended to advanced PDF parsing, video subtitle generation and alignment, speech-to-speech translation, and real-time language adaptation in Augmented Reality / Virtual Reality environments (Gu et al., 2025). These extensions are facilitated by enhanced node functionality and the inherent flexibility of workflows in resource allocation, quality monitoring, and human intervention.

Workflow platforms can evolve from basic human–machine collaboration to parallel cooperation involving multiple roles and models (Peter et al., 2024). Within this framework, language models may assume diverse functions at different workflow nodes, such as maintaining consistency in version control, providing decision support in consensus-building, or directly generating usable content for specific tasks. By integrating with writing assistants, marketing content platforms, and other content distribution systems, translation workflows can support end-to-end processes encompassing generation, localization, and publication, thereby advancing efficiency, quality, and business reach.

Translation workflows not only optimize individual translation tasks but also provide a scalable and portable technological pathway for cross-domain and cross-media language services, laying a solid foundation for future diversified applications.

References

Andersson, A., & Caracolias, V. (2024). *Unifying a large language model and company-specific terminology for enhanced translation in a company's multilingual landscape* [Master's thesis, Uppsala University]. https://urn.kb.se/resolve%3Furn%3Durn:nbn:se:uu:diva-534550

Baldwin, C. Y., & Clark, K. B. (2000). *Design rules: The power of modularity* volume 1. MIT Press.

Bowker, L. (2002). *Computer-aided translation technology: A practical introduction*. University of Ottawa Press.

Briakou, E., Luo, J., Cherry, C., & Freitag, M. (2024). Translating step-by-step: Decomposing the translation process for improved translation quality of long-form texts. *arXiv*. https://arxiv.org/abs/2409.06790

Chan, S. W. (2023). The development of translation technology: 1967–2023. In *Routledge encyclopedia of translation technology* (pp. 3–41). Routledge.

Fan, S., Cong, X., Fu, Y., Zhang, Z., Zhang, S., Liu, Y., … & Sun, M. (2024). WorkflowLLM: Enhancing workflow orchestration capability of large language models. arXiv. https://arxiv.org/abs/2411.05451

Fernandes, P., Deutsch, D., Finkelstein, M., Riley, P., Martins, A. F., Neubig, G., … & Firat, O. (2023). The devil is in the errors: Leveraging large language models for fine-grained machine translation evaluation. arXiv. https://arxiv.org/abs/2308.07286

Gao, D., Chen, K., Chen, B., Dai, H., Jin, L., Jiang, W., … & Wang, Z. (2024). LLMs-based machine translation for E-commerce. *Expert Systems with Applications, 258*, 125087.

Gu, Y., You, H., Cao, J., Yu, M., Fan, H., & Qian, S. (2025). Large language models for constructing and optimizing machine learning workflows: A survey. arXiv. https://arxiv.org/abs/2411.10478

Herbert, S., do Carmo, F., Gough, J., & Carnegie-Brown, A. (2023). From responsibilities to responsibility: A study of the effects of translation workflow automation. *Journal of Specialised Translation, 40*, 9–35.

Kaleigha, B., Glassford, B., Barros, C., & Stonebridge, O. (2024). Optimized machine translation of technical acronyms using large language models: A workflow-based approach. https://doi.org/10.31219/osf.io/9c5t6

Leviathan, Y., Kalman, M., & Matias, Y. (2023, July). Fast inference from transformers via speculative decoding. In *International Conference on Machine Learning* (pp. 19274–19286). PMLR.

Lewis, M., Liu, Y., Goyal, N., Ghazvininejad, M., Mohamed, A., Levy, O., Stoyanov, V., & Zettlemoyer, L. (2020). BART: Denoising sequence-to-sequence pre-training for natural language generation, translation, and comprehension. In D. Jurafsky, J. Chai, N. Schluter, & J. Tetreault (Eds.), *Proceedings of the 58th Annual Meeting of the Association for Computational Linguistics* (pp. 7871–7880). Association for Computational Linguistics.

Li, S., & Huang, Y. (2024). BAS-ALSTM: analyzing the efficiency of artificial intelligence-based English translation system. *Journal of Ambient Intelligence and Humanized Computing, 15*(1), 765–777.

Li, Z., Xu, S., Mei, K., Hua, W., Rama, B., Raheja, O., … & Zhang, Y. (2024). Autoflow: Automated workflow generation for large language model agents. arXiv. https://arxiv.org/abs/2407.12821

Liu, H., Li, R., Xiong, W., Zhou, Z., & Peng, W. (2025). WorkTeam: Constructing workflows from natural language with multi-agents. arXiv. https://arxiv.org/abs/2503.22473

Lyu, C., Du, Z., Xu, J., Duan, Y., Wu, M., Lynn, T., … & Wang, L. (2024). A paradigm shift: The future of machine translation lies with large language models. arXiv. https://arxiv.org/abs/2305.01181

Mohamed, Y. A., Khanan, A., Bashir, M., Mohamed, A. H. H., Adiel, M. A., & Elsadig, M. A. (2024). The impact of artificial intelligence on language translation: A review. *IEEE Access, 12*, 25553–25579.

Moorkens, J., & O'Brien, S. (2017). Assessing user interface needs of post-editors of machine translation. In *Human issues in translation technology* (pp. 127–148). Routledge.

Mu, Y., Reheman, A., Cao, Z., Fan, Y., Li, B., Li, Y., … & Zhu, J. (2023). Augmenting large language model translators via translation memories. arXiv. https://arxiv.org/abs/2305.17367

Omar, L. I., & Salih, A. A. (2024). Systematic review of English/Arabic machine translation postediting: Implications for AI application in translation research and pedagogy. *Informatics, 11*(2), 23.

Pérez, C. R. (2024). Re-thinking machine translation post-editing guidelines. *The Journal of Specialised Translation, 41*, 26–47.

Peter, A., Dang, M., Liu, M., Dominguez, J., & Lohia, N. (2024). Multi-agent translation team (MATT): Enhancing low-resource language translation through multi-agent workflow. *SMU Data Science Review, 8*(3), 3.

Pym, A., & Hao, Y. (2024). *How to augment language skills: Generative AI and machine translation in language learning and translator training.* Taylor & Francis.

Qian, M., & Kong, C. (2024). Enabling human-centered machine translation using concept-based large language model prompting and translation memory. In *International Conference on Human-Computer Interaction* (pp. 118–134). Springer Nature Switzerland.

Ramos, M. M., Fernandes, P., Agrawal, S., & Martins, A. F. (2025). Multilingual contextualization of large language models for document-level machine translation. arXiv. https://arxiv.org/abs/2504.12140

Reimers, N., & Gurevych, I. (2019). Sentence-BERT: Sentence embeddings using Siamese BERT-networks. https://arxiv.org/pdf/1908.10084

Reitenbach, S., Siggel, M., & Bolemant, M. (2024). Enhanced workflow management using an artificial intelligence chatbot. In *AIAA SCITECH 2024 Forum.* https://doi.org/10.2514/6.2024-0917

Rudan, S. M., Kelbert, E., Kovacevic, L., Reynolds, M., & Rudan, S. (2023). Augmenting and informing the translation process through workflow-enabled CALT tools. In *Computer-assisted literary translation* (pp. 258–281). Routledge.

Sculley, D., Holt, G., Golovin, D., Davydov, E., Phillips, T., Ebner, D., … & Dennison, D. (2015). Hidden technical debt in machine learning systems. *Advances in Neural Information Processing Systems, 28.*

Specia, L., Turchi, M., Cancedda, N., Cristianini, N., & Dymetman, M. (2009). Estimating the sentence-level quality of machine translation systems. In *Proceedings of the 13th Annual conference of the European Association for Machine Translation.*

Temizoz, O., & Gough, J. (2024). Translation process in concurrent, collaborative workflows. *Tradumàtica: traducció i tecnologies de la informació i la comunicació, 22*, 355–376.

Vieira, I., Allred, W., Lankford, S., Castilho, S., & Way, A. (2024). How much data is enough data? Fine-tuning large language models for in-house translation: Performance evaluation across multiple dataset sizes. arXiv. https://arxiv.org/abs/2409.03454

Wang, L., Du, Z., Jiao, W., Lyu, C., Pang, J., Cui, L., … & Tu, Z. (2024). Benchmarking and improving long-text translation with large language models. In *Findings of the Association for Computational Linguistics ACL 2024* (pp. 7175–7187).

Wang, L., Lyu, C., Ji, T., Zhang, Z., Yu, D., Shi, S., & Tu, Z. (2023). Document-level machine translation with large language models. arXiv. https://arxiv.org/abs/2304.02210

Weske, M. (2024). Business process management: Concepts, languages, architectures. Springer Nature.

Wu, M., Vu, T. T., Qu, L., Foster, G., & Haffari, G. (2024). Adapting large language models for document-level machine translation. arXiv. https://arxiv.org/abs/2401.06468

Wu, M., Xu, J., Yuan, Y., Haffari, G., Wang, L., Luo, W., & Zhang, K. (2024). (Perhaps) beyond human translation: Harnessing multi-agent collaboration for translating ultra-long literary texts. arXiv. https://arxiv.org/abs/2405.11804

Yue, R., Ortega, J. E., & Church, K. W. (2024). On translating technical terminology: A translation workflow for machine-translated acronyms. arXiv. https://arxiv.org/abs/2409.17943

Zhu, W., Liu, H., Dong, Q., Xu, J., Huang, S., Kong, L., … & Li, L. (2023). Multilingual machine translation with large language models: Empirical results and analysis. arXiv. https://arxiv.org/abs/2304.04675

Chapter 10
Structured and Intelligent Technical Writing

Abstract This chapter analyzes the transformation of technical writing into a structured, intelligence-enabled content engineering discipline. It first clarifies the functional, task-oriented nature of technical writing and differentiates it from broader multimodal technical communication. Core linguistic quality pillars (clarity, accuracy, consistency, lack of ambiguity) are situated within governance systems: style guides, controlled language (e.g., Aerospace and Defence Simplified English), and frameworks such as the Developing Quality Technical Information. The chapter then contrasts source-first translation workflows with multilingual co-authoring and hybrid/tiered models that elevate target-language fitness. Structured authoring principles—topic-based modularity (Darwin Information Typing Architecture), hierarchy, reuse, single sourcing, metadata, and component content management—recast documents as maintainable knowledge assets deployable across channels and contexts. AI capabilities now permeate drafting, semantic segmentation of legacy content, real-time terminology/style compliance, predictive impact analysis, and adaptive, context-aware delivery ("content as a service"). This shifts writers' roles from language producers to knowledge architects collaborating with product, user experience, engineering, and localization teams to design information architectures and embedded guidance. The chapter argues that combining controlled linguistic standards, modular engineering, multilingual strategy, and AI-driven automation produces scalable, safe, personalized, and continuously improvable documentation ecosystems.

In language services, technical writing is a structured, purpose-driven form of professional writing that prioritizes clarity and precision while placing greater emphasis on information architecture, usage context, and maintainability. With advances in intelligent technology, the toolchain, methodology, and delivery channels of technical writing are undergoing profound change. Artificial Intelligence (AI) is no longer merely a drafting aid; it now permeates multiple stages, including content component management (based on topic-oriented frameworks such as Darwin Information Typing Architecture (DITA) (Day et al., 2005), automated document structuring, and multi-channel publishing, thereby reshaping the field (Duin & Pedersen, 2023).

J. S. Yu and Y. Yao, *Intelligent Language Services*,
https://doi.org/10.1007/978-981-95-4632-9_10

The focus has thus moved from asking "What can AI generate?" to determining what technical writing requires and how to embed AI at each stage to meet those requirements.

1 Fundamentals of Technical Writing

As a branch of professional writing, technical writing connects specialized knowledge with practical use across domains. Unlike creative or routine administrative writing, it emphasizes functional orientation, structural stability, and operational language. Historically, it supported printed manuals and technical documents; today it has evolved into a cross-platform, multilingual, multi-format information service activity. Grasping its core definition, application scenarios, and relationship to technical communication establishes a foundation for subsequent analysis of AI integration (Reeves & Sylvia IV, 2024).

1.1 The Role and Industry Value of Technical Writing

At its core, technical writing converts complex material into clear, accurate, actionable information that enables a defined audience to complete tasks (Jordan, 2020). It spans the full product lifecycle—design, development, deployment, use, and maintenance—and forms a key component of technical communication. Its value lies in usability and sustainability rather than rhetorical flourish or emotional appeal (Jordan, 2020). Unlike creative writing (originality) or transactional business writing (throughput), technical writing stresses terminological consistency, coherent structure, and uniform expression, organizing content around user tasks and system principles.

In practice, documentation formats vary according to audience and context. End-user documentation—such as a home 3D printer manual—pairs plain language with visuals to guide layer users through assembly and software installation while reducing cognitive load. Industrial equipment manuals retain essential specifications while ensuring terminological precision for engineers. Instructions for children or older adults emphasize layout and visualization to enhance accessibility.

Documentation for maintenance personnel focuses on system principles, standard procedures, and troubleshooting. A network equipment maintenance guide, for example, details indicator light meanings, diagnostic steps, replacement procedures, safety notes, compliance requirements, and risk alerts. Specification documents (e.g., an embedded module datasheet) highlight static information—parameters, interfaces, electrical characteristics—critical for procurement, integration, and quality control.

Internal engineering documentation and Application Programming Interface (API) references are likewise central. Engineering documents capture architectural decisions, module responsibilities, and rationale, sustaining team continuity. API documentation specifies endpoints, parameters, authentication mechanisms, reusable code samples, and error handling. Automation can scaffold structure, yet human writers remain essential for semantic enrichment, disambiguation, and example refinement (Getto et al., 2025).

Technical writing also encompasses knowledge bases, training materials, regulatory and compliance documentation, accessibility statements, and internationalization guidelines. Internal FAQs and support knowledge bases reduce support cost; training materials accelerate onboarding; compliance documentation enables market entry and risk management; accessibility and internationalization guidelines extend reach to specialized user groups and multilingual markets.

For years, documentation was treated as ancillary until digitization and modular content made it integral to the product. In safety-critical domains (aviation, medical, industrial), comprehensive documentation is a prerequisite for market release; in software, coherent API documentation shapes ecosystem growth. A single-sourcing strategy combined with structured authoring enables efficient reuse across platforms, languages, and media, reducing maintenance cost and accelerating knowledge accumulation (Rockley & Kostur, 2003).

1.2 Technical Writing and Multimodal Technical Communication

Technical writing is a core branch of technical communication but not identical to it. Technical communication spans broader multimodal expression—imagery, symbols, interface, audio—and focuses on adaptation and integration across contexts and audiences. Technical writing emphasizes precision and structured exposition; technical communication foregrounds channel orchestration and holistic experience design. In practice, many writers also act as communication designers, connecting content structure, presentation form, and user experience.

Modern technical communication relies on three channels: visual, linguistic, and interactive. In the print era, users passively consulted text with limited illustrations. In digital environments, information is embedded in usage flows and operational experience. Visual assets (architecture diagrams, flowcharts, animations) help users internalize principles and steps without terminological barriers. Linguistic expression requires consistent terminology, concise sentences, and clear structure. Interactive expression provides real-time prompts and guidance—tooltip bubbles, guided question-answering (Q&A), and voice assistant feedback (Tham et al., 2023).

In software, the help ecosystem may combine quick-start videos, annotated screenshots, structured documents, inline tips, and interactive Q&A. These forms serve a shared knowledge model and must remain semantically and stylistically aligned, forming a coherent information system rather than a loose compilation.

Platform companies and smart device manufacturers now embed technical communication in product experience: online API documentation with interactive sandboxes for instant testing; industrial maintenance guidance refactored into mobile-optimized visual workflows; staged in-product learning paths guiding users to core capability mastery. All derive from systematic user-journey analysis and multimodal integration.

Advances in AI and human–computer interaction are driving documentation toward intelligence, contextualization, and personalization. Augmented Reality (AR) has transformed static maintenance manuals into real-time visual guidance: with a headset, an engineer sees 3D exploded views, procedural instructions, and risk alerts, improving efficiency and safety (Azuma, 1997). Context-aware systems deliver tailored content based on user role, interaction history, and current state—recommending diagnostic steps when a parameter misconfiguration occurs or supplying maintenance guidance when a smart-home device fails. Technical communication now extends beyond static documents into a dynamically adaptive knowledge system.

1.3 Role Reconfiguration of Technical Writers

Technical writing is shifting from static text production to systemic collaborative design. Documentation is embedded within product workflows and interfaces, becoming part of the knowledge architecture and experience. Writers must plan content models, information pathways, and presentation forms so documentation remains navigable, maintainable, and extensible.

This shift stems from embedding knowledge into operational flows: user interface (UI) hints, inline help, and contextual recommendations require language and interaction to evolve in tandem. Writers collaborate with product, user experience (UX), and algorithm teams to define information structures around cognitive paths and task flows, ensuring semantic consistency across media and touchpoints.

With deeper AI participation (Hart-Davidson et al., 2024), division of labor has sharpened: AI produces foundational drafts; human writers distill complex knowledge, design user-oriented architectures, and maintain cross-media semantic alignment (Bender et al., 2021). Analytical reasoning, cross-cultural interpretation, and discourse control skills enable writers to transform heterogeneous inputs into coherent knowledge units and tailor information pathways to audience profiles.

The role is evolving from language producer to knowledge architect and UX co-designer integrated with product and engineering (Tham et al., 2022). For example, maintenance knowledge for complex equipment can be decomposed into minimal procedural units and surfaced stepwise via AR cues, video, and text; platform API documentation can integrate an interactive sandbox plus diagnostic scripts, reducing developer–support friction.

Centered on tasks and scaffolded by terminology and concepts, technical writers co-design knowledge and experience with product, UX, and algorithm teams under constraints of cross-media consistency and data-driven evaluation. Content remains responsive to evolving contexts and—with AI assistance—durably reliable and evolvable.

2 Language Style and Standards in Technical Documentation

Expectations for language in technical documentation extend beyond basic fluency. It must support precise operations, convey unambiguous meaning, and remain consistent and usable across cultures and languages. These demands have produced institutionalized frameworks—style guides and controlled languages—moving practice beyond intuition (DeRespinis et al., 2011; Feng & Gao, 2017).

2.1 Core Linguistic Characteristics of Technical Documentation

The register of technical documentation is driven by function, not aesthetics. Unlike creative or advertising copy aimed at emotional impact, its goal is exact, executable information transfer (Microsoft Writing Style Guide, 2025). Users consult documentation to perform defined tasks—troubleshooting, completing procedures, interpreting system behavior—so language must deliver clarity, accuracy, consistency, and lack of ambiguity.

Clarity requires direct, logically ordered expression that avoids redundancy and vagueness. "Restart the device at an appropriate time" invites divergent interpretations, whereas "Restart the device immediately after replacing the battery" specifies condition and action (Redish, 2007), reducing cognitive load and execution variance.

Accuracy entails faithful representation of technical details and system behavior, factual correctness, and strict terminological uniformity. If a UI button reads "Start," the documentation should not alternate with "Open," "Activate," or "Begin" (Google Developer Documentation Style Guide, 2025). Inconsistency increases the risk of error, especially across languages and platforms.

Consistency underpins quality. Multi-author, iterative, multilingual workflows require uniform style, terminology, syntax, numbering, and labeling to preserve continuity and improve retrieval and translation efficiency.

Unambiguity is critical. Diverse user backgrounds produce divergent readings. "Shut down the device as soon as possible" is subjective; "After the error message appears three consecutive times, shut down the device immediately" removes interpretive latitude and mitigates risk.

Stylistically, technical documentation favors neutral, objective, fact-based statements. Instead of "highly powerful," use "This feature supports batch processing of up to 1,000 data units," which provides quantifiable information and aids translation and automation.

New writers, especially from humanities backgrounds, may conflate "clear" with "ornate," overusing modifiers or metaphors that obstruct comprehension. "This interface easily handles complex requests" lacks engineering value; "This interface supports asynchronous processing and pagination, suitable for high-concurrency scenarios" provides actionable insight.

Assessing compliance requires professional style guides, linguistic quality assurance (QA) tools, and peer review—not personal intuition—to verify it effectively. Clarity, accuracy, consistency, and unambiguity form the four linguistic cornerstones that distinguish technical writing.

2.2 *Quality Standards and Style Governance Systems for Technical Information*

In enterprise settings, several methods assess documentation quality. IBM's Developing Quality Technical Information (DQTI) framework is widely adopted (Hargis et al., 2004). Integrating user experience and information architecture, it defines three dimensions—Clarity, Findability, and Usefulness—as reference standards.

Clarity requires concise, precise, unambiguous language and structure so users obtain executable guidance. An installation guide should not say "Perform some settings first" but list concrete steps and parameters. Findability concerns organization—logical headings, keyword indexing, navigation, modularity—enabling rapid location. Usefulness demands alignment with user tasks: explicit steps, inputs and outputs, error handling, and expected results (e.g., "A flashing red LED indicates an over-temperature condition" plus remediation).

DQTI also articulates supporting principles: terminological consistency, audience orientation, task-based structure, and text–visual synergy. Consistently using "log in" (verb phrase) reduces ambiguity and facilitates translation. Audience orientation adjusts density and explanatory depth; task-based structure aligns with user goals ("Deploy," "Troubleshoot") rather than product modules. Visual synergy—flowcharts, screenshots—enhances immediacy and operational clarity.

The style guide system complements DQTI. A style guide is infrastructure ensuring consistency, maintainability, and professionalism (Microsoft Writing Style Guide, 2025). The Microsoft Manual of Style specifies terminology, UI wording, tone, and naming—preferring "Select Settings from the menu" to "click here" for clarity and translatability. The IBM Style Guide emphasizes structured authoring, separating conceptual, task, and reference topics, and integrating terminology databases for cross-language/version alignment.

Uniformity in syntax and formatting improves readability and enables automation. Standardizing alerts as "State + Cause + Action" supports multilingual generation and UI integration. Style guidelines often align with corporate visual identity so websites, product documentation, in-app tips, and notifications share tone and wording. Modern design systems (Google Material Design, Microsoft Fluent Design, IBM Carbon) co-design linguistic style and visual components for an integrated language–interface experience.

In distributed, multi-author environments, style guides prevent terminological drift and structural inconsistency and assist version tracking by filtering formatting noise. With AI in the workflow, their role expands: intelligent authoring platforms load custom rules to flag terminology, tone, and syntactic deviations (Getto et al., 2025), embedding governance in every production stage.

Under the combined scaffolding of quality standards and style governance, documentation attains accuracy and sound structure while preserving cross-platform and multilingual consistency and maintainability.

3 From Translation-Centric to Cross-Language Collaborative Multilingual Authoring

In global dissemination and multilingual service contexts, multilingual content creation has moved beyond a downstream translation step to a strategic authoring choice. Technical documentation, product instructions, websites, and marketing collateral must communicate efficiently, accurately, and appropriately across languages and cultures (Jiménez-Crespo, 2013). Traditional source-centric linear workflows often produce cultural misalignment and limit communicative effectiveness.

Research on multilingual authoring spans optimization for translation (Byrne, 2006) and collaborative "simultaneous multilingual generation" workflows. Practitioners must compare strengths and limitations across scenarios and align production strategy with project goals, language portfolio, and communication needs (Bowker, 2019).

3.1 The Necessity of Multilingual Authoring and Diverging Quality Standards

As multilingual dissemination becomes routine, focus shifts from a serial, single-source pipeline to architectures designed for simultaneous languages. Technology firms, international bodies, and educational platforms are experimenting with multilingual co-authoring to replace "write first, translate later" (Suojanen et al., 2014; Suojanen et al., 2015). The shift reflects movement toward target-language-oriented quality metrics and improved process efficiency and user experience.

International organizations (e.g., the United Nations, European Union) apply a principle of equal linguistic authenticity: all official language versions hold identical legal force. Drafting guidelines mandate early cross-lingual collaboration to surface ambiguity or cultural conflict and ensure structural and readability alignment across languages (Leal, 2020; European Parliament, Council of the European Union, and European Commission, 2015; United Nations, 2024). This institutional design advances front-loaded, ambiguity-reducing multilingual authoring.

In enterprise contexts, major technology firms (e.g., Microsoft) pursue "simultaneous shipping (Sim-ship)" so product and documentation launch concurrently across locales. This depends on controlled language (e.g., Aerospace and Defence Simplified English, ASD-STE100), unified termbases, and automated quality assurance (QA). Early multilingual planning anticipates linguistic divergence (German, Chinese, Japanese) and embeds adaptation in product and documentation architecture, reducing feature redundancy, content pruning, and stylistic fragmentation.

Source-dominant workflows often overlook target-language reading conventions and cultural logic. German legal sentence length reproduced in Japanese overloads processing; Spanish instructional materials favor everyday contextualization—linear English exposition may dampen resonance. The directive "click the button" typically gains a politeness particle in Chinese UI copy ("请单击该按钮", meaning "Please click the button"), may omit an explicit subject in Thai, and in Arabic must follow formal syntactic norms plus right-to-left layout. Such distinctions argue for embedding multilingual considerations during authoring rather than retrofitting them post-translation.

In the domains of publishing and knowledge dissemination, although internal practices vary, the industry prioritizes localized readability—adapting structure, tone, and examples through style guidelines, editorial policy, and translation collaboration. This shifts emphasis from a single "faithfulness" criterion toward intelligibility, acceptability, and utility in the target language (Suojanen et al., 2014; Suojanen et al., 2015).

Quality evaluation is shifting from "translation fidelity" to "target-language fitness." Defining multilingual goals at the authoring stage—and demonstrating structural, stylistic, and expressive sensitivity to linguistic and cultural reception—is becoming a new benchmark.

3.2 *Translation-Driven Writing Under a Source-First Strategy*

In multilingual content production, the source-language-first (translation-driven) model remains the dominant approach for international organizations, multinational enterprises, and publishers. A single pivot language (most often English) serves as the design anchor, and conditions for subsequent multilingual translation and release are engineered during scoping and drafting. The approach is shaped by workflow design as well as resource allocation and quality governance.

Translation-driven writing anticipates downstream translation at the drafting stage. It applies terminological standardization, structural discipline, and linguistic simplification to reduce ambiguity and increase translatability. For example, European Commission policy papers are drafted in English with controlled sentence length, harmonized wording (supported by the InterActive Terminology for Europe (IATE) database), and avoidance of vague expressions so they can be rendered efficiently and accurately into more than twenty official languages. The degree of source normalization directly affects translation effort and target quality.

In enterprise practice, companies such as Adobe use modular authoring tools (e.g., FrameMaker) to decompose content into reusable standardized components, while termbases and formatting conventions tighten source control (Bowker, 2019). Implementation typically integrates terminology management, controlled language, modular structures, and source annotations. Tools such as SDL MultiTerm or Acrolinx enforce lexical uniformity; standards such as Simplified Technical English (STE) reduce ambiguity and complexity; structural schemas like Darwin Information Typing Architecture enable modular reuse; and disambiguating notes (e.g., "implant (refers to surgical device, not action verb)") in medical device manuals prevent confusion between procedure and object in French or Chinese.

Key advantages include efficiency, control, and consistency. A well-engineered source combined with translation memories and termbases accelerates production of multiple language versions while preserving logic and structure. Tight integration with translation technology platforms (e.g., SDL Trados, XTM, MemoQ) enables parallel translation and simultaneous release, making it a de facto standard in global content operations.

Its limitations are equally clear—chiefly diminished naturalness and cultural fit in target languages. Substantial structural and stylistic distance can yield stilted translations or misaligned user expectations. For instance, English passives rendered literally into Chinese often read awkwardly; the direct tone of English marketing copy may clash with politeness conventions in Japanese or Arabic contexts. For example, a company's English user manual was criticized in Japanese for insufficient detail—not due to translation quality, but because the source assumed prior technical knowledge and concise exposition, overlooking readers' preference for gradual, fully elaborated explanations (Suokas, 2022).

Translation-driven writing remains a pragmatic choice for industrialized multilingual production, given its process standardization and cost control. However, because language conveys culture as well as information, source development should embed localization awareness, reserving room for cultural and stylistic adaptation to enhance usability and resonance across markets.

3.3 Collaborative Multilingual Co-authoring

Translation-driven writing still dominates global content operations, yet where multilingual dissemination must balance tight cross-language alignment with deep localization, multilingual co-authoring offers distinct advantages (Suojanen et al., 2015). Rather than a single source language, language teams draft in parallel around shared assets and common communication objectives.

For example, in UNESCO global policy handbooks the project team first consolidates key concepts, data, figures, and policy points into a shared information kit. Chinese, French, Arabic, and other language teams then author independently for their audiences. The resulting versions are parallel expositions—not translations—of the same thematic core. This model demands rigorous project management: real-time shared asset access, a unified termbase, and transparent progress tracking.

Terminology alignment is central. Without a fixed source, teams rely on a shared termbase plus scheduled consultations to sustain consistent conceptual understanding. Two chief benefits follow: (1) elevated localization quality—each team optimizes structure and register directly for local readers (Suokas, 2022); and (2) linguistic parity—mitigating source-language centrality and fostering balanced global reach. The trade-off is higher coordination overhead: experienced project management, adaptive terminology processes, and frequent communication.

Quality evaluation thus diverges from translation metrics. Assessment shifts from "faithfulness to source" toward intra-language quality and cross-language equivalence: Does the version fit local discourse norms? Is the register natural? Are core informational intents aligned?

Multilingual co-authoring does not supplant translation-driven writing; rather, it provides a flexible pathway for high-value, deeply localized communication. Many organizations now mix strategies by content type: controlled-source plus unified translation for technical instructions to ensure consistency; parallel native drafting for marketing copy, social media, or training to maximize cultural relevance. This hybrid—shared core intent with differentiated expression—preserves efficiency while boosting audience engagement.

Some international bodies and global education platforms employ a "tiered authoring" model: an English conceptual skeleton and key data precede parallel reconstruction by language teams—creating a semi-free rewriting layer between pure translation and full co-authoring (Suojanen et al., 2015). This retains a stable informational core while granting expressive latitude for cultural fit.

Elastic, strategy-aware workflow design is now a professional threshold: teams diagnose communicative purpose and language portfolio, then adjust authoring pathways and quality criteria rather than imposing a single model.

4 Controlled Language in Technical Writing

In multilingual technical documentation, controlled language is a primary instrument for ensuring quality and consistency. By systematically constraining vocabulary, grammar, and syntax, it promotes clarity, uniformity, machine parsability, automation readiness, and reliable cross-language transfer (Nyberg et al., 2008). Its intent is not to diminish expressiveness but to preempt redundancy, vagueness, and ambiguity, thereby improving communicative efficiency. Design principles reflect cognitive processing: limiting sentence length, simplifying structure, and reducing pronominal ambiguity lower reading burden and accelerate information uptake (Kintsch & van Dijk, 1978). Such optimization supports user comprehension while providing a stable substrate for multilingual collaboration and machine translation (Trippel, 2012).

4.1 Evolutionary Stages of Controlled Language

Controlled language has a centuries-long lineage in technical communication (Aikawa et al., 2007). In the 17th century, Urquhart (1653) proposed a simplified terminological scheme for artisans to reduce linguistic complexity and improve technical dissemination. In the early 20th century, Ogden (1930) advanced "Basic English" with 850 core words and a one-word-one-meaning principle. Although criticized for limited expressiveness and cultural bias, the simplification ethos strongly influenced later industrial standards.

In the 1970s, Caterpillar introduced Caterpillar Fundamental English as a manual standard to cut translation costs (Caterpillar Tractor Company, 1972). Soon after, the European aerospace sector developed Simplified Technical English, codifying roughly 53 linguistic rules and about 900 core words, later formalized as the international standard ASD-STE100 (Aerospace, Security and Defence Industries Association of Europe (ASD), n.d.).

In the 1990s, variants such as Bull Controlled English prioritized machine translation (MT) readability, introducing simplification rules to improve MT performance (Kuhn, 2014). Boeing's Simplified English Checker and similar tools embedded conformance validation into authoring platforms, increasing enforcement efficiency.

In the 21st century, controlled languages converged with natural language processing (NLP). Attempto Controlled English emerged, supporting direct mapping to logical forms and automated reasoning (Fuchs et al., 2008). Concurrently, automated conformance tools (e.g., Boeing's and Congree's solutions) integrated rule checking into authoring, and the aerospace sector's Modified Natural Language sought a balance between human readability and machine parsability.

Across these stages—simplification, enterprise standardization, MT optimization, and NLP/logical integration—controlled language has consistently used rule-based constraints to raise linguistic quality and cross-language operability, securing its foundational role in contemporary technical writing.

4.2 Standardized Controlled Language in Technical Writing

ASD-STE100 (STE) is among the most prominent controlled language standards. Originating in the 1980s aerospace imperative for standardized, globally intelligible multilingual documentation, it systematically constrains lexis, syntax, and expression—reducing comprehension barriers, improving translation efficiency, and reshaping production and governance models.

Its philosophy is not subtraction but the conversion of linguistic flexibility into verifiable, operational design constraints. ASD-STE100 treats uncontrolled expressive variability as a primary source of complexity; only explicit, uniform rules can sustain consistency across cultures and teams. Thus it recasts authoring from an individual craft into an engineered, automatable process.

Lexically, ASD-STE100 restricts the core inventory to roughly 900 approved words, each with a single sanctioned part of speech and meaning, disallowing synonyms and polysemy. Domain terms may be added when necessary but must be defined at first use and remain stable. Multi-word verbs and complex constructions are reduced to base forms to ease cross-language transfer; selection favors high frequency and global familiarity for unambiguous expression.

Syntactically, the rules privilege short sentences (typically $\leq$20 words) and active voice, tightly limiting embedded clauses; conjunctions and conditional patterns are regulated. This reduces cognitive and translation load and improves machine parsing. Passive constructions are reserved for unknown or non-human agents to preserve directness. Figurative language is excluded. Numerals, units, dates, and times follow international conventions, and punctuation is explicitly specified.

Its advantages lie not only in rule design but also in implementable governance: checklists and automated validators enable process control and auditability. Writers typically undergo formal training; periodic updates and associated training services deliver sustained support and revenue, reinforcing influence through co-evolution with industry practices.

Advances in AI and NLP now permit real-time conformance checking and optimization suggestions, markedly improving authoring and quality control efficiency. ASD-STE100 sees broad adoption in aerospace, defense, and other high-compliance domains, measurably enhancing comprehensibility, translation throughput, and maintenance sustainability.

Its practice shows that simplification and standardization expand rather than constrain communicative efficacy—amplifying global reach and usability. The engineered, operable, automatable rule set now forms a methodological and technological foundation for modern technical writing and language services.

4.3 AI-Driven Linguistic Standardization and Compliance

Traditionally, linguistic standards—grammar, spelling, terminology, style, tone—were enforced through author expertise or editorial gatekeeping and documented in static manuals or term lists. Reliance on post-hoc human review constrained efficiency. With generative AI embedded in workflows, these norms are evolving from static prescriptions to dynamic, interactive feedback loops (Bender et al., 2021), turning standards into real-time control parameters.

AI-enabled style platforms convert static rules into live feedback. Grammarly Business, for instance, operationalizes parameters like tone consistency and audience appropriateness against a custom style guide, flagging deviations during composition. In multilingual authoring, DeepL Write suggests stylistic and syntactic refinements during reformulation. Feedback thus shifts from end-stage correction to continuous optimization.

Stylistic consistency underpins team collaboration and brand voice. Increasingly, organizations employ prompt conditioning or sample-based adaptation so AI reflects institutional style. Notion AI can generate harmonized prose from uploaded project documents or style guides; Writer.com uses exemplars plus prompt design to approximate team voice and support style transfer without full model retraining. This controllable generation capability is especially valuable in domains—public relations, technical documentation, legal—where tonal uniformity is critical.

Style governance now intersects with content quality assurance. In a Docs-as-Code model, documentation is authored in structured plaintext (e.g., Markdown, AsciiDoc), and open-source linters such as Vale apply rule sets. These can integrate with custom rule engines or language models to automate linguistic QA within Continuous Integration/Continuous Delivery (CI/CD) pipelines.

In knowledge management and conversational systems, organizations embed style exemplars and tonal directives into prompt templates so output remains both accurate and brand-conformant. Software as a Service (SaaS) support bots, for instance, may enforce standardized salutations, neutral tone, and avoidance of first-person pronouns—codified through iterative prompt engineering.

Linguistic compliance and style control have become integral quality safeguards. Large language models now enable automated enforcement and adaptive application of stylistic norms, advancing workflow formalization and professionalization. Capabilities vary across products, however, so advanced customization still requires organization-specific optimization.

5 Structuring in Technical Documentation

In a complex, continuously evolving product and service landscape, technical documentation has shifted from static explanation to maintainable, reusable, deliverable structured knowledge. Quality depends not only on accuracy and clarity but critically on structural soundness (Wixom & Todd, 2005). Task-oriented users—of manuals, developer guides, API references, and Standard Operating Procedures (SOPs)—skip redundancy to locate goal-relevant fragments, behavior consistent with information foraging theory (Pirolli & Card, 1999). Structures enabling rapid navigation, logical transparency, and extensible recomposition enhance experience while improving maintainability and reuse.

5.1 Design Principles for Technical Documentation Structure

In expository technical documents, structure governs information exposure and thus usability. Because objectives are problem-solving and task support, readers rarely proceed linearly; they scan with intent. Structural design should therefore prioritize efficient navigation, scannability, and maintainability to minimize cognitive and operational cost (Johnson, 1998).

Navigability is primary: users "arrive with a question and should leave with an answer." This requires precise, user-centric headings and coherent navigation. Vague or inconsistent titling undermines retrieval. Scannability then drives acquisition speed. A troubleshooting template—"Problem Description / Impact Scope / Possible Causes / Resolution Steps"—lets users jump directly to needed blocks (Krug, 2000). Dense, monolithic paragraphs, by contrast, slow search and increase frustration under time pressure.

Consistency across a documentation corpus accelerates orientation and reduces update errors. Standard templates (e.g., "Business Context / System Setup / Procedure Path / Cautions") promote rapid transfer across modules. Structure should also weave a knowledge network: inline links from a procedure to configuration syntax, credential management, or diagnostic methods enable seamless lateral movement. New users rely on structural guidance for progressive learning; experts treat structure as a high-speed index—design must satisfy both.

Structural failure can be life-critical. During Ethiopian Airlines Flight ET302 (Boeing 737 MAX), pilots repeatedly consulted manuals seeking the procedure to disable the automatic nose-down Maneuvering Characteristics Augmentation System (MCAS) and manually re-trim the stabilizer, but never completed the action. Although they cut electric trim per procedure, excessive speed and aerodynamic load prevented manual wheel operation; reverting to electric trim allowed MCAS to reactivate, culminating in the crash (Ethiopian Accident Investigation Bureau (EAIB), 2022). This multi-factor accident (sensor failure, system design, high workload) illustrates how unclear structure in high-stress conditions can prove fatal.

Effectiveness reflects not only authoring skill but organizational culture. Clear, retrievable, cognitively aligned structures require integrated collaboration among design, engineering, QA, and documentation, with "documentation as product" embedded culturally. Cross-functional teams internalize user task contexts and cognitive load, layering domain expertise and risk foresight so information remains rapidly accessible and executable across scenarios.

AI augments accessibility and retrieval, yet in safety-critical or decision-critical contexts it is assistive rather than a sole dependency. Automation can fail through interruption, latency, or misjudgment; users then rely on inherently intelligible, directly actionable documentation. Structured, normalized content is both AI-friendly and resilient offline. Clear hierarchy, direct navigation pathways, and explicit high-risk cues form the minimum design baseline linking technical communication to safety assurance.

5.2 *Hierarchical and Modular Structural Strategies*

Structure in expository documentation governs presentation and directly affects usability, maintainability, and long-term extensibility. Unlike linear prose, technical content must accommodate non-linear navigation: rapid step lookup, immediate task execution, and cross-document sharing. Hierarchy, modularization, and reuse therefore form the strategic core of modern documentation systems.

Hierarchy builds a progression from topic to task to supporting detail. A document may segment by functional domain (e.g., network configuration, user management), drill into tasks (add user, set permissions), then embed "Steps / Examples / Cautions" modules beneath each task. Layered tables of contents, anchor links, or grouped indexes let users form a mental map and reduce navigational hops.

Modularization decomposes content into self-contained functional units (overview, prerequisites, procedure, result description, code example, cautions). Users enter only the needed module without whole-document reading, increasing efficiency; teams update only impacted units, avoiding full rewrites. Predictable module patterns also reinforce consistency across products.

Reusability extends hierarchy and modularization—"write less, trust more"—while sustaining consistency and version control across product variants, locales, and delivery platforms. Common tactics include:

- Template reuse: standardized callouts (warnings, permissions, cautions) as callable templates to ensure visual and logical uniformity and reduce manual error.
- Direct inclusion (single-sourcing): centrally stored core content is referenced elsewhere so updates synchronize automatically—analogous to module imports in software.
- Indirect referenced reuse: localized adjustments layered on referenced material with source attribution and update prompts—suited to platform or regional variants.
- Variable substitution: volatile items (product name, version, brand) abstracted as variables for build-time replacement.
- Conditional publishing: display conditions keyed to audience, version, or scenario; one source yields differentiated outputs (DITA natively supports such filtering).

Combined structural and reuse architectures parallel modular software design—enabling standardized management, rapid recomposition, and automated output. Under conditions of rapid iteration, cross-platform deployment, or simultaneous multilingual release, they reduce update cost while safeguarding consistency and brand alignment.

Conversely, unstructured text blocks degrade retrieval, erode experience, and raise maintenance risk—version drift, latent inaccuracies, and obsolete content—particularly dangerous in safety, compliance, or high-risk operational contexts.

Structure and reuse embody product thinking, not mere stylistic technique. Technical writers architect user pathways and build durable content assets. Early involvement in content architecture—alongside product, engineering, QA, and localization—is essential to establish a scalable management framework.

5.3 Structured Authoring Languages and DITA-Based Content Engineering

The usability of technical documentation depends not only on clarity and modular design but also on the rigor of the underlying markup. The emergence of structured authoring languages signals a shift from producing documents to engineering knowledge systems. Through elements, attributes, and hierarchical relationships, content becomes machine-processable: systems can identify semantic modules for precise retrieval while maintainability and scalability improve.

Early web practice showed that mixing structure and presentation undermines maintainability. Original HyperText Markup Language (HTML) targeted structure (headings, paragraphs, lists); escalating layout demands led to misuse of presentational tags, eroding structural clarity and accessibility. The separation introduced by Extensibile HyperText Markup Language (XHTML plus Cascading Style Sheets (CSS) restored the division: structure states "what it is," presentation controls "how it looks." Contemporary technical communication extends this principle, privileging semantic relationships and logical hierarchy over page layout and enabling a single source to generate web, PDF, mobile help, and augmented/virtual reality outputs—"write once, use everywhere."

Within this ecosystem, approaches fill distinct niches. Lightweight syntaxes such as Markdown are terse and easy to learn—well suited for READMEs, blogs, and engineering journals—but lack the semantic richness and reuse governance required for large documentation portfolios. In contrast, Extensible Markup Language (XML) and its derivatives provide extensible structural expressiveness foundational to industrial-scale documentation. XML frameworks like DocBook were once prevalent for books and long manuals, but extensive tag sets and a steep learning curve have yielded ground to the more flexible architectural standard DITA.

DITA's core principle is topic-based authoring in place of linear composition. Content is decomposed into minimal semantic units typed as Concept, Task, Reference, and other standardized topic classes, each aligned to a distinct user intent. A security guide, for instance, can explain principles in Concept topics, prescribe actions in Task topics, and enumerate configuration parameters in Reference topics. The map mechanism assembles, orders, filters, and publishes these modules independently of sequence, fully decoupling content from structure. An "Installation Procedure" module can appear in a quick start guide and a support manual simultaneously; a single update propagates globally, eliminating duplication and version drift.

This fusion of modularity and structure yields strategic advantages:

- Create once, reuse broadly: cross-document and cross-channel referencing cuts maintenance cost.
- Multi-channel, multi-variant publishing: output to HTML, PDF, EPUB, and more; apply conditional filters by market, role, or version.
- Consistency and governed quality: standardized structures enable automated validation, terminology control, and style enforcement.
- Multilingual and localization readiness: conditional attributes plus modular granularity support synchronized updates and variant releases efficiently.
- Long-term knowledge asset accumulation: portable DITA modules form a maintainable knowledge base integrable with AI search, recommendation, and translation for intelligent content services.

In high-reliability, compliance-intensive, multilingual domains—aviation, medical devices, manufacturing, large-scale IT—DITA has become a de facto global standard. It streamlines authoring workflows and elevates documentation to a systemic content engineering discipline, recasting writers as content architects who shape knowledge organization, delivery, and long-term stewardship.

5.4 A Structured Workflow for Modern Technical Documentation

Understanding the value of DITA and related frameworks reframes workflow goals from "finishing a document" to "building a sustainable content asset." Structured methodology partitions the lifecycle into planning, authoring, management, and publishing, instituting traceable, automated controls at each stage so that updates resemble disciplined software versioning.

During planning, information architects define the content model and structural blueprint, decomposing information into functionally scoped modules (procedural steps, risk notices, code examples, parameter tables). Each module is created with metadata, a unique identifier, and contextual relationships to ensure precise retrieval, reuse, and recomposition. An industrial automation firm, for example, treats "Device

Initialization Procedure" as a global module cited in manuals, training, online help, and compliance documents; a single source edit synchronizes all consuming locations.

Authoring operationalizes the design. Writers populate Concept, Task, and Reference topics in a DITA (or lightweight DITA) environment to mirror user task flows. Controlled language, centralized termbases, and style guides reduce ambiguity and inconsistency, preserving clarity across versions and languages. Localization teams can engage once a module stabilizes, eliminating the sequential delay inherent in "author–translate–assemble" pipelines.

The management phase relies on a Content Management System (CMS) or Component Content Management System (CCMS) to enforce version control and update traceability across teams. When a module is modified, the system flags its impact and routes it for targeted review or approval. In medical device documentation, high-risk modules (e.g., "Emergency Shutdown Steps," "Chemical Handling Warning") may require mandatory legal and compliance review to ensure rapid propagation of regulatory or process changes across documents and training assets.

Publishing showcases multi-channel leverage: the same source renders to HTML, PDF, mobile help, or embedded micro-documentation. A SaaS platform, for instance, dynamically assembles role-based views—new users see core steps and cautions; administrators receive advanced configuration guidance and Application Programming Interface (API) references. Conditional filtering maximizes contextual relevance and task efficiency.

Underlying all phases is a reengineered collaboration model: authors, template engineers, translators, developers, and compliance reviewers work in parallel within a unified framework with clearly defined interfaces, reducing rework and silos. AI further strengthens discoverability and analytical oversight by surfacing terminology deviations and recommending contextually relevant modules or prior iterations, reducing manual search and decision overhead.

The normalization produced by structured authoring constitutes an engineered production paradigm: information remains accurate and consistent amid rapid product or regulatory change, while forming a future-ready knowledge asset base. This synthesis of methodology and workflow is becoming the shared operational language of high-quality technical communication in complex content ecosystems.

5.5 Artificial Intelligence and Structured Technical Authoring

Structured authoring stresses logical partitioning, modular independence, and governed consistency, yet traditional workflows expend significant effort on markup maintenance, terminology enforcement, and formatting compliance. With large-model document intelligence tools (Kandepu & Harry, 2023), the discipline is accelerating toward higher automation and collaborative augmentation. AI reduces friction in structural transformation, markup governance, and standards validation, increasing efficiency, precision, and auditability and making it a primary productivity lever for documentation teams (Aljedaani, 2024).

AI excels at reconstructing unstructured corpora. It can perform semantic segmentation on maintenance manuals, email threads, and technical reports to extract procedural steps, cautions, and conditional constraints (Laxmanan, 2025), then draft template-conforming structured content. A medical device firm, for example, parses design dossiers and test reports, maps results into predefined templates via automated workflows, and mass-produces compliant documents—reducing labor by roughly 75% while preserving accuracy and regulatory conformity. Manufacturers similarly apply large language models to convert legacy PDF guides into DITA-compliant modular assets, revitalizing dormant linguistic capital.

AI likewise transforms terminology and style governance. Manual line-by-line review is slow and error-prone; embedding termbases and style guides directly in the authoring environment enables real-time alerts for inconsistent usage or tonal deviation (Kumar, 2024). Early detection shrinks downstream rework and elevates consistency in large documentation programs.

In content creation, AI serves as an assistive amplifier—auto-completing procedural fields, generating examples, or expanding caution sections from semantic prompts (Kandepu & Harry, 2023). Within DITA toolchains it can recommend topic-appropriate components, broadening coverage and tightening structural integrity. Human-AI coauthoring accelerates turnaround and increases cross-version and cross-language reuse.

AI is also reshaping lifecycle governance. Enterprise content platforms can monitor product changes and user feedback, automatically flag impacted modules, propose revisions, and push synchronized updates to support or training channels. This "predictive maintenance" shifts documentation from reactive correction to proactive optimization, sustaining accuracy and currency across the lifecycle.

AI augments structured authoring not by displacing professional judgment but by amplifying capability in organization, quality assurance, and multi-channel delivery. With AI support, structured authoring is evolving from document production into an adaptive content engineering discipline that underpins durable knowledge asset management and competitive differentiation.

6 Content Management and Distribution

Content management is not a post-writing afterthought but a higher-order extension of structured authoring (Rickenberg et al., 2012). As digital products and services evolve, technical documentation has moved beyond static manuals to become a dynamic component of user interaction. Content must update in near real time, adapt across devices, and support personalized, on-demand delivery. Structured authoring toolchains, content management systems, single sourcing, and intelligent distribution together form the technological substrate of modern content engineering.

6.1 Structuring and Engineering Management of Content Assets

Rooted in publishing (Paivarinta & Munkvold, 2005), content management initially targeted accuracy and consistency across multi-stage, multi-version workflows—drafting, editing, typesetting, proofing. As knowledge-centric operations expanded, the paradigm generalized to enterprise knowledge bases, training, marketing collateral, and customer support (Alalwan & Weistroffer, 2012; Rickenberg et al., 2012), and matured into robust technical practices in software development, engineering manufacture, and regulated pharma domains (Laumer et al., 2013).

These domains impose distinctive demands: precision, consistency, traceability, cross-platform synchronicity, multilingual support, long lifecycle, frequent updates. A complex device manual may coexist as print, PDF, web knowledge base, and mobile help—yet must remain version-aligned. Whole-document management is inefficient for multi-channel rapid iteration and inhibits cross-team collaboration. Fine-grained management—at module, paragraph, or even term level—supports reuse, substitution, and traceability.

The expansion of web and digital publishing accelerated the shift. Corporate sites and apps now integrate text, imagery, video, interactive charts, structured data, Search Engine Optimization tags, and access controls. Hand-maintained HTML cannot scale; the Content Management System (CMS) emerged to decouple content from presentation, centralize orchestration, and facilitate multi-channel distribution—mirroring the logic of structured technical authoring.

In this model, content becomes a metadata-rich asset: each paragraph, figure, or table carries descriptors (applicable scenario, target user, language variant, release date, revision state). Metadata detaches content from any single page, turning it into identifiable, traceable, callable knowledge nodes. A "Login Flow Description" module can serve multiple products—maintained once in a central repository with version/platform tags. When the flow changes, updates propagate automatically to all referencing outputs.

This "content + metadata" construct underpins assetization and engineered management. Precise information modeling plus cross-functional collaboration (development, design, architecture, operations) enables fluid knowledge flow across platforms and endpoints while supporting multi-form publishing. The result is rapid response to market or regulatory change and productized, sustainable knowledge operations (Rickenberg et al., 2012).

6.2 Structured Content Publishing and Single Sourcing

The spread of structured authoring is shifting technical publishing from page-centric pipelines to content-centric intelligent distribution (Hackos, 2002). Historically, the page was the atomic unit—linear content embedded in layout and re-exported wholesale after any change, imposing high cost and latency. The page also acted as an implicit boundary, trapping information in layout and impeding systematic classification or recomposition across devices, variants, and fast release cycles.

Structured management dissolves these constraints. Semantically tagged, metadata-rich modules exist independently of pages and can be assembled on demand. Functional module types (procedures, API descriptions, error hints) can feed manuals, mobile help, embedded device overlays, intelligent support, or recommendation systems (Bellamy et al., 2012). Distribution shifts from single-endpoint export to multi-node lifecycle orchestration.

Single sourcing encapsulates this logic: create once, reference broadly, publish everywhere (Ament, 2002). Modular units act as globally addressable resources; document assemblies become compositional constructs. If a software product adds phone-number login, updating the base "Login Function" module synchronizes manuals, help, and training materials, eliminating divergence and redundant maintenance.

This capability rests on combining modular construction with a referencing architecture. Modules carry content plus metadata (applicable version, audience, language state). Authors embed modules by reference, not duplication. Mature standards such as DITA provide structural clarity and flexible invocation (Kimber, 2012; Evia et al., 2016). In multilingual, multi-format pipelines, single sourcing is amplified: source language content passes through a Translation Management System (TMS) and slots directly into localized frameworks while preserving structure; the same module set can be transformed (e.g., via DITA Open Toolkit) into PDF, HTML, mobile micro-help, or API references.

At the technical layer, a Component Content Management System (CCMS) manages modules as atomic units, enabling semantic annotation, reference tracking, and version control. Structured editors (e.g., oXygen, XMetaL) enforce schema compliance; the TMS orchestrates multilingual workflows; build engines perform automated rendering. Task management, review systems, and content analytics round out an end-to-end workflow ecosystem.

Challenges are frequently organizational: effective reuse depends on clear content boundaries and naming discipline; divergent interpretations across teams erode portability (Mamishev & Williams, 2011). Shared modules must reconcile variant needs—expanded exposition for training versus concise phrasing for maintenance—testing design flexibility and variant governance. Approval latency also constrains value; in agile cadences, protracted review chains cause documentation lag.

Although enabling technologies are essential, successful adoption is equally an exercise in organizational design and process optimization. Documentation teams must institutionalize collaboration with product, engineering, marketing, and support so the module library maintains coherence while accommodating scenario diversity. Policy, process, and tooling alignment together sustain high-efficiency reuse and continuous evolution toward intelligent, service-oriented content.

6.3 Embedded Content and the Shift to Content as a Service

Structured foundations enable multi-channel publishing and efficient governance—and allow content to embed within product interaction as a real-time, context-aware service component. Traditional manuals and help centers require user-initiated navigation, imposing long retrieval paths and offering generalized, non-situational guidance.

Contemporary content service models prioritize immediacy, contextual relevance, and task utility. Documentation transforms into an active interaction layer: on first use, repeated failure, or specific error states, the system surfaces targeted modules as tooltips, illustrated step cards, animations, or micro-videos directly in situ. Such just-in-time guidance becomes a first-class product element, not an external reading detour.

This shift relies on structural plus semantic scaffolding. Beyond core text, modules carry rich metadata—applicable model, feature version, user role, locale, difficulty. An orchestration layer matches "interaction path + user state + profile" to the most relevant module. A manufacturing firm, for instance, decomposed legacy print/PDF manuals into thousands of callable modules and embedded state-aware logic in the device UI. If a critical step is executed out of sequence, the system overlays a module tagged "maintenance role + current model + urgent correction" with annotated visuals and concise text. All modules draw from a single source, so a single update propagates across all channels via single sourcing, eliminating multi-version divergence.

This "context trigger + precision dispatch" paradigm resembles a recommendation engine, but optimizes for task completion and error resolution rather than clicks or dwell time. In intelligent support channels, the same mechanism returns an embedded module (e.g., "new user + wireless setup + illustrated steps") inside the chat interface instead of redirecting to an external knowledge base.

Embedded delivery depends on a Content as a Service (CaaS) architecture. Via API calls, structured modules are dynamically requested by web clients, mobile apps, embedded terminals, or third-party systems, with adaptive rendering—full procedural detail on desktop, condensed prompts on mobile, single-line directives on wearables. Content shifts from a published artifact to an orchestrable resource, integrating with lifecycle management, behavioral analytics, and diagnostic systems.

This service orientation blurs the boundary between "documentation" and "function." Users no longer perceive a distinction between reading instructions and using the product; information access is integral to task execution. Authors must therefore design for contextual embedding and interaction integration from the outset—ensuring each module is semantically crisp, structurally independent, and composable under varied triggers.

Combining structural rigor with embedded delivery elevates documentation from static text to dynamic service—advancing from external knowledge support to an integrated intelligent assistant. The model both enhances user experience and sustains content asset value within the product ecosystem.

7 Conclusion

With AI and content engineering advancing, technical writing is shifting from recording information to constructing information systems. Writer responsibilities now span structural planning, workflow orchestration, and intelligent delivery, embedding the role in enterprise content ecosystems. Understanding documentation's position across the information lifecycle has become a core professional competency.

In planning, classification and structural design are foundational. Frameworks like DITA partition content into Concept, Task, and Reference types, clarifying functional boundaries and usage context. Accurate typing sharpens logical clarity and lays an extensible base for maintenance, reuse, and cross-platform publishing.

Organizationally, documentation is moving from linear sequencing to non-linear orchestration. Map mechanisms assemble modules into persona-specific journeys while preserving global synchronization on update. Writers must command boundary definition, naming conventions, and scenario-driven information flow design.

Technically, structured authoring rests on XML-family markup—elements, attributes, content models—and benefits from a data modeling mindset for schema compliance and system integration across engineering, support, and marketing. AI extends this collaboration—supporting terminology checks, module generation, and version tracking—to sustain responsiveness amid rapid product evolution.

In delivery, structured content transcends manuals and web pages, auto-adapting to in-app guidance, conversational responses, embedded hints, and e-learning modules. Authors must align content form and timing with channel interaction patterns and user information paths.

For language service professionals, progression entails evolving into information architects: defining modular logic and referencing rules at inception, co-governing version and update strategies, and planning automated distribution plus interface adaptation at delivery. Structured authoring heightens linguistic order while strengthening manageability, addressability, and adaptability. As documentation becomes a dynamic service, the discipline advances from specialized craft to systemic capability—gradually yet fundamentally redefining professional scope and identity.

References

Aikawa, T., Schwartz, L., King, R., Corston-Oliver, M., & Lozano, C. (2007). Impact of controlled language on translation quality and post-editing in a statistical machine translation environment. In *Proceedings of Machine Translation Summit XI: Papers*. https://aclanthology.org/2007.mtsummit-papers.1.pdf

Alalwan, J. A., & Weistroffer, H. R. (2012). Enterprise content management research: A comprehensive review. *Journal of Enterprise Information Management, 25*(5), 441–461.

Aljedaani, S. M. (2024). Utilizing artificial intelligence techniques in supporting enterprise content management systems. *American Academic & Scholarly Research Journal, 14*(8).

Ament, K. (2002). *Single sourcing: Building modular documentation.* William Andrew.

Aerospace, Security and Defence Industries Association of Europe (ASD). (n.d.). *Simplified Technical English (STE). ASD-STE100*. https://www.asd-europe.org/standards-specifications/simplified-technical-english/

Azuma, R. T. (1997). A survey of augmented reality. *Presence: Teleoperators & Virtual Environments, 6*(4), 355–385. https://doi.org/10.1162/pres.1997.6.4.355

Bellamy, L., Carey, M., & Schlotfeldt, J. (2012). *DITA best practices: A roadmap for writing, editing, and architecting in DITA*. IBM Press.

Bender, E. M., Gebru, T., McMillan-Major, A., & Shmitchell, S. (2021, March). On the dangers of stochastic parrots: Can language models be too big? In *Proceedings of the 2021 ACM Conference on Fairness, Accountability, and Transparency* (pp. 610–623). Association for Computing Machinery. https://doi.org/10.1145/3442188.3445922

Byrne, J. (2006). Assessing usability. In *Technical translation* (pp.177–252). Springer.

Bowker, L. (2019). Fit-for-purpose translation. In *The Routledge handbook of translation and technology* (pp. 453–468). Routledge.

Caterpillar Tractor Company. (1972). *Caterpillar fundamental English*. Caterpillar Tractor Co.

Day, D., Priestley, M., & Schell, D. (2005). *Introduction to the Darwin information typing architecture*. IBM Corporation.

DeRespinis, F., Hayward, P., Jenkins, J., Laird, A., McDonald, L., & Radzinski, E. (2011). *The IBM style guide: Conventions for writers and editors*. IBM Press.

Duin, A. H., & Pedersen, I. (2023). *Augmentation technologies and artificial intelligence in technical communication: Designing ethical futures*. Routledge.

Ethiopian Ministry of Transport and Logistics, Aircraft Accident Investigation Bureau. (2022). *Investigation report on accident to the B737-MAX8 Reg. ET-AVJ operated by Ethiopian Airlines (Report No. AI-01/19). https://bea.aero/fileadmin/user_upload/ET_302__B737-8MAX_ACCIDENT_FINAL_REPORT.pdf*

European Commission: Legal service. (2015). *Joint practical guide of the European Parliament, the Council and the Commission for persons involved in the drafting of European Union legislation*. Publications Office of the European Union. https://data.europa.eu/doi/10.2880/5575.

Evia, C., Tech, V., & Priestley, M. (2016). Structured authoring without XML: Evaluating lightweight DITA for technical documentation. *Technical Communication, 63*(1), 23–37.

Fuchs, N. E., Kaljurand, K., & Kuhn, T. (2008). Attempto controlled English for knowledge representation. In A. Editor & B. Editor (Eds.), *Reasoning Web: 4th International Summer School 2008, Tutorial lectures* (pp. 104–124). Springer.

Feng, Q. G., & Gao, L. (2017). The impact of controlled-language-based pre-editing on machine translation [基于受控语言的译前编辑对机器翻译的影响]. Contemporary Foreign Language Studies [当代外语研究], (2), 63–68.

Getto, G., Kelley, S., & Vance, B. (2025). How to write with GenAI: A framework for using generative AI to automate writing tasks in technical communication. *Journal of Technical Writing and Communication, 0*(0). https://doi.org/10.1177/00472816251332208

Google Developer Documentation Style Guide. (2025). *Google for Developers*. https://developers.google.com/style

Hackos, J. T. (2002). *Content management for dynamic web delivery*. John Wiley & Sons Inc.

Hargis, G., Carey, M., Hernandez, A. K., Hughes, P., Longo, D., Rouiller, S., & Wilde, E. (2004). *Developing quality technical information: A handbook for writers and editors*. Pearson Education.

Hart-Davidson, B., Ristich, M., McArdle, C., & Potts, L. (2024). The history of technical communication and the future of generative AI. In *Proceedings of the 42nd ACM International Conference on Design of Communication* (pp. 253–258). Association for Computing Machinery.

Jiménez-Crespo, M. A. (2013). *Translation and web localization*. Routledge.

Johnson, B. T. (1998). Minimalism Beyond the Nurnberg Funnel. *Issues in Science and Technology Librarianship, 19*.

Jordan, P. W. (2020). *An introduction to usability*. CRC Press.

Kandepu, R. K., & Harry, A. (2023). The rise of AI in content management: Reimagining intelligent workflows. *American Journal of Engineering, Mechanics and Architecture, 1*(7), 78–85.

Kimber, E. (2012). *DITA for Practitioners Volume 1: Architecture and Technology*. XML Press.

Kintsch, W., & Van Dijk, T. A. (1978). Toward a model of text comprehension and production. *Psychological Review, 85*(5), 363.

Krug, S. (2000). *Don't make me think!: A common sense approach to Web usability*. Pearson Education India.

Kuhn, T. (2014). A survey and classification of controlled natural languages. *Computational Linguistics, 40*(1), 121–170. https://doi.org/10.1162/COLI_a_00168

Kumar, D. (2024). AI-driven automation in administrative processes: enhancing efficiency and accuracy. *International Journal of Engineering Science and Humanities, 14*(Special Issue 1), 256–265.

Laumer, S., Beimborn, D., Maier, C., & Weinert, C. (2013). Enterprise content management. *Business & Information Systems Engineering, 5*, 449–452.

Laxmanan, K. V. (2025). Intelligent content management systems leveraging AI to revolutionize data organization and user experience in dynamic platforms. *Journal ID, 6283*, 7415.

Leal, A. (2020). Multilingualism and translation in the European Union. In E. Bielsa & D. Kapsaskis (Eds.), The Routledge handbook of translation and globalisation (pp. 483–497). Routledge. https://doi.org/10.4324/9781003121848-39

Microsoft Writing Style Guide. (2025). *Microsoft style guide*. Retrieved July 8, 2025, from https://learn.microsoft.com/en-us/style-guide

Mamishev, A., & Williams, S. (2011). *Technical writing for teams: The STREAM tools handbook*. John Wiley & Sons.

Nyberg, E., Mitamura, T., & Huijsen, W. O. (2008). Controlled language for authoring and translation. In *Computers and Translation: A translator's guide* (pp. 245–281). John Benjamins Publishing Company.

Ogden, C. K. (1930). *Basic English: A general introduction with rules and grammar*.

Paivarinta, T., & Munkvold, B. E. (2005). Enterprise content management: An integrated perspective on information management. In *Proceedings of the 38th annual Hawaii international conference on system sciences* (pp. 96–96). IEEE.

Pirolli, P., & Card, S. (1999). Information foraging. *Psychological Review, 106*(4), 643.

Redish, J. G. (2007). *Letting go of the words: Writing web content that works*. Morgan Kaufmann.

Reeves, C., & Sylvia, J. J., IV. (2024). Generative AI in technical communication: A review of research from 2023 to 2024. *Journal of Technical Writing and Communication, 54*(4), 439–462.

Rickenberg, T. A., Neumann, M., Hohler, B., & Breitner, M. H. (2012). Enterprise content management—A literature review. In *Proceedings of the 18th Americas Conference on Information Systems (AMCIS 2012)*. Association for Information Systems. https://aisel.aisnet.org/amcis2012/proceedings/DataInfoQuality/10

Rockley, A., & Kostur, P. (2003). *Managing enterprise content: A unified content strategy*. New Riders.

Suokas, J. (2022). *User-centered translation and practical application of usability methods* [Doctoral dissertation, University of Eastern Finland]. https://erepo.uef.fi/server/api/core/bitstreams/78515248-3e6e-4488-be6d-631c20c7e31a/content

Suojanen, T., Koskinen, K., & Tuominen, T. (2014). *User-centered translation*. Routledge.

Suojanen, T., Koskinen, K., & Tuominen, T. (2015). Usability as a focus of multiprofessional collaboration: A teaching case study on user-centered translation. *Connexions: International Professional Communication Journal, 3*(2), 147–166.

Tham, J., Howard, T., & Verhulsdonck, G. (2022). Extending design thinking, content strategy, and artificial intelligence into technical communication and user experience design programs: Further pedagogical implications. *Journal of Technical Writing and Communication, 52*(4), 428–459. https://doi.org/10.1177/00472816211072533

Tham, J. C., Howard, T., & Verhulsdonck, G. (2023). *UX Writing: Designing user-centered content*. Routledge.

Trippel, T. (2012). Controlled language structures in technical communication. In A. Mehler & L. Romary (Eds.), *Handbook of technical communication* (pp. 121–140). De Gruyter Mouton. https://doi.org/10.1515/9783110224948.121

Urquhart, T. (1653). Logopandecteision, or an introduction to the universal language. Internet Archive. Retrieved July 9, 2025, from https://archive.org/details/bim_early-english-books-1641-1700_logopandecteision-or-an_urquhart-sir-thomas_1653/page/n5/mode/2up

United Nations. (2024). *United Nations editorial manual*. Department for General Assembly and Conference Management. https://www.un.org/dgacm/en/content/editorial-manual

Wixom, B. H., & Todd, P. A. (2005). A theoretical integration of user satisfaction and technology acceptance. *Information Systems Research, 16*(1), 85–102.

Chapter 11
Exploration of Multimodal Language Services

Abstract This chapter surveys the emergence, technological foundations, application paradigms, and professional implications of multimodal language services in the AI era. It traces the evolution of "multimodality" from cognitive and discourse studies to contemporary large language model (LLM) and Aritificial Intelligence (AI)-Generated Content ecosystems that integrate text, speech, image, video, and spatial signals. Core advances—multimodal LLMs, diffusion and generative architectures, agent orchestration, and retrieval-augmented pipelines—enable cross-modal understanding, transformation, reasoning, and generation (e.g., text-to-image, text-to-audio, and text-to-video, multimodal translation, adaptive subtitling, and real-time interpreting). The chapter highlights prompt engineering as a controllability lever, redefining workflows via structured semantic specification. Application domains span education, accessibility, cultural dissemination, product localization, conferencing, Augmented Reality and Virtual Reality navigation, digital humans, and new media "media matrix" distribution models. It contrasts single-modal baselines with multimodal semantic reconstruction focused on actionability and immersion. Governance challenges (hallucination, factuality, cultural alignment, provenance, ethical steering) motivate human–AI collaborative quality regimes. Finally, the professional role shifts from linear translation to multimodal adaptation design—encompassing product thinking, process engineering, cultural risk management, and iterative co-creation with intelligent agents.

Multimodal language services are emerging as a major force in the era of artificial intelligence (Feher, 2025). Each major technological wave in information technology and software has reshaped the industry structure and catalyzed new business models. Localization accelerated as evolving channels of dissemination and software architectures intersected with globalization. Today, the rapid advances of large language models (LLMs) and Artificial Intelligence Generated Content (AIGC) technologies provide unprecedented momentum (Anthropic, 2024; Gozalo-Brizuela & Garrido-Merchán, 2023). "Multimodal" here spans text, speech, images, and video, signaling a shift beyond single-form information toward broader application scenarios. As AIGC's generative and interpretive capacities expand—from

J. S. Yu and Y. Yao, *Intelligent Language Services*,
https://doi.org/10.1007/978-981-95-4632-9_11

creative writing to real-time translation, immersive interaction, and context-aware content generation—the form of language services is undergoing profound change (Liang et al., 2024). These developments open diverse commercial opportunities while continually extending technical boundaries and future possibilities.

1 The Rise of Multimodal Language Services

The notion of "multimodality" originated in perception and cognitive science to describe how humans integrate visual, auditory, linguistic, and other sensory channels when acquiring and interpreting information (Gogate, 2018). It was subsequently broadened in linguistics, communication studies, and psychology to stress that interaction relies not only on verbal language but also on gesture, facial expression, bodily movement, and the visual environment. With technological progress, the concept entered artificial intelligence and language services, denoting the fusion of textual, speech, image, and video signals for transmission, comprehension, and generation (Baltrušaitis et al., 2017; Nazarieh et al., 2024).

By the late twentieth century, multimodal corpora had become a research focus. Scholars collected audio, video, and textual channels to capture naturalistic interaction; for example, the Lancaster Multimodal Corpus synchronously records speech, movement, and facial expressions to support discourse analysis. In the 2000s, increased computing power and maturing automation tools enabled scalable processing and modeling of multimodal data. Deep learning advanced joint modeling of images, audio, and text (Shen et al., 2024), and the advent of large language models plus AIGC technologies pushed multimodal language services into applied domains, supporting creative generation, intelligent translation, and immersive interaction.

Although "multimodal" and "multimedia" often overlap in practice, their emphases differ. Multimedia focuses on the presentation layer—the coordinated display of media elements (e.g., integrated audio and video in instructional slides or news pages). Multimodality concentrates on processes of acquisition and understanding, emphasizing cross-channel synergy and semantic alignment. A multimodal machine translation system, for instance, jointly interprets speech, imagery, and text for greater accuracy. Put simply, multimedia furnishes data and scenarios, whereas multimodality adds cognitive depth and intelligent processing.

As translation tasks extend to video subtitling, voice narration, image description, and Augmented Reality (AR) guidance, the operational contours of multimodal language services are crystallizing (Lv et al., 2025). This broadens task scope and reframes service logic—from decoding isolated text to reconstructing meaning under multi-sensory input (Caglayan et al., 2019)—requiring coordinated control of temporal rhythm, medium, and situational context. Beyond semantic accuracy, providers must manage subtitle time slicing, perspective shifts, and synchronization between spoken output and auditory pacing (Penyameen et al., 2025). Language thus functions as the core integrative layer of cross-modal expression rather than a mere symbolic vehicle.

Single-modal methods retain advantages of simplicity and efficiency for structurally clear, low-context tasks (e.g., plain text translation or single-channel Automatic Speech Recognition (ASR)). However, real applications commonly entangle modalities—speech recognition in noisy settings or speaker differentiation in multi-party dialogue—where a single channel proves inadequate. Integrating image, text, and speech inputs enhances robustness and improves user experience.

For deployment, expanding modalities is insufficient; providers must also secure semantic completeness and explicitness across channels and maintain cross-modal consistency. Should an on-screen operational cue also appear as text? How should speech and subtitles be synchronized? Addressing such questions entails deep coordination of semantic structure and interaction rhythm layered on basic multi-channel transfer.

The value of multimodal language services ultimately lies in perceptible, usable adaptation. Beyond accurate linguistic transfer, the key question is whether users can act on outputs—critical in online education, global product localization, and AR navigation (Chen, 2025). Users must not only comprehend content but also receive actionable feedback at the intersection of language and medium.

With advances in multimodal large language models (e.g., GPT-4V, Gemini, Claude 3 Opus) and agent frameworks (e.g., LangChain, AutoGen) (Wu et al., 2023; Gemini Team et al., 2023; OpenAI, 2023; Anthropic, 2024; Yao et al., 2025), language services are becoming integrated and automated. These models interpret and generate multimodal content and can plan task sequences and optimize outputs according to user intent (Wang et al., 2024), extending service boundaries toward intelligent systems.

Technological evolution is altering practitioner roles. Providers are no longer mere textual translators; they must command language modeling, modality alignment, tooling, and interaction design, including how language is perceived and used across media. Consequently, "translation" is evolving into adaptive design, with language serving as a bridge for cross-modal interaction systems rather than an endpoint.

The future of multimodal language services will rest on productization. Modular architectures, configurable systems, low-code interfaces, and agent collaboration mechanisms lower adoption barriers and raise flexibility (Yao et al., 2025), enabling sustainable services that shift from content conversion to cognitive linkage and intelligent interaction.

1.1 AIGC: Cross-Modal Synesthesia and Perceptual Transfer

Breakthroughs in AIGC technologies provide a new framework for multimodal language services. Generation methods based on diffusion models and large language models move beyond cross-modal translation to direct transformations that reconstruct information (Li et al., 2024; Rombach et al., 2022; Zhai et al., 2024). The objective is not to preserve surface form but to leverage large-scale statistical modeling and semantic disentanglement to convey underlying meaning via an alternative perceptual system.

When converting classical poetry into an image, a model must interpret the density of imagery and realize it through diffusion sampling. Generating a soundtrack for video requires extracting spatiotemporal patterns from frame sequences and mapping them to melodic parameters (Agostinelli et al., 2023). Producing descriptive text from image sequences activates visual–linguistic cross-modal representations (Yao & Wan, 2020). These tasks compel machines to internalize semantics across forms, extend expressive boundaries, and emulate human synesthetic and perceptual transfer mechanisms to re-create information across senses.

1.2 Cross-Modal Transformation and Generation

Cross-modal content transformation and generation represent a leading frontier in agent design. Models must interpret source structure and affect while constructing novel target-modal expression. Pairing classical poetry with imagery, for example, depends on cultural symbolism and the visual reconstitution of poetic ambience. Language serves as an inter-sensory mediator, establishing a shared semantic space for alignment as surveyed in recent work on multimodal alignment and fusion.

The value of modality transformation lies in extending expressive and interpretive boundaries, presenting information more richly and immersively. In education, text–image or video synergy deepens comprehension; in cultural dissemination, comics or short drama amplify narrative resonance; in accessibility, scene data can be converted to speech or haptics so users with differing abilities share core content.

The challenge is not simple mapping but deep modeling of source semantics, structure, and affect, followed by context-coherent, stylistically consistent re-expression in the target modality. Representative academic and industrial tasks cluster into: (1) modality understanding and interpretation (image captioning, visual question answering, speech recognition); (2) cross-modal generation (text-to-image, text-to-audio, text-to-video); (3) cross-modal reasoning and fusion (affect, event, or causal inference across inputs); and (4) cross-modal retrieval (querying one modality to locate another).

In the past two years, paradigms have shifted from rule-based or shallow features to unified "pretrain + generative" frameworks. OpenAI's GPT-4and GPT-5 series, Google's Gemini series, and Anthropic's Claude 3 series integrate text, image, and audio within a shared interaction loop while improving latency, long-context handling, and instruction fidelity. Image and music generators—DALL·E, Stable Diffusion, Midjourney, MusicLM, Suno—continue to lower creative barriers while advancing stylistic consistency and affective expression.

Multi-task orchestration and agent-based workflows are becoming standard. "Illustrate a classical poem and produce an explanatory video" can be decomposed into affect and imagery analysis, element extraction, shot planning, image generation, script drafting, voice synthesis, and editing, with frameworks such as LangChain and AutoGen coordinating these stages for human-AI collaboration.

Human specialists in language and culture remain indispensable. While AIGC scales multilingual tasks efficiently, human review markedly improves reliability in emotional strategy, cultural adaptation, and contextual disambiguation. Hallucinations, cross-modal consistency issues, and alignment bias remain active research topics requiring retrieval augmentation, factual validation, and human feedback.

Methodologically, systemic thinking and task decomposition are core to deploying multimodal agents. Explicit decomposition and search, exemplified by Tree of Thoughts, have yielded a "plan–execute–reflect–retrieve" engineering loop in multi-agent and planning research that aligns closely with pipeline production of multimodal tasks.

Cross-modal transformation and generation are not only technical endeavors but also a coordinated reconstruction of linguistic, visual, and auditory expression. With effective decomposition and tooling, language serves as a bridge that converts heterogeneous signals into coherent, usable content naturally instantiated across media.

1.3 Prompts That Drive Cross-Modal Generation

Achieving faithful transformation across modalities requires linguistic proficiency plus understanding of visual, auditory, and spatial logics. High-quality prompt design, retrieval integration, and tool composition—together with observable task decomposition—are crucial for semantic transfer. Language maps multimodal inputs into operational semantic structures that drive stylistic reconstruction in target media. In practice, clearly specified inputs, outputs, and evaluation metrics should pair with human-in-the-loop review as pipelines scale to long, multi-role, multimodal workflows.

Cross-modal prompts are not simplistic commands; their informational richness and structural logic shape accuracy, controllability, and aesthetics. Effective prompts precisely encode human intent while steering generation and aesthetic direction, demanding linguistic skill, media sensitivity, and a firm grasp of target structure and style.

Prompt construction must reflect target-modality traits. For images, specifying subject, salient details, and stylistic features—"subject–details–style"—improves coherence and fidelity (e.g., "a medieval city at sunset, viewed from a high tower, cinematic style, warm tones"). Audio prompts highlight tempo, timbre, and mood ("a calm ambient track with slow piano chords and soft rain sounds"). Video, animation, and speech synthesis prompts are more complex, spanning temporal cadence, character intonation, and situational change (Brooks et al., 2024). In multimodal generation, modality-specific directives (e.g., "adjust image lighting" alongside "maintain a gentle audio tempo") foster coordinated outputs.

Each modality has domain-specific descriptors: "cinematic lighting," "flat composition," or "surreal style" guide image models; "uptempo beat with lo-fi texture" conveys musical rhythm and stylistic character. Mastery of such lexical sets underpins effective prompt authoring.

An effective approach is the "subject–details–style" strategy: subject (core entities/actions), details (color, composition, attire), and style (e.g., "Baroque," "1980s manga"). For instance: "a young woman in traditional Hanfu, standing beside a lake with falling petals, misty mountains in the background, painted in soft ink wash style."

Prompt design should be iterative. Techniques such as Chain-of-Thought can guide progressive integration of multimodal cues; successive refinements to wording and structure improve coherence and aesthetics.

Multiple strategies build prompt proficiency. Community platforms (PromptHero, PromptBase) support template curation and analysis; generators (Midjourney, DALL·E) allow iterative variation to assess parameter impact; optimization tools (PromptPerfect) refine multimodal inputs. Systematic practices integrate frameworks (LangChain, Orq.ai, PromptLayer) for multimodal prompt aggregation, version control, and testable validation.

Sustained practice develops cross-modal sensitivity: distill imagery into concise language, iteratively revise toward target outputs, or analyze and vary existing prompts. Coupling this with routine translation and writing cultivates dual competencies in linguistic and media perception.

Prompt craftsmanship should evolve with expanding knowledge and aesthetics. Insights from art history, photographic composition, film language, and music theory inject stylistic inspiration and structural depth. Since multimodal models are trained on extensive human creative corpora, analyzing cross-media linguistic patterns becomes a reverse exploration of the model's semantic space, strengthening expressive leverage in prompt design.

2 New Paradigms in Multimodal Translation Services

With multimodal technologies, translation has expanded from pure text conversion to seamless interaction across speech, image, and video—encompassing speech transcription, image recognition with subtitle generation, dubbing, and lip synchronization. Translation now entails cross-sensory semantic reconstruction and transmission; technological convergence improves accuracy and efficiency while markedly enhancing immersion.

Against this backdrop, translation has moved beyond document processing into multi-dimensional video, speech, image, and interactive spaces, prompting a comprehensive conceptual and operational overhaul. Large language models and multimodal models underpin this shift (Wang et al., 2024). Within a cognitive framework of multimodal translation, language is the core orchestrator and modalities are carriers; subtitles, speech, image descriptions, and AR overlays all ultimately center on linguistic coordination.

Cognitively, translation is semantic reconstruction. In multimodal settings it spans visual, auditory, and spatial channels under temporal, interactive, and environmental constraints, demanding precise cross-modal adaptation (Xiao et al., 2025). Three challenges arise: (1) semantic completeness and visibility across modalities (e.g., visual action cues may need textual explanation for cross-lingual transfer); (2) unit and temporal control (subtitle segmentation, real-time AR cue updates, speech synthesis pacing); and (3) inter-modal consistency (subtitle–audio synchronization, spatial tag–device mapping, speech–lip alignment).

The goal is not to transplant legacy methods into new media, but to enable real-time, perceptible, and actionable cross-lingual transmission across diverse modalities and interactive contexts. Traditional translation targets "reading comprehension"; multimodal translation targets "action participation," ensuring users can understand, apply, and operate immersively (Xia, 2024). This logic underlies synchronized subtitles and speech on streaming or conferencing platforms, integrated text-image-video support in post-sales localization, and AR navigation or decision support with real-time spatial tagging in tourism, industrial maintenance, and defense.

Translation is shifting from an information conduit to the semantic engine of cross-domain systems, spawning service forms and workflows closer to application needs.

2.1 Subtitle Translation from a Multimodal Perspective

In multimodal dissemination, subtitles have moved beyond simple linguistic substitution. While conventional subtitles support comprehension by converting speech to target-language text, multimodal contexts assign them a coordinating role—linking semantic consistency and fluent presentation across visual, auditory, and linguistic layers. Audiences now seek immersive, interactive, multi-sensory engagement.

This evolution rests on advances in computer vision and large language models, particularly in multimodal subtitle generation (Striuk & Hordiienko, 2025; Yu et al., 2025). The dynamic "bullet comments" (danmu) on Bilibili exemplify real-time viewer–content interaction; their motion, rhythm, and register heighten immediacy and participation. Compared with static subtitles, they illustrate the shift from ancillary language to an interaction mechanism.

Generating multimodal subtitles extends beyond transcription and translation to incorporate scene recognition, gestures, and prosodic context (Lv et al., 2025). Rapid shot changes and complex sound design in film require precise temporal and semantic alignment. Large language models can modulate meaning and affect to maintain cohesion between verbal and non-verbal signals (Wang et al., 2025; Xu et al., 2023).

Medical continuing education videos add further complexity: vision models detect procedural steps, patient responses, and instrument usage, while large language models generate professional, clear, tone-appropriate subtitles to aid precise comprehension (Penyameen et al., 2025). Product tutorial videos likewise demand rapid subtitle updates aligned with feature presentation pacing. LLMs synchronize subtitles with temporal markers, context, and style (Malaviya et al., 2024).

LLMs excel at adaptive contextualization. Compared with traditional machine translation, they adjust subtitle output to video context and audience culture (Cui et al., 2024). Subject matter and learner age influence emotional tone and technical depth, making subtitles a finely tuned layer of cross-lingual, cross-cultural mediation.

In production settings, source subtitles are often incomplete or noisy—educational videos may reflect spontaneous, disfluent speech. Subtitle translation therefore extends to discourse reconstruction for clarity and instructional precision. Such refinement can occur intra-lingually, with source rewrites improving linguistic quality and communicative effect (Poncelet, 2025).

Subtitle translation in multimodal contexts synthesizes technology, linguistics, and communication strategy. Its value lies in precise information transfer coupled with agile modulation of context, affect, and style to deliver coherent viewer comprehension.

2.2 Multimodal Interpreting Services

Advances in multimodal large models and speech technologies are reshaping the technical foundation and application modes of interpreting (Marangoz, 2023). The pipeline has evolved from basic speech-to-text and text-to-speech into conference systems integrating ASR, machine translation, and subtitle generation, forming architectures centered on multimodal capability.

Dialogue systems powered by large models from OpenAI or Qwen embed ASR and Text-to-Speech as core automation mechanisms. Spoken input is transcribed, translated, and synthesized into target-language speech in real time (Guo et al., 2024), now routine in international conferences, remote collaboration, and cross-border communication.

Building on this, intelligent meeting subtitle systems expand functional scope by transcribing and translating speech into multiple languages for synchronous display. Multimodal large models integrate speech, text, and visual cues to identify speakers, intonation shifts, and paralinguistic signals (laughter, pauses), improving contextual fidelity (Gutiérrez 2025; Gomez & Pinazo, 2025).

For professional interpreters, multimodal tools now augment cognition and information handling—term extraction, turn ordering, and summarization accompany subtitle and translation output, reducing cognitive load and streamlining record keeping (Yin, 2025).

LLMs broaden interpreting from linear linguistic conversion to contextual processing. In multilingual virtual meetings they dynamically adjust subtitle sequencing and presentation, semantically analyze shared materials, and insert clarifying text. Speech–lip synchronization further heightens multi-sensory coherence and immersion (Defrancq, 2024).

Multimodal systems improve target-language quality, processing speed, and task adaptability while offering interpreters more operable collaboration platforms. As model capabilities grow, interpreting will become increasingly intelligent and context-sensitive, crystallizing into human–AI collaborative workflows.

Interpreter roles are shifting from direct language converters to supervisors and calibrators. Although some task volume may decline, workload intensity drops while quality and stability improve.

2.3 From Digital Humans to Metaverse Language Services

Multimodal technologies and generative AI are redefining language services in virtual environments. Digital humanities have shifted from text processing to multimodal integration, transforming organizational forms and operational logic (Feng and Zhang 2023). Scenarios now range from voice-driven, lip-synchronized virtual anchors to immersive linguistic interactions in virtual worlds, expanding applicability while redefining content and value (Forbes Tech Council 2024).

Digital human platforms—Alibaba Cloud's Intelligent Digital Human, JD's Yanxi, Microsoft Azure AI Avatar, and Synthesia—support multilingual dubbing with lip and expression synchronization (capabilities varying by platform/version). They accelerate production of international promotional, product, and training videos while adapting speech rate, prosody, and style for cultural fit (Whittaker et al., 2025).

Synthesia, for example, lets users customize gender, accent, expressions, and gestures, and output multilingual subtitles for culturally localized presentations. Language professionals still review scripts and audio to ensure terminological precision, emotional authenticity, and cultural appropriateness.

Digital humans need not be fully anthropomorphic. A navigation platform like Amap, with nearly one billion users, now integrates large-model voice agents for real-time, context-aware travel recommendations. Massive data resources and strong scenario coupling promise substantial practical utility.

Proliferation of AR/VR brings language services into immersive environments. Microsoft Mesh and Teams provide multilingual captions and interpreting; Meta's Horizon Worlds enables user-generated content and avatars, though multilingual interaction often still depends on external tools. Head-mounted displays enable dialogue with virtual guides in museums, corporate showrooms, or meeting spaces (Taşdan Doğan, 2023). Professional fields such as healthcare and law are likewise building cross-lingual collaboration via virtual interaction (Zhu et al., 2023).

Challenges include simultaneous linguistic conversion and real-time adaptation to spatial context, user behavior, and dynamic data. During a virtual tour, narration must adjust language and depth based on location and dwell path, adding cultural notes or affective cues as needed. Models such as GPT-4o/5 and Gemini 2.5 support multimodal input and multilingual output, combining speech synthesis with subtitle generation to heighten immersion and accessibility.

A higher tier involves personalized virtual dialogue. Platforms such as Character.AI and Replika enable natural multilingual conversations with preference-retentive personas that adjust tone dynamically (Whittaker et al., 2025). In training, cross-border marketing, and healthcare, organizations can explain complex information while tailoring discourse to cultural and professional profiles for clarity and rapport.

In virtual contexts, language services now extend beyond barrier removal to cultural adaptation and cognitive assistance. Roles shift from translator or voice artist to multimodal interaction designer, virtual content auditor, and cross-cultural experience planner—embedded in AI generation and interaction, curating script structure, cultural symbols, and domain expression.

Language services in virtual spaces are a natural extension of human communicative needs. Despite digital humans, virtual tours, and metaverse scenarios, linguistic and cultural gaps persist. Bridging them for authentic, fluid mutual understanding still requires deep language service expertise.

3 AIGC-Driven Language Expression in New Media

AIGC is rapidly reshaping new media content formats and dissemination models, propelling writing and expression beyond text-only paradigms toward highly interactive, cross-platform, cross-media configurations (Forbes Tech Council 2024). Large language models now underpin journalism, social engagement, and brand communication by enabling real-time multilingual generation and globally synchronized release. Consequently, language service providers are adopting a holistic focus on expressive innovation, cultural adaptation, and credibility management. Traditional translators and editors are evolving into content strategists and co-designers of cross-cultural communication, with linguistic and cultural literacy now pivotal to this transition.

3.1 AIGC-Driven Language Services in New Media

Within a cross-media ecosystem spanning Weibo, Bilibili, WeChat Official Accounts, Douyin, YouTube, and TikTok, users participate actively via danmu (on-screen comments), likes, comments, and tipping. Bilibili reinforces fan co-creation through danmu and its "Charging Plan," YouTube enables live interaction through Super Chat and Super Stickers, and TikTok facilitates direct creator–audience exchange through its Gifts system. These interaction features have reconfigured platform communication models, making users active contributors to both content production and linguistic exchange.

AIGC is restructuring production workflows and linguistic mediation. Data-driven verticals such as financial and business news have long adopted automated authoring and data triggers (e.g., the Associated Press automated earnings reports and Reuters' Lynx Insight). Between 2023 and 2025, generative AI increasingly entered human–AI collaborative pipelines for topic selection, drafting, and multilingual distribution, reinforced by editorial protocols and human review to safeguard factual accuracy and pragmatic appropriateness.

Short-form and long-form video platforms are embedding generative capabilities directly into creative toolchains. Between 2024 and 2025, YouTube integrated Dream Screen and the Veo model family to auto-generate Shorts backgrounds and label provenance with SynthID watermarks and "AI-generated" notices; its auto-dubbing feature was also extended to more creators to broaden multilingual reach. In virtual anchoring, Xinhua introduced an "AI news anchor" as early as 2018, and commercial platforms such as Synthesia and Azure AI Avatar now deliver scalable multilingual speech synthesis with lip synchronization for global content production.

Creators and brands employ models such as GPT-4/5, Claude, DeepSeek, and Qwen to optimize tone, narrative reframing, and multilingual distribution efficiency. However, human oversight remains essential for cross-cultural adaptation and pragmatic precision; localized editing and cultural review are still critical pre-market steps. Multiple industry and academic reports emphasize increasing process transparency and instituting auditable editorial standards to prevent misdirection and cultural friction.

Concurrently, AIGC introduces governance challenges: content homogenization, unauthorized paraphrasing, deepfake fabrication, and AI-generated flooding of comments and danmu streams. Platforms are responding with disclosure and labeling regimes. For example, starting in 2024 YouTube required labels for potentially misleading synthetic or AI content and in 2025 extended SynthID watermarking to AI-generated Shorts. However, disparities in labeling standards and enforcement rigor persist across platforms.

Human–AI collaboration is now the prevailing governance paradigm. Since 2017, Xinhua's "Media Brain" initiative has coupled data pipelines and algorithms with human verification to enhance news production and distribution efficiency; international platforms likewise combine machine learning with manual review to refine oversight of generated content. Within this architecture, language services extend beyond translation and editing to credibility management, cultural adaptation strategy, and pragmatic risk control.

Linguistic interaction in new media is shifting from linear distribution to a multidirectional, multimodal, and real-time feedback network. Auto-dubbing, generative backgrounds and video, and interactive tools shorten the feedback–revision loop. Achieving smooth cross-cultural comprehension and affective resonance still requires deep intervention by language professionals in structural design, interaction logic, and cultural modulation.

3.2 *Content Production and Cultural Adaptation Enabled by Large Language Models*

Large language models are accelerating the reconfiguration of content creation and distribution, demonstrating efficient, flexible, multilingual production and dissemination in rapid news response, brand storytelling, and knowledge outreach (AlKhamissi et al., 2024). These capabilities reduce latency and cost while enabling audience segmentation through channel- and cohort-specific expression.

In data-driven journalism, automated authoring and data triggers have operated for years (e.g., the Associated Press (AP) automated earnings-coverage system and Reuters' AI-assisted Lynx Insight platform). Between 2023 and 2025, generative AI further penetrated collaborative workflows for topic ideation, drafting, and multilingual distribution, underpinned by explicit editorial standards and human oversight to balance speed and credibility. Video platforms embedded generative tools: YouTube linked Dream Screen with the Veo model family to create Shorts visuals, adding SynthID and "AI-generated" labels for provenance; auto-dubbing was opened to more creators for multilingual reach. Virtual anchoring—from Xinhua's 2018 "AI anchor" to commercial offerings by Synthesia and Azure AI Avatar—now provides scalable multilingual dubbing with lip synchronization for global dissemination and training.

Brands leverage LLMs to extend content lifespan and enhance localization capability. Models generate tailored copy aligned with linguistic and cultural preferences, simulate Frequently Asked Questions and sentiment responses, and support synchronized multi-market releases within unified governance, reinforcing consistency and responsiveness (Pranida et al., 2025). With GPT-4/5, Claude, DeepSeek, and Qwen, creators and organizations rapidly adjust tone and narrative perspective for multilingual rollout, while in-market review remains essential to ensure terminological accuracy and pragmatic appropriateness.

Knowledge dissemination likewise benefits. Models generate popular-science articles, instructional explainers, and FAQs grounded in domain knowledge and current public concerns, producing tiered versions for children, adolescents, or adults. Multilingual auto-generation enables simultaneous global access, allowing medical, environmental, and scientific domains to narrow information gaps through multilingual summaries, visual explanations, and interactive question-answering (Q&A) (Liu et al., 2025).

Content generation is advancing toward deeper contextual comprehension and cultural adaptation. Alibaba Cloud's CultureVLM targets cultural perception capabilities, while the CultureVerse benchmark reveals cross-cultural performance differentials that underscore the importance of diverse training data. For multilingual brand narratives, models autonomously select local symbols and festive motifs, adjust pacing and phrasing, and avoid mistranslations (Acharya, 2022). In public relations and customer support, models detect emotional tenor and soften tone, using neutral or empathetic language to de-escalate conflict and preserve trust.

Production and distribution workflows are being re-architected around model capabilities. Given a theme, setting, or character profile, models generate shot lists, dialogue, and scene descriptions, accelerating documentary, short-video, and micro-film pipelines from concept to script. In event and knowledge management, models produce multilingual session synopses, speaker biographies, and minutes, adjusting depth to audience expertise. In social and news comment threads, they conduct Q&A and extract key points, facilitating cross-lingual dialogue.

Cross-platform, multi-style, stratified batch distribution around a single theme produces a "media matrix." LLMs amplify reach and penetration by recomposing content, transferring styles, and enabling multilingual variants, improving marginal efficiency and impact. This model also raises ethical and regulatory pressures: boundaries between homogenization, information steering, and opinion shaping can blur, and authentic expression becomes harder to distinguish from engineered output. Accordingly, provenance transparency, labeling, and watermarking must pair with traceable editorial workflows to build human–AI collaborative review systems that balance efficiency with public accountability.

As infrastructural components of the new media era, LLMs underpin rapid production, segmented reach, and localized expression. Language professionals' responsibilities have expanded from translation and editing to semantic design, cultural adaptation, and pragmatic risk management across scripting, interaction logic, and in-market review—balancing speed, quality, and cultural comprehension.

4 Conclusion

The convergence of AIGC and new media dissemination is driving language services toward productization and proceduralization. They now extend beyond "translation" or "copywriting," becoming modular, reusable functions embedded in news summarization, short-video dubbing, multilingual commenting, global live streaming, and product promotion—readily deployable within brand, public relations, and educational communication pipelines.

The spread of SaaS (Software as a Service) platforms accelerates this shift. Numerous cloud services now offer one-stop multilingual generation, review, and distribution—covering translation, dubbing, subtitling, terminology management, and style customization. Platforms such as Alibaba Cloud and Microsoft Azure enable end-to-end execution within a single system, markedly improving delivery efficiency and expanding cross-team and cross-project collaboration opportunities for language professionals.

Human–AI collaboration is becoming the default production model. Language specialists conduct review and refinement, contribute to structural design, narrative strategy, and audience analysis, and prepare datasets for model fine-tuning. For instance, AI anchors on short-video platforms adapt delivery dynamically to viewer feedback and regional linguistic norms through close expert–system coordination:

experts define strategy and contextual boundaries, while AI handles generation, distribution, and feedback capture for real-time adaptation.

In major news organizations, AIGC produces draft stories, contextual background, and multilingual summaries, while editors focus on fact-checking, value judgments, and stylistic coherence. On international e-commerce platforms, AIGC batch-translates and localizes product descriptions; language teams adjust keywords and marketing tone based on market feedback to reduce semantic drift and cultural mismatch.

Under this model, competency profiles are shifting toward multi-skill integration. Practitioners need product thinking, process design capability, understanding of AI strengths and constraints, and the ability to formulate multilingual communication strategies and quality benchmarks. In managing a multinational brand's social content matrix, a language professional may oversee data integration, feedback analysis, and sentiment response simultaneously, maintaining efficiency, accuracy, and cultural alignment.

As content ecosystems become more intelligent and specialized, language professionals will act as pivotal intermediaries between AI systems and human communication—driving innovation while ensuring clarity, credibility, and adaptability in global dissemination.

References

Acharya, A. (2022). *Integrating cultural knowledge into artificially intelligent systems: Human experiments and computational implementations* (Doctoral dissertation, Florida International University). FIU Electronic Theses and Dissertations. https://digitalcommons.fiu.edu/etd/5083

Agostinelli, A., Denk, T. I., Borsos, Z., Engel, J., Verzetti, M., Caillon, A., Huang, Q., Jansen, A., Roberts, A., Tagliasacchi, M., Sharifi, M., Zeghidour, N., & Frank, C. (2023). *MusicLM: Generating music from text*. arXiv. https://doi.org/10.48550/arXiv.2301.11325

AlKhamissi, B., ElNokrashy, M., AlKhamissi, M., & Diab, M. (2024). *Investigating cultural alignment of large language models*. https://aclanthology.org/2024.acl-long.671.pdf

Anthropic. (2024). *Introducing the next generation of Claude*. https://www.anthropic.com/news/claude-3-family

Baltrušaitis, T., Ahuja, C., & Morency, L. P. (2017). *Multimodal machine learning: A survey and taxonomy*. arXiv. https://doi.org/10.48550/arXiv.1705.09406

Brooks, T., Peebles, B., Holmes, C., DePue, W., Yu, W., Li, J., Aditya, R. et al. (2024). *Video generation models as world simulators*. OpenAI. https://openai.com/research/video-generation-models-as-world-simulators

Caglayan, O., Madhyastha, P., Specia, L., & Barrault, L. (2019). Probing the need for visual context in multimodal machine translation. In J. Burstein, C. Doran, & T. Solorio (Eds.), In P*roceedings of the 2019 conference of the North American chapter of the association for computational linguistics: Human language technologies* (Vol. 1, Long and Short Papers, pp. 4159–4170). Association for Computational Linguistics. https://doi.org/10.18653/v1/N19-1422

Cela Gutiérrez, C. (2025). AI-assisted interpreting: Valuable tool for professional interpreters or job displacement? *Traduction et Langues, 24*(1), 263–281. https://asjp.cerist.dz/en/article/271727

Chen, Q. (2025). Enhancing cross-cultural educational awareness: Experimental study on immersive experiences using virtual reality. *British Educational Research Journal, 51*(2), 687–704. https://doi.org/10.1002/berj.4089

Cui, W., Yu, D., Jiao, X., Meng, Z., Zhang, G., Wang, Q., & King, I. et al. (2024). *Recent advances in speech language models: A survey*. arXiv. https://doi.org/10.48550/arXiv.2410.03751

Defrancq, B. (2024). Conference interpreting in AI settings: New skills and ethical challenges. In *Handbook of the language industry: Contexts, resources and profiles* (Vol. 20, p. 473).

Feher, K. (2025). Generative AI, media, and society. Routeledge. https://doi.org/10.4324/9781003591023

Forbes Technology Council. (2024). *Beyond large language models: How multimodal AI is unlocking human-like intelligence*. Forbes. https://www.forbes.com/councils/forbestechcouncil/2024/12/30/beyond-large-language-models-how-multimodal-ai-is-unlocking-human-like-intelligence/

Gogate, L. (Ed.). (2018). Multisensory *perception and communication: Brain, behaviour, Environment interaction, and development in the early years* (1st ed.). Routledge. https://doi.org/10.4324/9780429470899

Gomez, L. P., & Pinazo, E. P. (2025). Artificial intelligence in the training of public service interpreters. *Language & Communication, 103*, 86–107. https://doi.org/10.1016/j.langcom.2025.04.002

Gozalo-Brizuela, R., & Garrido-Merchán, E. C. (2023). *A survey of generative AI applications*. https://arxiv.org/html/2306.02781#:~:text=In%20this%20paper%2C%20we%20present%20a%20comprehensive%20survey,of%20various%20unimodal%20and%20even%20multimodal%20generative%20AIs.

Guo, S., Zhang, S., Ma, Z., Zhang, M., & Feng, Y. (2024). *SiLLM: Large language models for simultaneous machine translation*. https://arxiv.org/pdf/2402.13036

Li, Z., Li, J., Shi, Y., Ling, H., Chen, J., Wang, R., & Huang, S. (2024). Cross-modal generation and alignment via attribute-guided prompt for unsupervised text-based person retrieval. In *Proceedings of the international joint conference on artificial intelligence* (pp. 1047–1055).

Liang, Z., Xu, Y., Hong, Y., Shang, P., Wang, Q., Fu, Q., & Liu, K. (2024). A survey of multimodel large language models. In *Proceedings of the 3rd International Conference on Computer, Artificial Intelligence and Control Engineering (CAICE '24)* (pp. 405–409). Association for Computing Machinery. https://doi.org/10.1145/3672758.3672824

Liu, S., Jin, Y., Li, C., Wong, D. F., Wen, Q., Sun, L., & Wang, J. et al. (2025). CultureVLM: Characterizing and improving cultural understanding of vision-language models for over 100 countries. arXiv. https://doi.org/10.48550/arXiv.2501.01282

Lv, J., Chen, J., Long, Z., Fu, X., & Chen, Y. (2025). *TopicVD: A topic-based dataset of video-guided multimodal machine translation for documentaries*. arXiv. https://doi.org/10.48550/arXiv.2505.05714

Malaviya, P., Patel, D., & Bharti, S. (2024). Video captioning using large language models. In *2024 3rd International Conference for Innovation in Technology (INOCON)* (pp. 1–7). IEEE. https://doi.org/10.1109/INOCON60754.2024.10512233

Marangoz, E. Ö. (2023). The transformative role of artificial intelligence and machine learning in interpreting and language services. *RumeliDE Dil ve Edebiyat Araştırmaları Dergisi*, (36), 1591–1598. https://doi.org/10.29000/rumelide.1372500

Nazarieh, F., Feng, Z., Awais, M., Wang, W., & Kittler, J. (2024). A survey of cross-modal visual content generation. *IEEE Transactions on Circuits and Systems for Video Technology, 34*(8), 6814–6832. https://doi.org/10.1109/TCSVT.2024.3351601

OpenAI. (2023). *GPT-4V(ision) system card*. https://openai.com/research/gpt-4v-system-card

Penyameen, K., Rajan, G. S. S., Ahamed, A. A., Ram, S. Y., Shiny, J. J., & Nayaki, A. P. (2025). AI-based automated subtitle generation system for multilingual video transcription and embedding. In *2025 3rd international conference on intelligent data communication technologies and internet of things (IDCIoT)* (pp. 1096–1101). IEEE. https://doi.org/10.1109/IDCIOT64235.2025.10914946

Poncelet, J., & Van Hamme, H. (2025). *Leveraging broadcast media subtitle transcripts for automatic speech recognition and subtitling*. arXiv. https://doi.org/10.48550/arXiv.2502.03212

Pranida, S. Z., Genadi, R. A., & Koto, F. (2025). *Synthetic data generation for culturally nuanced commonsense reasoning in low-resource languages*. arXiv. https://doi.org/10.48550/arXiv.2502.12932

Rombach, R., Blattmann, A., Lorenz, D., Esser, P., & Ommer, B. (2022). High-resolution image synthesis with latent diffusion models. In *Proceedings of the IEEE/CVF conference on computer vision and pattern recognition* (pp. 10684–10695). https://openaccess.thecvf.com/content/CVPR2022/papers/Rombach_High-Resolution_Image_Synthesis_With_Latent_Diffusion_Models_CVPR_2022_paper.pdf

Shen, H., Shao, L., Li, W., Lan, Z., Liu, Z., & Su, J. (2024). *A survey on multi-modal machine translation: Tasks, methods and challenges*. arXiv. https://doi.org/10.48550/arXiv.2405.12669

Striuk, A. M., & Hordiienko, V. V. (2025). Research and development of a subtitle management system using artificial intelligence. In *CEUR Workshop Proceedings* (pp. 415–427). https://ceur-ws.org/Vol-3917/paper61.pdf

Taşdan Doğan, T. (2023). Translating and interpreting in the Metaverse: Potential opportunities and challenges. *RumeliDE Dil ve Edebiyat Araştırmaları Dergisi*. https://doi.org/10.29000/rumelide.1346642

Gemini Team, Anil, R., Borgeaud, S., Alayrac, J.-B., Yu, J., Soricut, R., Schalkwyk, J., Dai, A. M., Hauth, A., Millican, K., Silver, D., Johnson, M., Antonoglou, I., Schrittwieser, J., Glaese, A., Chen, J., Pitler, E., Lillicrap, T., Lazaridou, A., Chen, X. et al. (2023). *Gemini: A family of highly capable multimodal models* [Preprint]. arXiv. https://doi.org/10.48550/arXiv.2312.11805

Wang, J., Jiang, H., Liu, Y., Ma, C., Zhang, X., Pan, Y., & Zhang, S. et al. (2024). *A comprehensive review of multimodal large language models: Performance and challenges across different tasks*. arXiv. https://doi.org/10.48550/arXiv.2408.01319

Wang, Y., Liu, Y., Zhou, S., Huang, Y., Tang, C., Zhou, W., & Chen, Z. (2025). Emotion-oriented cross-modal prompting and alignment for human-centric emotional video captioning. *IEEE Transactions on Multimedia*. https://doi.org/10.1109/TMM.2025.3535292

Wang, Y., Wang, L., Zhou, Q., Wang, Z., Li, H., Hua, G., & Tang, W. (2024). *Multimodal LLM enhanced cross-lingual cross-modal retrieval*. arXiv. https://arxiv.org/abs/2409.19961

Whittaker, L., Weismueller, J., & Pallant, J. (2025). *Avatars, assemble! Digital human avatars for public figure engagement and marketing*. Business Horizons. Advance online publication. https://doi.org/10.1016/j.bushor.2025.06.004

Wu, Q., Bansal, G., Zhang, J., Wu, Y., Li, B., Zhu, E., & Wang, C. et al. (2023). *Autogen: Enabling next-gen LLM applications via multi-agent conversation*. https://www.microsoft.com/en-us/research/wp-content/uploads/2023/08/LLM_agent.pdf?msockid=289fdc1018d664273522ca43192e654e

Xia, W. (2024). Research on the international dissemination of Tang poetry from the perspective of digital language service. *Journal of Trends in Arts and Humanities, 13*. http://www.upubscience.com/upload/20240903101028.pdf

Xiao, B., Shen, Q., & Wang, D. Z. (2025). From text to multi-modal: Advancing low-resource-language translation through synthetic data generation and cross-modal alignments. In *Proceedings of the eighth workshop on technologies for machine translation of low-resource languages (LoResMT 2025)* (pp. 24–35). https://doi.org/10.18653/v1/2025.loresmt-1.4

Xu, Y., Chen, H., Yu, J., Huang, Q., Wu, Z., Zhang, S., Li, G., Luo, Y., & Gu, R. (2023). *SECap: Speech emotion captioning with large language model*. arXiv preprint arXiv:2312.10381. https://arxiv.org/abs/2312.10381

Yao, S., & Wan, X. (2020). Multimodal transformer for multimodal machine translation. In D. Jurafsky, J. Chai, N. Schluter, & J. Tetreault (Eds.), In *Proceedings of the 58th annual meeting of the association for computational linguistics* (pp. 4346–4350). Association for Computational Linguistics. https://doi.org/10.18653/v1/2020.acl-main.400

Yao, Y., Yu, T., Zhang, A., Wang, C., Cui, J., Zhu, H., & Sun, M. et al. (2025). Efficient GPT-4V level multimodal large language model for deployment on edge devices. *Nature Communications, 16*(1), 5509. https://doi.org/10.1038/s41467-025-61040-5

Yin, T. (2025). Has the use of AI-translated live captions in simultaneous interpreting changed the role of the interpreter? A study based on professional interpreters' perceptions. *The Translator, 31*(2), 214–231. https://doi.org/10.1080/13556509.2024.2412923

Yu, H., Lu, J., Wang, Y., Li, Y., Wang, H., Huang, C., & Li, B. (2025). *Eve: Towards end-to-end video subtitle extraction with vision-language models*. arXiv. https://doi.org/10.48550/arXiv.2503.04058

Zhai, Y., Zeng, Y., Huang, Z., Qin, Z., Jin, X., & Cao, D. (2024). Multi-prompts learning with cross-modal alignment for attribute-based person re-identification. In *Proceedings of the AAAI Conference on Artificial Intelligence* (Vol. 38, No. 7, pp. 6979–6987). https://doi.org/10.48550/arXiv.2312.16797

Zhu, S., Xie, H., & Wan, M. (2023). A study on the development of remote interpreting from a metaverse perspective [元宇宙视域下远程口译发展探究. *Journal of Beijing International Studies University* [北京第二外国语学院学报], *45*(2), 60–73.

Chapter 12
Language Service Management and Operations

Abstract This chapter examines how intelligent technologies are restructuring language service management and operations. It frames modern workflows as modular, node-based systems in which process nodes (ingestion, preprocessing, assignment, execution, consolidation, feedback) are dynamically reconfigurable and instrumented with quality, time, and risk indicators. Large Language Models and agent architectures shift coordination from file-centric handoffs to semantic connectivity, enabling context graphs, automated resource orchestration, and adaptive scheduling. Business models evolve from labor and per-word pricing to platform productization, capability-bundled, risk-aware pricing, and data asset monetization. Client management expands beyond textual quality toward experience visibility, customization, lifecycle communication, and retention analytics. Team structures move from discrete translator–editor roles to hybrid human–AI collaboration, adding new functions (prompt engineering, data stewardship, workflow orchestration). Operational intelligence rests on governed linguistic/data assets, modular platform integration, and observability pipelines that capture micro-behaviors, power experimentation (A/B, canary deployment), and drive algorithmic feedback loops for continuous optimization. The chapter highlights systemic thinking, data governance, and human value amplification as emerging differentiators in a platform-anchored, AI-mediated ecosystem.

Language services are a knowledge-intensive domain grounded in professional judgment and collaborative mechanisms. From real-time interpreting to workflow-based document translation, effective delivery relies on the coordinated integration of project management, technological tools, talent, and a coherent value system. As intelligent technologies deepen, the ecosystem is being rapidly reconfigured (Crangasu, 2025; Cui, 2025; Lionbridge, 2023). Automation continually reshapes task boundaries; data has displaced traditional resources as the central asset; and service formats are shifting toward platform and product architectures. Organizing and managing language services extends beyond operational oversight. Understanding these evolving models clarifies operative mechanisms and the sector's likely trajectory under technological momentum.

J. S. Yu and Y. Yao, *Intelligent Language Services*,
https://doi.org/10.1007/978-981-95-4632-9_12

1 Principles of Language Service Management

Language services are not simply a linear chain of receiving, translating, and delivering; they are highly structured, collaboration-dependent, technology-enabled knowledge-intensive activities. As scope broadens and complexity rises, organizational models, process design, and scheduling mechanisms increasingly shape project outcomes.

1.1 Process Nodes in Multilingual Projects

In multilingual language services, process nodes are critical control points along the execution chain. Each node integrates a clear objective, defined tasks, and technical interfaces. They function as checkpoints for quality and schedule and as focal points for risk control and resource coordination. Although sequenced, they are not rigidly linear and can be dynamically reconfigured to meet project needs.

Multilingual projects often follow a "central intake—language-specific execution – consolidated delivery" pattern, while execution paths diverge by language due to resource availability, client requirements, and linguistic characteristics. For example, in a pharmaceutical marketing initiative at a multinational company, English source materials must be converted into dozens of target language versions, meet each country's regulatory policies, and adapt to local marketing strategies. Every language presents distinct challenges in compliance review, market positioning, and resource coordination, and these differences are reflected in the design of individual process nodes (Montalt & Muñoz-Miquel, 2024).

At project initiation, the objective is to establish the framework and execution baseline. Clients submit source documents plus term bases, figures, and reference materials. The project manager confirms target languages, content categories (e.g., compliance, medical, marketing), delivery formats, and cadence, then configures task structures, alerts, and resource allocation in the management platform. The key is translating business objectives into an executable multilingual task network.

At the document preprocessing and task decomposition node, all source files undergo standardized handling before translation to ensure downstream stability and control. Steps include unlocking locked layers, removing hidden content, extracting editable text, and segmenting. Unlocking layers enables computer-assisted translation (CAT) tools to detect and replace text; removing hidden content prevents irrelevant material from polluting output. Translation memories and terminology tools support automated batch processing, while extraction tools generate initial glossaries per language. Task splitting must preserve semantic unit integrity to improve translation and review accuracy (Kappus, 2024).

At the resource scheduling and task assignment node, requirements are matched to translators by specialization, availability, and performance history. Low-resource languages or specialized domains (e.g., medical) require early resource locking and calibrated workload allocation; the resource management platform surfaces real-time availability for decisions (Brandt, 2024).

At the execution and synchronized-review node, translators work in the designated CAT platform while the system logs edits and terminology updates; reviewers monitor changes in real time, focusing on terminology consistency, linguistic fluency, and regulatory conformity (Carmo & Koponen, 2024). For related languages, teams may share translation memories to harmonize expression.

At the quality consolidation and delivery node, the desktop publishing (DTP) team standardizes formatting across languages and restores integrated text–image structures. CAT tools interoperate with layout software to reduce formatting errors, producing delivery-ready PDFs plus editable files. Manual proofreading is added where needed to ensure visual and linguistic consistency.

At the feedback and improvement node, client revisions feed back into repositories and translator evaluation systems, updating term bases and style guides to sustain a continuous improvement loop.

Process nodes are modular and adjustable. If a pharmaceutical client advances a deadline, the project manager can insert an expedited terminology review node and re-architect the flow. Mastery of node functions and interfaces directly determines responsiveness and adaptability. Intelligent orchestration and embedded node intelligence are mutually reinforcing.

1.2 *Semantic Connectivity of Translation Content and Intelligent Resource Orchestration*

Language services have long relied on files for collaboration and handoff. A file-centric model provided a verifiable container readable across tools: carrying text units and structural tags, terminology and version metadata, and word counts and match ratios used for quoting and settlement. XML Localization Interchange File Format transports content and metadata among CAT tools; Translation Memory aggregates bilingual pairs with timestamps and domain attributes; TermBase eXchange preserves terminology and usage constraints; project management systems then split tasks and track progress. Files thus became boundaries of delivery and accountability—any stakeholder can reproduce outcomes or reconcile accounts from the same snapshot.

The challenge is that files poorly convey context. User Interface (UI) linkages, engineering diagrams, image annotations, and business context such as regulatory domains or user personas are difficult to capture in a single file. Tools interpret standards inconsistently, causing loss of comments, tags, or term attributes. Large projects therefore rely on engineers' scripts or plugins to bridge gaps, with communication and maintenance costs scaling upward. More critically, many errors arise not from lexical misjudgment but from missing situational context: a static snapshot cannot express task intent, temporal constraints, or change history—factors that materially affect quality and consistency.

Large language models and agent technologies are shifting connectivity from file and data layers to task and semantic layers. An agent orients around project intent, maintains a unified representation of goals, state, and constraints, and maps these to callable actions. After receiving a project description, it parses language distribution and layout, invokes optical character recognition (OCR) for image-rich PDFs, normalizes paragraphs, tags, and annotations into a unified dataset, and injects them directly into the designated CAT workspace. Permissions and templates govern visibility and intervention timing. The process becomes request–response rather than interface clicking and manual import/export. Multimodal control protocols provide an abstract intent-to-action mapping, conferring composability, rollback, and auditability (Volk & Läubli, 2024).

This semantic connectivity mitigates context loss. Agents can fuse source channels, target users, regulatory requirements, and reference assets into a continuously updated context graph that travels with the task. In pharmaceutical promotion, a single instruction—"Extract table paragraphs related to side effects and import them into the designated Trados Cloud project mapped to regulatory terminology"—enables detection, extraction, terminology alignment, and repository ingestion, then triggers subsequent review and consistency checks on status changes. Translators and reviewers work within a shared evolving context; interface switching and file shuttling decline sharply, refocusing attention on linguistic quality and cultural fit. Open-design and video-platform application programming interfaces (APIs) allow agents to read objects, modify layers, and batch-replace text, further reducing multimodal localization friction (Kappus, 2024).

In translation projects, resources comprise human expertise, linguistic assets, tool capabilities, and temporal and budget constraints. Semantic connectivity and agents shift scheduling from people and files to articulated task intents and constraints. Processes run as a chain of monitorable nodes, each bound to explicit inputs, actions, and acceptance criteria—forming a semantics-driven, orchestrable system.

An agent first produces a task profile summarizing domain, risk level, and engineering complexity, then executes a single-hop resource-graph match to propose language pair and team selection, memory and terminology loading schemes, whether to adopt an English pivot route, and the need for pre-terminology validation or sample review. The key is codifying these decisions into reusable nodes—terminology sprint, sample review, main batch, rollback—so task semantics map directly to resource invocation and quality control.

Multilingual synchronization best illustrates node-based orchestration. For a multi-market medical device launch, the system first triggers terminology sprints and sample reviews for regulation-sensitive languages before the main batch. Scarce languages follow a pivot route to enforce consistency; resource-rich languages proceed directly, accelerating throughput. If the launch date is advanced, the agent inserts expedited consistency and terminology re-validation nodes, prioritizing high-risk languages to prevent systemic stall.

Resources extend beyond personnel. Translation memories and term bases are orchestrable assets version-selected by relevance and freshness with controlled write permissions. Tools and compute surface as executable nodes. For a PDF with images containing translatable text, an OCR pipeline localizes layout and text blocks with coordinates, performs language detection and character correction, outputs anchored JSON for CAT import with terminology validation, then restores content by anchors while DTP reconstructs layout from coordinates. Time and budget are represented as constraint nodes; the system searches feasible configurations balancing quality thresholds and cost.

Time control and contingency are integrated with scheduling. Using historical and real-time data, the platform builds a temporal risk map, outputs delay probabilities per language group, and recommends parallel paths or backups at early warning signs. Organizations pre-establish contingency pools; on critical path alerts, reinforcements auto-deploy based on task profiles. When justified, a compliant large language model produces a controlled draft, applies automated terminology corrections, then hands off for human review. Event-triggered node reconfiguration sustains cadence, maintaining throughput, quality, and traceability under high concurrency and cross-time-zone conditions.

2 Restructuring of Language Service Business Models

The industry's business model is undergoing systemic reconstruction. Traditional translation firms anchored value in labor supply and project management, whereas platform-centric entrants integrate data, algorithms, and human expertise to reshape service structure (Carreira, 2024) and profit model. The adoption of Aritificial Intelligence (AI) accelerates productization and platformization, resetting pricing mechanisms, cost structures, and value boundaries. The industry is moving from a linear "project–delivery" model toward an "asset–platform" ecosystem (Moorkens & Guerberof Arenas, 2024), altering delivery modalities and compelling participants to reassess positioning, strategy, and sustainability.

2.1 *Platform Reconfiguration and Resource Reallocation*

Language services are shifting from an outsourcing-driven project business to a data-driven, human–AI collaborative knowledge system. Drivers include continued content globalization, diffusion of generative AI, and heightened expectations for automation and data security (Koskinen, 2020). Core competence is moving from "fulfilling orders" to "building platforms," reshaping service units, delivery modes, and value sources.

RWS's 2020 acquisition of SDL marked this pivot. RWS excelled in technical translation, intellectual property (IP) support, and process standardization;

SDL contributed strengths in CAT tooling (Trados, MultiTerm), content management system integration, and neural machine translation (MT) and data platforms. Post-merger, the former divide between service provider and tool vendor converged into a unified language technology platform with simultaneous product and organizational reconfiguration (Araghi et al., 2024; Sánchez-Castany, 2024). A Tridion-centered ecosystem channels authoring, review, terminology management, translation, and publishing through one pipeline. The platform absorbs portions of project management; human effort concentrates on quality and compliance; accumulated high-quality corpora feed MT and retrieval evaluation models (Orlando et al., 2024).

Platformization recombines data, compute, and human expertise into a composable capability stack. Data shifts from by-product to strategic asset, determining MT precision, stylistic consistency, and semantic safety boundaries. Firms build proprietary corpora and localized style repositories to govern terminology and pragmatics while mitigating generic-model bias and leakage risk. Compute moves from tool adjunct to process core—spanning MT training, semantic search, quality prediction, and content moderation—with cloud integration providing elastic scaling and on-demand orchestration. Human roles evolve from single-track translators to hybrid contributors who exercise linguistic judgment, govern data, and design workflows—value migrates from processing text to steering data and training loops.

Operational differentiation manifests in closed-loop capability. Terminology and memories are continually refreshed; model invocation and evaluation, post-editing and DTP, publishing and audit connect via unified interfaces and permissions. Corpora and metrics cycle back at each stage, generating traceable quality and cost curves. RWS's IP services show one platform supporting multilingual synchronization and compliance while enabling cross-project data reuse for higher long-term marginal returns (Orlando et al., 2024).

The value chain is decoupling. Corpus construction, model training and evaluation, post-editing, automated delivery, and data feedback can be distributed across actors and coordinated via standard interfaces. In international regulatory scenarios, specialized teams handle annotation and training; providers concentrate on post-editing and consistency; outputs enter master data systems via APIs; IT manages deployment and audit. Each stage can become a profit node, extending boundaries upstream into data engineering and downstream into content governance. Firms failing to transform face declining volumes and unit prices (Carreira, 2024).

The industry trajectory is clarifying. Providers modularize AI model invocation, data annotation and review, quality evaluation, and style governance, embedding them as platform capabilities monetized by subscription or usage. Platforms convert language services from replaceable outsourcing to sticky embedded capability, easing integration with enterprise content and security architectures. Competitive focus shifts from headcount and single-project efficiency to corpus quality and availability, compute and integration maturity, and process embedding depth (Nimdzi, 2023b).

2.2 AI-Driven Productization and Pricing Reconstruction

Pricing mediates supply and demand and mirrors product form and delivery mode. Under AI influence, language services are moving from labor-centric per-piece pricing to product systems centered on algorithmic capability and workflow configuration (Sakamoto & Bawa Mason, 2024). Pricing now bundles capabilities, risks, and ongoing operations rather than simply converting effort.

Language services are being decomposed into configurable, combinable, continuously optimizable modules. The traditional per-thousand-words rate distorted once post-editing expanded. Effort no longer scales linearly with volume, while clients expect process observability, terminology control, and quality traceability. Tiered pricing now treats machine translation, light human review, style harmonization, terminology tagging, deep polishing, and audit logging as selectable units. Clients pay for required quality and transparency—not raw volume.

Subscription models embed language services in daily operations. Unbabel offers monthly packages priced by interaction frequency and service span—email support, FAQ generation, localization pre-checks—so clients acquire scalable language operations capability rather than one-off output. Platform tools reinforce this model: GlobalLink centralizes ingestion, configuration, processing, and monitoring; clients upload files, select editing depth, or connect via API—price and process become jointly visible, increasing price elasticity and collaboration efficiency.

With large language models embedded, pricing must account for model invocation costs, corpus construction, and human review. Model services are billed per character or call; integrators balance caching strategies with quality assurance. Legal platforms often use a "model call fee + review labor + risk premium" structure reflecting sensitivity, error impact, and compliance burden. Explicit cost–risk linkage improves decision transparency.

Cost structures are being rewritten. After model training, marginal inference cost approaches compute consumption—far below repetitive human translation. Platforms can price basic services very low—or at zero—and shift monetization to terminology governance, quality assurance, and API integration (Andrews, 2024). Compute and operations still incur expense; high-fidelity, terminology-sensitive content accumulates hidden iteration costs. The cost profile now shows higher upstream and downstream expenditure with reduced midstream bulk processing. Firms front-load investment into data preparation and model construction and back-load governance into customized delivery and quality control, using granular decomposition and data governance to optimize margin (Beninatto and Varga 2025).

Profit centers are shifting. Instead of relying on efficiency gains and compressed review cycles, value migrates to data asset operations, platform capability output, and relationship design. After acquiring SDL, RWS productized large corpora, licensing data to localization platforms and AI training entities—creating recurring "language data as a service" revenue (Orlando et al., 2024; Sánchez-Castany, 2024; Tomedes, 2025). Software-as-a-service subscriptions distribute fixed costs; Phrase tiers plans and overage billing to achieve scale effects, decoupling client growth from headcount.

Increasingly, enterprises expect providers to support the full content lifecycle as "language infrastructure," sustained by API integration and service agreements—raising expectations for data security, platform stability, and operational elasticity (LinguaLinx, 2025).

Within this framework, coherent pricing and product design follow three lines: capability stratification—distinguishing basic automation, enhanced human–AI collaboration, and high assurance tiers with auditable metrics; usage intensity—hybrid subscription plus consumption billing leveraging caching and reuse to damp volatility; and risk and compliance—translating sensitivity, terminology consistency, and audit needs into transparent premiums enabling explainable trade-offs.

Shifting from selling labor to delivering capability units—and from pricing text to subscribing to algorithms and governance modules—language services are entering a product-centric, configuration-driven, data-supported phase. Mastery of technical parameters, decomposition of cost and risk, and participation in service design and packaging are emerging sources of competitive advantage.

3 Client Relationship and Service Experience Management

The core value of language services lies in accurate, efficient transformation—and in the interaction experience during delivery. Intensifying competition and pervasive AI adoption keep reshaping client expectations. Clients assess not only output quality but also response speed, process transparency, and collaboration flexibility. Providers must move beyond a narrow technical-delivery mindset, systematize relationship and experience management, and build sustainable differentiated capability (Koskinen, 2020).

3.1 From Quality Management to Experience Management

Traditional quality management provides the content foundation—standards, sampling, and scoring ensuring accuracy and consistency—but remains text-centric and engineering-oriented, only marginally addressing business context and outcomes.

Content-oriented evaluation treats static text, often overlooking real-world complexity. Terminology may be correct and the text acceptable yet fail to support downstream compliance, publication, or user comprehension. Hybrid AI scoring plus human review improves efficiency and consistency but still centers on textual adequacy, leaving unresolved whether the service solved the client's problem (Lommel et al., 2024).

Modern quality now extends to experience. Clients emphasize responsiveness, process visibility, and collaborative flexibility. Experience management makes systemic capability and responsiveness perceptible through structured processes

(Bernardini et al., 2020). Providers must internalize business context, move beyond transfer, rapidly match resources across requirement tiers, collaborate flexibly, and adapt structures as conditions shift. Experience is evidenced by efficiently resolving complex requests rather than conversational smoothness alone.

A compliance project for a multinational life sciences firm illustrates this. The client initially requested translation and layout, but the source format was intricate, regulations and terminology interlaced, and updates frequent. Standard workflows produced correct translations yet failed to support compliance review. An experience assessment led to adding terminology co-development, regulatory interpretation, incremental update handling, and version comparison—realigning with the client's process and making experience the primary value metric (Al-Tarawneh & Kanan, 2025).

Operationalizing experience management depends on transparent, explainable structures. Service charters, process diagrams, and status dashboards help clients grasp system scope and influence long-term commitment. Organizationally, experience management must be embedded in capability building: diversified standards, preconfigured contingencies, and cross-team coordination keep processes orderly amid change.

Quality management remains the prerequisite; experience management links it to business objectives. Scenario-oriented design and transparent collaboration ensure content adequacy while sustaining orderly, stable, predictable delivery under change. Client participation, perceived controllability, and outcome predictability are becoming key value dimensions.

3.2 *Demand-Driven and Customized Language Services*

Quality control systems provide foundational safeguards, yet acceptable output alone seldom sustains long-term relationships. Clients interpret "acceptable" differently; project goals, content types, and industry context shape preferences and evaluative criteria (Ruokonen & Svahn, 2022).

As demands diversify, process-standardization and reuse models show limitations. Clients expect problem solving, not mere linguistic conversion. In law, concern extends beyond terminological consistency to enforceability; a mistranslated force majeure clause can invalidate a contract and cause severe losses (Huang et al., 2024). Legal translation's core is functional legal equivalence, not surface fluency.

Medical texts balance clinical precision with patient readability (Barwise et al., 2024). E-commerce emphasizes conversion: language must align with platform algorithms and user search behavior; grammatically correct translations may still underperform. Value is shifting from correctness to goal attainment, requiring practitioners to integrate domain knowledge, digital tools, and business insight to identify and address real needs proactively.

Project content should be stratified: critical segments receive premium human translation and review; less critical portions leverage MT to optimize flow

(Novozhilova et al., 2025). Mature providers build client knowledge graphs aggregating terminology preferences and revision histories and apply large models for style prediction and auto-matching, improving responsiveness and quality.

Customization spans linguistic, procedural, and technical layers. Workflows adjust to urgency and quality thresholds—elastic for rapid drafts plus later refinement, or multi-round review with integrated quality assurance (QA) for high-stakes tasks. Key accounts often have dedicated teams for stylistic consistency and efficient communication. Providers build client-specific term bases, style guides, and corpora, dynamically invoked to accumulate and reuse knowledge.

For long-term or large-scale projects, customization extends to interaction platforms and bespoke interfaces. Dedicated workspaces enable automatic dispatch, progress tracking, and real-time communication. Deliverables diversify—terminology lists, cultural adaptation reports, style analyses—enhancing overall experience.

At its core, customization hinges on precise resource allocation and flexible process adaptation. Demand-driven design and technological enablement integrate language services into client business systems, shifting from standalone output to value co-creation.

3.3 Client Communication Management

In day-to-day language service operations, client communication management is the linchpin of sustained quality and continuity. It secures accurate information flow and underpins trust, client experience, and process optimization. While deliverables often draw primary attention, the depth of requirement understanding typically determines satisfaction. Many quality disputes arise not during execution but from misalignment at the requirements phase (Koskinen, 2020).

Conventional workflows span requirements clarification, in-process feedback, and post-delivery review. Early gathering—via email, forms, or meetings—of target languages, file formats, deadlines, and stylistic preferences appears orderly yet is fraught with incomplete inputs, vague intent, and jargon asymmetries. Seemingly "basic" errors usually reflect expectation gaps rather than operational faults.

Enhancing communication requires structured elicitation rather than simply adding additional form fields. Providers should probe across business objectives, audience profiles, and distribution channels. For a corporate website, priority distinctions—brand positioning, conversion, or search visibility—guide linguistic strategy. Clarifying scope and intent upfront enables targeted language solutions (Koskinen, 2020).

During execution, proactive feedback loops outperform linear "deliver–comment–revise" cycles. Mid-phase checkpoints and sample approvals realign style and terminology early, cutting rework and strengthening engagement and trust.

Artificial intelligence now automates requirement extraction, status reporting, and query handling through natural language processing (NLP) and large language models. Systems mine client emails to draft initialization forms for validation (Cui, 2025; Moorkens & Guerberof Arenas, 2024). Platforms also generate briefs, profile stylistic preferences, and infer latent delivery aims—especially valuable for large, heterogeneous project streams—thereby reducing manual load.

In retrospective phases, AI clusters recurrent edits, surfaces stylistic trends, and contrasts revisions against initial briefs to reveal systemic weaknesses—capabilities once reliant on senior managers now increasingly automated (Barzizza et al., 2024).

Technology cannot displace interpretive and strategic layers. AI accelerates extraction, yet nuanced context still demands human judgment. Effective communication fuses automated processing with expert framing to yield an adaptive, continuously improving service system that reduces error, deepens collaboration, and amplifies professional value.

3.4 Visualization of Service Experience and Intelligent Client Retention

Perceptibility of service experience and long-term relationship stewardship now forms the nexus between client perception and operational delivery. Output-centric quality control gives way to process alignment with client expectations—trust built through transparent interaction, scope breadth, depth of issue resolution, and proactive discovery of latent needs (Koskinen, 2020).

Because experience resists direct measurement, engineered perception signals—progress bars, terminology review status, revision histories, and preference tags—provide real-time visibility, strengthen engagement, and embed experience as a continuous layer. Platforms such as memoQ, Smartling, and Lokalise already deliver multidimensional views of progress, review activity, and linguistic assets; experience is therefore treated not as an endpoint but as an attribute of every service node.

AI further digitizes and augments experience: NLP and LLMs accelerate requirement extraction, status tracking, automated responses, and complex query resolution. Systems mine emails, forms, and prior exchanges to prefill project setup for validation (Cui, 2025; Moorkens & Guerberof Arenas, 2024). Across iterative feedback cycles, AI flags decision points, consolidates revision trails, and preserves auditability—reducing misunderstanding and redundant exchanges.

In Service Level Agreement (SLA) design, AI shifts static clauses on response times and delivery milestones toward dynamic, data-driven commitments. Historical usage patterns enable tailored remediation triggers and value-added advisory layers. Emerging tiers—basic, collaborative, intelligent—leverage LLMs and multilingual analytics to provide style coaching, contextual optimization, and strategic guidance.

Quantification has become more granular: beyond Net Promoter Score, behavioral indicators—edit frequency, task dwell time, and content abandonment—enrich evaluation. AI performs attribution and clustering, combining patterns with explicit feedback to surface pain points and improvement levers (Barzizza et al., 2024).

Making experience explicit and structuring agreements propel the shift from outsourced execution to collaborative co-creation. Visualization and intelligent analytics increase transparency and control for clients while enabling providers to iteratively refine processes as durable partners in efficiency and knowledge gains.

Durable client relationships constitute the primary competitive moat. Legacy reliance on individual project managers' tacit skills does not scale. Intelligent platforms use data modeling and modular service design to identify high-value accounts, optimize engagement cadence, and adjust information flows dynamically. GlobalLink (TransPerfect) embeds language workflows into client content management, increasing operational stickiness and enabling deeper collaboration.

AI also transforms churn prediction by monitoring initiation intervals, feedback density, complaint counts, and project mix. When composite risk thresholds trigger, stakeholders are alerted for intervention. Lifecycle segmentation (new, active, at-risk) supports stage-specific playbooks for proactive retention.

Relationship capital derives from progressively deeper business understanding forged across scenarios. AI and data tooling enhance adaptive insight and flexible embedded collaboration. High-quality experience coupled with disciplined lifecycle management is steering the sector toward data-driven, transparent, goal-aligned operations.

4 Team Management and Collaboration in Language Services

The industry has transitioned from "individual craft" to team-, process-, and platform-centric collaboration. Large programs span multiple languages, stages, and systems across geographies, making individual capacity insufficient for efficiency and quality assurance. Thus, team management and coordination architectures are foundational. Deep AI integration is redefining the division of labor: translator–AI synergy, distributed scheduling by project managers, and continuous professional development now anchor organizational and technical design (Bernardini et al., 2020; Moorkens & Guerberof Arenas, 2024).

4.1 Redefining Roles and Structures in Human–AI Collaboration

Historically, core roles—translator, editor, and project manager—were distinctly bounded; some firms added terminologists or DTP engineers. With deep AI—especially LLM—adoption, workflows are being re-architected, altering organizational structure and responsibilities (Briva-Iglesias, 2023; Krüger, 2025; Lion People Global, 2025).

Machine pre-translation now dominates, with fully human translation retained only for narrow high-stakes domains (Sakamoto & Bawa Mason, 2024). Translators increasingly act as evaluators and post-editors, requiring linguistic depth plus model literacy—anticipating failure modes, refining prompts, and sometimes contributing to fine-tuning. New roles—prompt engineer and AI linguistic optimizer—focus on raising overall human–AI throughput (Briva-Iglesias & O'Brien, 2022).

Editors ensure linguistic accuracy and stylistic coherence, interpret generative logic, surface latent biases, and recommend refinements. They are evolving from final gatekeepers to pivotal data quality stewards whose judgments feed iterative model enhancement (Sánchez-Castany, 2024).

Project management is expanding toward orchestration of automation and technical resources. Managers now need competencies in model configuration, API coordination, and workflow design, bridging business objectives and engineering constraints (Mankauskienė, 2024).

Technical roles underpin stability, security, and scalability—covering model deployment, retrieval-augmented generation (RAG) pipelines, SLA monitoring, multilingual knowledge bases, and translation memory stewardship. Boundaries between engineers and linguists are blurring as they collaborate on automated terminology extraction, style model training, and corpus preprocessing.

AI tools function as virtual teammates. In platform organizations, embedded automation selects LLM summarization, neural machine translation plus post-editing, or AI style diagnostics as needed—both substituting discrete tasks and enabling parallelized distributed execution (Volk & Läubli, 2024).

Organizational change extends beyond tool adoption; it rewires operating logic. Capability interfaces, data literacy, systemic service orientation, and multidimensional collaboration models now define team value.

4.2 Workflow Collaboration and Task Interface Management

In language service systems, workflow modeling and interface specification directly shape efficiency and quality. Legacy reliance on manual orchestration yields semi-structured flows prone to latency and blurred accountability. As volume, role diversity, and AI integration scale, finer task granularity and standardized interfaces become pivotal (Risku, 2008).

Workflow modeling decomposes projects into functional units with defined inputs and outputs: source ingestion, corpus preprocessing, terminology extraction, translation (machine pre-translation plus post-editing), quality evaluation, and layout. Each node specifies inputs, a human or AI processor, outputs, and constraints—shifting from tacit practice to system logic (van der Meer, 2024).

Deeper AI adoption introduces automated, parallelizable nodes—summarization, style detection, terminology consistency auditing—shifting mental models from linear chains to graph structures. Data and temporal dependencies drive scheduling;

state-aware adjustments optimize performance without compromising quality. Early interface rigor ensures scalable, sustainable collaboration.

Clear interfaces underpin efficiency. Each service unit stipulates I/O schemas, quality thresholds, and exception handling, enabling seamless tool or team substitution. Unified specifications shift control from ad hoc practice to platform governance (Sánchez-Gijón et al., 2015).

Technically, multiple interface protocols are emerging. Anthropic's Model Context Protocol (2024) standardizes LLM connectivity with external tools and databases, enabling dynamic access to terminology and knowledge bases to improve translation and localization efficiency (Secara et al., 2025). Google's Agent-to-Agent (A2A) protocol treats roles, tools, and models as agents negotiating intent, yielding adaptive multi-project, multi-model orchestration.

As outlined in the "Intelligent Agents and Workflows" chapter, evolution converts organizational logic into inter-agent task negotiation. Model Context Protocol, A2A, and related standards all pursue clear interfaces and unified protocols for interactive, schedulable, monitorable collaboration graphs. Effective management hinges on reproducible role behaviors, explicit task boundaries, and auditable exchanges—anchored in standardized processes and systematic interface governance.

4.3 Distributed and Cross-Cultural Remote Collaboration

The sector is inherently international: translation, interpreting, localization, and review span time zones, cultures, and platforms. Remote distribution reduces costs and increases flexibility yet introduces communication friction, process inconsistency, cultural misreading, and temporal coordination challenges.

Time zone separation creates immediate risk: multilingual tasks require precise handoffs in narrow overlap windows; delays cascade. Asynchronous, node-based collaboration on standardized platforms mitigates this, while detailed briefs, acceptance criteria, and documented workflows reduce ambiguity.

Cultural divergence exerts subtler effects: notions of quality, delivery rigor, and feedback vary; expression norms and accountability expectations can clash. Static documentation, templates, and episodic training seldom keep pace. Intelligent tooling offers adaptive mediation (Orlando et al., 2024).

LLM-based communication mediators rephrase briefs, feedback, and handoff notes to align with recipients' linguistic and cultural expectations. Terminology change rationales can be tailored by native language or stylistic profile to improve pragmatic fit.

Agent systems also orchestrate cadence by mapping resource availability to optimized assignment and notification timing. Before a new task window opens, they compile and preliminarily validate prior time zone outputs to extend effective downstream working time.

Platforms monitor bottlenecks, diagnosing recurrent delays via interaction logs—such as divergent interpretations of stylistic consistency—and respond by refining instructions or attaching exemplars to narrow variance.

Remote collaboration ultimately depends on sensing and aligning cognitive and behavioral patterns. AI adds value by modeling interaction and modulating expression for continuous, designable cross-cultural optimization. Teams must pair linguistic and tooling skills with structured collaboration mindsets and cultural adaptability to convert global potential into operational leverage.

5 Operational Intelligence in Language Services

Amid platformization and intelligent transformation, the industry is integrating fragmented information assets, legacy toolchains, and algorithmic capabilities to reconfigure operating models and service capacity (Day Translations, 2025). Operational intelligence extends beyond tool upgrades—requiring data governance, platform interoperability, and embedded algorithms. Fine-grained linguistic and operational data management, modular platform integration, and in-flow algorithmic augmentation are driving structural change and reframing strategic understanding.

5.1 Management of Linguistic and Data Assets

The sector is intrinsically data-rich: each phase yields bilingual corpora, terminology bases, style guides, project metadata, QA records, client feedback, and task logs—assets whose systematic governance underpins platform intelligence (Nimdzi, 2023a). Robust data stewardship is now a core competitive differentiator.

Execution phases generate the highest-quality linguistic data. Source–target pairs deliver domain specificity for model training and reuse. Without granular tagging and metadata, value is lost. Leading firms employ Translation Management Systems (TMS) for automated synchronization and multidimensional archiving (client, domain, time), enabling intelligent reuse within Computer-Assisted Translation environments. In pharmaceutical localization, labeled document-type corpora support specialized sub-models or prompt optimization, boosting terminological fidelity and stylistic stability. Carefully fine-tuned small models can outperform generic LLMs, becoming proprietary assets.

Terminology and style datafication are multifaceted. Terms originate from client submissions or iterative accumulation via editing and QA. Extraction tools apply frequency and alignment heuristics to propose candidates for human curation (Chataut et al., 2024). Style guides crystallize from recurrent edits and client revisions, with platform modules (e.g., Trados "Linguistic Feedback") aggregating signals to generate targeted improvement recommendations.

Quality evaluation data management likewise exhibits intelligence—modern systems capture scores with multi-source error tagging to power trend analytics and model refinement (Zhao et al., 2024). One game localization provider tracked imperative-sentence mistranslations structurally, injecting bespoke prompts during training to improve draft quality and post-editing efficiency.

For personalization, unstructured interaction text—emails, summaries, and reviews—encodes terminology usage, stylistic preferences, and sensitivity hotspots. Automated summarization and semantic tagging structure these signals for intelligent linguist matching, prompt customization, and evaluative benchmarking (Liu et al., 2025).

Lifecycle management underwrites sustained data value. Trust levels evolve: repeatedly reused, unedited segments gain confidence; heavily revised items require re-annotation. Conflicting term usages warrant contextual qualifiers. Rigorous state governance mitigates risk from legacy misapplication.

In a mature model, governance creates a value loop: feeding model training, automated quality assessment, and tailored prompt optimization while driving iterative operational intelligence. At project initiation, correlated analysis of quality tags, feedback, and term preferences can auto-generate guidance, allocate resources, select style templates, and steer terminology curation.

Real value lies in structured, traceable, decision-enabling data. Preserving, contextualizing, and exploiting process-embedded assets is foundational for competitive leverage in platform-intelligent transformation.

5.2 *Modular Platform Systems and Tool Integration*

Modern platforms employ modular architectures to unify business flows, eliminating silos and aligning information with functional execution. Multi-tool orchestration is now standard; isolated tools cannot meet complex scalability needs. Modularity elevates efficiency while enabling standardization and capability extension.

Typical stacks encompass CAT tools, TMS, Language Quality Assessment (LQA) platforms, terminology and corpus management, AI augmentation modules (machine translation, intelligent rewriting, prompt generation), and permission/user layers. These modules cooperate dynamically: TMS dispatches tasks and injects terminology; CAT integrates translation memory and AI engines for draft generation and post-editing; quality scoring and archiving loop back into resource systems.

Interface design ensures continuity. Replacing static file handoffs, modular integration supports API-based dynamic loading of terminology and memories with automatic project and permission validation—maintaining synchronization and security.

Intelligent platforms emphasize feedback loops and self-optimization (Chkirbene et al., 2024). An upgraded service fused translation memory with LLM capabilities for asynchronous, sentence-level batch retrieval plus fuzzy matching layered with multi-tier quality scoring and contextual analysis. Returned segments include the closest historical matches and LLM-generated enhancements. Translators receive context-reconstructed, quality-annotated suggestions rather than raw matches—expanding traditional memory boundaries while sustaining high-quality throughput with reduced cognitive load.

Coordinated permission and user architectures secure the platform and enable efficient AI operation. Role-based and field-level controls govern client, project manager, translator, reviewer, terminologist, and algorithm invoker access, enforcing safe corpus and terminology usage. Large programs require multi-organization identity mapping and provenance tracking, so AI-generated or modified content remains attributable.

Modularity's chief benefit is furnishing a standardized substrate for rapid AI expansion. Unified interfaces, schemas, workflow templates, and quality rules allow plug-and-play integration of AI components (terminology extraction, intelligent evaluation, automated rewriting), elevating the platform to an operating-system role.

Developing and integrating AI tools constitute structural redesign of business architecture and service flows. Real-time data and logic interlinking across modules create resilient feedback loops, enabling continuous operational optimization and accelerated adaptive evolution—sustaining competitive advantage amid industry transformation.

5.3 *Observability and Algorithm-Driven Operational Feedback Loops*

In intelligent language service platforms, combining observability with algorithmic capability transforms operations from merely executable into perceivable, schedulable, and self-optimizing dynamic systems. Modular architectures and integrated tools capture interaction events at each stage, convert them into observability signals, and assemble end-to-end real-time monitoring—providing the prerequisite for continuous platform evolution.

From a management perspective, each modular workflow node maps to quantifiable key indicators: turnaround time, cost, staffing pattern, quality score, terminology match rate, percentage of machine translation, and loci of human intervention. Fine-grained logging is foundational. Beyond standard action records, "micro-behaviors" (edit frequency, suggestion acceptance ratio, undo counts) must be captured. In prompt-driven AI rewriting, user acceptance, modification, or rejection of suggestions are critical signals of model effectiveness. Correlating these with final delivery analysis enables the platform to localize error patterns and refine prompt strategies.

A/B testing and canary (staged) deployments provide an experimental framework for model and workflow optimization. Alternative translation engines, prompt sets, or quality evaluation algorithms can be compared under comparable task conditions to quantify performance deltas. Unlike many traditional sectors, testing in language services must incorporate content type, user profile, and task tagging for accurate attribution and targeted optimization.

Deep algorithmic embedding shifts observability from passive recording to active regulation. Large-model-driven automated scoring systems can structure quality assessment across semantic accuracy, stylistic consistency, fidelity, and client preference dimensions, approaching expert judgment for accuracy while exceeding manual evaluation in stability and consistency (Mohammed & Aljanabi, 2024). Feeding scores back into the workflow allows retraining to flag high-risk segments and trigger targeted human review—thereby helping balance labor cost against quality assurance.

Semantic similarity models supply the intelligence layer for resource reuse and task scheduling. Sentence-embedding retrieval not only identifies surface-level matches but also captures deeper semantic relations—raising efficiency in terminology alignment, translation memory leverage, and segment recommendation. On this basis, the platform can auto-recommend project configurations, optimal linguists, or refined prompts, shifting decisions from experience-driven to data-driven.

Recommender systems extend beyond e-commerce or short-form media; their core value is intelligent allocation. By modeling multidimensional relationships between translator profiles and task attributes—and applying attention mechanisms to weight historical performance and feedback—the platform can execute high-precision automatic assignment and contingency reassignment. Compared with manual scheduling based on project manager intuition, this substantially improves resource utilization and completion rates.

Within this system, virtually every translator action—accepting or editing AI suggestions, adjusting output, submitting quality ratings—is logged and transformed into structured data for performance evaluation, coaching insights, and ongoing model training (Algaraady & Mahyoob, 2025). Thus, routine human–AI collaboration continuously accumulates high-value data and organically forms a "co-evolution" feedback loop.

To realize this loop, the platform requires flexible model ingress and a microservices architecture that supports dynamic loading and parallel deployment of multiple algorithmic modules, coupled with low-latency feedback channels that accelerate cycles of model refinement and workflow adjustment (Owusu Boateng et al., 2024).

6 Conclusion

Intelligent and platform-based transformation is reshaping role structures and operational logic in language services (Tavares et al., 2023). The traditional "craft workshop" model grounded in experiential accumulation is giving way to a process-framed, platform-anchored, data- and algorithm-driven operational system. AI now absorbs many foundational tasks, allowing human contribution to concentrate on complex judgment, workflow architecture, cross-team coordination, and client communication.

In this environment, talent development shifts from passive accumulation to structured task curation and role empowerment. Organizations should design progression pathways: involving translators in terminology system building, engaging editors in client style alignment, and assigning project assistants to multilingual coordination—cultivating members with systemic perspective and hybrid capability. New roles such as "workflow advisor," "quality mentor," and "data strategy liaison" create differentiated growth tracks and promote knowledge circulation and institutional memory.

Intelligent platforms increase efficiency and reconfigure organizational practice: tasks are further decomposed, collaboration nodes diversify, and decision processes become more data- and algorithm-dependent. Workflows progressively acquire traits of structure, observability, measurability, and capacity for optimization. Quality management ensures reproducible delivery; emerging business models expand scope; systematized client experience strengthens perceived value; and coordinated teams sustain complex cross-cultural, cross-regional engagements.

Future competitiveness will rest not only on technical capability but also on systemic thinking and operational literacy. Language services now constitute a socially distributed collaboration system under continuous technological reconstruction. Practitioners must keep identifying uniquely human value and the optimal balance of intelligent collaboration amid data-driven, platform-mediated, human–AI integrated conditions. Those who can connect linguistic expertise, technology, and system logic will occupy pivotal positions in the next phase of industry evolution.

References

Algaraady, J., & Mahyoob, M. (2025). Exploring ChatGPT's potential for augmenting post-editing in machine translation across multiple domains: Challenges and opportunities. *Frontiers in Artificial Intelligence, 8*, 1526293. https://doi.org/10.3389/frai.2025.1526293

Al-Tarawneh, A., & Kanan, M. (2025). The economics of legal translation: Cost-benefit analysis and quality assurance. In A. M. A. Musleh Al-Sartawi, M. Al-Okaily, A. A. Al-Qudah, & F. Shihadeh (Eds.), *From machine learning to artificial intelligence* (Studies in systems, decision and control, Vol. 572). Springer. https://doi.org/10.1007/978-3-031-76011-2_95

Andrews, T. (2024). *A.I. and the evolution of language services—a 2024 update*. Interpreters and Translators, Inc. https://ititranslates.com/a-i-and-the-evolution-of-language-services/

Anthropic. (2024). *Introducing the model context protocol*. Anthropic. https://www.anthropic.com/news/model-context-protocol

Araghi, S., Palangkaraya, A., & Webster, E. (2024). The impact of language translation quality on commerce: The example of patents. *Journal of International Business Policy, 7*(2), 224–246. https://doi.org/10.1057/s42214-023-00157-0

Barwise, A. K., Curtis, S., Diedrich, D. A., & Pickering, B. W. (2024). Using artificial intelligence to promote equitable care for inpatients with language barriers and complex medical needs: Clinical stakeholder perspectives. *Journal of the American Medical Informatics Association, 31*(3), 611–621. https://doi.org/10.1093/jamia/ocad224

Barzizza, E., Campbell, S., Ceccato, R., Dobosz, A., Haag, M., Martins, R., & Salmaso, L. (2024). A data-driven approach to understanding customer satisfaction. *Journal of Machine Intelligence and Data Science, 5*, 1–7.

Beninatto, R., & Varga, L. K. (2025). *The language industry curve.* Nimdzi Insights. https://www.nimdzi.com/the-language-industry-curve/

Bernardini, S., Bouillon, P., Ciobanu, D., Hansen-Schirra, S., O'Brien, S., Steiner, E., & Teich, E. (2020). Language service provision in the 21st century: Challenges, opportunities and educational perspectives for translation studies. *Bologna Process Beyond 2020,* 297–303. https://www.academia.edu/110527056/Language_service_provision_in_the_21st_century_challenges_opportunities_and_educational_perspectives_for_translation_studies

Crangasu, A. (2025). *How AI is changing the translation service industry in 2025.* https://www.getblend.com/blog/artificial-intelligence-changing-the-translation-services-industry/

Brandt, A. (2024). Translation and localization project and process managers. In G. Massey, M. Ehrensberger-Dow, & E. Angelone (Eds.), *Handbook of the language industry: Contexts, resources and profiles* (pp. 143–178). De Gruyter Mouton. https://doi.org/10.1515/9783110716047-008

Briva-Iglesias, V., & O'Brien, S. (2022). The language engineer: A transversal, emerging role for the automation age. *Quaderns De Filologia: Estudis Lingüístics, 27,* 17–48. https://doi.org/10.7203/QF.27.24622

Briva-Iglesias, V. (2023). Translation technologies advancements: From inception to the automation age. *La Família Humana: Perspectives Multidisciplinàries de La Investigació En Ciències Humanes i Socials,* 137–152.

Carreira, O. (2024). Market concentration in the language services industry and working conditions for translators. *Perspectives, 32*(5), 889–904. https://doi.org/10.1080/0907676X.2023.2214318

Carmo, F. D., & Koponen, M. (2024). Revisers and post-editors: The guardians of quality. In G. Massey, M. Ehrensberger-Dow, & E. Angelone (Eds.), *Handbook of the language industry: Contexts, resources and profiles* (pp. 203–224). De Gruyter Mouton. https://doi.org/10.1515/9783110716047-010

Chataut, S., Do, T., Gurung, B. D. S., Aryal, S., Khanal, A., Lushbough, C., & Gnimpieba, E. (2024). *Comparative study of domain driven terms extraction using large language models.* arXiv. https://doi.org/10.48550/arXiv.2404.02330

Chkirbene, Z., Hamila, R., Gouissem, A., & Devrim, U. (2024). Large language models (LLM) in industry: A survey of applications, challenges, and trends. In *2024 IEEE 21st international conference on smart communities: Improving quality of life using AI, Robotics and IoT (HONET)* (pp. 229–234). IEEE. https://doi.org/10.1109/HONET63146.2024.10822885

Cui, Q. (2025). Development trends of language services industry in the era of artificial intelligence. *Journal of Beijing International Studies University, 47*(1), 62–72.

Day Translations. (2025). *How AI is changing the translation service industry in 2025.* Day Translations Blog. https://www.daytranslations.com/blog/how-ai-is-changing-the-translation-service-industry-in-2025/

Huang, L., Zhao, C., Chen, S., & Zeng, L. (2024). Blockchain: A promising technology for judicial translation services in cases with foreign elements. *Aslib Journal of Information Management, 76*(5), 713–735. https://doi.org/10.1108/AJIM-11-2022-0485

Kappus, M. (2024). Language technology developers. In G. Massey, M. Ehrensberger-Dow, & E. Angelone (Eds.), *Handbook of the language industry: Contexts, resources and profiles* (pp. 121–141). De Gruyter Mouton. https://doi.org/10.1515/9783110716047

Koskinen, K. (2020). Tailoring translation services for clients and users. In *The Bloomsbury companion to language industry studies* (pp. 139–152). Bloomsbury. https://www.bloomsburycollections.com/encyclopedia-chapter?docid=b-9781350024960&tocid=b-9781350024960-chapter7

Krüger, R. (2025). Implementing generative artificial intelligence technologies in language industry workflows–a competence perspective. *Lebende Sprachen, 70*(1), 11–38. https://doi.org/10.1515/les-2025-0002

Liu, H., Tahmasbi, A., Haque, E. S., & Jain, P. (2025). *LLMs for customized marketing content generation and evaluation at scale.* arXiv. https://doi.org/10.48550/arXiv.2506.17863

LinguaLinx. (2025). *The future of language service providers: Trends to watch in 2026*. https://www.lingualinx.com/blog/the-future-of-language-service-providers-trends-to-watch-in-2025

Lion People Global. (2025). *Essential skills to develop for new roles in translation and localization in 2025*. Lion People Global Blog. https://lionpeopleglobal.com/essential-skills-to-develop-for-new-roles-in-translation-and-localization-in-2025/

Lionbridge. (2023). *The future of localization*. https://www.lionbridge.com/content/dam/lionbridge/pages/blogs/translation-localization/lionbridge-ai-loc-e-book-blog/ai-business-the-future-of-localization-ebook-chinese-simplified.pdf

Lommel, A., Gladkoff, S., Melby, A., Wright, S. E., Strandvik, I., Gasova, K., & Nenadic, G. et al. (2024). *The multi-range theory of translation quality measurement: MQM scoring models and statistical quality control*. arXiv. https://doi.org/10.48550/arXiv.2405.16969

Mankauskienė, D. (2024). Mastering translation project management: What, when, and where. *Perspectives*, 1–21. https://doi.org/10.1080/0907676X.2024.2349944

Meer, A.-M. van der. (2024). Evolution of the language industry. In G. Massey, M. Ehrensberger-Dow, & E. Angelone (Eds.), *Handbook of the language industry: Contexts, resources and profiles* (pp. 33–48). De Gruyter Mouton. https://doi.org/10.1515/9783110716047-003

Mohammed, S. Y., & Aljanabi, M. (2024). Advancing translation quality assessment: Integrating AI models for real-time feedback. *EDRAAK, 2024*, 1–7. https://doi.org/10.70470/EDRAAK/2024/001

Montalt, V., & Muñoz-Miquel, A. (2024). Translators in medical and health settings. In G. Massey, M. Ehrensberger-Dow, & E. Angelone (Eds.), *Handbook of the language industry: Contexts, resources and profiles* (pp. 375–402). De Gruyter Mouton. https://doi.org/10.1515/9783110716047-017

Moorkens, J., & Guerberof Arenas, A. (2024). Artificial intelligence, automation and the language industry. In G. Massey, M. Ehrensberger-Dow, & E. Angelone (Eds.), *Handbook of the language industry: Contexts, resources and profiles* (pp. 71–100). De Gruyter Mouton.

Nimdzi. (2023a). *The 2023 Nimdzi language technology atlas*. Nimdzi Research. https://www.nimdzi.com/language-technology-atlas/

Nimdzi. (2023b). *The rise of AI-driven applications in translation feat. Stefan Huyghe*. https://www.nimdzi.com/live-the-rise-of-ai-drive-applications-in-translation-feat-stefan-huyghe/

Novozhilova, A.A., Volkova, I.D., Naumova, A.P. (2025). Legal support for investing in AI technologies (using machine translation of legal video content as an example). In: Inshakova, A., Matytsin, D., & Baltutite, I. (Eds.) *LegalTech and Legal-AI in business. Intelligent systems reference library* (Vol. 276). Springer. https://doi.org/10.1007/978-3-031-93474-2_18

Orlando, M., Liao, S., & Kruger, J. L. (2024). Translation and interpreting technologies and their impact on the industry. In G. Massey, M. Ehrensberger-Dow, & E. Angelone (Eds.), *Handbook of the language industry: Contexts, resources and profiles*. De Gruyter Mouton.

Owusu Boateng, G., Sami, H., Alagha, A., Elmekki, H., Hammoud, A., Mizouni, R., Mourad, A., Otrok, H., Bentahar, J., Muhaidat, S., Talhi, C., Dziong, Z., & Guizani, M. (2024). *A survey on large language models for communication, network, and service management: Application insights, challenges, and future directions*. arXiv. https://doi.org/10.48550/arXiv.2412.19823

Risku, H. (2008). The role of technology in translation management. In *Doubts and directions in translation studies* (pp. 85–97). John Benjamins Publishing Company. https://doi.org/10.1075/btl.72.10ris

Ruokonen, M., & Svahn, E. (2022). Comparative research into translator status: Finland and Sweden as a case in point. *Perspectives, 30*(5), 859–875. https://doi.org/10.1080/0907676X.2021.1953546

Sakamoto, A., & Bawa Mason, S. (2024). In search of a fair MTPE pricing model: LSPs' reflections and the implications for translators. *Perspectives, 32*(3), 460–476. https://doi.org/10.1080/0907676X.2023.2292572

Sánchez-Castany, R. (2024). Industry insights about translation technologies: Current needs and future trends. In Y. Peng, H. Huang, & D. Li (Eds.), *New advances in translation technology* (*New frontiers in translation studies*). Springer. https://doi.org/10.1007/978-981-97-2958-6_6

Sánchez-Gijón, P., Mesa-Lao, B., Torres-Hostench, O., & Do Carmo, F. E. M. (2015). *Conducting research in translation technologies*. Peter Lang.

Secara, A., Ginel, I. R., Toral, A., Guerberof, A., Ciobanu, D. I., Brockmann, J., ... & Rossi, C. (2025, February). *LT-LiDER language technology map-Technologies in translation practice and their impact on the skills needed*.

Tarawneh, A., & Al-Badawi, M. (2025). The importance of accurate translation in corporate legal documents. In *Artificial intelligence, sustainable technologies, and business innovation: Opportunities and challenges of digital transformation* (pp. 231–239). Springer. https://doi.org/10.1007/978-3-031-77925-1_20

Tavares, C., Oliveira, L., Duarte, P., & da Silva, M. M. (2023). Artificial intelligence: A blessing or a threat for language service providers in Portugal. *Informatics, 10*(4), 81. https://doi.org/10.3390/informatics10040081

Tomedes. (2025). *The future of language: Emerging top translation trends for 2025*. https://www.tomedes.com/translator-hub/translation-industry-trends

Volk, M., & Läubli, S. (2024). MT developers. In G. Massey, M. Ehrensberger-Dow, & E. Angelone (Eds.), *Handbook of the language industry: Contexts, resources and profiles* (pp. 101–120). De Gruyter Mouton. https://doi.org/10.1515/9783110716047-006

Zhao, H., Liu, Y., Tao, S., Meng, W., Chen, Y., Geng, X., & Yang, H. et al. (2024). From handcrafted features to llms: A brief survey for machine translation quality estimation. In *2024 International Joint Conference on Neural Networks (IJCNN)* (pp. 1–10). IEEE. https://doi.org/10.1109/IJCNN60899.2024.10650457

Chapter 13
Quality, Compliance, and Ethical Responsibility

Abstract This chapter analyzes how artificial intelligence reshapes the language services ecosystem across four interconnected dimensions: quality standards, compliance, professional ethics, and language (cultural) sovereignty. It traces the shift from intuition-based judgment to process standards (developed by the International Organization for Standardization, and ASTM International), multidimensional frameworks such as Multidimensional Quality Metrics and ISO 5060, and intelligent feedback loops combining automated and human evaluation. Compliance is reframed as end-to-end data governance covering ownership, provenance, privacy (General Data Protection Regulation; China's Personal Information Security Specification, GB/T 35,273-2020), cross-border transfer, platform logging, and contractual allocation of rights for AI-assisted outputs. Ethical responsibility moves from narrow textual fidelity to task fitness, transparent human–AI collaboration, auditable processes, and reoriented education emphasizing workflow design, data stewardship, and decision competence. Social impact analysis highlights cultural reproduction, equity for low-resource languages and users with impairments, and emerging trust architectures. The sovereignty discussion addresses community-led data stewardship, Indigenous revitalization cases, and polycentric negotiation of value alignment in AI ethics. Sustainable competitiveness depends on adaptive standards, verifiable compliance infrastructures, participatory ethical frameworks, and protection of expressive diversity—aligning technical efficiency with social justice and cultural dignity.

The language services sector is undergoing a profound shift from manual workflows to AI-enabled, technology-driven production (Borgonovi et al., 2023; Chan & Tang, 2024; Tavares et al., 2023). Artificial intelligence (AI) now permeates corpus acquisition, content generation, and distribution, accelerating automation, enhancing evaluation capabilities, and enabling real-time feedback while raising expectations for quality assessment, standards adaptation, and management strategy. This transformation pressures existing compliance and ethics frameworks, blurring legal–ethical boundaries around data use, cross-border transfer, and content ownership. The sector

J. S. Yu and Y. Yao, *Intelligent Language Services*,
https://doi.org/10.1007/978-981-95-4632-9_13

therefore must continually balance innovation and compliance while reassessing fairness, expressive rights, and professional norms.

1 Quality Standards Framework for Language Services in the Intelligent Era

In an era of pervasive intelligent enablement, quality standards serve as the central mechanism for continual improvement and trust formation. The standards architecture mirrors shifts in technology, process, and role division while accommodating expanding scenarios and finer accountability. Generative AI has transformed production paradigms and introduced new evaluative criteria and practices. The reconstruction, adaptation, and continual innovation of standards are now pivotal to sustainable development.

1.1 Quality Standards for Language Services and Their Adaptation Logic

Quality management rests on an operational standards system that underpins adequacy judgments and enables multi-stakeholder collaboration and process interoperability. As service portfolios diversify and delivery grows more complex with deep AI embedding, legacy standards face mounting transformation pressure. The evolution from experiential heuristics to process formalization, structural modeling, and intelligent augmentation has progressively aligned with current industry needs.

Early translation quality management relied on shared professional intuition. The Chinese triad of "faithfulness, expressiveness, elegance" served as a literary ideal yet lacked measurable, reproducible criteria. Digitization shifted priorities toward standardization and proceduralization. In the 1990s, the Localization Industry Standards Association (LISA) Quality Assurance (QA) Model introduced error categorization and weighted scoring, generating cumulative indices despite limited flexibility and granularity (O'Brien, 2012). International standards then matured: ISO 17100:2015 superseded EN 15,038:2006 by extending focus from the translated text to end-to-end process and capability assurance—covering qualifications, task division, documentation, and client feedback (International Organization for Standardization, 2015). ISO 18587:2017 clarified human post-editing requirements (International Organization for Standardization, 2017), and ISO 20607:2019 refined linguistic and formatting safety for technical documentation (International Organization for Standardization, 2019). Collectively, these standards shifted quality management from outcome judgment to full lifecycle control, strengthening traceability and procedural rigor.

Building on process standards, Multidimensional Quality Metrics (MQM) introduced a structured dimension-by-severity matrix (accuracy, fluency, terminology, locale-specific conventions, style, authenticity, formatting, internationalization), each weightable (Lommel, 2018). Its full application suits complex programs; selective subsets address commercial efficiency. Cross-border e-commerce emphasizes terminology uniformity and interface formatting, whereas game localization elevates dialogue style and authenticity. MQM functions both as an evaluation instrument and a shared "metalanguage" for aligning objectives and interpreting errors (Han, 2020; Mariana, 2014; Thelen, 2019).

AI is accelerating a shift toward intelligent and institutionalized quality management. Natural language processing (NLP) and large language models (LLMs) enable automatic detection of spelling, grammar, terminology consistency, and semantic alignment so reviewers can focus on high-risk and stylistic issues (Çetiner, 2021; Han et al., 2021). ISO 5060:2024 institutionalizes MQM's multidimensional error schema—specifying sampling, annotation, scoring, and reporting, enabling cross-project mutual recognition, reserving interfaces for automated annotation, and embedding inter-rater consistency controls (International Organization for Standardization, 2024).

Among major standards, ISO 17100:2015 serves as an institutional benchmark for process and personnel qualification, widely adopted in high-compliance fields. Organizations augment it with dual review and terminology consistency to enhance transparency and risk control. ASTM F2575-23, as a guidance standard, emphasizes upfront negotiation of purpose, audience, style, budget, and terminology (ASTM International, 2023), fitting localization and creative tasks. Its flexibility reduces disagreement and rework yet imposes fewer execution constraints, relying on self-regulation. A prevalent hybrid pairs ISO 17100:2015 for procedural accountability with ASTM F2575-23 for customization. With digital toolchains, automated checking, structured error tagging, and adaptive baselines have established a closed loop linking AI output, human review, and structured feedback (Huang et al., 2023; Kocmi & Federmann, 2023).

The purpose of standards is less to label outputs than to codify processes and responsibility. A complete loop comprises a process baseline, structured multidimensional evaluation, data- and AI-enabled instrumentation, and scenario-specific adaptation. High-risk domains emphasize strict compliance and traceability; marketing and creative work prize flexibility; technical documentation foregrounds terminology and formatting consistency. Subtitling and interpreting demand dynamic adjustment aligned with tools and practice.

The path evolves from experiential consensus to process governance and then to multidimensional, intelligent evaluation. ISO and ASTM frame baseline processes and negotiation; MQM and ISO 5060:2024 enable structured expression tightly integrated with automation. Future emphasis will shift toward dynamic in-process control, knowledge capture, and pervasive AI enablement to advance efficiency, sustainability, and diversification (National Institute of Standards & Technology, 2023).

1.2 *Quality Evaluation and Adaptation of Generative Content*

AI-driven generation has sharply increased production efficiency while challenging traditional evaluation. Historically, quality judgments centered on terminology, fluency, and formatting. The scale of machine translation, summarization, and intelligent authoring now exceeds the capacity for human coverage, particularly in high-frequency multilingual settings.

Focus has shifted from terminal inspection to dynamic, embedded mechanisms spanning the generation lifecycle. Automated quality prediction now forms core infrastructure. Cross-border e-commerce platforms assign risk scores via terminology matching, style consistency analysis, and numeral validation, prioritizing high-risk items for review. Historical data iteratively refines scoring logic, improving risk control and response speed.

Automated metrics have redefined boundaries. Early n-gram overlap scores such as BLEU (Bilingual Evaluation Understudy) enabled large-scale filtering but missed semantic and stylistic nuance. Semantic and neural evaluation metrics—such as COMET (Crosslingual Optimized Metric for Evaluation of Translation), BLEURT (a learned BERT-based quality metric), and BERTScore (a contextual embedding precision/recall/F1 metric using BERT)—have shown improved correlation with human judgments in reference-based settings, yet still struggle in reference-free, low-resource, or specialized domains owing to misalignment and limited explainability.

"LLM-as-a-Judge" approaches now match or surpass traditional metrics and rapid human scoring, yet introduce biases (model familiarity, length, answer position). Mitigation blends debiasing, cross-model adjudication, and fine-grained annotation (Guo et al., 2024; Huang et al., 2023; Kocmi & Federmann, 2023). Human evaluation remains the anchor while multi-source metrics are triangulated and weighted by task type: stable, reference-rich contexts favor reference metrics plus MQM sampling; open or creative tasks rely on LLM scoring with expert review; specialized domains add fact verification and terminology checks (Mehandru et al., 2023; Yang et al., 2023).

In intelligent authoring, outputs must balance factual accuracy, tone, and stylistic coherence. A financial institution, for example, encountered misunderstandings caused by tonal misalignment in AI-generated emails, prompting an expert-labeled machine learning pipeline tagging "credible tone" and "risk expressions" to steer models toward operational needs (Habib Lantyer, 2025; Ji et al., 2023).

AI-assisted writing elevates soft dimensions—affect, tone, audience fit—that are resistant to full quantification. Some organizations fuse behavioral feedback (satisfaction, complaints) into adaptive scoring. Yet many systems still predict proxy performance rather than interpret underlying needs, thus preserving the necessity of hybrid human–automation oversight. (Weidinger et al., 2022).

Operationally, human–automation synergy is standard. Automated scoring stratifies content and calibrates post-editing depth. Standardized checklists (brand consistency, persuasive impact) build empirical baselines. These mechanisms, while not replacing judgment, materially improve controllability and reuse efficiency.

Quality governance is moving from binary correctness toward task fitness and contextual applicability, e.g., marketing copy evaluated for persuasive impact rather than literal fidelity. Human and AI contributions now co-define and iteratively adjust acceptability boundaries. Standards thus function both as assessment instruments and adaptive decision frameworks for configuring collaboration, task diversity, and risk management.

1.3 Evolution of Quality Standards for Language Services in the Intelligent Era

With AI deeply embedded, standards have shifted from end-stage control to foundational mechanisms for explanation and feedback. Static scores alone cannot sustain process improvement across translation, authoring, or moderation. Effective management relies on a detect–explain–adjust loop embedding structured feedback into workflows.

Single quantitative scores localize issues but rarely expose root causes. Providers therefore deliver structured bundles—error type, causal analysis, recommended correction—with explanatory tags and exemplars. This accelerates practitioner development and supplies high-value data for model refinement. Annotated contrasts similarly guide AI authoring toward authentic brand tone, building shared human–AI knowledge (Ginel & Moorkens, 2025; Moorkens, 2022).

In multi-party projects, explanatory feedback narrows divergent quality definitions. Consensus quality agreements at initiation clarify standards and responsibilities, reducing later contention. Integrated into training, automated scoring plus causal analysis bridges rule internalization and skill acquisition, paralleling human feedback loops in model alignment and enabling iterative optimization.

As noted, evaluation is moving from unified standards to elastic management. Satisfaction depends on timeliness, communicative efficiency, and industry context—often outweighing narrow linguistic precision, especially in literary or marketing domains where style–intent alignment dominates. From initiation, teams should surface priorities and integrate tailored indicators (publication readiness, advertising resonance). During execution, co-constructed multi-metric systems preserve adaptability, repositioning providers from executors to collaborators (Li, 2023; Mutashar, 2024; Zhang, 2024).

In operational governance, a minimal consistency baseline with tiered control is pragmatic: sentence-level review for high-risk content; moderated stylistic latitude for low-impact tasks; AI pre-filtering to focus human scrutiny. Process paths adapt to archetypes (game localization, technical documentation, social media) with differentiated controls and tolerance thresholds. Decision mechanisms recast standards from constraint into scenario-specific floors plus strategy.

The value of standards lies in enabling explanation, feedback, and adaptive recalibration across diverse tasks. Mature systems avoid rigid uniformity, combining structured interpretation, flexible feedback, and multidimensional adaptation to preserve safeguards while responding rapidly to situational needs. Recognizing their relativity and elasticity is key to effective human–AI collaboration and ongoing optimization.

2 Compliance Management in Language Services

Compliance now spans law, technical architecture, data processing, and service workflow. Ownership, storage, corpus provenance, and cross-border enforceability are core operational questions shaping liability, technology deployment, and process design.

2.1 Data Boundaries, Content Ownership, and Responsibility in the AI Era

As intelligence deepens, defining data boundaries and accountability is central. The sector processes large volumes of personal information, trade secrets, and sensitive material; clarifying legitimate use while sustaining compliance amid innovation is unavoidable.

Effective protection is multi-layered. De-identification reduces linkage risk but cannot, on its own, preclude re-identification, requiring governance (independent review, traceability) for transparency (State Administration for Market Regulation and Standardization Administration of China, 2019; State Administration for Market Regulation and Standardization Administration of China, 2020). Data minimization confines collection, storage, and use to stated purposes. Access control using permission segmentation, auditing, and isolation limits exposure. Advancing these in tandem builds a resilient compliance shield.

China's Personal Information Security Specification (GB/T 35,273-2020) establishes baselines—minimal collection, shortest retention, anonymization, and safeguards—to mitigate processing risk (State Administration for Market Regulation and Standardization Administration of China, 2020). The European Union (EU)'s GDPR (General Data Protection Regulation) likewise embeds minimization, security, and heightened accountability, requiring organizations both to comply and to evidence compliance (European Parliament and Council of the European Union, 2016).

Privacy protection is a legal obligation and a strategic foundation for trust and sustainability. Under environmental, social, and governance (ESG) imperatives, data privacy compliance is integral to corporate responsibility and investor and user confidence.

Content ownership has grown more complex. AI—particularly large language models—blends client source material, provider prompts, third-party outputs, and external corpora, blurring boundaries among proprietary data, open-source licensing, and client rights, especially in fine-tuning and reuse (Dai & Jin, 2023; Hugenholtz & Quintais, 2021; Wan & Lu, 2021; Lucchi, 2024; U.S. Copyright Office, 2023).

AI-generated content and reusc carry parallel risks. Unauthorized internal training on client data may infringe intellectual property rights or trade secrets, especially in sensitive sectors. Caching and API (application programming interface) invocation introduce leakage vectors. Open-source and third-party assets require precise license scope delineation (commercial versus non-commercial, attribution, derivative rights). Distinctive stylistic replication may trigger derivative work claims; provenance tracking and anonymization are thus essential.

Jurisdictions diverge: the EU emphasizes human creativity; U.S. practice recognizes substantial human contribution; China stresses originality and independence. Purely automated outputs often fail protection thresholds; minimally edited AI-assisted translations may weaken downstream enforceability.

Enterprises should contractually define ownership, usage rights, and reuse boundaries for AI-assisted outputs; maintain traceability for data flows, training events, and attribution; and pair anonymization, access controls, and compliance screening to mitigate risk. Legal horizon scanning, industry self-discipline, and transparent client engagement form the practical foundation for safeguarding rights.

Language services mediate responsibility and entitlement in content transformation and knowledge redistribution. In the AI era, "who owns, who may reuse, who is accountable" forms the governance core across every processing and production stage.

2.2 *Platform Compliance and Cross-Border Data Governance*

With large language models embedded, data ownership and movement sit at the center of compliance. Platforms have evolved into orchestration layers integrating models, interfaces, permissions, and logs, with each action carrying allocable liability. Submitted content may be transiently stored, cached, used for training, or routed to third-party APIs, creating leakage and ownership ambiguity (Weidinger et al., 2022). This erodes traditional control and complicates liability demarcation.

High compliance standards are now prerequisites for sensitive engagements. Robust platforms classify ingress and usage, provide transparent notices, and support modes such as immediate processing, no caching, and exclusion from training.

For sensitive content they enable on-premise inference, masking, segregated logs, encryption, and automated purging.

Each model invocation and access event must be discretely configurable, auditable, and traceable to deter misuse. Permission management underpins segregation; fine-grained visibility and localized deployment enable sensitive operations. Cross-border flows require proactive alerts and scoped routing via data sandboxes and localized processing nodes (State Administration for Market Regulation and Standardization Administration of China, 2019).

Cross-border operations heighten complexity. The EU's GDPR mandates a lawful basis and transparency; consent is only one option (Voigt & Bussche, 2017). Transfers depend on adequacy decisions, Standard Contractual Clauses, and, where needed, risk assessments plus safeguards. China's Personal Information Protection Law requires localization for Critical Information Infrastructure operators and important data; others may rely on security assessment, standard contracts, or certification (Standing Committee of the National People's Congress, 2021).

Enterprises should dynamically adapt: apply layered storage and minimization by purpose, sensitivity, and geography; prioritize on-premise inference and regional encryption for sensitive data; perform de-identification and impact assessment before cross-border invocation; and bind foreign processors with auditable logs. Layered, controllable governance reconciles innovation and regulation and sustains high-risk protection.

Modern compliance emphasizes data sovereignty: localized sandboxes and edge nodes confining processing to national boundaries without persistent artifacts, plus monitoring and accountability tracing. Data Processing Agreements formalize mutual responsibilities, while pre-project assessments align risk with procedural and technical paths.

Multi-stage collaboration introduces additional liable parties. Comprehensive flow supervision—logging each access, transformation, and call with attribution—improves control and reduces ambiguity risk. Regulatory volatility demands translation of legal mandates into enforceable platform rules. Compliance is intrinsic to architecture and workflow; proactive governance now shapes competitiveness and trust.

At the core of cross-jurisdictional compliance is enabling lawful data flow. Only by integrating governance with platform design, service processes, and technical safeguards can enterprises navigate global, multi-regulatory, AI-intensive contexts and sustain trust among high-sensitivity, high-expectation clients (European Parliament and Council of the European Union, 2016; National Institute of Standards & Technology, 2023).

3 Social Impact and Ethical Responsibility of Language Services

Language services are moving from manual practice to platform- and model-driven production, while language itself is increasingly conceived as social infrastructure rather than a simple information conduit (Poibeau, 2023). This shift foregrounds the ethical boundaries and societal implications of language technologies. Beyond professional technique, linguistic circulation now entails cultural reconstruction, social equity, redistributed responsibility, and platform-based trust architectures. Understanding these dynamics is not merely reactive to technological change; it is essential to redefining the sector's role and social responsibility in the intelligent era.

3.1 Cultural Reproduction and Expressive Autonomy in the Algorithmic Era

The value of language services extends well beyond interlingual transfer; they actively reproduce cultural meaning and reshape cognitive structures. Language molds thought and expression, bearing historical memory, collective identity, and social experience. Mother-tongue education remains irreplaceable for cultivating analytical rigor, literary proficiency, and critical awareness. In Singapore, for example, bilingual policy has strengthened international communication yet weakened the depth of native expression and cultural attunement: individuals gradually lose mother-tongue-rooted advantages—deep reasoning, nuanced emotional articulation, and culturally grounded judgment (Wee, 2018). Surface diversification of linguistic skills can therefore mask an erosion of cultural depth and cognitive breadth.

As multilingual technologies interweave with global content dissemination, dominant platforms center on high-resource languages (notably English), standardizing production, circulation, and evaluation. Consequently, professional competence must extend beyond foreign-language proficiency to a mother-tongue anchor for cultural judgment and dissemination strategies. Native mastery underpins the sensitivity and creativity with which translators, editors, and planners handle complex texts, convey cultural inflection, and decode implicit meaning (Li, 2023; Zhang, 2024). As large models extend operational boundaries, the irreplaceable core returns to deep command of the mother tongue and local culture.

Translation and localization sit at the frontline of cultural value reproduction. Across literature, audiovisual media, branding, and cross-border e-commerce, language services restructure, reinterpret, and refashion source cultures (Venuti, 2017). Practitioners weigh audience expectations, communicative aims, and technological context to decide what to retain, transform, adapt, or—when warranted—strategically rewrite for specific markets. Agencies and individuals thus move from passive mediation to secondary cultural authorship (Li, 2023; Moorkens, 2022).

Recent deep integration of AI and algorithmic platforms has altered this ecology. Machine translation, automatic summarization, and generative tools accelerate multilingual circulation yet remain insensitive to fine cultural nuance. Literary allusions, social critique, humor, wordplay, and localized policy terms are often flattened into "translatable yet unusable" or superficially equivalent but distorted outputs (Al Rousan et al., 2025; Puppel, 2024). Creators on TikTok and YouTube iteratively adjust text, palette, imagery, and voice-over—often de-localizing elements—to respond to heterogeneous audience feedback.

Algorithmic curation is quietly reshaping cultural expression. Beyond individual creators, media outlets and brands recalibrate discourse to satisfy ranking and translation heuristics—eschewing intricate rhetoric, metaphor, and regionally marked usage in favor of direct, standardized, predictable forms. Platform algorithms privilege "high translatability" and "searchability," reshaping production logics and aesthetic norms (Gillespie, 2016). Over time this fosters homogenization, superficiality, and symbolic flattening, while context-rich or critical local expressions risk marginalization or disappearance (Noble, 2018).

Recommendation systems—especially for short video—are not value neutral. Traffic, breadth, and commercial potential dominate ranking, prompting creators to preconfigure a global mainstream audience and adopt standardized styles. To stay machine-filterable and translation-friendly, some preemptively avoid local issues or complex discourse, compressing diversity into a "least common denominator," constraining innovation and shrinking space for peripheral practices (Cotter, 2019; Tao et al., 2024).

Accordingly, the sector must reassess its positioning. While efficiency and reach have expanded, durable competitiveness depends on safeguarding and renewing cultural distinctiveness and expressive pluralism. Practitioners must combine algorithmic literacy with mother-tongue-centered interpretation and proactive amplification of local cultural value (Li, 2023; Zhang, 2024).

Culture-rooted linguistic discernment remains a distinctly human advantage. At the intersection of humanistic intent, technological affordance, and social meaning, language services must employ technology for global adaptability while preserving cultural depth—establishing a sustainable position between globalization and diversity.

3.2 Technology-Driven Equity in Language Services

Artificial intelligence continues to advance language service systems while exposing inequities in resource distribution and accessibility. Users in remote regions, speakers of resource-scarce languages, and individuals with sensory or expressive impairments frequently face technical bottlenecks to access services. Although translation, automatic speech recognition (ASR), and assistive reading capabilities have matured, achieving broad coverage and equitable application still poses a persistent engineering challenge.

Uneven distribution of language resources directly constrains technological coverage. Large technology companies and research institutions continue investing to enhance performance for low-resource and marginalized languages. Meta's No Language Left Behind model (NLLB-200) delivers high-quality translation for 200 languages, markedly extending applicability and embedding fairness considerations in universal design (Team et al., 2022). Speech recognition has followed a similar trajectory. AfriSpeech-200 provides standardized resources and baselines for clinical and general ASR; SautiDB-Naija is a Nigerian English accent dataset for accent recognition and adaptation; more recently, AfriMed-QA illustrates a cross-institutional benchmarking effort for African medical question answering.

Accessible language services have expanded through multimodal technologies. Users with visual impairments depend on converting visual inputs into linguistic descriptions, raising expectations for clarity and specificity. Microsoft's Seeing AI project integrates image recognition with natural language generation, allowing users to obtain salient daily information via mobile devices. During training, engineers incorporate assistance-styled data to improve the relevance and utility of generated language. Ongoing research continues to propose approaches that optimize interaction for users with diverse impairments (Khan et al., 2020).

Users with hearing impairments rely more heavily on speech transcription in educational and public settings. Automatic captioning systems must robustly handle accent variation and background noise. Platforms such as Zoom and Microsoft integrate multilingual ASR with custom vocabularies and real-time editing interfaces, thereby building service mechanisms for heterogeneous user groups. These measures enhance overall robustness and offer practical pathways toward technological fairness.

In multilingual societies, localized model optimization has become a pivotal strategy. "HKGAI V1" and "港話通" (Ganghuatong, a Cantonese communication pilot) were showcased at a 2025 exhibition as pilots for local scenario optimization; however, no authoritative announcement confirms large-scale governmental deployment. Development has emphasized fine-grained identification of usage patterns and institutional alignment of system functions, providing a technical foundation for improved local service quality.

In engineering practice, deployability, maintainability, and adaptability have become core design objectives. Given heterogeneous devices, marked structural differences among languages, and layered user needs, systems must be resilient. Although the global distribution of language resources cannot be rebalanced quickly, iterative loops linking data collection, model training, and user feedback now provide a pathway toward broader reach and fairness (Guo et al., 2024; Weidinger et al., 2022).

3.3 Redefining Professional Responsibility and Rebuilding Trust Mechanisms

Professional ethics in language services are undergoing profound adjustment. Historically, a fidelity-to-source norm underpinned professional judgment, privileging accurate meaning transfer and formal equivalence. In conference interpreting, technical documentation, and software localization, rigid fidelity standards no longer meet task demands. A task orientation is displacing strict textual equivalence: translators adjust strategies to stakeholders, scenarios, and delivery goals. Professional awareness is shifting ethical responsibility from text-level equivalence to communicative outcomes.

A task orientation does not imply neglect of the source but requires precise alignment with communicative goals. Terminological standardization in EU legal translation and cultural reframing in cross-border medical encounters are legitimate task-driven adaptations. In these processes, the translator demonstrates responsibility rather than mechanical mirroring. This outcome-focused shift has strengthened translators' capacity to steer and intervene in overall communication (Ginel & Moorkens, 2025; Zhang, 2024).

Deeper integration of AI tools has complicated ethical structures. Machine-assisted translation, automatic captioning, and ASR are shifting services toward human–AI collaboration. Responsibility now spans model behavior, engineering configuration, and user interaction rather than resting solely on the translator. Designers add confidence annotations and interactive correction mechanisms to help practitioners locate risk sources and maintain process control. In European Parliament workflows, AI produces drafts while linguists handle terminology alignment, contextual adaptation, and stylistic refinement. The role moves from text producer to outcome controller, with duties centered on validating and adjusting machine output (Moorkens, 2022; Mutashar, 2024).

This structural shift creates institutional pressure. Traditional codes centered on the translator cannot cover multi-actor chains after AI integration. Skewed training data, poor platform configuration, or missing feedback loops can become ethical risks. Consequently, platforms are issuing usage policies demarcating boundaries between AI output and human revision to clarify responsibility chains.

Trust mechanisms likewise require reconstruction. Traditional trust rested on reputation, stylistic consistency, and long-term collaboration. Under human–AI collaboration, platforms, tools, and models introduce additional nodes, shifting trust from individuals to processes. Transparency—explicit labeling, delivery notes, terminology logs—renders workflows and responsibility visible. Some tools now trace generation paths ("machine translation + human post-editing") to increase explainability. Quality statements are integral to sensitive domains, specifying model involvement and the extent of human intervention.

Platform-level logging furnishes evidence for workflow audits. Translation platforms (e.g., Tencent) implement version tracking and action logs to support attribution and dispute resolution. Concurrently, model-level confidence feedback helps translators gauge reliability. Rationale prompts and confidence scores in systems such as Microsoft's provide algorithmic grounding for oversight, complementing risk control (Huang et al., 2023; Kocmi & Federmann, 2023).

Restructuring professional responsibility requires technological adaptation and renewed professional logic. Translators must grasp task objectives, understand technological affordances, and embed responsibility in collaborative mechanisms. Trust shifts from résumés to transparent, auditable processes. This transition reflects technological evolution and deepens professional self-understanding.

3.4 Strategic Reorientation of Language Service Education

Language service education long centered on linguistic competence and translation skills, structuring curricula around equivalence, text types, and domain knowledge. As large models and intelligent tools permeate workflows, a lag has become evident. The gap between instruction and practice is driving a shift toward more systemic, innovation-oriented development—an active effort to reconfigure industry boundaries and redefine talent value (Alharbi, 2024; Li & Liu, 2025; Zhang, 2024).

Universities now commonly integrate AI collaboration modules (Aleedy et al., 2025). Students work with machine translation engines, corpus systems, and terminology tools, experiencing end-to-end human–machine collaboration. This elevates technical proficiency and reframes their understanding of translator roles. Once large models perform preliminary semantic transfer, translators must lead quality control, discourse restructuring, and pragmatic adaptation. If training still centers solely on "how to translate," students will struggle to see their multidimensional roles (Alyami & Alzubi, 2025; Li & Liu, 2025).

Pedagogy is likewise shifting. Traditional instruction emphasized syntactic drills, terminology accumulation, and procedural standardization, whereas real projects are fast-paced and contextually complex. Project-based learning is becoming mainstream, simulating medical localization, subtitle alignment, and multilingual legal review. Students assume multiple roles—execution, review feedback, terminology management, client communication—accelerating a transition from skill operators to service collaborators (Parrilla Gómez & Postigo Pinazo, 2025).

Course objectives are shifting from skill training to service design. Some courses begin with real business problems, have students investigate multilingual bottlenecks, and design integrated solutions combining human interventions with automation. The training focus moves from mastering conversion to systemic responsiveness in workflow design, resource allocation, and user needs—embedding a service mindset as a marker of pedagogical upgrading.

Assessment now emphasizes process dimensions and system control. Evaluation has moved from linguistic accuracy and stylistic fit to delivery completeness, user feedback, and task responsiveness; students also submit reflective reports explaining technical and strategic choices and attributing responsibility. This mirrors industry practice and underscores controllability and ethical awareness. External certification standards broaden content: exposure to standardized management and data governance reframes language services from text handling to structured responsibility allocation.

Technological progress and industry demand jointly propel this transition. Education is moving beyond traditional drills toward a systemic model centered on workflow design, service innovation, and decision competence. Students shift from executors to participants and designers of complex systems; educators evolve from tool demonstrators to mentors fostering autonomous judgment under uncertainty. This restructuring will underpin future competitiveness.

4 Language Sovereignty and Cultural Governance in the AI Era

Language services involve information transfer while implicating underlying power relations. With pervasive AI adoption, professionals increasingly participate in cultural governance. Understanding language sovereignty requires examining everyday practices and technological decision nodes, not abstract theorizing. Language now functions both as a medium and a component of technical systems; platforms and algorithms reshape linguistic ecologies. It thus reemerges as a core dimension of cultural sovereignty—a key resource for preserving diversity and promoting equity.

4.1 Reconfiguring the Global Language Ecology and Technological Fairness

Rapid advances in language technologies are reshaping the global linguistic ecology. Generative AI, typified by large language models, depends heavily on open-web corpora dominated by high-resource languages, especially English. English reportedly accounts for nearly half of web content; major corpora such as Common Crawl show similar distributions (commoncrawl.github.io). This structure elevates performance for dominant languages while marginalizing medium, minor, and low-resource languages through data scarcity (Guo et al., 2024).

The imbalance appears not only in translation accuracy and generation fluency but also in expressive rights and participatory capacity. When platforms fail to recognize or generate a language, users face barriers to information access and service uptake. In healthcare, law, and education, technological absence amplifies inequities. Even where speaker populations grow, weak support can further erode expressive capacity and cultural influence.

To mitigate disparities, multilingual models such as No Language Left Behind (NLLB-200) leverage parameter sharing and cross-lingual transfer to enhance the performance of low-resource languages, narrowing some gaps; yet corpus composition and expressive diversity still constrain balance (Guo et al., 2024). Digital texts for low-resource languages cluster in formal registers, lacking colloquial material, which limits adaptability and transfer. Communities maintaining oral traditions or adopting cautious digitization further shape data accumulation and technological fit.

Speech technologies show a similar disparity. Systems like Whisper have broadened coverage yet still underperform on low-resource languages, dialects, and non-standard accents. Mainstream platforms prioritize commercially promising languages. Although Tamazight, Lingala, and others have been added to Google Translate, higher-tier features—speech, captioning, personalization—remain limited. Entrenched product gaps continue to raise access thresholds for low-resource language users.

Digital representation of low-resource languages has implications for cultural power. Languages outside large-model coverage experience compression of discursive space and transmission capacity. Evaluation frameworks that privilege semantic equivalence underrepresent cultural context and diversity, entrenching a hierarchy of digital expression (Blodgett et al., 2020).

In response, initiatives explore alternative pathways. The Google Endangered Languages Project uses community co-creation and open archiving to sustain endangered languages, stressing local participation and open data governance (Google, 2012). Policy frameworks likewise foreground accessibility: the EU Artificial Intelligence Act imposes understandability and language support requirements for high-risk systems, nudging platforms toward stronger multilingual inclusion (Giagkou et al., 2023).

Rebuilding language technology infrastructure and elevating multilingual support are central to protecting diversity and digital equity. Determining who can be seen and heard is now a shared concern of language services, technology development, and cultural governance.

4.2 The Sovereignty Debate in Artificial Intelligence

The reconfiguration of the global language ecology unfolds through concrete communities and applied practice. The circumstances of minority languages in the AI era make language sovereignty an unavoidable global issue. The Māori experience illuminates the interplay among technological development, revitalization, and cultural justice.

AI technologies create revitalization opportunities while provoking debate over data ownership, cultural expression rights, and technological ethics. Whisper reportedly incorporated over a thousand hours of Māori audio without prior community consent. Although recognition improved, this sparked calls for Māori data and algorithmic sovereignty (Mahelona et al., 2023). Advocates assert that the collection, stewardship, and use of linguistic data must be community-led and grounded in participation and cultural respect (Brown et al., 2023; Kukutai et al., 2023).

These sovereignty claims do not reject external expertise but insist on community-first participation. Māori recognize language as a medium and vessel of history, identity, and worldview. A colonial legacy of marginalization heightens the need to steer linguistic destiny (Chandran, 2023). Training data shape algorithmic interpretations of culture; collection and openness practices condition representation. Without participation, even well-intentioned research risks contextual loss, expressive simplification, or commercialization.

In response to external corporate involvement, Māori actors assert technological autonomy. Te Hiku Media leveraged three decades of speech archives to build a Māori ASR system surpassing several major firms in accuracy. Emphasizing community stewardship, it collaborates with media, universities, and other Polynesian language groups to advance transcription and voice applications. Community-led development is viewed as protecting cultural sovereignty while improving practical impact (Li, 2023; Zhang, 2024).

Balancing technology and culture is evident in concrete innovation. A Gisborne initiative using Azure AI developed a voice assistant fluent in the local Nāti dialect and a virtual elder to transmit traditional knowledge. These efforts show that community-anchored, culturally adaptive design enables AI to support revitalization and continuity. Media and public commentary praise such cases for transcending a "progress versus preservation" binary.

Māori stakeholders further advocate agreement-first collaboration, requiring ethical and ownership frameworks that guarantee participation, informed status, and consent. Leadership is framed not as exclusion but as securing primary narrative authority. This stance responds to critiques by emphasizing that external involvement is acceptable when it respects autonomous choice, intellectual property, and values.

The Māori experience articulates multiple dimensions of sovereignty—usage rights, data stewardship, technological governance—advocating prioritized participation and co-construction. Unpermitted research, however well-intentioned, risks contextual erasure, misreading, leakage, and uncontrolled application. Community leadership thus becomes a mechanism for digital equality and cultural justice.

This logic is not unique to Māori. For marginalized linguistic and cultural groups worldwide, the AI-era question of decision authority is increasingly urgent. Community-led governance may guide language protection, knowledge representation, and cultural justice. Co-creation, shared governance, and open collaboration help ensure technology serves linguistic diversity and cultural fairness.

4.3 Cultural Subjects and the Authority to Define AI Ethics

Deciding a language's digital fate has implications for technological ethics and linguistic justice. As AI spreads, ostensibly neutral decisions—corpus collection, annotation, training configurations—become pivotal nodes shaping cultural visibility and expressive authority. Digitization now reorganizes cultural experience and reconfigures power. Genuine plurality requires recognizing cultural subjects as primary decision-makers and interpreters.

Every language encodes distinctive epistemologies and cultural logic—cyclical temporalities, layered memory in place names, myth, ritual, landscape. Mainstream standards rarely capture these depths. When external actors control digitization, language risks reduction to surface code and loss of deeper meaning structures, fostering deculturalization and marginalization.

Digitization reconfigures power. Training data function as digital capital: languages prioritized for collection, annotation, and inclusion gain visibility. Under the guise of "technical efficiency," platforms allocate support and features, deciding whose voices are amplified. Dominant languages reinforce advantages while peripheral languages lose expressive and reproductive space. Without leadership, historical patterns of representation and simplification are algorithmically reenacted (Guo et al., 2024; Weidinger et al., 2022).

Leadership does not entail exclusion. Responsible collaboration rests on equitable negotiation and sustained participation, preserving voice and interpretive authority across system design, corpus governance, and model updates. Instruments such as Te Hiku Media's data sovereignty agreements and Canadian Indigenous protocol tags institutionalize "negotiate-first" principles. Digitization should stage cultural agency and narrative integrity.

This logic extends to definitions of justice and political correctness. Māori insistence on data and algorithmic sovereignty—tribal permission and value alignment—is lauded as decolonial progress. Cultural specificity is recognized when technology meets vulnerable cultures. Yet similar claims by powerful actors (e.g., aligning algorithms with local values or security criteria) are reframed as censorship or ideological interference.

This bias shows that technological neutrality is bounded by dominant norms. Euro-American influence over governance, journals, and open-source ecosystems limits recognition of diverse value systems. Cases where Chinese open-source models are retrained and republished after removing local alignment illustrate contests over output standards. Despite assets in data, modeling, and cultural sovereignty, narrative sovereignty and multilateral ethical negotiation remain challenging.

AI ethics are not mere technical specifications but a negotiation over cultural governance and discursive authority. Justice should emerge from intercultural deliberation. If Indigenous sovereignty is accepted in AI development, other civilizations should likewise be recognized as entitled to articulate and embed local value propositions. This asserts dignity and collective experience rather than monopolizing economic benefit.

Future AI governance and platform architecture must rest on polycentric negotiation to build inclusive cultural expression. Standards, platform policies, and model architectures should enhance transparency, openness, and configurability, enabling communities to co-define localized value constraints instead of absorbing a single global narrative. Only when cultural subjects author first can digital language and ethical justice reconcile diversity, historicity, and fairness (Li, 2023; Mutashar, 2024; Zhang, 2024).

5 Conclusion

In the era of AI and big data, quality management, legal compliance, social ethics, and cultural sovereignty are increasingly intertwined, driving systemic transformation. Standards provide technical control and systematic risk anticipation. Compliance now extends from contracts and document review to end-to-end oversight of data acquisition, cross-platform governance, and algorithmic explainability, tightening stewardship of data ownership, privacy, and content security and encouraging proactive adaptation.

Meanwhile, social ethics and cultural sovereignty move to the foreground. Ubiquitous AI-generated content challenges expressive autonomy, cultural identity, and multilingual equity. Algorithms, platforms, and standards become arenas for negotiating expressive rights and group identity. Tensions between dominant norms and local claims prompt reassessment of universality and inclusiveness, underscoring priority participation and interpretive authority. Balanced stakeholder dialogue is essential to prevent efficiency and scale from eroding diversity and fairness.

Future ethical governance will hinge on openness, collaboration, and plural coexistence. Quality management, compliance, ethics, and cultural sovereignty must evolve within complementary frameworks. Ongoing innovation must be anchored in social justice, cultural dignity, and technological fairness, embedding diverse value claims into workflows, platform architectures, and education. Only then can the sector fulfill a dual commitment to technological progress and humanistic value.

References

Alharbi, W. (2024). Future translators' linguistic and non-linguistic competencies and skills in the age of neural machine translation and artificial intelligence: A content analysis. *International Journal of Linguistics, Literature & Translation*, *7*(4). https://doi.org/10.32996/ijllt.2024.7.4.16

Al Rousan, R., Jaradat, R., & Malkawi, M. (2025). ChatGPT translation vs. human translation: An examination of a literary text. *Cogent Social Sciences*, *11*(1), 2472916. https://doi.org/10.1080/23311886.2025.2472916

Aleedy, M., Alshihri, F., Meshoul, S., Al-Harthi, M., Alramlawi, S., Aldaihani, B., Shaiba, H., & Atwell, E. (2025). Designing AI-powered translation education tools: A framework for parallel sentence generation using SauLTC and LLMs. *PeerJ Computer Science, 11*, Article e2788. https://doi.org/10.7717/peerj-cs.2788

Alyami, N., & Alzubi, A. A. F. (2025). The evolving role of human translators in the age of artificial intelligence: Perceptions, challenges, and adaptation strategies. *International Journal of Linguistics, Literature and Translation, 8*(5), 45–56. https://doi.org/10.32996/ijllt.2025.8.5.5

ASTM International. (2023). *Standard practice for language translation* (ASTM Standard no. F2575–23). ASTM International. https://doi.org/10.1520/F2575-23

Blodgett, S. L., Barocas, S., Daumé III, H., & Wallach, H. (2020). *Language (technology) is power: A critical survey of "bias" in NLP*. arXiv. https://doi.org/10.48550/arXiv.2005.14050

Borgonovi, F., Hervé, J., & Seitz, H. (2023). Not lost in translation: The implications of machine translation technologies for language professionals and for broader society. *OECD Social, Employment, and Migration Working Papers*, (291), 0_1–60. https://doi.org/10.1787/e1d1d170-en

Brown, P. T., Wilson, D., West, K., Escott, K. R., Basabas, K., Ritchie, B., & Keegan, T. T. et al. (2023). *Maori algorithmic sovereignty: Idea, principles, and use*. arXiv3. https://doi.org/10.48550/arXiv.2311.15473

Çetiner, C. (2021). Evaluating quality assurance (QA) checks in CAT tools in relation to professional quality standards. https://www.researchgate.net/profile/Caner-Cetiner/publication/353719751_Evaluating_Quality_Assurance_QA_Checks_in_CAT_tools_in_Relation_to_Professional_Quality_Standards/links/610c48831e95fe241ab38d81/Evaluating-Quality-Assurance-QA-Checks-in-CAT-tools-in-Relation-to-Professional-Quality-Standards.pdf

Chan, V., & Tang, W. K. W. (2024). GPT for translation: A systematic literature review. *SN Computer Science, 5*(8), 986. https://doi.org/10.1007/s42979-024-03340-z

Chandran, R. (2023). *Indigenous groups in NZ, US fear colonisation as AI learns languages*. RNZ. https://www.rnz.co.nz/news/te-manu-korihi/487275/indigenous-groups-in-nz-us-fear-colonisation-as-ai-learns-languages

Cotter, K. (2019). Playing the visibility game: How digital influencers and algorithms negotiate influence on Instagram. *New Media & Society, 21*(4), 895–913.

Dai, Z., & Jin, B. (2023). The copyright protection of AI-generated works under Chinese law. *Juridical Tribune-Review of Comparative and International Law, 13*(2), 241–260.

European Parliament & Council of the European Union. (2016). Regulation (EU) 2016/679 of the European Parliament and of the Council of 27 April 2016 on the protection of natural persons with regard to the processing of personal data and on the free movement of such data, and repealing Directive 95/46/EC (General Data Protection Regulation). *Official Journal of the European Union*, L 119(1), 1–88

Giagkou, M., Lynn, T., Dunne, J., Piperidis, S., & Rehm, G. (2023). European language technology in 2022/2023. In *European language equality: A strategic agenda for digital language equality* (pp. 75–94). Springer. https://doi.org/10.1007/978-3-031-28819-7_4

Gillespie, T. (2016). #trendingistrending: When algorithms become culture. In *Algorithmic cultures* (pp. 64–87). Routledge.

Ginel, M. I. R., & Moorkens, J. (2025). Translators' trust and distrust in the times of GenAI. *Translation Studies*, 1–17. https://doi.org/10.1080/14781700.2025.2507594

Google. (2012). *Endangered languages project*. https://www.endangeredlanguages.com

Guo, Y., Guo, M., Su, J., Yang, Z., Zhu, M., Li, H., & Liu, S. S. et al. (2024). *Bias in large language models: Origin, evaluation, and mitigation*. arXiv. https://doi.org/10.48550/arXiv.2411.10915

Habib Lantyer, V. (2025). The Phantom Menace: Generative AI Hallucinations and Their Legal Implications. *SSRN*. https://doi.org/10.2139/ssrn.5167036

Han, C. (2020). Translation quality assessment: A critical methodological review. *The Translator, 26*(3), 257–273. https://doi.org/10.1080/13556509.2020.1834751

Han, L., Jones, G. J., & Smeaton, A. F. (2021). *Translation quality assessment: A brief survey on manual and automatic methods*. arXiv:2105.03311

Huang, H., Wu, S., Liang, X., Wang, B., Shi, Y., Wu, P., & Yang, M. (2023). Towards making the most of LLM for translation quality estimation. In F. Liu, N. Duan, Q. Xu, & Y. Hong (Eds.), *Natural language processing and Chinese computing (NLPCC 2023, Lecture Notes in Computer Science*, Vol. 14302). Springer. https://doi.org/10.1007/978-3-031-44693-1_30

Hugenholtz, P. B., & Quintais, J. P. (2021). Copyright and artificial creation: Does EU copyright law protect AI-assisted output? *IIC-International Review of Intellectual Property and Competition Law, 52*(9), 1190–1216. https://doi.org/10.1007/s40319-021-01115-0

International Organization for Standardization. (2024). *ISO 5060:2024 Translation services—Evaluation of translation output—General guidance*. ISO.

International Organization for Standardization. (2017). *ISO 18587:2017, Translation services—Post-editing of machine translation output—Requirements*. ISO.

International Organization for Standardization. (2015). *ISO 17100:2015, Translation services—Requirements for translation services*. ISO.

International Organization for Standardization. (2019). *ISO 20607:2019, Safety of machinery—Instruction handbook—General drafting principles*. ISO.

Ji, Z., Lee, N., Frieske, R., Yu, T., Su, D., Xu, Y., & Fung, P. et al. (2023). Survey of hallucination in natural language generation. *ACM Computing Surveys, 55*(12), 1–38. https://doi.org/10.1145/3571730

Khan, M. A., Paul, P., Rashid, M., Hossain, M., & Ahad, M. A. R. (2020). An AI-based visual aid with integrated reading assistant for the completely blind. *IEEE Transactions on Human-Machine Systems, 50*(6), 507–517. https://doi.org/10.1109/THMS.2020.3027534

Kocmi, T., & Federmann, C. (2023). *Large language models are state-of-the-art evaluators of translation quality*. arXiv. https://doi.org/10.48550/arXiv.2302.14520

Kukutai, T., Cassim, S., Clark, V., Jones, N., Mika, J., Morar, R., Muru-Lanning, M., Pouwhare, R., Teague, V., Tuffery Huria, L., Watts, D., & Sterling, R. (2023). Māori data sovereignty and privacy. *Te Ngira Institute for Population Research*. https://doi.org/10.15663/j21.35481

Li, B. (2023). Ethical issues for literary translation in the era of artificial intelligence. *Babel, 69*(4), 529–545. https://doi.org/10.1075/babel.00334.li

Li, B., & Liu, Y. (2025). Ethical issues in translation education in the AI era. In *Translation studies in the age of artificial intelligence* (pp. 210–229). Routledge.

Lommel, A. (2018). Metrics for translation quality assessment: A case for standardising error typologies. In J. Moorkens, S. Castilho, F. Gaspari, & S. Doherty (Eds.), *Translation quality assessment : From principles to practice (pp. 109-127)*. Springer. https://doi.org/10.1007/978-3-319-91241-7_6

Lucchi, N. (2024). ChatGPT: A case study on copyright challenges for generative artificial intelligence systems. *European Journal of Risk Regulation, 15*(3), 602–624. https://doi.org/10.1017/err.2023.59

Mahelona, K., Leoni, G., Duncan, S., & Thompson, M. (2023). *OpenAI's Whisper is another case study in Colonisation*. Papareo Blog. https://blog.papareo.nz/whisper-is-another-case-study-in-colonisation/

Mariana, V. R. (2014). *The Multidimensional Quality Metric (MQM) framework: A new framework for translation quality assessment* (Master's thesis, Brigham Young University). BYU ScholarsArchive. https://scholarsarchive.byu.edu/etd/4312

Mehandru, N., Agrawal, S., Xiao, Y., Khoong, E. C., Gao, G., Carpuat, M., & Salehi, N. (2023). *Physician detection of clinical harm in machine translation: Quality estimation aids in reliance and backtranslation identifies critical errors*. arXiv. https://doi.org/10.48550/arXiv.2310.16924

Moorkens, J. (2022). Ethics and machine translation. In D. Kenny (Ed.), *Machine translation for everyone: Empowering users in the age of artificial intelligence* (pp. 121–140). Language Science Press.

Mutashar, M. K. (2024). Navigating ethics in AI-driven translation for a human-centric future. *Academia Open, 9*(2), 10–21070. https://doi.org/10.21070/acopen.9.2024.9407

National Institute of Standards and Technology. (2023). *Artificial intelligence risk management framework (AI RMF 1.0) (NIST AI 100–1)*. U.S. Department of Commerce. https://doi.org/10.6028/NIST.AI.100-1

Noble, S. U. (2018). *Algorithms of oppression: How search engines reinforce racism*. New York University Press. https://doi.org/10.18574/nyu/9781479833641.001.0001

O'Brien, S. (2012). Towards a dynamic quality evaluation model for translation. *The Journal of Specialised Translation, 17*, 55–77.

Parrilla Gómez, L., & Postigo Pinazo, E. (2025). Artificial intelligence in the training of public service interpreters. *Language & Communication, 103*, 86–107. https://doi.org/10.1016/j.langcom.2025.04.002

Poibeau, T. (2023). *How machine translation changed the translation industry*. Paper presented at The Responsible AI Forum, Technical University of Munich, Munich, Germany. https://hal.science/hal-04242026

Puppel, M. (2024). *A comparative study of technical and creative text translation: Evaluating the performance of ChatGPT* [Master's thesis, University of Malta].

Standing Committee of the National People's Congress. (2021). *Personal information protection law of the People's Republic of China*. The National People's Congress of the People's Republic of China.

State Administration for Market Regulation, & Standardization Administration of China[国家市场监督管理总局, 国家标准化管理委员会]. (2020). *GB/T 35273–2020 [Information security technology—Personal information security specification.* [信息安全技术 个人信息安全规范]Standard of the People's Republic of China.

State Administration for Market Regulation, & Standardization Administration of China [国家市场监督管理总局, 国家标准化管理委员会]. (2019). *GB/T 37964–2019 Information security technology—Guidelines for de-identification of personal information* [信息安全技术 个人信息去标识化指南]. Standard of the People's Republic of China.

Tao, Y., Viberg, O., Baker, R. S., & Kizilcec, R. F. (2024). Cultural bias and cultural alignment of large language models. *PNAS Nexus*, *3*(9), 346. https://doi.org/10.1093/pnasnexus/pgae346

Tavares, C., Oliveira, L., Duarte, P., & Da Silva, M. M. (2023). Artificial intelligence: A blessing or a threat for language service providers in Portugal. In *Informatics* (Vol. 10, No. 4, p. 81). MDPI. https://doi.org/10.3390/informatics10040081

Team, N. L. L. B., Costa-Jussà, M. R., Cross, J., Çelebi, O., Elbayad, M., Heafield, K., & Wang, J. et al. (2022). *No language left behind: Scaling human-centered machine translation*. arXiv2. https://doi.org/10.48550/arXiv.2207.04672

Thelen, M. (2019). Quality and quality assessment in translation: Paradigms in perspective. In *Quality assurance and assessment practices in translation and interpreting* (pp. 1–25). IGI Global Scientific Publishing. https://doi.org/10.4018/978-1-5225-5225-3.ch001

U.S. Copyright Office. (2023). Copyright registration guidance: Works containing material generated by artificial intelligence. *Federal Register*, *88*(59), 16190–16194. https://www.federalregister.gov/documents/2023/03/16/2023-05321/copyright-registration-guidance-works-containing-material-generated-by-artificial-intelligence

Venuti, L. (2017). *The translator's invisibility: A history of translation*. Routledge.

Voigt, P., & von dem Bussche, A. (2017). The EU general data protection regulation (GDPR). *Springer*. https://doi.org/10.1007/978-3-319-57959-7

Wan, Y., & Lu, H. (2021). Copyright protection for AI-generated outputs: The experience from China. *Computer Law & Security Review, 42*, Article 105581. https://doi.org/10.1016/j.clsr.2021.105581

Wee, L. (2018). *The Singlish controversy: Language, culture and identity in a globalizing world*. Cambridge University Press.

Weidinger, L., Uesato, J., Rauh, M., Griffin, C., Huang, P. S., Mellor, J., & Gabriel, I. et al. (2022). Taxonomy of risks posed by language models. In *Proceedings of the 2022 ACM Conference on Fairness, Accountability, and Transparency* (pp. 214–229). https://doi.org/10.1145/3531146.3533088

Yang, X., Zhan, R., Wong, D. F., Wu, J., & Chao, L. S. (2023). *Human-in-the-loop machine translation with large language model*. arXiv. https://doi.org/10.48550/arXiv.2310.08908

Zhang, W. (2024). Translation ethics. *Asia Pacific Translation and Intercultural Studies, 11*(3), 312–318. https://doi.org/10.1080/23306343.2024.2437731

Glossary

A/B testing Experimental method comparing two versions of content to determine which performs better, widely used in NLP for optimizing text, interfaces, and algorithms.

AI customer service The use of artificial intelligence technologies—such as chatbots, natural language processing, and speech recognition—to provide automated or semi-automated customer support, often across multiple languages and channels.

AI interaction interfaces User interfaces designed for interacting with artificial intelligence (AI) systems, involving natural language processing (NLP) and user experience design.

algorithm transparency The practice of making AI algorithms and their decision-making processes understandable and explainable to users and stakeholders.

annotation guidelines Detailed instructions and rules for human annotators to ensure consistent and accurate labeling of data in language intelligence projects.

annotation process The stage in data preparation where linguistic data is labeled or tagged with metadata, crucial for supervised learning in NLP and machine translation systems.

annotation protocol A standardized set of guidelines and procedures for labeling data, crucial for training machine learning models in NLP and speech recognition tasks.

annotation tool Software used to label or tag language data with linguistic information, such as part-of-speech, named entities, or semantic roles, for machine learning training.

attention mechanism A neural-network module that assigns weights to input elements to form a context vector, enabling the model to focus on the most relevant parts of a sequence.

automatic speech recognition (ASR) Technology that converts spoken language into text using computational methods, commonly used in voice assistants and transcription systems.

automatic summarization (AS) The process of using algorithms to generate a concise and coherent summary of a longer text automatically.

J. S. Yu and Y. Yao, *Intelligent Language Services*,
https://doi.org/10.1007/978-981-95-4632-9

autoregressive generation (AR) A sequence generation approach where each token is produced step by step, conditioned on previously generated tokens, widely used in language modeling, translation, and text generation.

autoregressive language model A type of language model that predicts the next token in a sequence based on previous context using unidirectional processing. Commonly implemented in architectures like GPT for text generation tasks.

back-translation A quality-assurance method that translates a target-language text back into the source language to reveal and correct errors.

bias evaluation framework A structured approach for assessing and mitigating biases in AI systems, particularly in language models and algorithms.

Bidirectional Encoder Representations from Transformers (BERT) A transformer-based language model pre-trained with bidirectional context to produce deep contextualized word representations.

Bidirectional LSTM with Conditional Random Field (BiLSTM-CRF) A hybrid architecture that combines a bidirectional LSTM encoder with a conditional random field layer for sequence labeling.

bidirectional masked model A bidirectional language model trained by masking selected tokens and predicting them from surrounding context.

Bilingual Evaluation Understudy (BLEU) An automatic machine-translation metric that compares n-gram overlap between a system output and reference translations.

bilingual parallel corpus A set of aligned text pairs in two languages, used to train and evaluate machine-translation systems.

byte-pair encoding A subword tokenization method that repeatedly merges the most frequent character pairs to build a vocabulary.

CAMEL framework A multi-agent collaboration framework that uses role-based interactions and goal conflicts to shape consistent behaviors and value orientations.

catastrophic forgetting The tendency of a neural network to lose previously learned knowledge when trained on new data or tasks.

Chain-of-Thought (CoT) A prompting technique that elicits intermediate reasoning steps to improve performance on multi-step problems.

clickbait Content designed with sensationalist headlines to attract clicks and attention, a common issue in text classification and content filtering systems.

cognitive labor Mental work involving understanding, processing, and generating language, central to AI linguistics and natural language understanding tasks.

COMET A neural machine-translation evaluation metric that uses cross-lingual pre-trained encoders to score translation quality from the source, hypothesis, and reference.

complex contexts Situations involving intricate linguistic or situational factors that challenge automated language processing systems.

computational linguistics An interdisciplinary field that develops computational methods for analyzing and processing natural language, combining linguistics and computer science.

consecutive interpreting A mode of interpretation where the interpreter speaks after the source language speaker has finished, relying on memory and note-taking to reproduce the message.

context The linguistic environment or surrounding text that influences the meaning and interpretation of words or phrases in natural language processing.

context-sensitive representations Vector representations that are computed from surrounding context, so a unit's meaning varies with its input sequence.

controlled language A restricted subset of natural language with simplified grammar and vocabulary rules designed to improve clarity and reduce ambiguity in technical communication.

coreference resolution mechanism A method that identifies and links mentions that refer to the same entity within a text or discourse.

corpus annotation The process of adding linguistic labels to a text corpus (e.g., POS tags, syntax, semantics, entities) for training and evaluation.

corpus annotation The process of adding metadata or labels to text data to make it suitable for training machine learning models in NLP applications.

corpus modeling The process of building and analyzing linguistic corpora for natural language processing and computational linguistics applications.

cross-modal generation Generating content in one modality from another (e.g., text-to-image or text-to-audio) using learned cross-modal mappings.

cultural bias Systematic errors or preferences in language models that reflect cultural assumptions or stereotypes, often leading to unfair or inaccurate outputs in NLP applications.

data aggregation The collection and combination of data from multiple sources, a key function in machine learning and natural language processing systems.

deep semantic representation High-dimensional learned representations that encode semantic meaning and relationships for language processing.

dense embedding A continuous vector representation of text units that encodes semantic and/or syntactic information.

dense retrieval retrieval method that represents queries and documents as embeddings and ranks them by similarity in a shared vector space.

dependency tree analysis A syntactic parsing approach that builds a tree to represent dependency relations between words in a sentence.

diffusion algorithm A generative method that learns to reverse a gradual noising process to produce data, widely used in text-to-image generation.

ELMo model A contextualized word-representation model that uses bidirectional LSTMs to generate embeddings conditioned on surrounding context.

embedding vector A dense vector representation of discrete items (e.g., words) in a continuous space, where similar items are mapped to nearby points.

emoji Digital icons or symbols used to express emotions, ideas, or concepts in electronic communication, enhancing textual meaning with visual cues.

entity extraction An NLP technique that identifies and classifies named entities (e.g., people, organizations, locations, dates) in text.

entity linking The task of mapping entity mentions in text to the correct entries in a knowledge base by disambiguating and normalizing them.

extractive summarization A summarization method that selects and concatenates sentences or passages from the source document to form a summary.

FAISS (Facebook AI Similarity Search) A library for efficient similarity search and clustering of dense vectors, optimized for large-scale high-dimensional data.

faithful reproduction A translation approach that aims to accurately and precisely reproduce the original text without significant alteration.

few-shot learning A learning setting in which a model performs a task using only a small number of labeled examples (often 1–5 per class).

fine-tuning Further training a pre-trained model on a smaller, task-specific dataset to adapt it to a downstream task.

Generative Pre-trained Transformer (GPT) A large-scale autoregressive language model pre-trained on text for natural language understanding and generation.

generative summarization An abstractive summarization approach in which a model generates new sentences to convey a document's key content.

glossary A list of specialized terms with definitions, used in translation and localization to ensure consistency and accuracy in technical domains.

graph retrieval-augmented generation (GraphRAG) A retrieval-augmented generation approach that uses graph-structured knowledge to retrieve evidence and guide generation.

hallucination The tendency of a generative model to produce plausible-sounding but incorrect or unsupported content.

hierarchical navigable small world algorithm (HNSW) An approximate nearest-neighbor search method that builds a hierarchical graph for efficient similarity search in high-dimensional spaces.

high-quality corpus A collection of text data that is carefully curated, accurate, and representative, used as training data for language models in NLP tasks.

human–AI collaboration The interaction and cooperation between humans and AI systems to enhance performance and decision-making.

human–AI collaboration model A framework where humans and AI systems work together, essential in hybrid approaches for translation, speech processing, and NLP tasks.

in-context learning A capability of large language models to learn from examples in the input context without updating model parameters.

intelligent knowledge service A service that leverages artificial intelligence and automation to provide knowledge-based solutions, such as information retrieval, content generation, or decision support in domains like NLP and AI.

intelligent system A computer-based system that uses AI techniques to perform tasks that typically require human intelligence.

intent recognition The process of identifying the user's purpose or goal from natural language input, a fundamental task in dialogue systems and NLP.

internationalization The design and development of a product, application, or document content that enables easy localization for target audiences that vary in culture, region, or language.

interpreting The real-time translation of spoken or signed language from a source language to a target language. In the context of artificial intelligence, it is a multidisciplinary field that integrates automatic speech recognition (ASR), machine translation (MT), and text-to-speech (TTS) technologies.

knowledge engineering The process of building knowledge-based systems that capture and utilize expert knowledge, fundamental to artificial intelligence and natural language processing.

knowledge graph A structured knowledge base that represents entities and their relations as a graph for semantic understanding and reasoning.

language barrier Obstacles in communication or understanding caused by differences between languages, often addressed in machine translation and cross-lingual NLP.

language data Data consisting of linguistic content, often used as training material for NLP models, machine translation systems, and other language intelligence applications.

language model A model that assigns probabilities to token sequences and can generate text, typically learned from large corpora to capture syntax, semantics, and context.

language modeling The task of predicting the next token from preceding context, serving as a core objective for many language models.

language processing The computational handling and manipulation of linguistic data, encompassing tasks like parsing, analysis, and transformation in NLP systems.

language service industry The sector encompassing professional services related to language technologies, including translation, localization, interpretation, and language technology development.

language service professionals Specialized personnel in language-related services including translation, localization, and language technology applications.

language specification A set of rules and standards governing the structure, usage, and implementation of a language, crucial in NLP and computational linguistics for consistency and interoperability.

language tasks Specific activities or operations involving language processing, such as translation, annotation, or speech recognition, in NLP and AI contexts.

language translation The process of converting text or speech from one language to another while preserving meaning and context.

large language model (LLM) A neural language model trained on massive text corpora, typically with billions of parameters, to generate text and perform diverse NLP tasks.

linguistic knowledge Understanding of language structures, semantics, and usage, fundamental to natural language processing and computational linguistics.

linguistic precision The accuracy and exactness in language processing, translation, or generation, crucial for effective communication in NLP and AI systems.

LLaMA (Large Language Model Meta AI) A family of transformer-based large language models released by Meta, designed for strong performance with relatively efficient model sizes.

LLM-as-a-Judge An evaluation approach that uses a large language model to rate or compare generated outputs according to specified criteria.

localization (L10n) The process of adapting products, software, or content to the linguistic, cultural, and technical requirements of a specific target market or locale. Beyond simple translation, it involves comprehensive adjustments to ensure cultural relevance and functional usability, serving as a critical component of global language services and AI-driven content adaptation.

long short-term memory (LSTM) A recurrent neural network architecture with gating mechanisms that captures long-range dependencies and mitigates vanishing gradients.

machine translation (MT) Automated translation between languages using computational methods, including statistical and neural models.

machine-generated Produced automatically by artificial intelligence systems. In translation studies, this term typically refers to raw machine translation output generated without human involvement, often serving as a starting point for post-editing.

masked language model (MLM) A training objective where some input tokens are masked and the model predicts them from surrounding context.

masked tokens Tokens deliberately hidden or replaced during training so a model learns to predict them from context.

model A computational framework in AI that processes and generates language data, often trained on large datasets for specific tasks.

model distillation A technique where a smaller model learns to imitate a larger model to reduce size and cost while retaining performance.

model fine-tuning The process of adjusting pre-trained AI models (e.g., in machine learning) for specific tasks or domains to improve performance.

multilingual Pertaining to the ability of a system, model, or individual to support or process multiple languages. In artificial intelligence, it specifically refers to models (e.g., Multilingual LLMs) trained on diverse linguistic datasets, enabling cross-lingual transfer and the handling of various language pairs within a single framework.

multilingual BERT (mBERT) A multilingual BERT trained on 104-language Wikipedia with a shared vocabulary for cross-lingual transfer.

multilingual knowledge graph A knowledge graph that links entities and relations across languages for cross-lingual retrieval and reasoning.

multimodal Pertaining to systems or models capable of processing, integrating, and generating information from multiple types of data, or modalities, such as text, images, audio, and video.

multimodal corpus A dataset combining text with audio/visual signals for training and evaluating multimodal NLP systems.

multimodal generation model A model that generates outputs across modalities (e.g., text and images) from shared cross-modal representations.

multimodal generation task Tasks that require generating coordinated content across modalities, such as text-to-image generation or captioning.

multimodal integration Aligning and fusing information from multiple modalities using neural fusion or attention mechanisms.

multimodal large model A large-scale model that processes multiple modalities with shared encoders and cross-modal attention.

multimodal machine translation (MMT) A translation approach that integrates multiple input modalities—such as text, images, or speech—to improve accuracy and contextual understanding beyond text-only translation.

multi-turn dialogue system A conversational AI that sustains multi-turn interactions by tracking context and keeping responses coherent.

named entity recognition (NER) A task that detects entity spans in text and labels them as types like person, organization, or location.

natural language processing (NLP) AI methods for understanding and generating human language from text or speech.

natural language to SQL (NL2SQL) A task that translates natural-language questions into executable SQL queries over a database.

neural machine translation (NMT) Neural models that translate between languages end-to-end, often using encoder–decoder architectures with attention.

neural network language model A neural model that estimates word/token probabilities in context using learned vector representations.

neural networks Computational architectures inspired by biological neural networks, widely used in modern AI for language modeling and translation tasks.

next token prediction Training where a model predicts the next token from prior context to learn language patterns.

n-gram model A Markov language model that predicts the next token using counts of the previous $n-1$ tokens.

NLLB-200 (No Language Left Behind) Meta's translation model covering 200 languages, designed for broad multilingual MT quality.

parallel corpus Aligned multilingual texts used to train and evaluate translation and cross-lingual models.

parallel processing A computational approach where multiple tasks are executed simultaneously to improve efficiency, applied in translation and NLP pipelines.

Porter stemmer A English rule-based stemmer that strips common suffixes to reduce words to stems.

post-editing (PE) The process of reviewing and correcting machine-translated output to improve accuracy, fluency, and terminology consistency.

pragmatic rules Principles governing language use in context, including speech acts, implicature, and politeness strategies, essential for natural language understanding and dialogue systems.

pragmatics The branch of linguistics that deals with how context contributes to meaning, including speaker intent and implied meanings in language understanding systems.

pre-trained language model (PLM) A model pre-trained on large text to learn general language patterns, then adapted to tasks.

pre-training Training first on large unlabeled data to learn general representations before task-specific fine-tuning.

pre-training fine-tuning paradigm A workflow that pre-trains on broad data and then fine-tunes on a specific task dataset.

probabilistic language model A model that assigns probabilities to word sequences based on statistics learned from data.

prompt Input text or instructions given to a language model to guide its behavior or output generation in AI systems.

prompt engineering Designing and refining prompts to steer a model's outputs toward a desired goal.

quality control The systematic process of monitoring and maintaining standards in language output and translation quality within intelligent platforms.

RAG pipeline (Retrieval-Augmented Generation pipeline) Retrieval-augmented generation that fetches external info to ground and improve generated answers.

RAG-Fusion A RAG approach that issues multiple queries and fuses retrieved results to improve coverage and ranking.

ReAct prompting A prompting method that interleaves reasoning with explicit actions like tool use or retrieval.

recurrent neural network (RNN) A neural network for sequences that uses recurrence to carry information across time steps.

register and style automatic recognition Automatically identifying a text's register and style by analyzing word choice, syntax, and discourse cues.

Reinforcement Learning from Human Feedback (RLHF) Training models with human preference feedback (often via reward models) to better align outputs with people.

remote interpreting Interpreting provided over distance using technology, typically involving real-time language translation between parties not physically co-located.

Reranker model A model that re-sorts retrieved candidates using deeper semantic matching to improve final ranking.

Retrieval-Augmented Generation (RAG) A system that retrieves external documents and conditions generation on them to improve grounded answers.

reuse The practice of utilizing existing content, modules, or linguistic resources multiple times in different contexts or applications within language intelligence systems.

robustness A model's ability to stay reliable under noise, distribution shifts, or adversarial inputs.

rule-based Systems or approaches that rely on predefined linguistic rules and patterns for processing language, commonly used in early NLP systems.

scaling law Empirical relationships showing how performance changes with model size, data, and compute.

self-attention mechanism An attention layer where each token weighs other tokens to build contextual representations.

self-verification mechanism Techniques that make a model check and revise its own reasoning to reduce errors and hallucinations.

semantic labels Annotations or tags that capture the meaning, sentiment, or intent of text segments, used in NLP for training and evaluation of models.

semantic prediction The ability to anticipate the meaning or content of upcoming speech based on context, a key skill in real-time language processing and interpretation.

semantic similarity model A model that compares meanings by embedding texts and computing similarity in vector space.

semantics The study of meaning in language, focusing on how words, phrases, and sentences convey information and relationships in computational linguistics.

sentence embedding A fixed-length dense vector representation of a sentence that encodes its overall semantic meaning in a continuous vector space, enabling semantic similarity computation.

Sentence-Bidirectional Encoder Representations from Transformers/Sentence-BERT (SBERT) A sentence embedding model derived from BERT that uses siamese or triplet network architectures to generate semantically comparable sentence representations.

sentiment analysis The computational analysis of opinions, emotions, and attitudes expressed in text, used to determine positive, negative, or neutral sentiment.

sentiment classification A natural language processing task that automatically assigns sentiment polarity or emotion categories to text using machine learning models.

simultaneous interpreting A mode of interpretating where the interpreter translates in real-time as the speaker talks, typically used in conferences and large events with specialized equipment.

sociolinguistics The study of how language varies and changes in social groups, relevant for understanding language use patterns in NLP applications.

speech synthesis, text-to-speech (TTS) A computational technique that converts written text into synthetic spoken language by generating speech waveforms from linguistic input.

speech technology Technologies related to the processing, recognition, synthesis, or analysis of human speech, including speech recognition and text-to-speech systems.

statistical language model A probabilistic model that estimates the likelihood of word sequences based on statistical patterns learned from large text corpora.

supervised fine-tuning (SFT) A training approach that adapts a pre-trained language model to specific tasks by further training it on labeled datasets.

syntactic analysis The computational analysis of sentence structure to identify grammatical relations among words using parsing techniques.

syntactic dependency relations Grammatical relations between words in a sentence, typically modeled as directed arcs from heads to dependents, and extracted via dependency parsing algorithms.

synthesized speech Artificially generated speech produced by text-to-speech (TTS) systems, commonly used in NLP and speech technology applications.

system tuning The process of optimizing language processing systems by adjusting parameters and configurations to improve performance and accuracy.

terminology Specialized vocabulary and expressions used in specific domains such as medicine and technology, requiring precise translation and standardization.

terminology consistency Maintaining uniform use of terms across documents or systems, fundamental in machine translation and terminology management for accuracy.

terminology standardization The process of establishing and maintaining consistent terminology definitions and usage across languages and domains, crucial for NLP and localization.

terminology system A structured collection of domain-specific terms and their relationships, crucial for NLP and knowledge representation.

token A basic unit of text used in NLP after segmentation, such as a word, subword, or character; tokens are produced by tokenization for downstream processing.

tokenization The procedure that segments text into tokens (e.g., words, subwords, characters), providing the discrete units required by NLP models and pipelines.

tokenization method An algorithmic strategy for mapping raw text to tokens, specifying segmentation rules (word-, subword-, or character-level) and the resulting vocabulary.

Transformer An attention-based neural architecture that models sequences without recurrence or convolution, enabling parallel computation and strong performance in many NLP tasks.

translation memory A database of aligned source–target segments that supports reuse of prior translations to improve consistency and efficiency in translation and localization workflows.

Tree of Thoughts (ToT) A reasoning paradigm that expands problem solving into a branching search over intermediate steps, supporting deliberate exploration, evaluation, and backtracking.

unigram language model A probabilistic model that assumes token independence and assigns sequence likelihood as the product of individual token probabilities, often used in subword segmentation.

vector search Similarity-based retrieval over vector embeddings using distance metrics (e.g., cosine or Euclidean), commonly applied to semantic search and nearest-neighbor retrieval.

video remote interpreting Interpreting service delivered via video conferencing technology, providing visual cues alongside audio for enhanced communication.

virtual assistant Software agent that performs tasks or services for users based on voice or text commands, often using NLP technologies.

Whisper model An OpenAI automatic speech recognition system based on Transformer architectures, trained on large-scale multilingual and multitask speech data for transcription and translation.

word segmentation The computational task of splitting raw text into word units or tokens; it is especially difficult for languages such as Chinese that lack explicit word boundary markers.

word sense disambiguation (WSD) The task of identifying the intended meaning of a polysemous word in context, typically by selecting the correct sense from an inventory using contextual cues.

Word2Vec A neural embedding approach that learns dense word vectors from co-occurrence patterns, yielding representations that encode semantic and syntactic regularities.

WordPiece A subword tokenization algorithm that builds a vocabulary by iteratively merging units to improve likelihood, producing subword pieces widely used in BERT-style models.

zero-shot prompting A prompting setting in which a model performs a task given only an instruction or description, without any in-context examples.

zero-shot reasoning The ability to solve novel tasks without task-specific training data, relying on generalization from pretraining and instruction signals to infer required reasoning steps.